PRAISE FOR *APSARA ENGINE*

"An astonishing collection of stories that expand and pulse into galaxy-sized moments of strangeness and wonder."

—**KELLY LINK,** author of *Get in Trouble*

"Imaginative and poetic, *Apsara Engine* is powered by a fiercely complex heart. Bishakh Som builds a world in which queer and trans South Asians not only survive but map the very future. Som is lighting the way forward with a stunning blend of mythology, futurity, and courageous tenderness."

—**FRANNY CHOI,** author of *Soft Science*

"The eight pieces here sprawl far larger than the two-hundred-odd pages that contain them. They slip in and out of time and telling; conversation, seduction, and the fantastic are their method, their object the elusive connections between people. *Apsara Engine* opens a new comics universe, one painted in the blood of someone incisive and hilarious and warm and intense and brilliant: say yes to it."

—**JEANNE THORNTON,** author of *The Black Emerald*

"This remarkable book does something rare and exhilarating: the stories the words tell are individual, familiar, and meaningful, but the images take the reader to situations and worlds that are alien, strange, dark, or numinous. Stories like these reveal the limits of what we consider 'realism'—and perhaps more, they remind us that the world is not always what we think it is."

—**RACHEL POLLACK,** author of *The Beatrix Gates*

"Bishakh Som's comics astonish me with beauty and invention; *Apsara Engine* opens up the medium to possibilities never before imagined. Luckily, Som has enough imagination for all of us."

—**JASON ADAM KATZENSTEIN,** illustrator of *Camp Midnight*

"A sweet mix of late nineteenth-century morals upended by early twenty-first-century juxtapositions, *Apsara Engine* is a set of uncanny shorts full of uniquely camouflaged and slow-moving yet effective trapdoors. Wish fulfillment is the book's true engine, but—as in ancient tales—wishes are fulfilled in unhappy or muted or at least prickly fashion. Dichotomies—particularly those of gender or of the Global North and South—get less subverted than softly imploded. A welcome blueprint for a side entrance into an only recently imagined utopia."

—**EUGENE LIM,** author of *Dear Cyborgs*

APSARA ENGINE

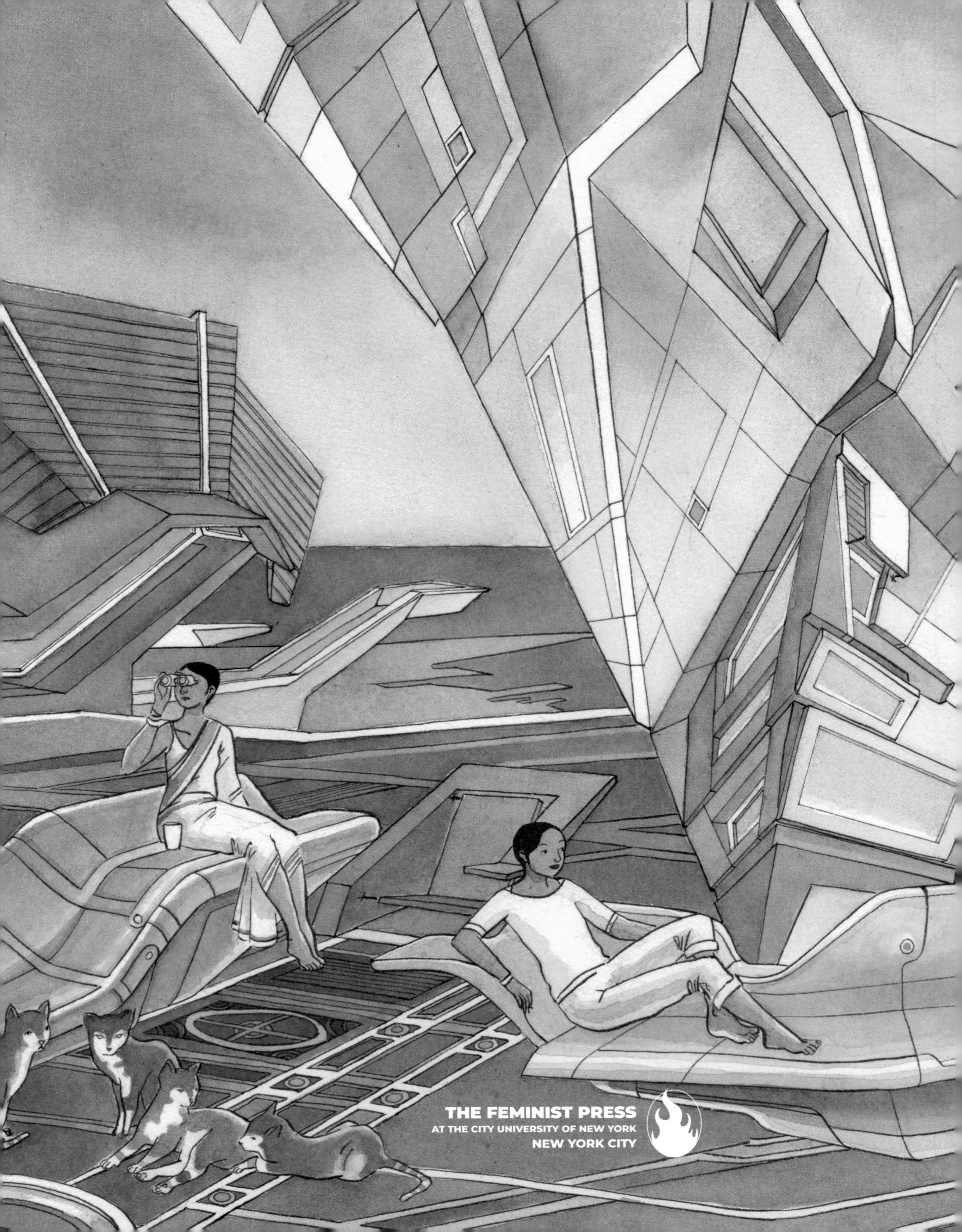

THE FEMINIST PRESS
AT THE CITY UNIVERSITY OF NEW YORK
NEW YORK CITY

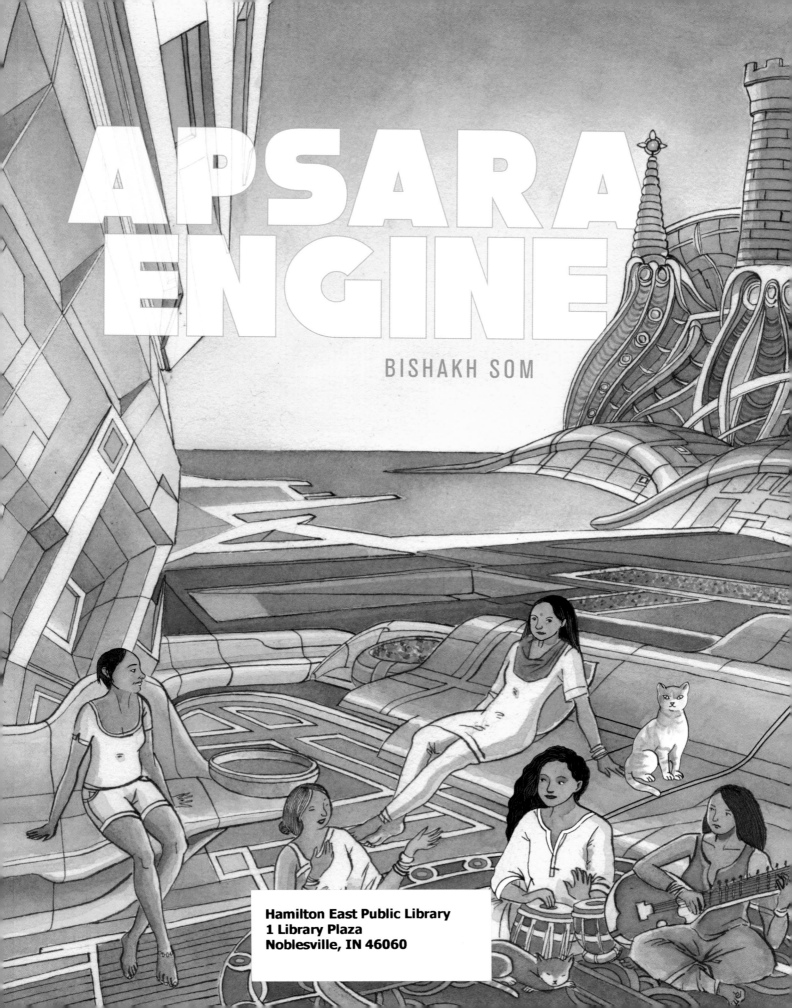

APSARA ENGINE

BISHAKH SOM

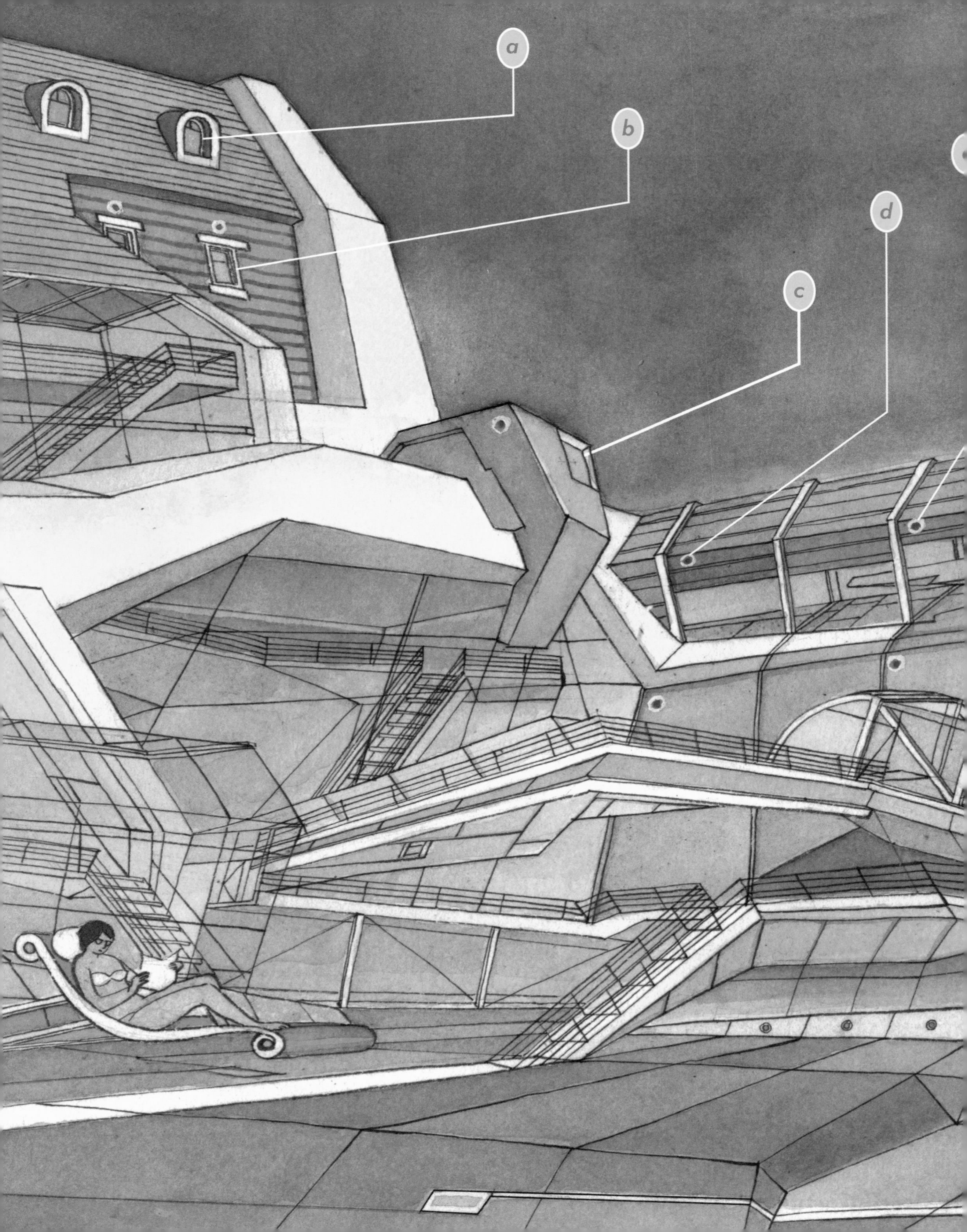
a
b
c
d

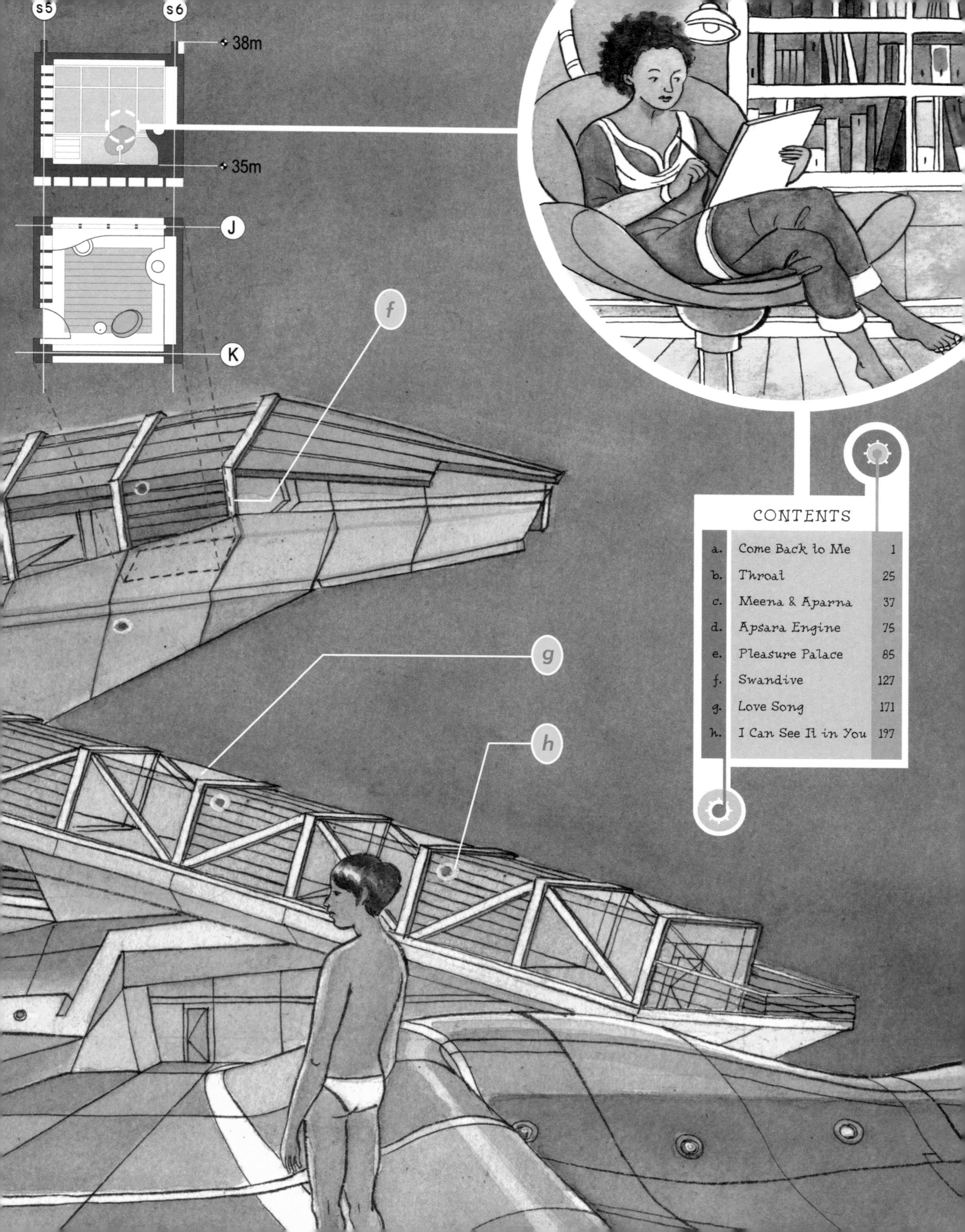
s5
s6
38m
35m
J
K
f
g
h

CONTENTS

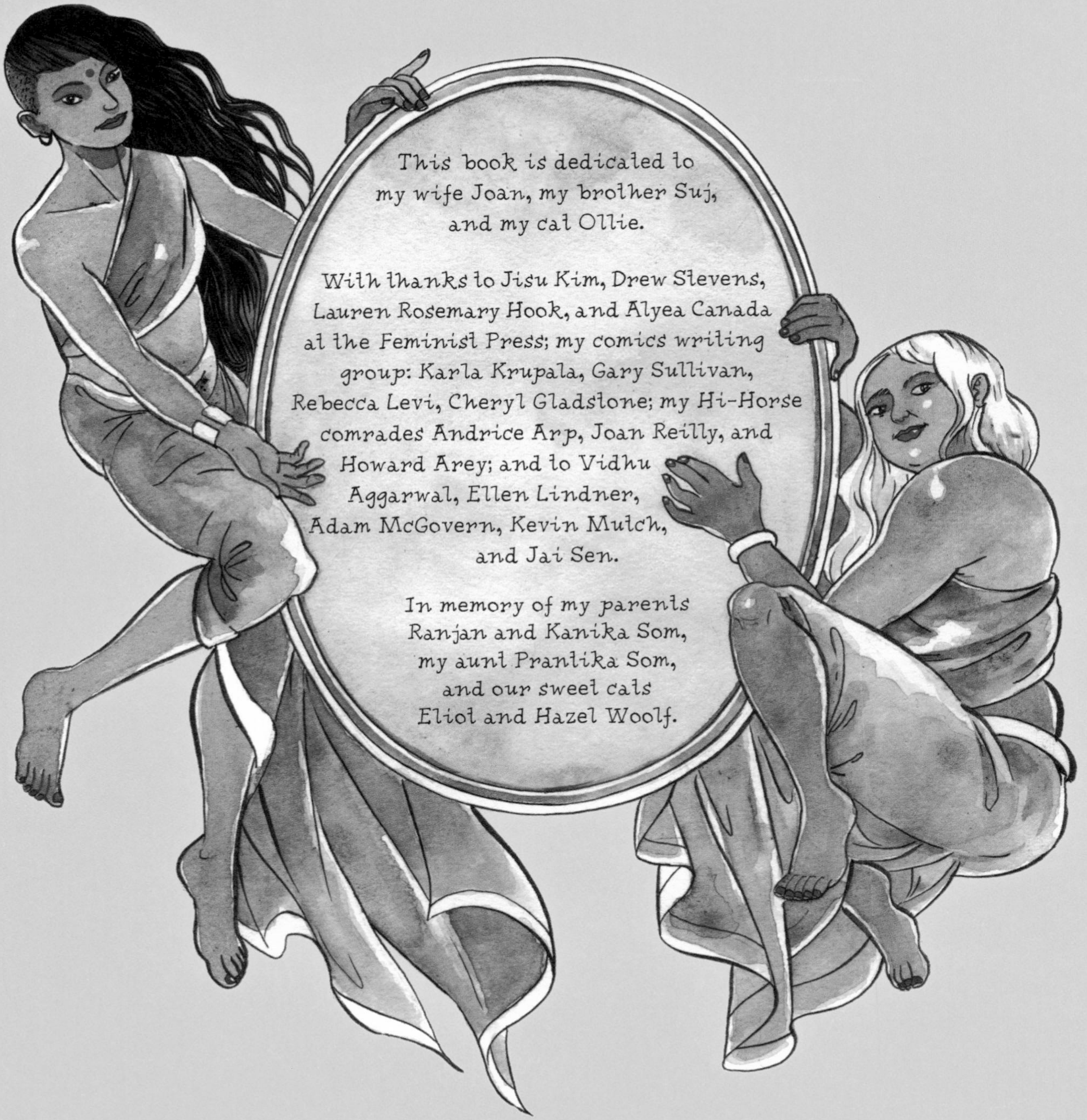
This book is dedicated to
my wife Joan, my brother Suj,
and my cat Ollie.
With thanks to Jisu Kim, Drew Stevens,
Lauren Rosemary Hook, and Alyea Canada
at the Feminist Press; my comics writing
group: Karla Krupala, Gary Sullivan,
Rebecca Levi, Cheryl Gladstone; my Hi-Horse
comrades Andrice Arp, Joan Reilly, and
Howard Arey; and to Vidhu
Aggarwal, Ellen Lindner,
Adam McGovern, Kevin Mutch,
and Jai Sen.
In memory of my parents
Ranjan and Kanika Som,
my aunt Prantika Som,
and our sweet cats
Eliot and Hazel Woolf.

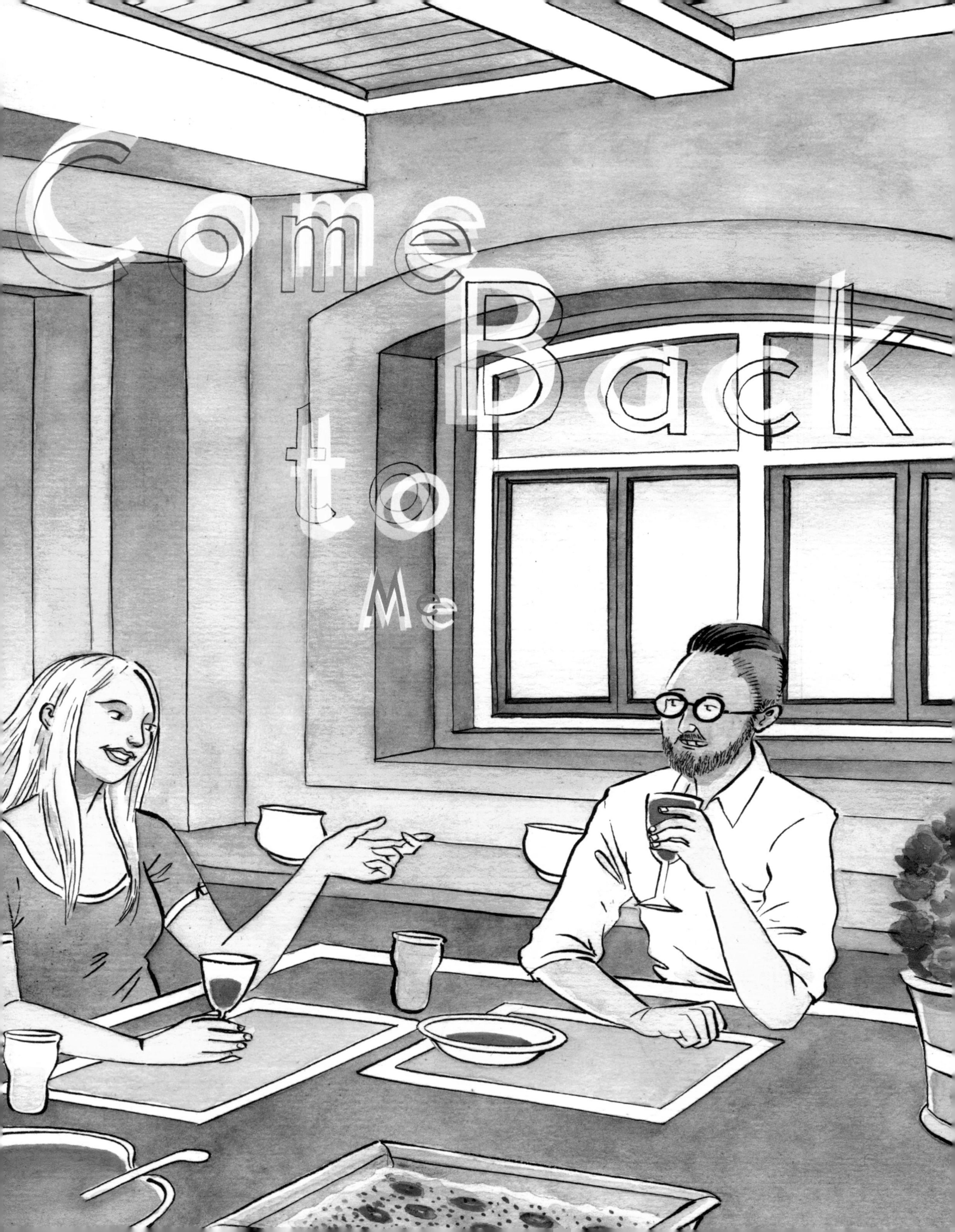
Come Back to Me

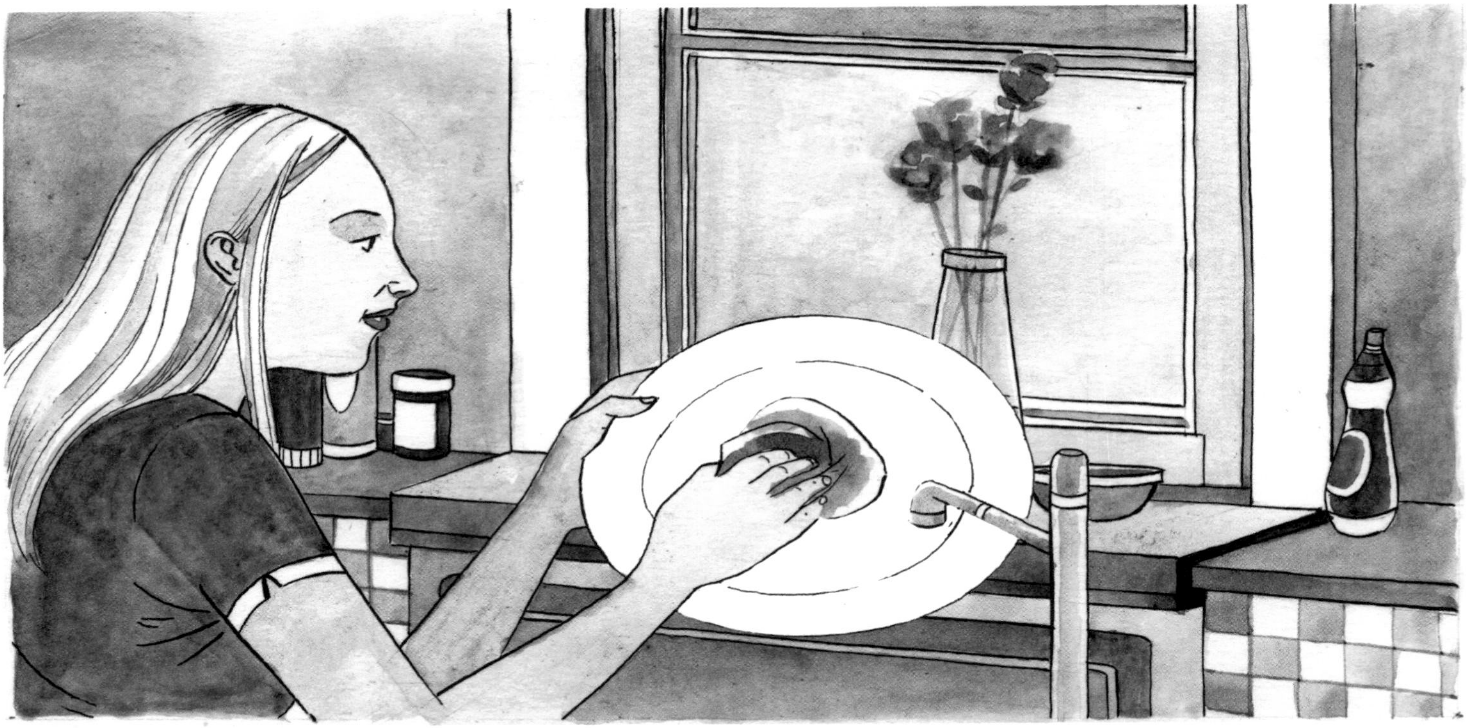

We bought the house two years ago.

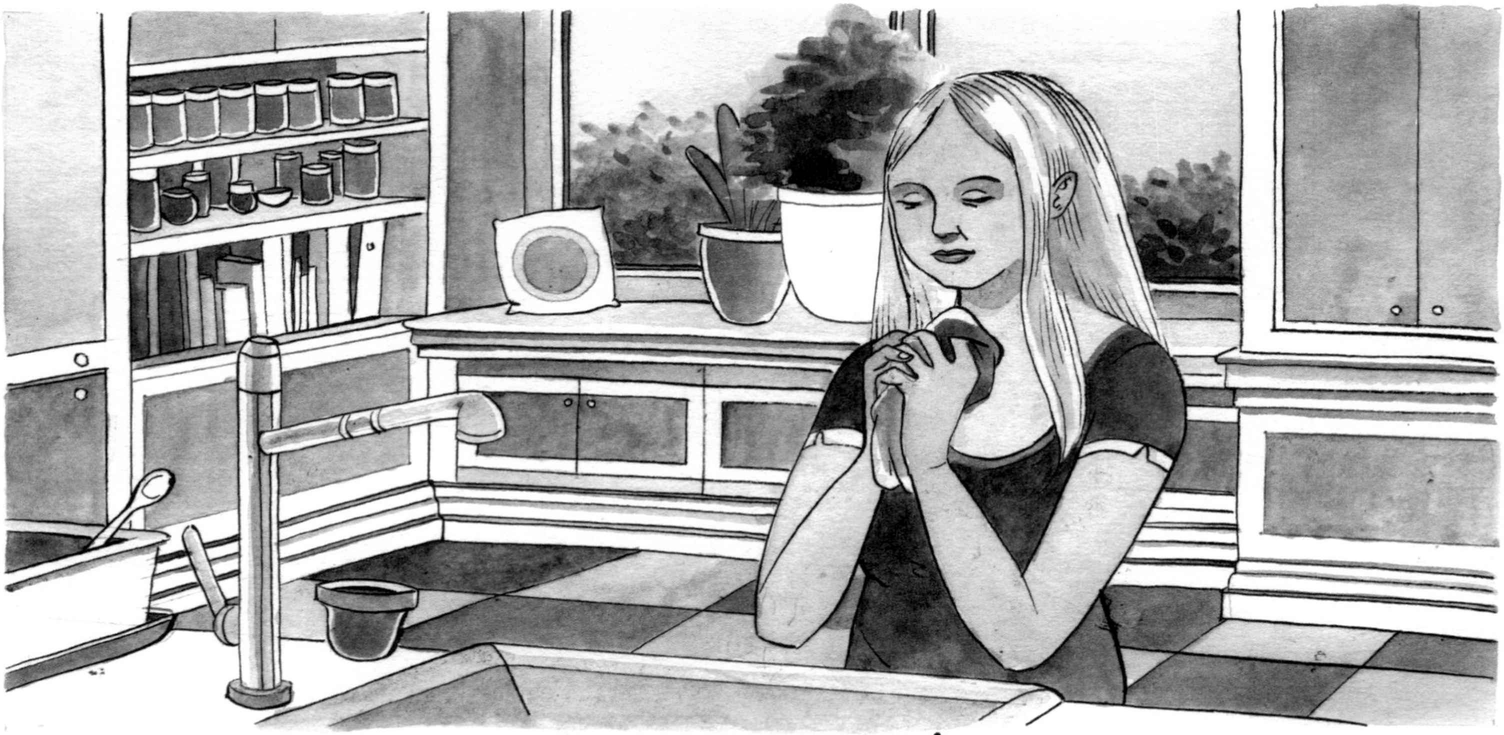

We'd been saving money for a while—cutting down on fancy dinners out, buying shoes on a whim, taking cabs, and all that. But James's parents helped us out with the bulk of the down payment—it was a godsend.

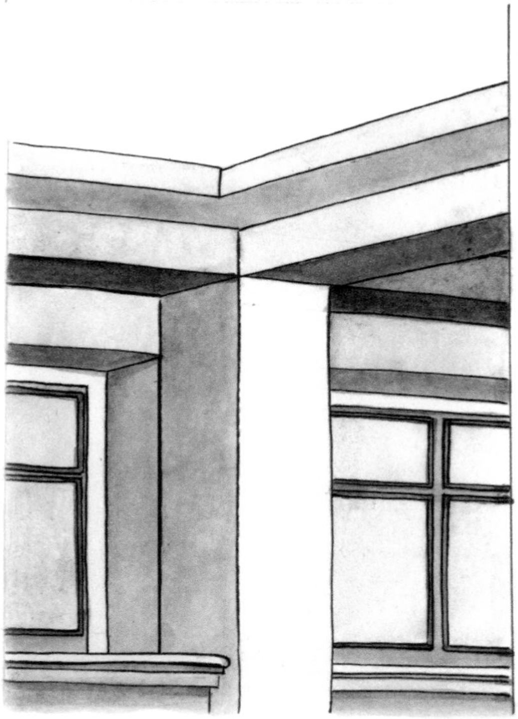

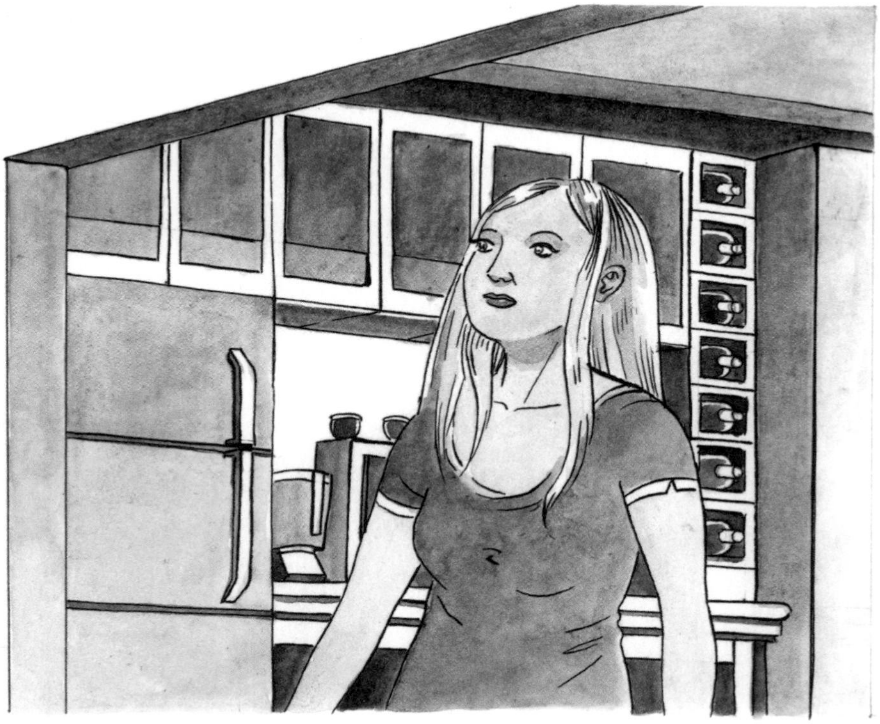

Summers had become so hot in the city and we'd been spending most weekends at the beach anyway, at a rental with friends. One weekend James said, "Yeah, well, we're not twenty-five anymore, are we? Maybe it's time to get our own place."

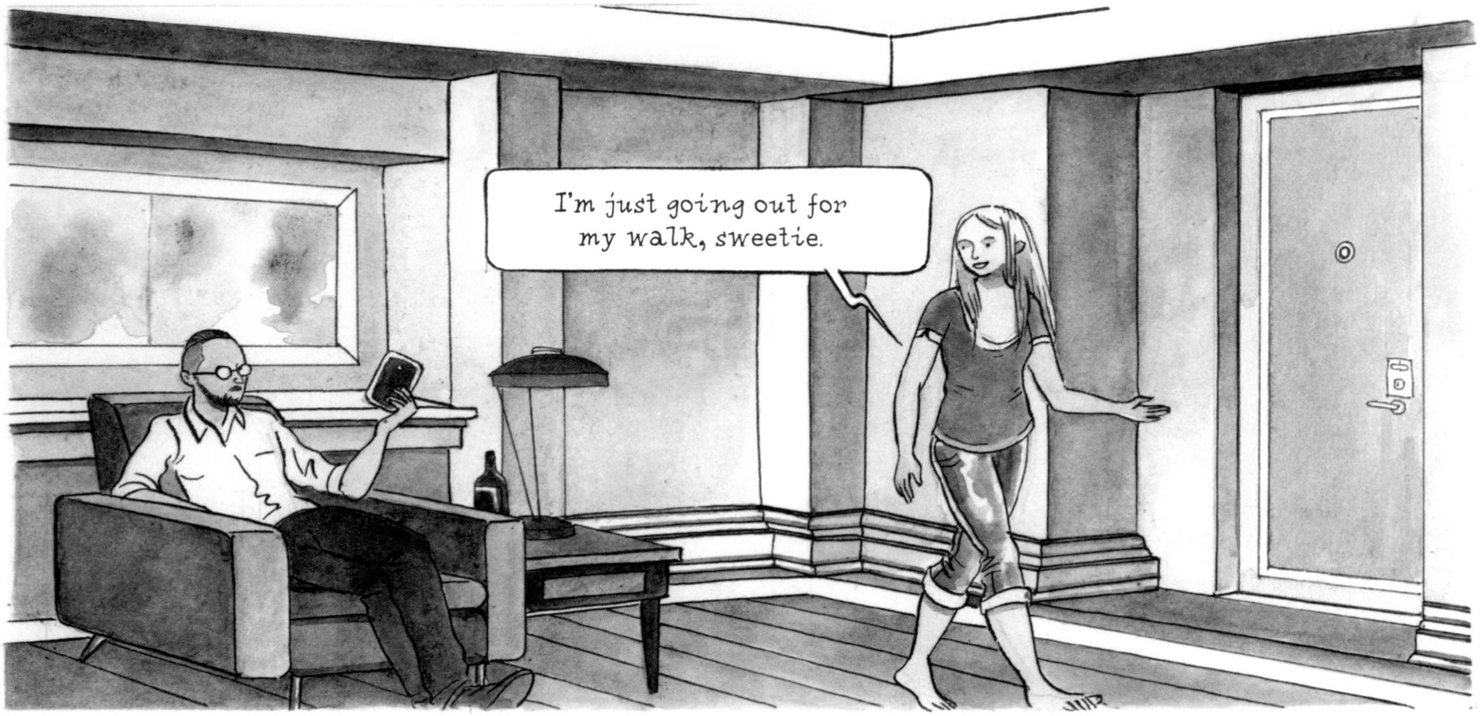
I'm just going out for my walk, sweetie.

We'd set down roots in the city, but we both loved the ocean so much and wanted to be closer to it, to feel—I don't know—moored to it, I guess.

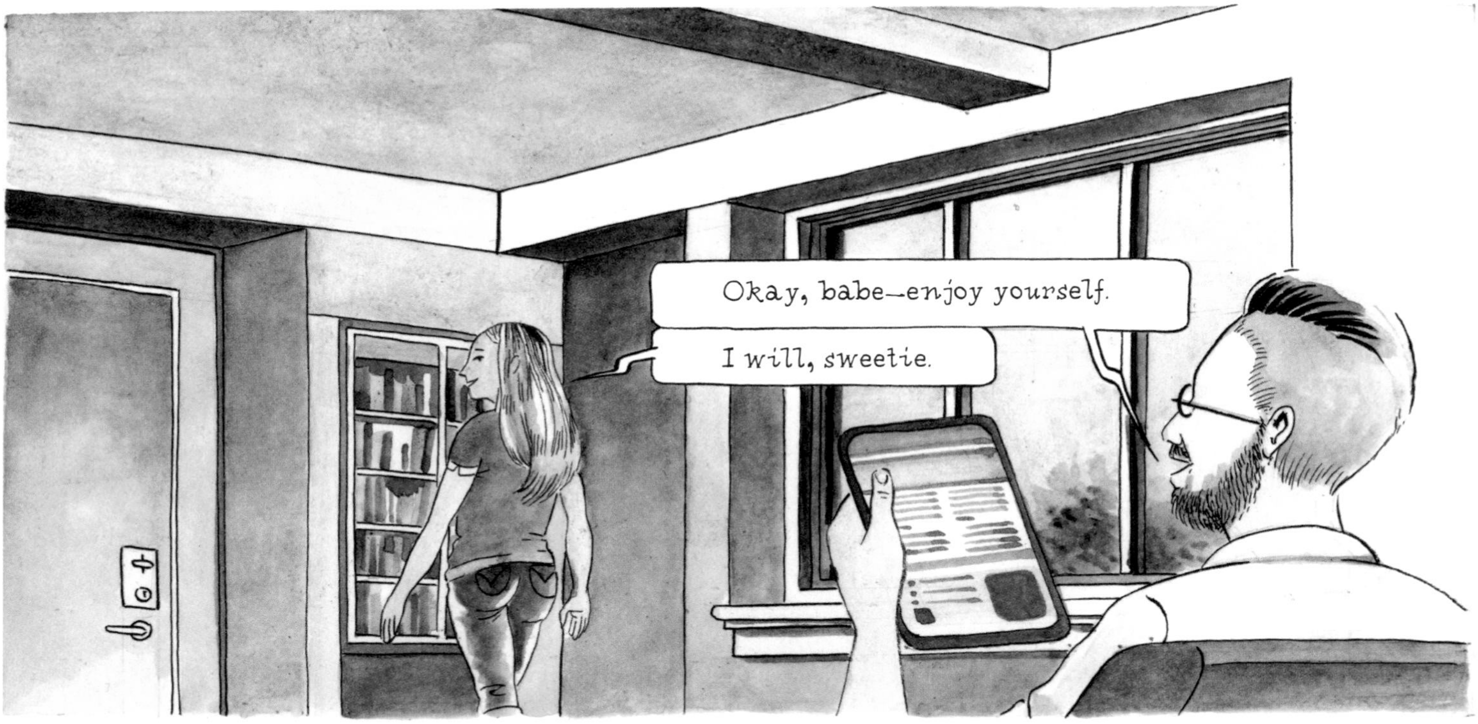
Okay, babe—enjoy yourself.
I will, sweetie.

Poor James. He'd grown up in Maine, near the ocean, and was always looking to get back to it. I'd never really spent much time by the water until I met James. I was too busy with Friday-night mojitos downtown and weekend brunches on Smith Street.

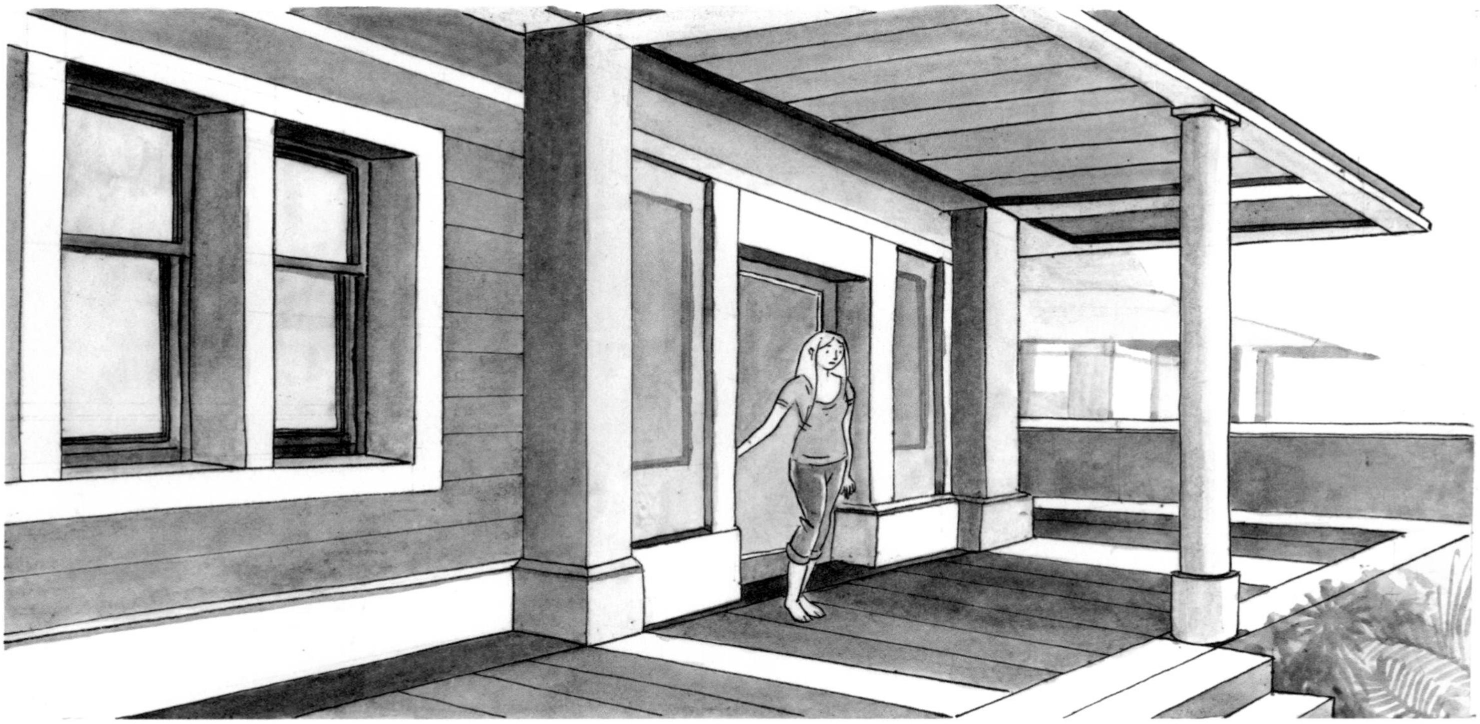

That all seems like another life now. Oh, I'll still meet up with Maisie and Gretchen after work, once in a while. But god knows even that's become an exercise in time management.

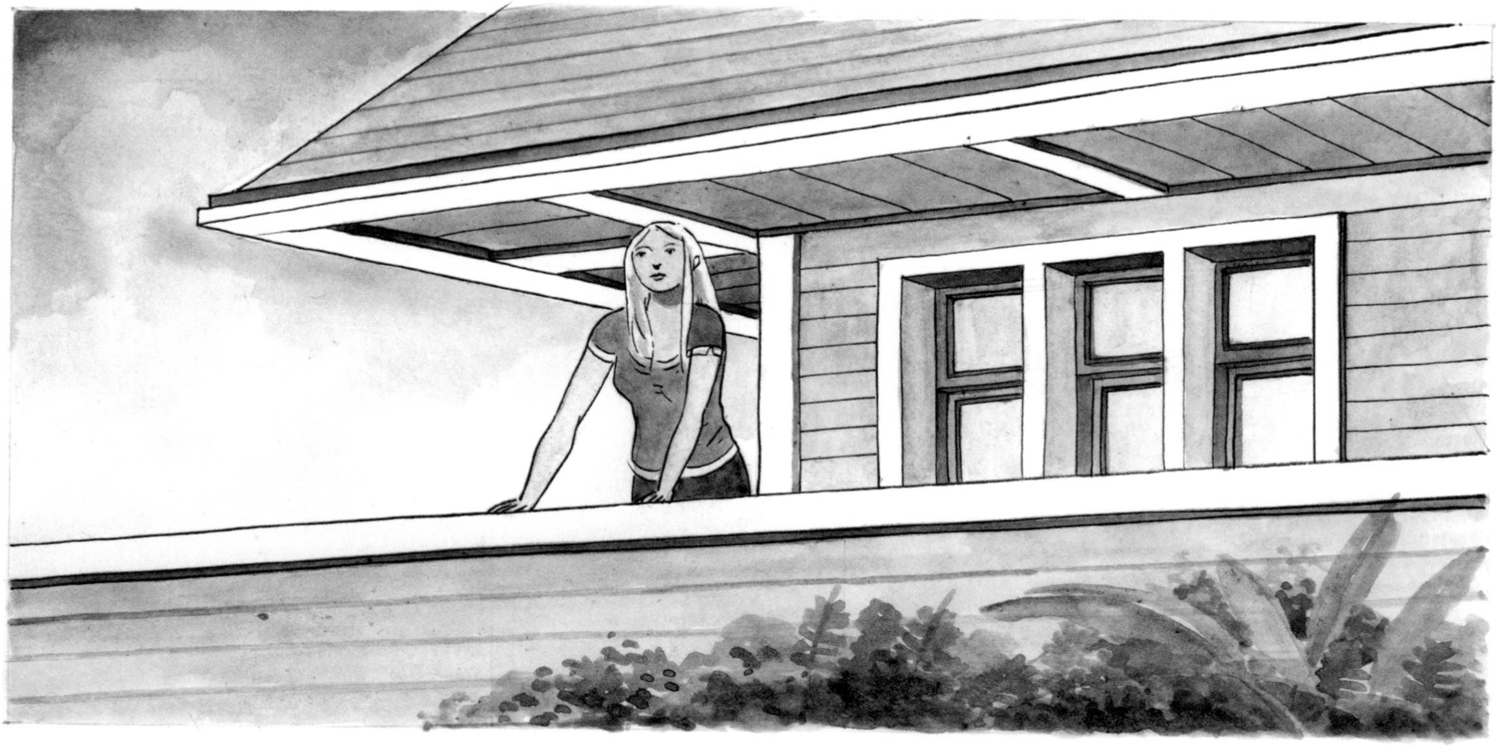

I do wonder if they envy or pity me, being the last of our little gang to still be unburdened by motherhood. I keep telling them James and I aren't ready yet and they start up with the *tick-tick-ticking* sounds and I'm all like, "Have another drink, bitches," and we all laugh.

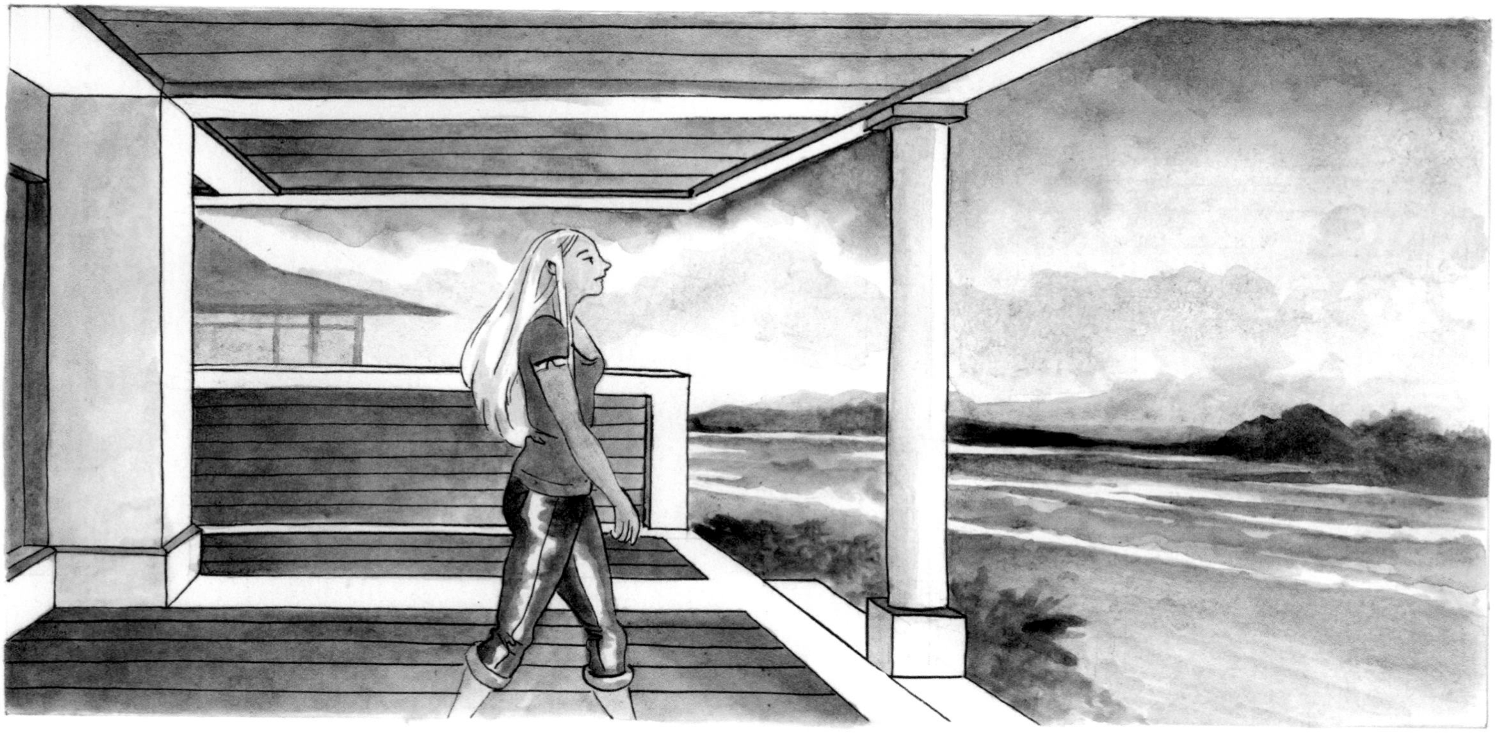

Anyway, I forget about all that when it's twilight and there's a salty breeze on the beach and the sand is still warm underfoot . . . I could just walk for hours, not having to focus on any one thing in particular.

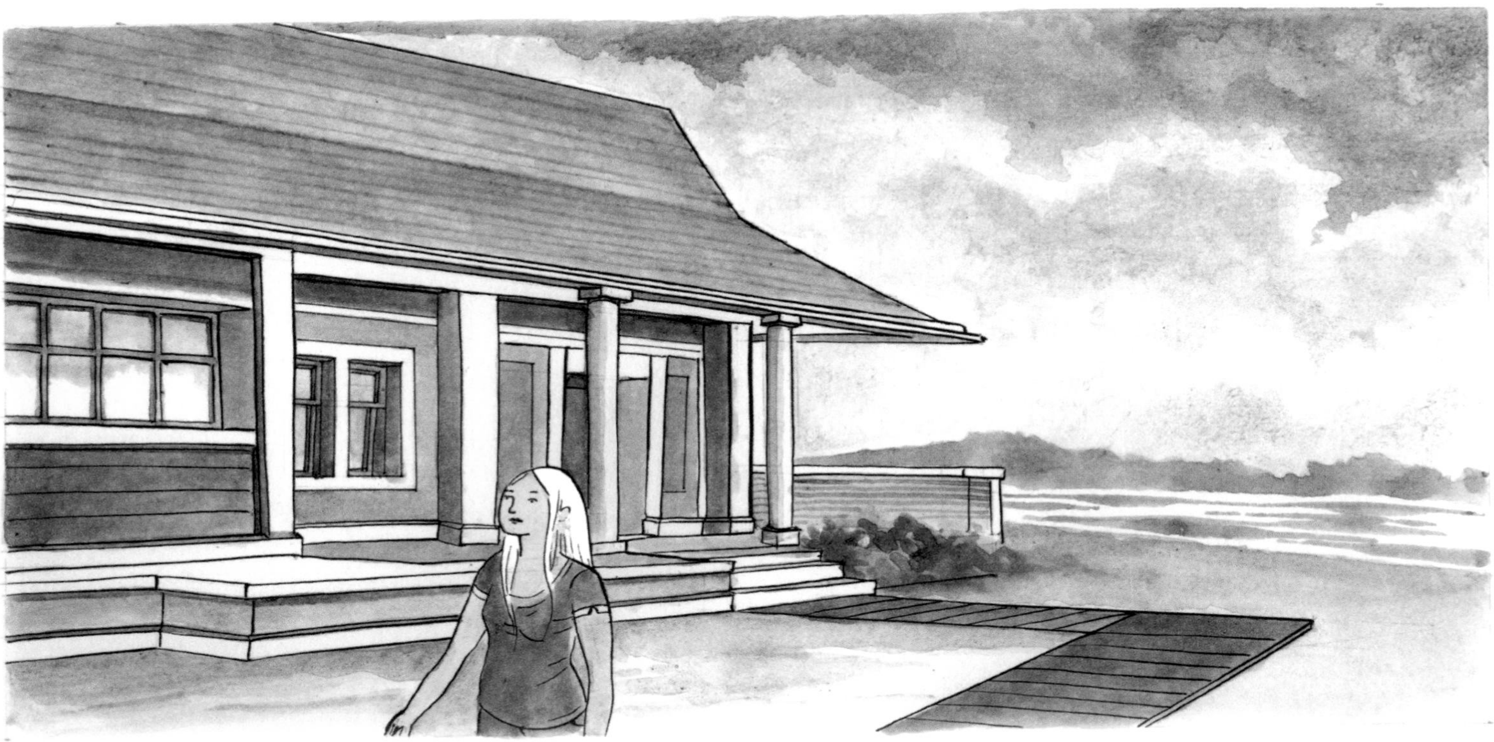

James prefers morning walks, when the light on the ocean is glimmering, flickering rapidly like thousands of diamonds popping in and out of existence. But my evening walks are my own.

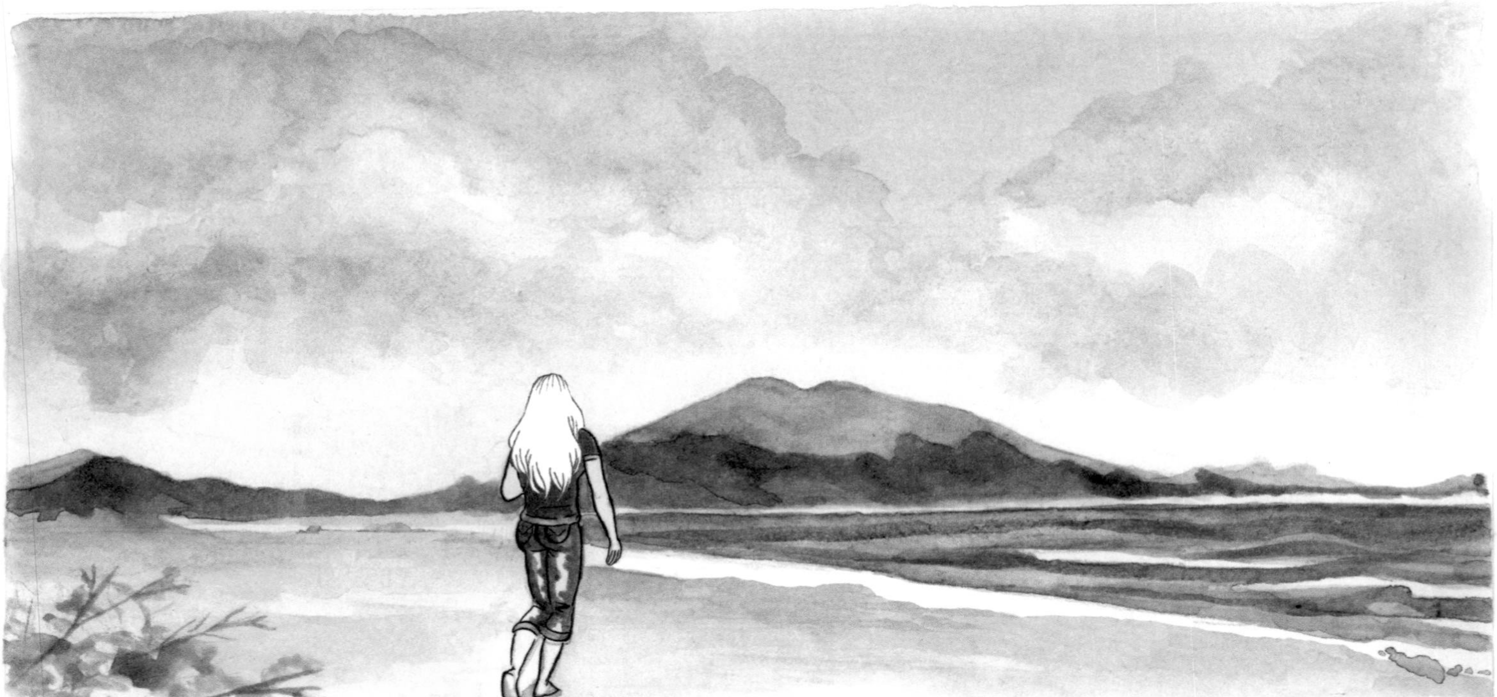

I feel a glorious nothing inside. No mindless mental chatter, no internal dialogue, a great absence of this and that.

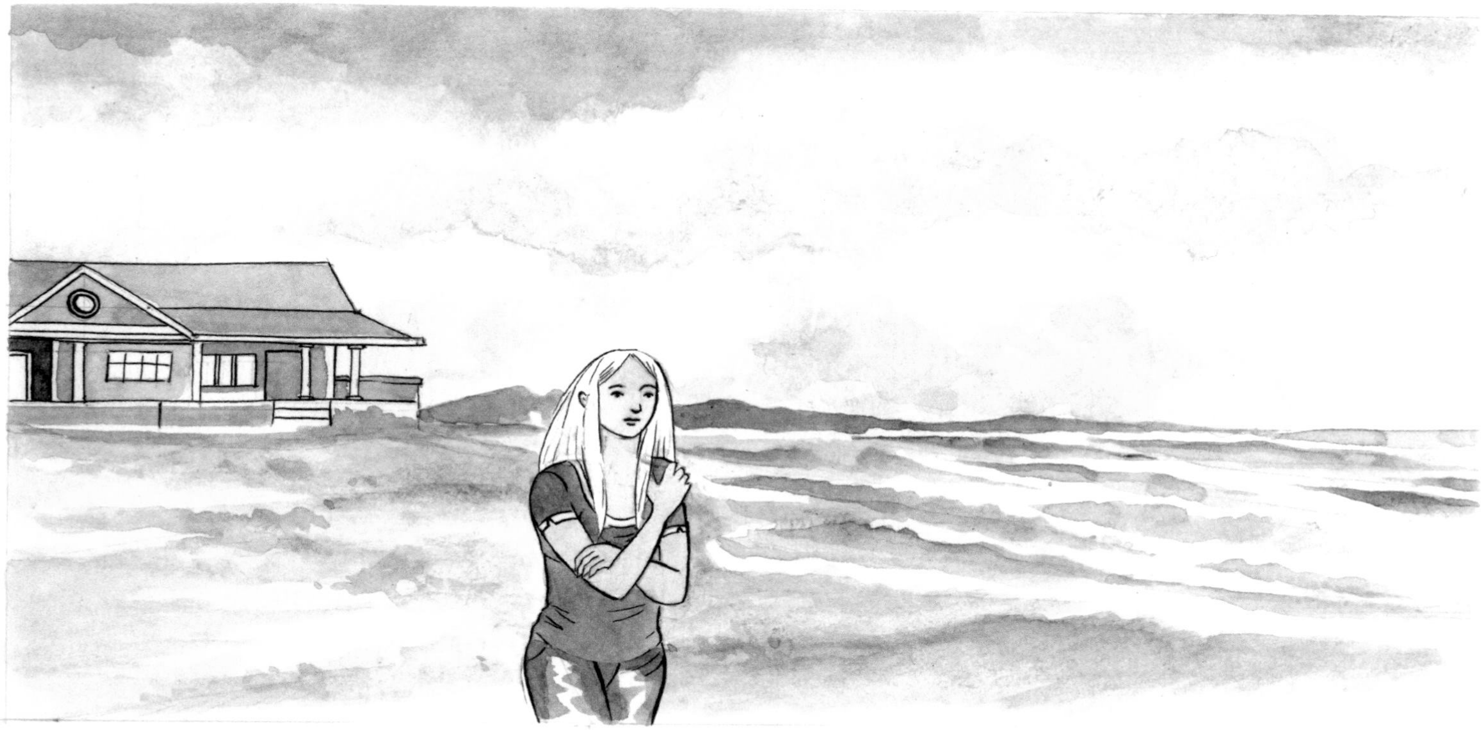

It was hard to get to this point though. Time was when I'd come out for my walk and still be thinking about Sunday antiques shopping or who to invite to James's birthday party or how James had seemed more stressed than usual, and on and on.

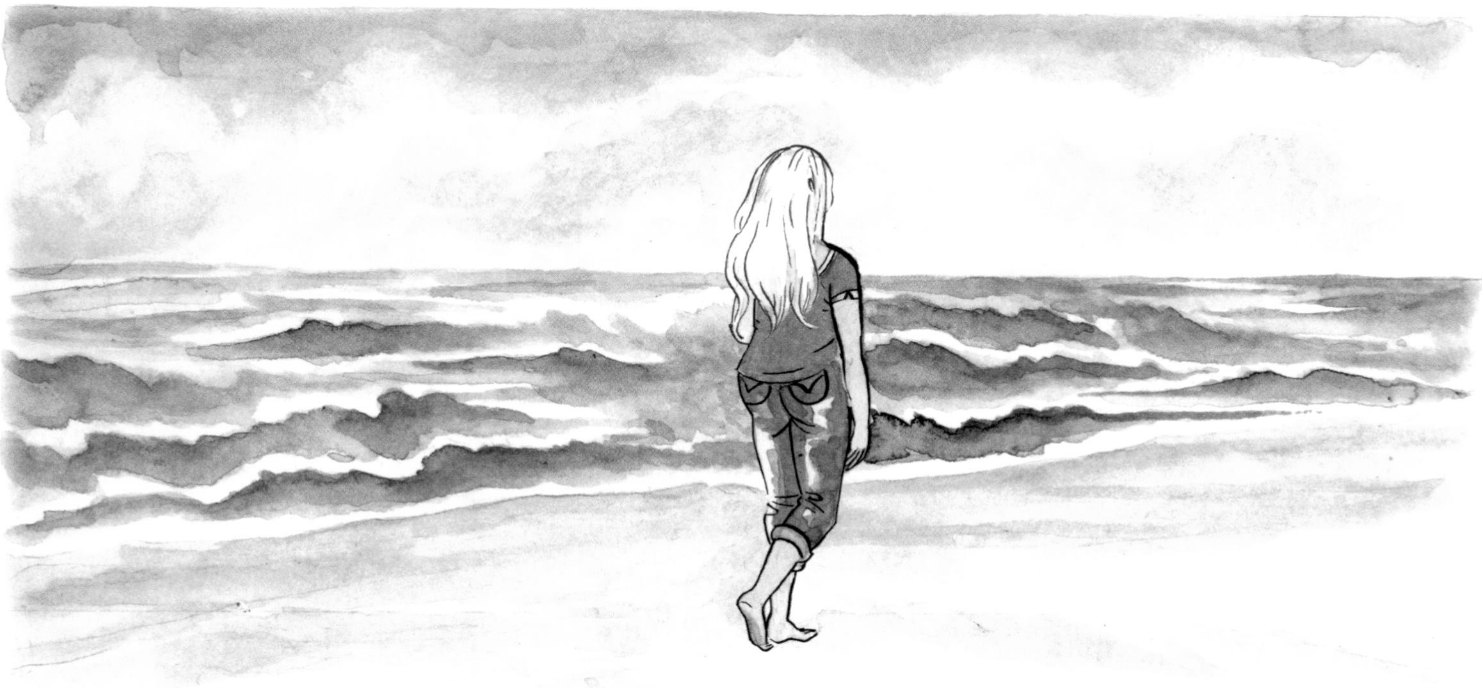

And cutting off that constant stream of thoughts—why was that so difficult? My yoga teacher used to say we should stop being so scared of the idea of nothing and embrace it instead.

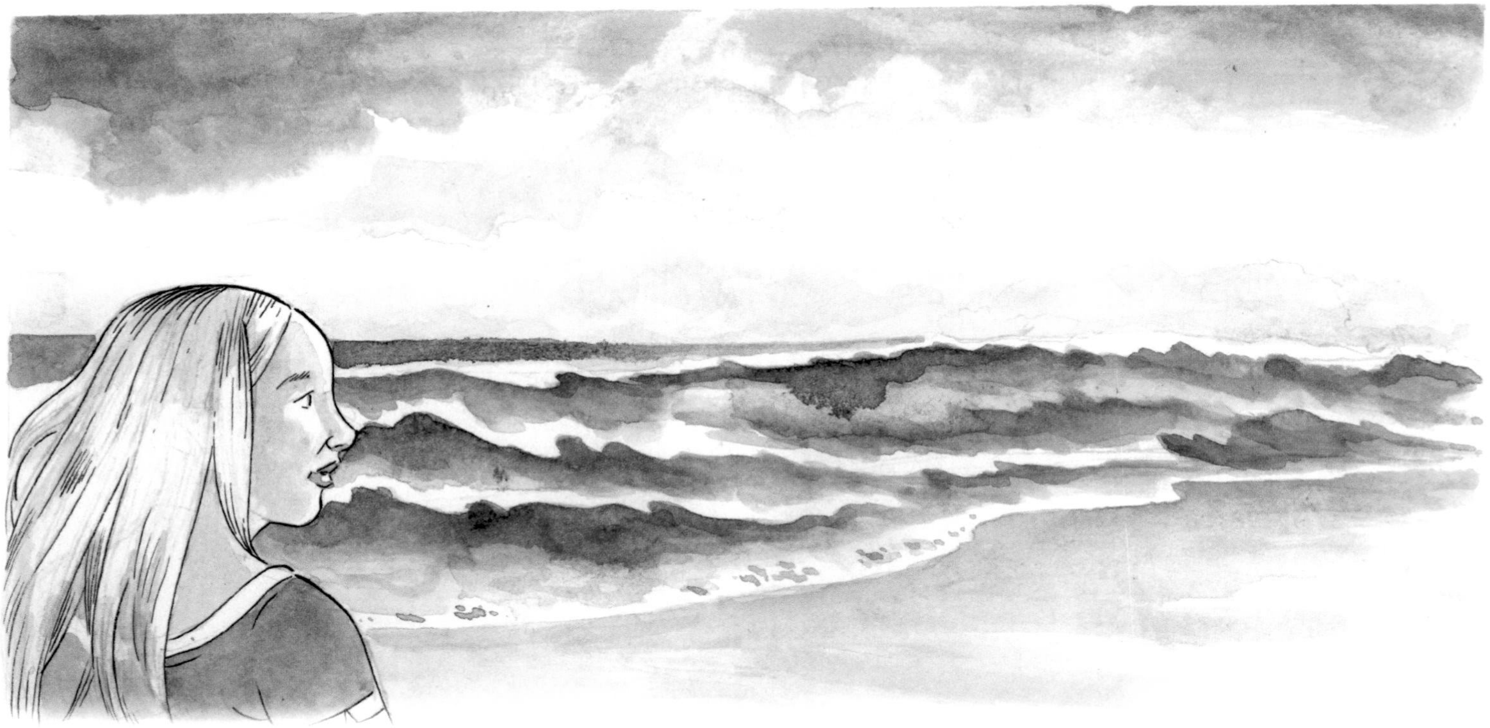

I don't know if that's what I've done. All I need to know during this time is the sound of waves, the call of gulls, the line of the horizon, the flight of clouds.

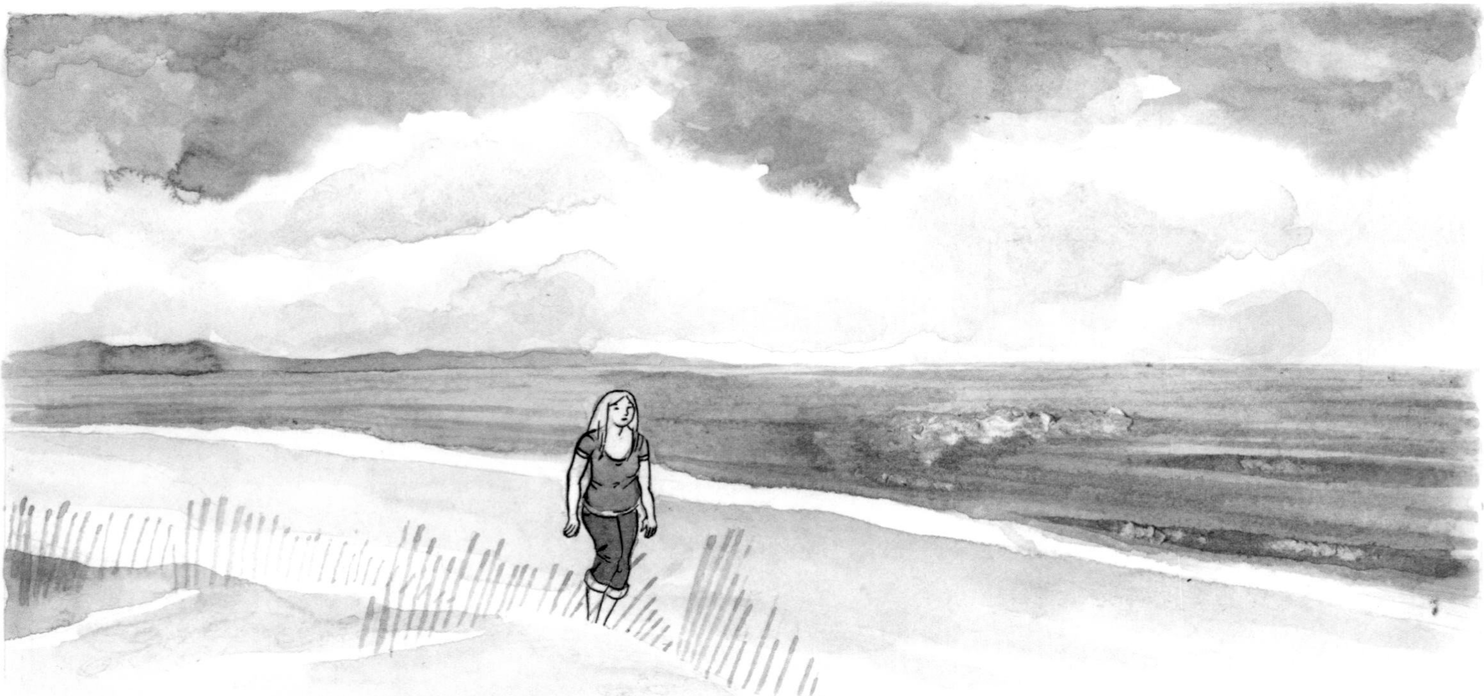

I don't really talk to James about this kind of stuff. Not that he wouldn't understand, but I'd sound like an ass to myself going on about it.

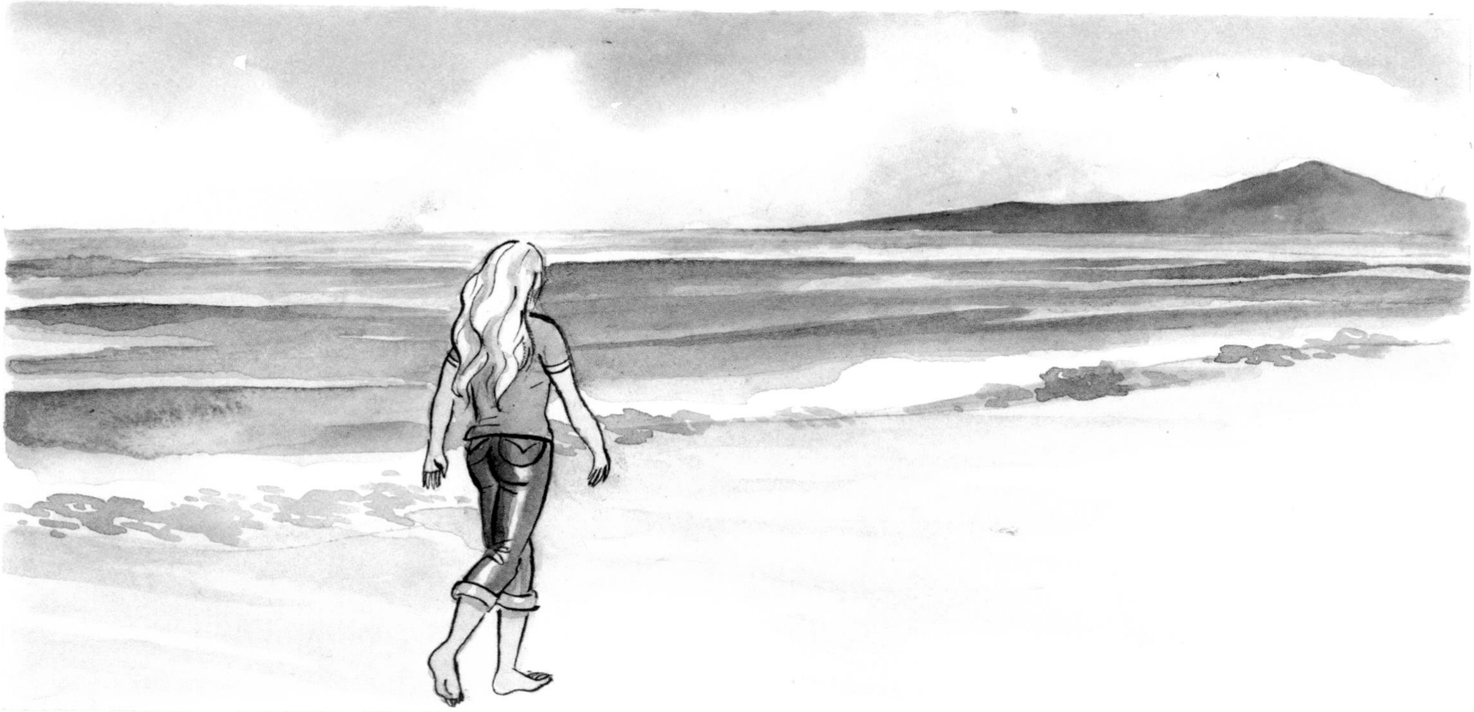

And it's not even as if I'm uncomfortable with it because it seems vaguely spiritual or religious—and therefore wacky. It's more a practical matter to me to be able to feel a calm.

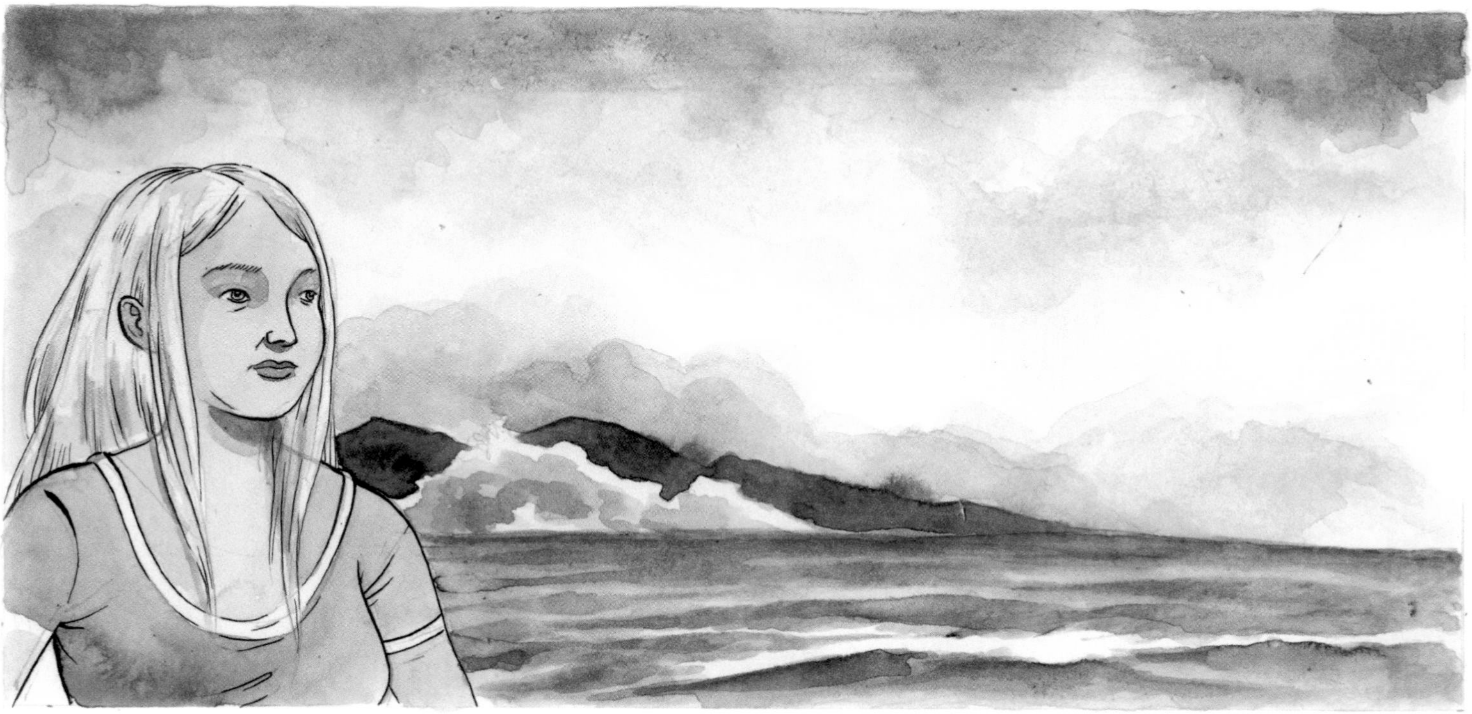

James would say I was really starting to shed my old skin, talking about walks on the beach this way. Which is fine by me—at least I'm not hanging around at singles bars anymore.

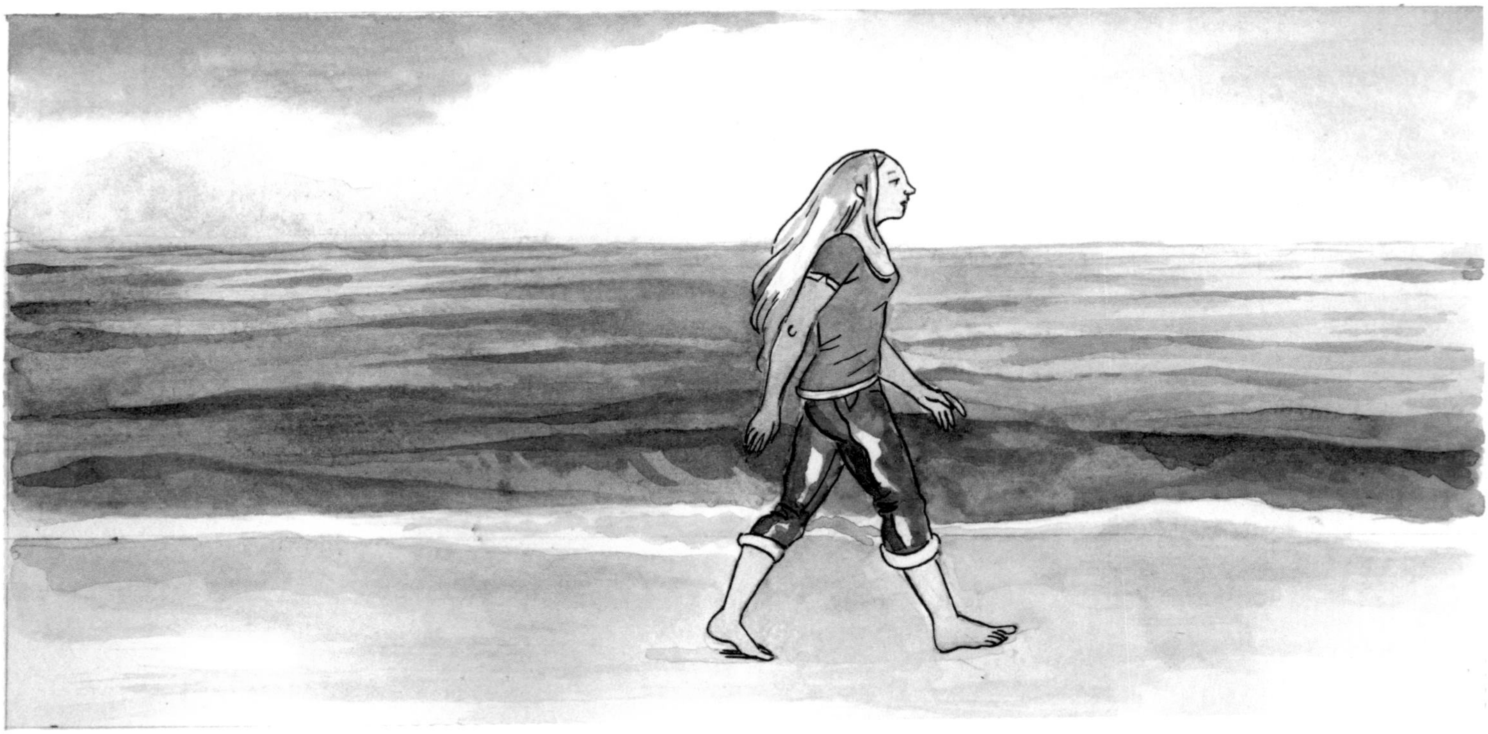

Ha ha! James would say the very same thing. When we first got together, we'd spend evenings at his apartment, drinking wine and laughing, laughing—"Thank you for saving me!" he'd say. The inevitable weekends out with his buddies were becoming tedious.

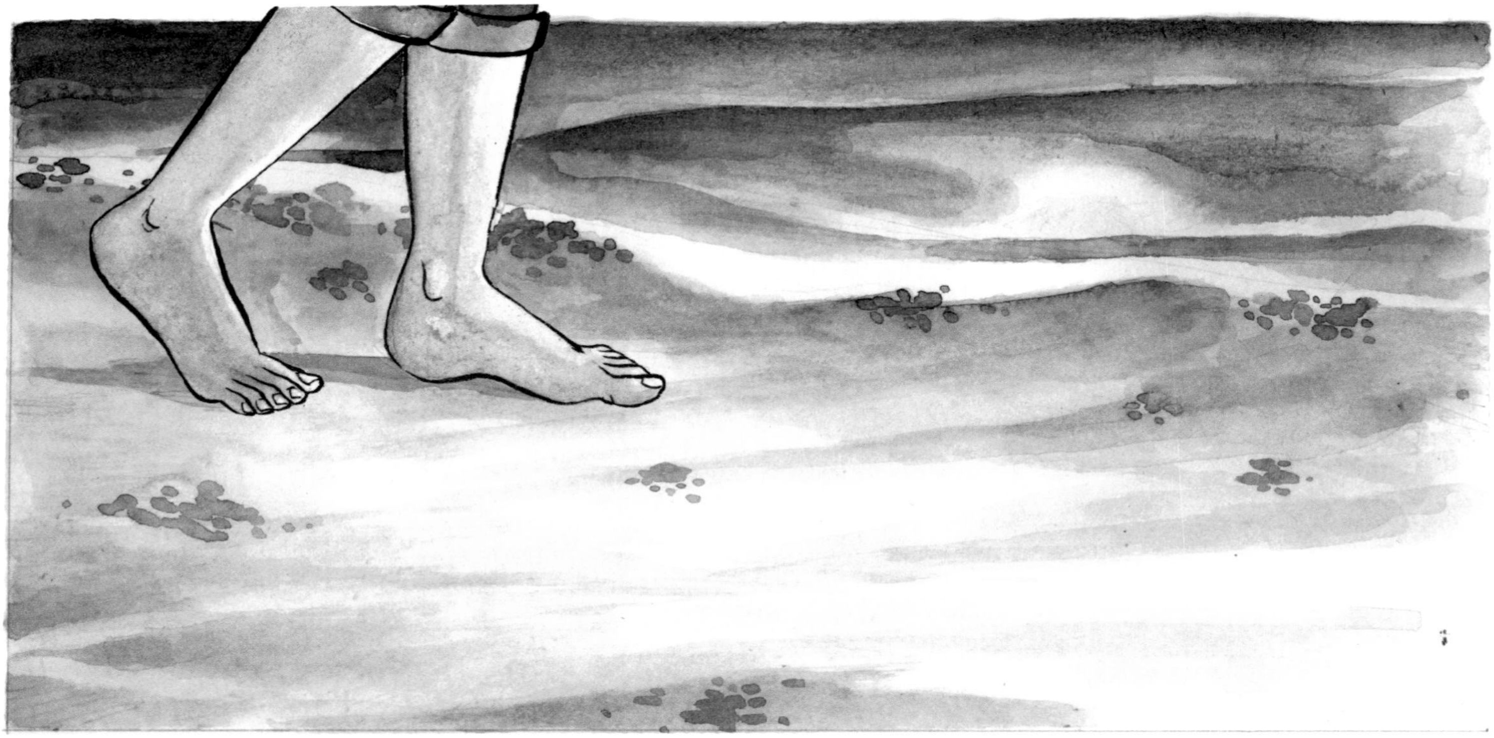

And unlike a lot of guys, he really wanted to settle down early—even before I did. Not that I minded. I was so happy the day he asked me. God, I was delirious. It wasn't a surprise; we'd been together nearly a year. But still!

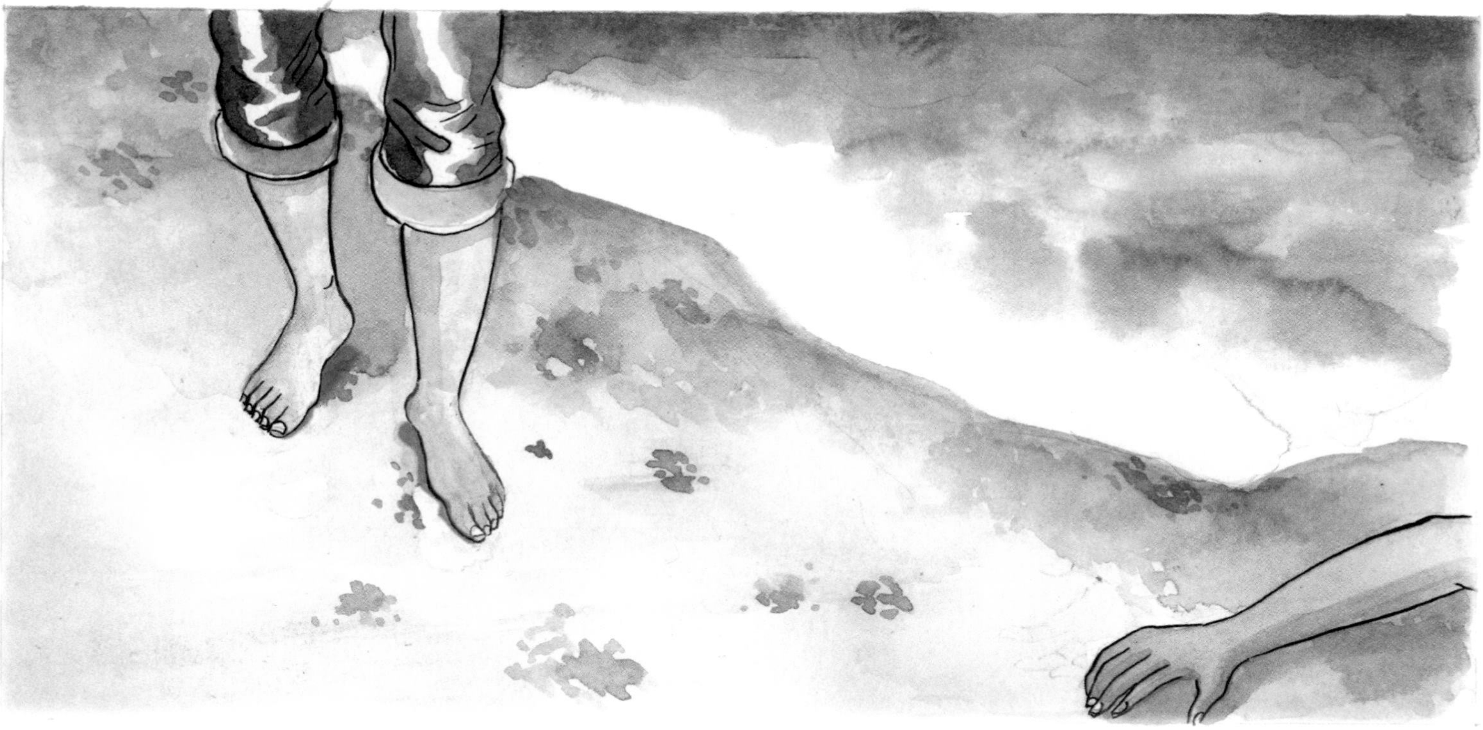

He kissed me: on my forehead, my nose, my lips, my neck, my chest, my stomach; on both thighs, knees, and then—both my feet. Who else would have done that?

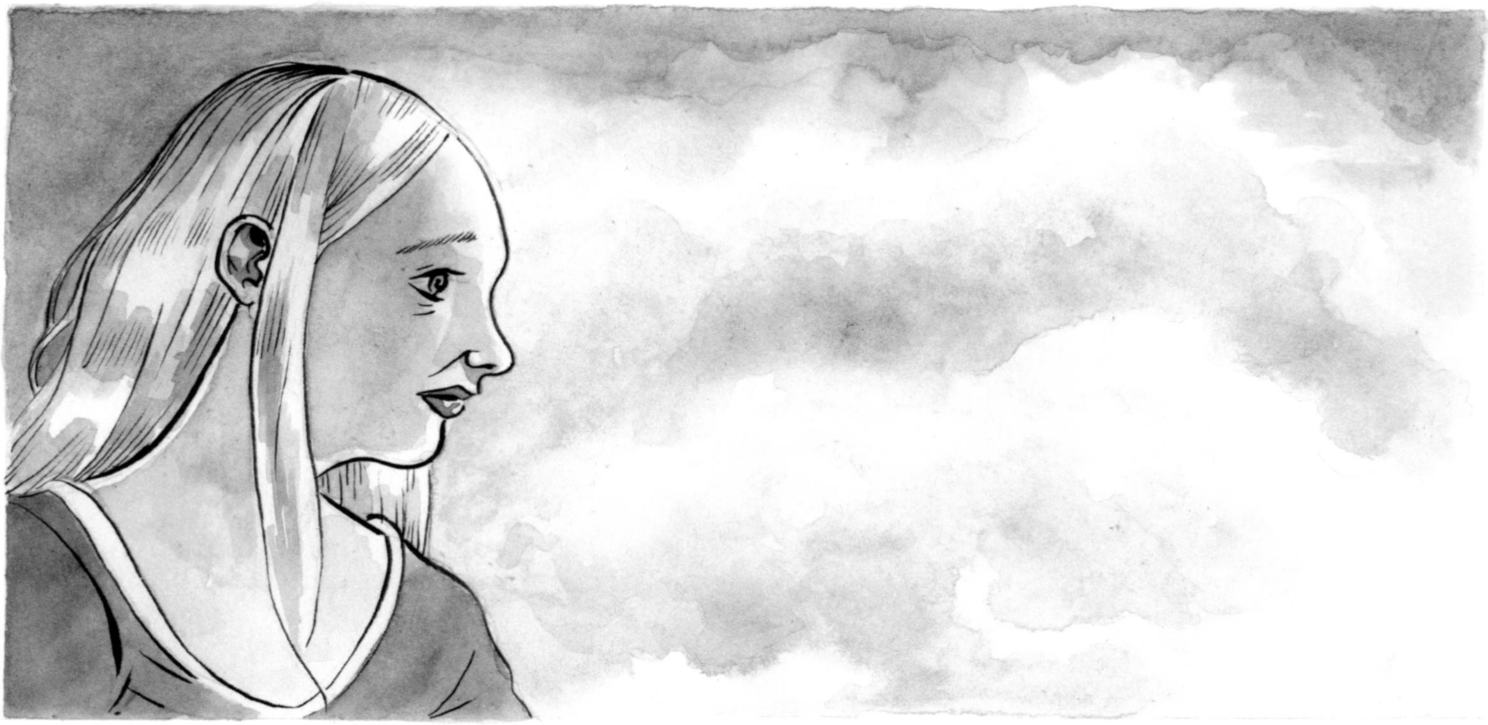

Then he asked me and I said yes and we both just started laughing. We were both so happy and I held his hands and kissed them, one finger at a time, over and over again.

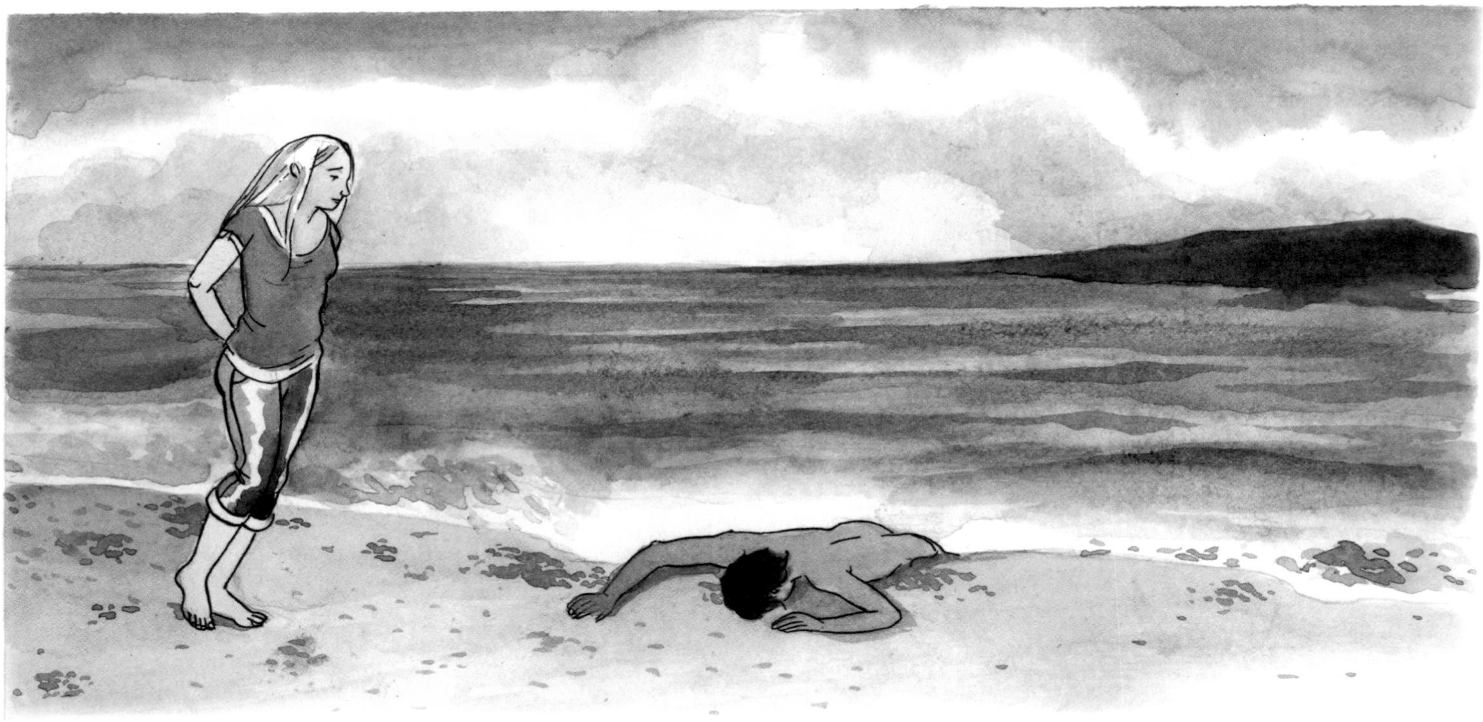

At first, things went pretty quickly. My mom started planning as soon as she got off the phone with me, I'm sure.

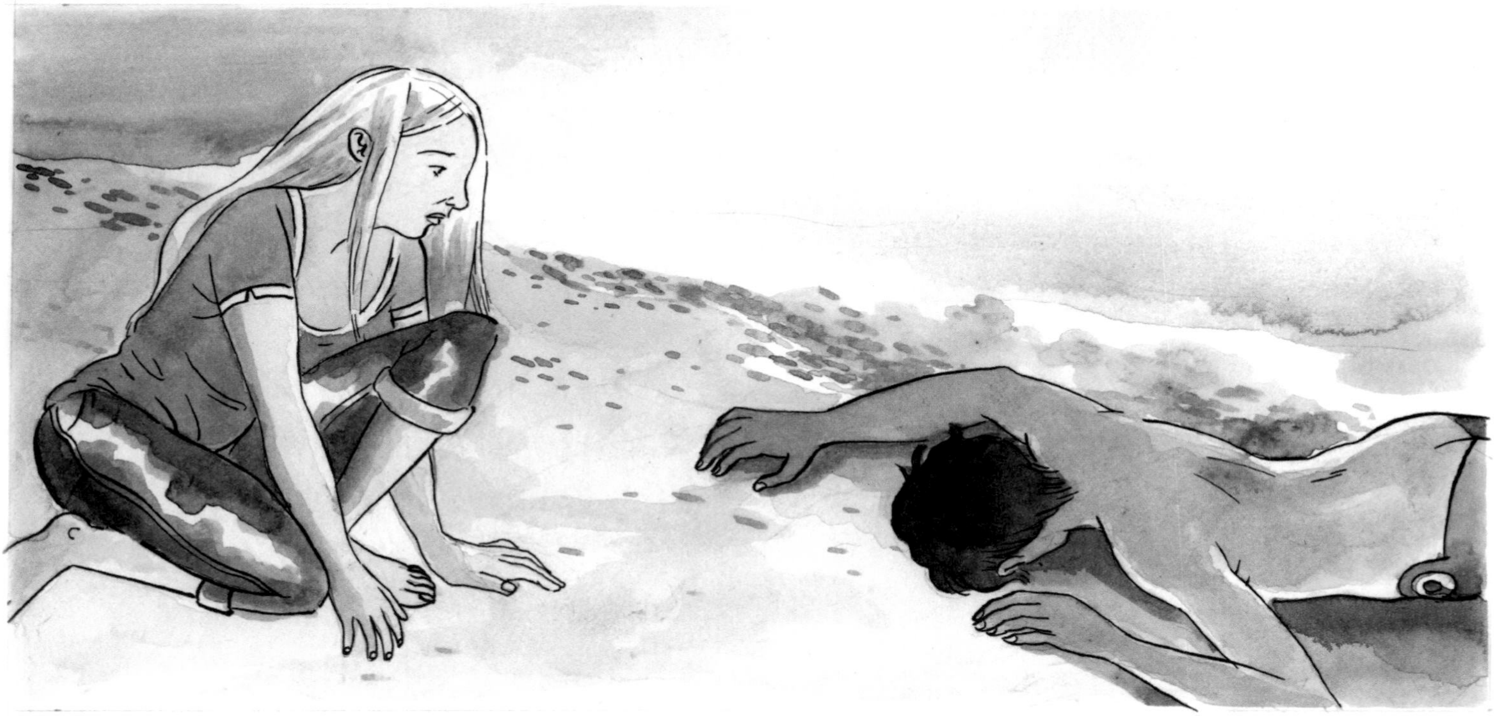

I was all like, "Ma, come on, please—we'll take care of it, seriously," which of course did absolutely no good at all.

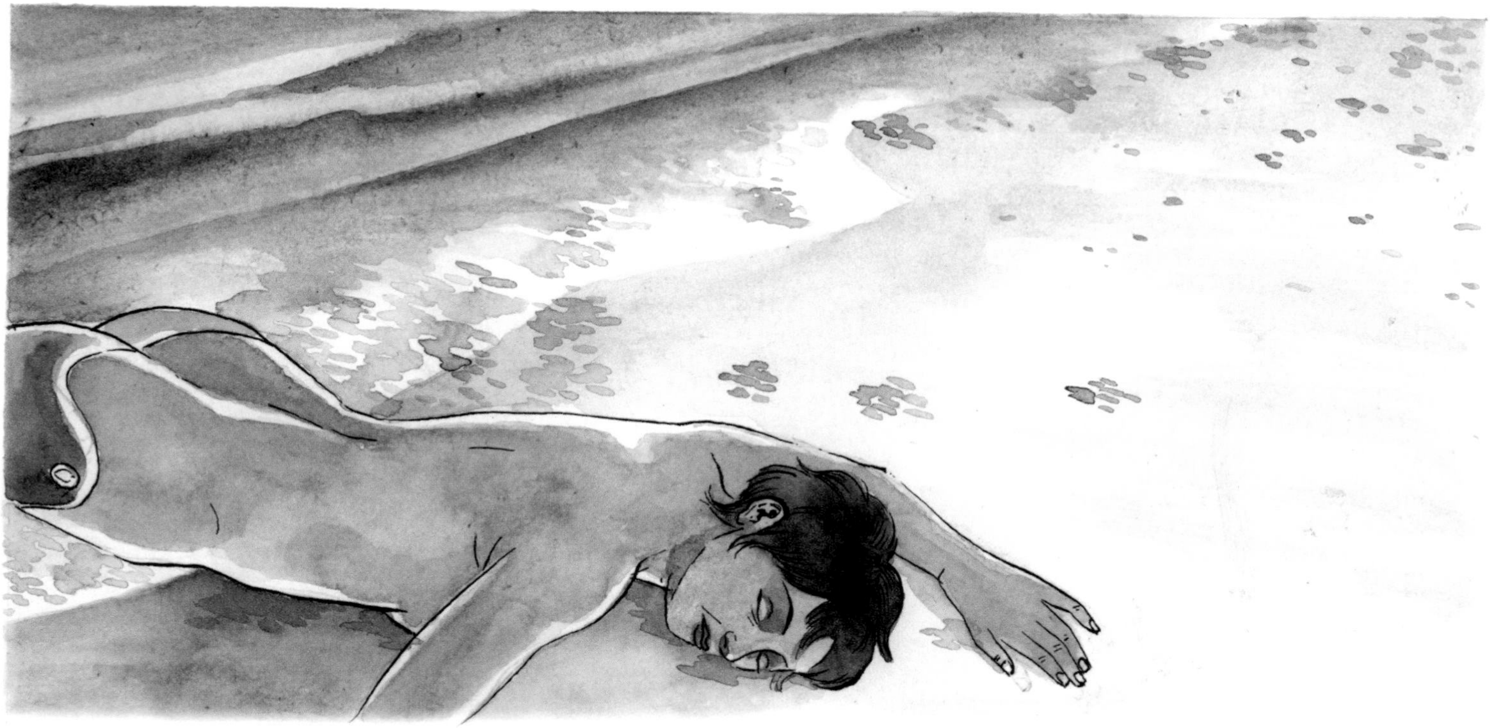

And I guess we did take care of it eventually. And thereby set a new record for "longest and strangest engagement ever!"

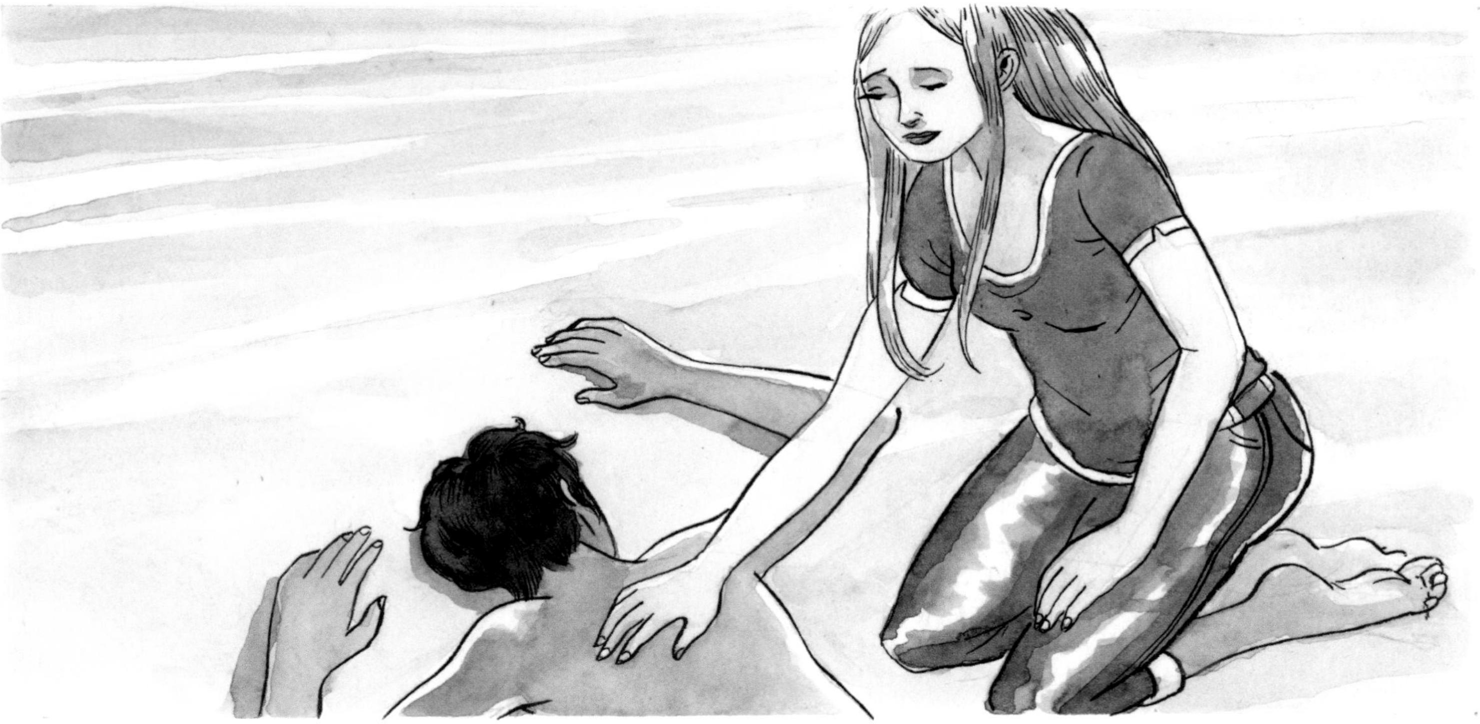

It's good to be able to laugh about it now. It wasn't so funny back then.

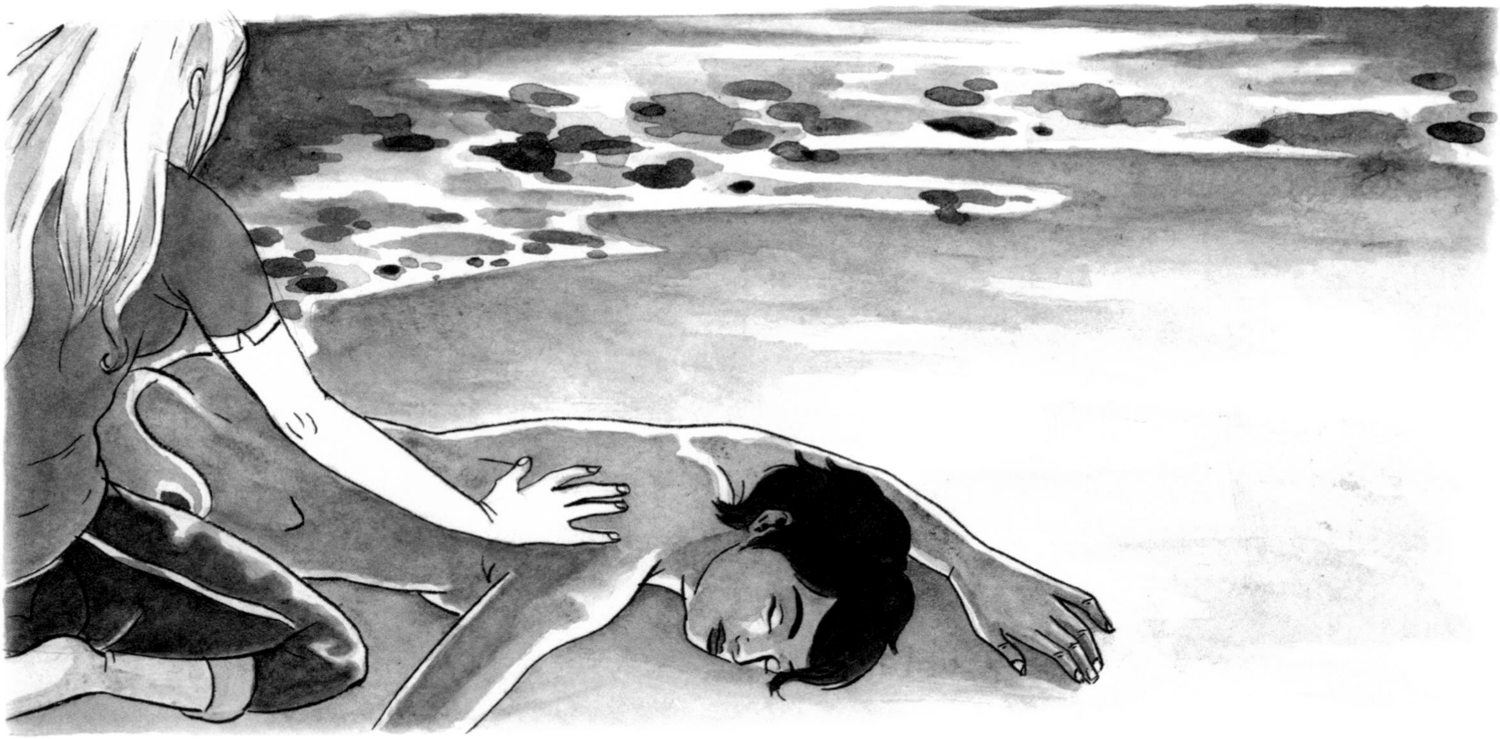

No, it was a long and stressful time for both of us. James was suddenly called away for weeks at a time—off to Tokyo, Bangkok, Shanghai—to deal with a flurry of projects that he'd been trying to manage for a while.

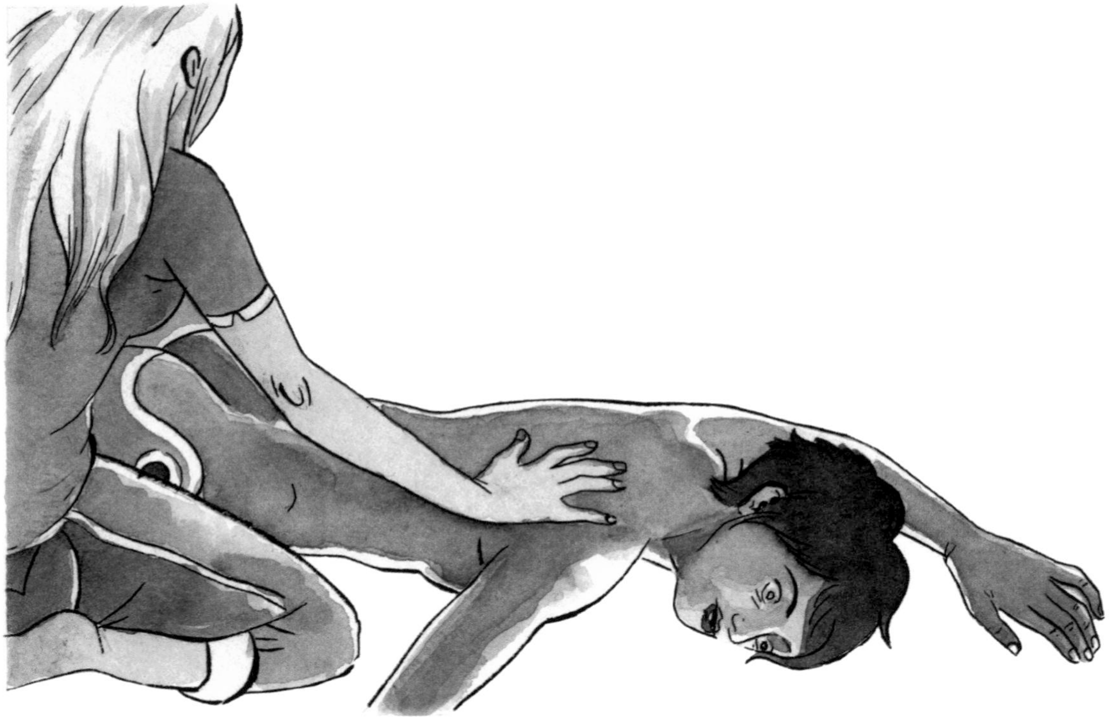

It was an amazing turning point in his career. He was obviously starting to be taken very seriously, and for us and our future, that meant only good things. But for me—alone for great yawning stretches—well, I was bored. So I'd call up Maisie and Gretchen and they'd feel bad for me and we briefly revived our Friday-night routine, which was all pretty funny, until . . .

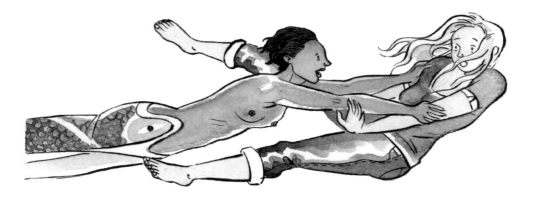

He was pretty shy and nervous. He'd been dragged to the bar by his buddies. I was, well, pretty drunk and I thought he was cute—tall, thin, boyish, slightly geeky—and I came on to him pretty aggressively.

And no, I didn't know what I was doing. I wasn't really thinking. Like I said, I was bored, bored, bored.

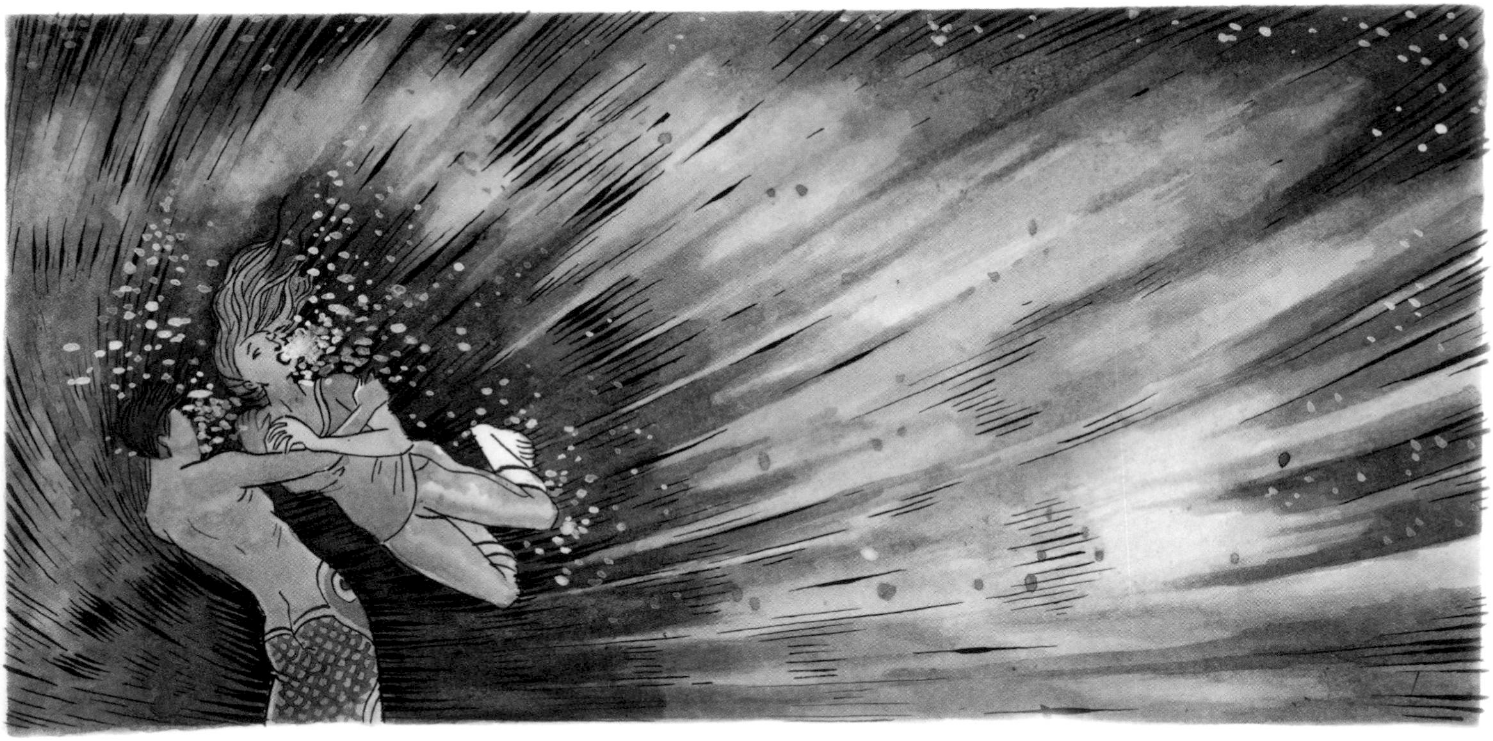

Anyway, I took him home. Of course it was strange. Instead of James, muscly and hard, there was this gangly child next to me.

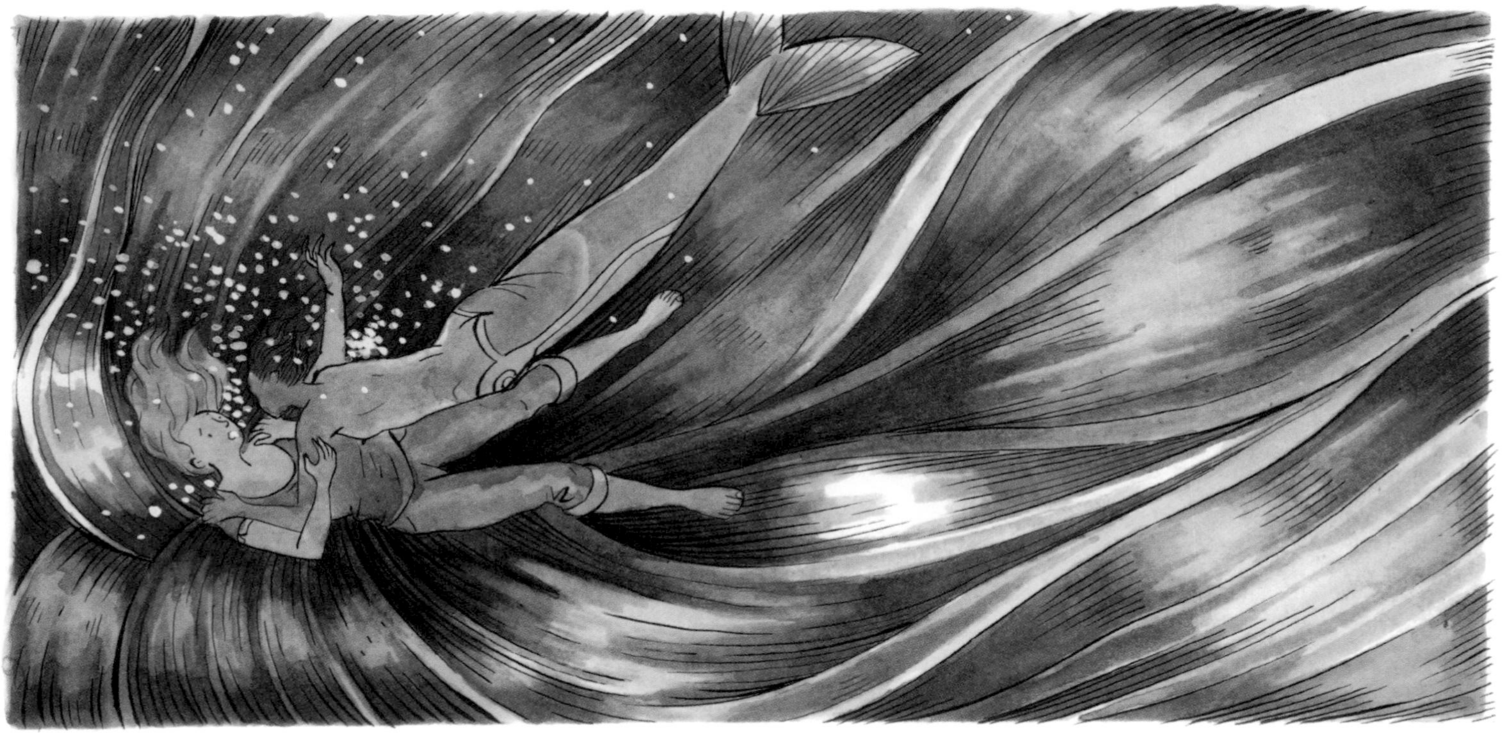

I don't think he knew what hit him. Although I tempered my approach after that night, I'd cook him dinners (he was happy to have someone feed him) and he'd tell me about his band, his jobs, his mom.

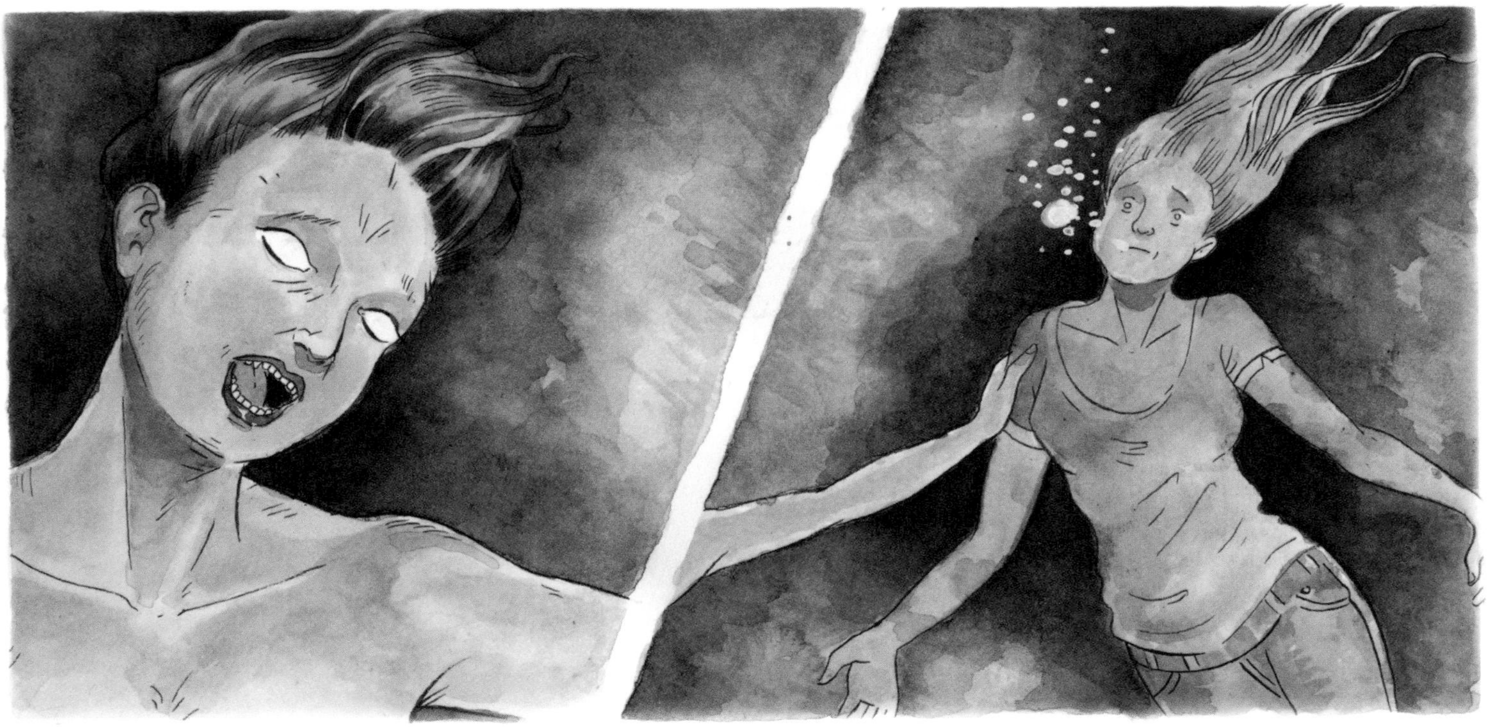

I'd go to see his band play and buy drinks for him and his friends.
I felt silly and immature but that, I guess, was the point.

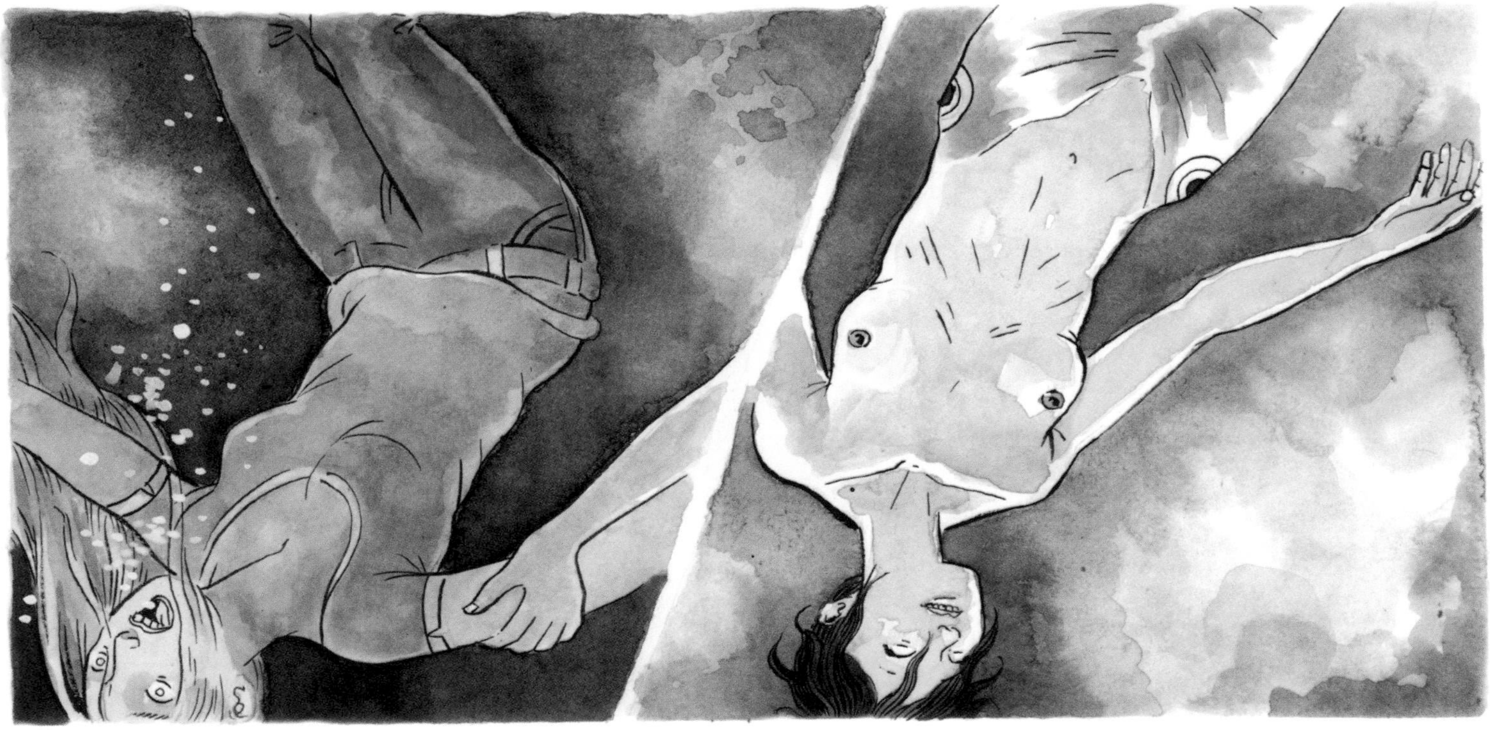

He did. He said it once. Which only added to his charm. He said he loved me and that he felt bad about the situation, but at the same time, we were both thrilled. And for a while, a short while, I thought about what it would be like to stretch out this giggle.

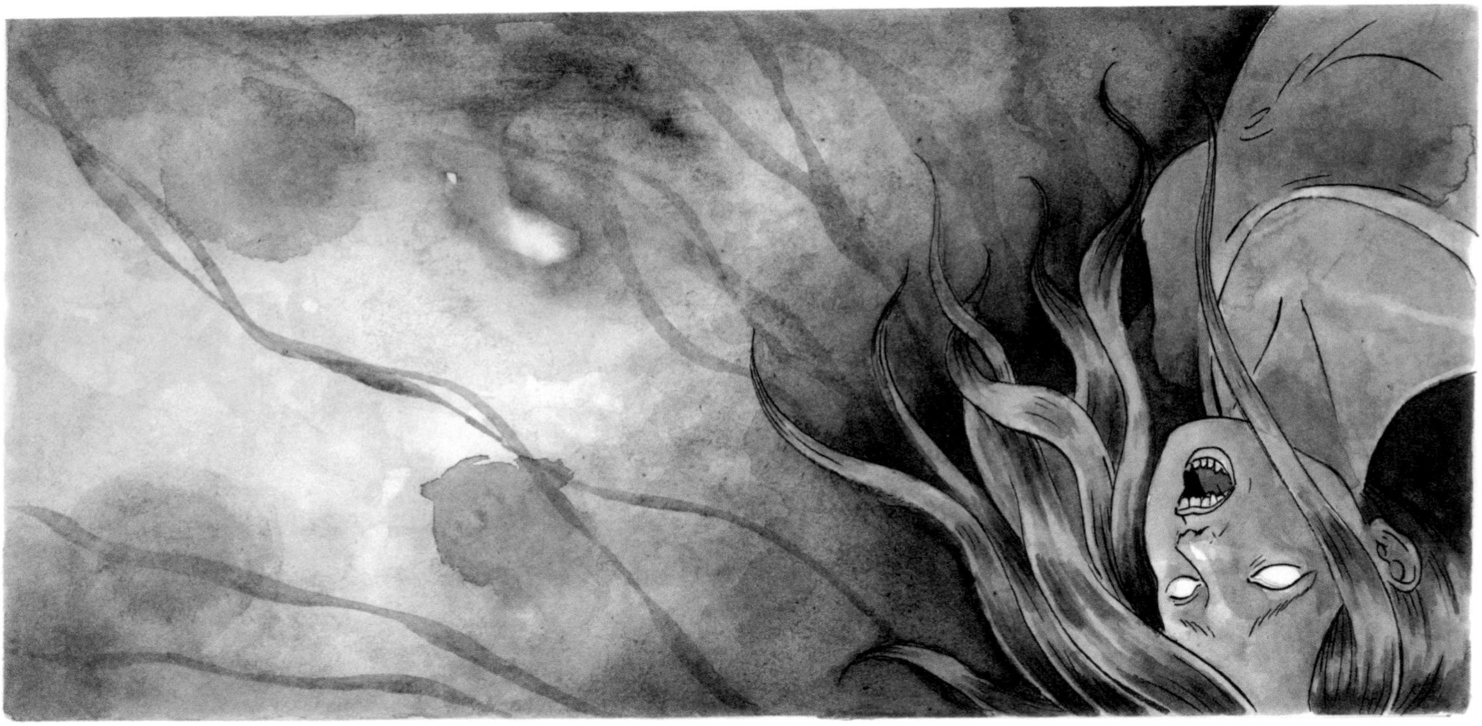

James phoned one night in September to say he was off the overseas projects, after much negotiation and complaints of battle fatigue, and that he was coming home for good.

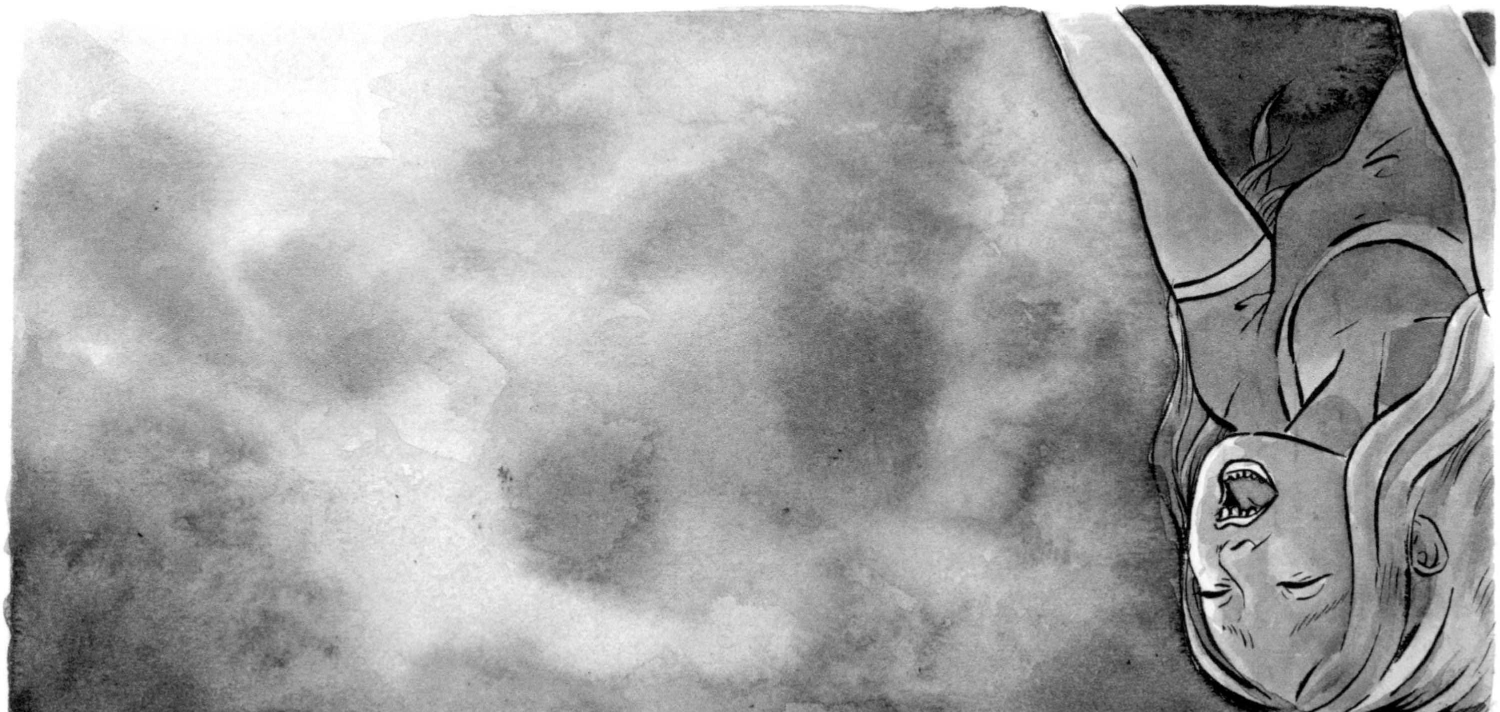

So that ended that. I let my little man-child go and he went, reluctantly and not without a small fight, but nothing painful, thank god.

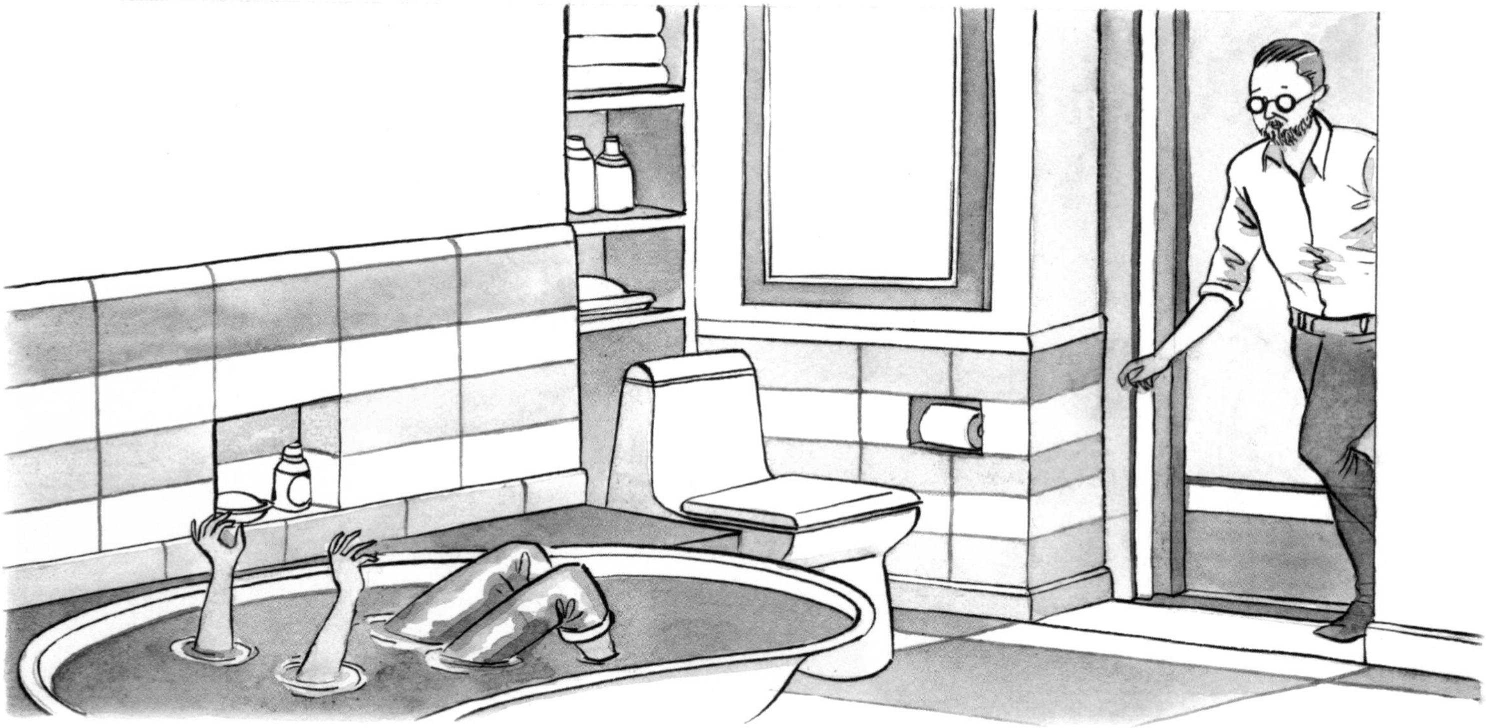

James doesn't know anything about it. There was no point in telling him. It would have killed our relationship, our future—for the sake of what, I don't know, a sort of slavish allegiance to "the truth"?

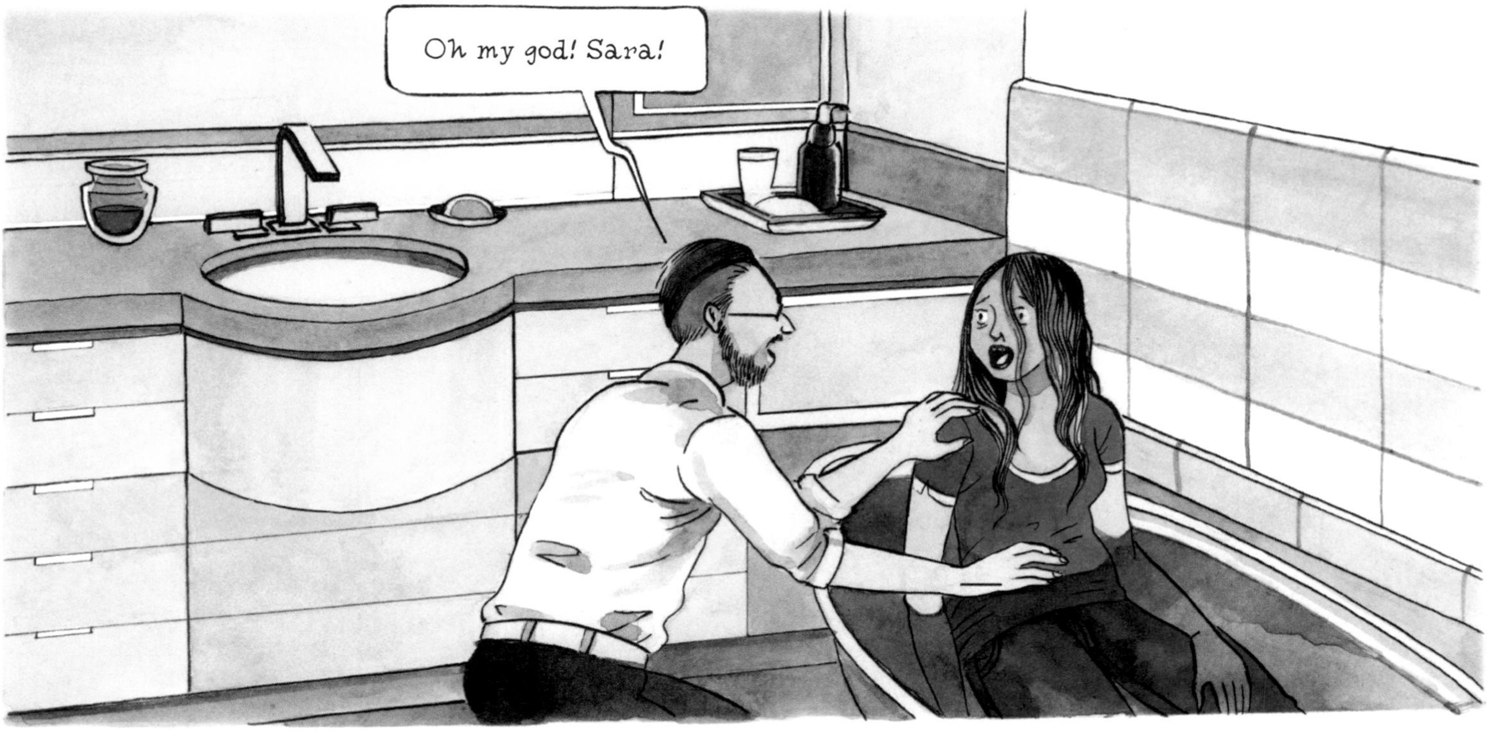
Oh my god! Sara!

Anyway, I'm sure he was off with some Asian beauty at some point. And I'm sure he wouldn't tell me if he had been—he knows I'd fall apart.

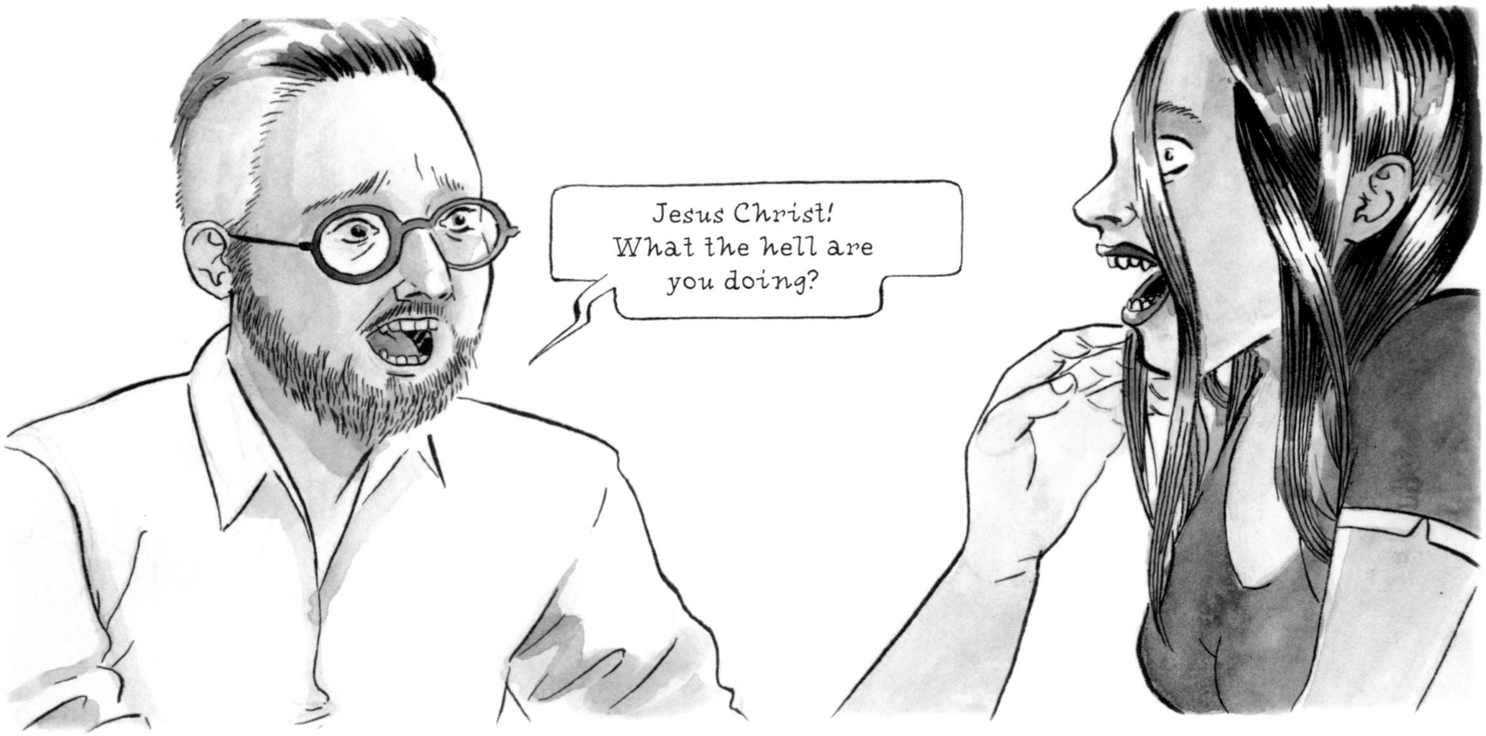
Jesus Christ! What the hell are you doing?

But that, and so many other things, is all history and has very little to do with how things are now. And now is where I want to be.

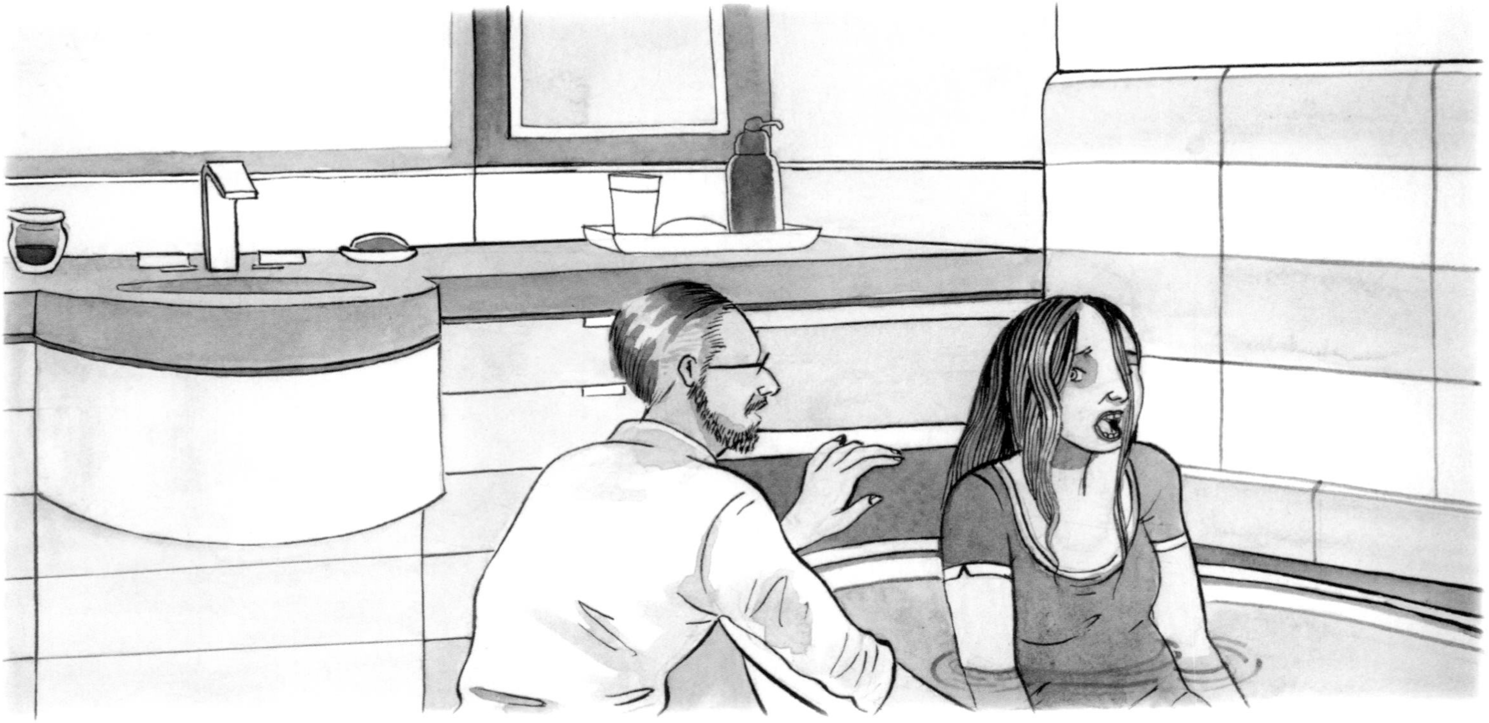

Now, with its intermittent surprises and minor triumphs. Now, with an eye to tomorrow, this weekend, next summer, full of lots of little nows.

I want a future of love and goodness: a summer in Provence, moonlit dinners, birthday parties, bubble baths, and yes, someday—a baby.

But for tonight . . .

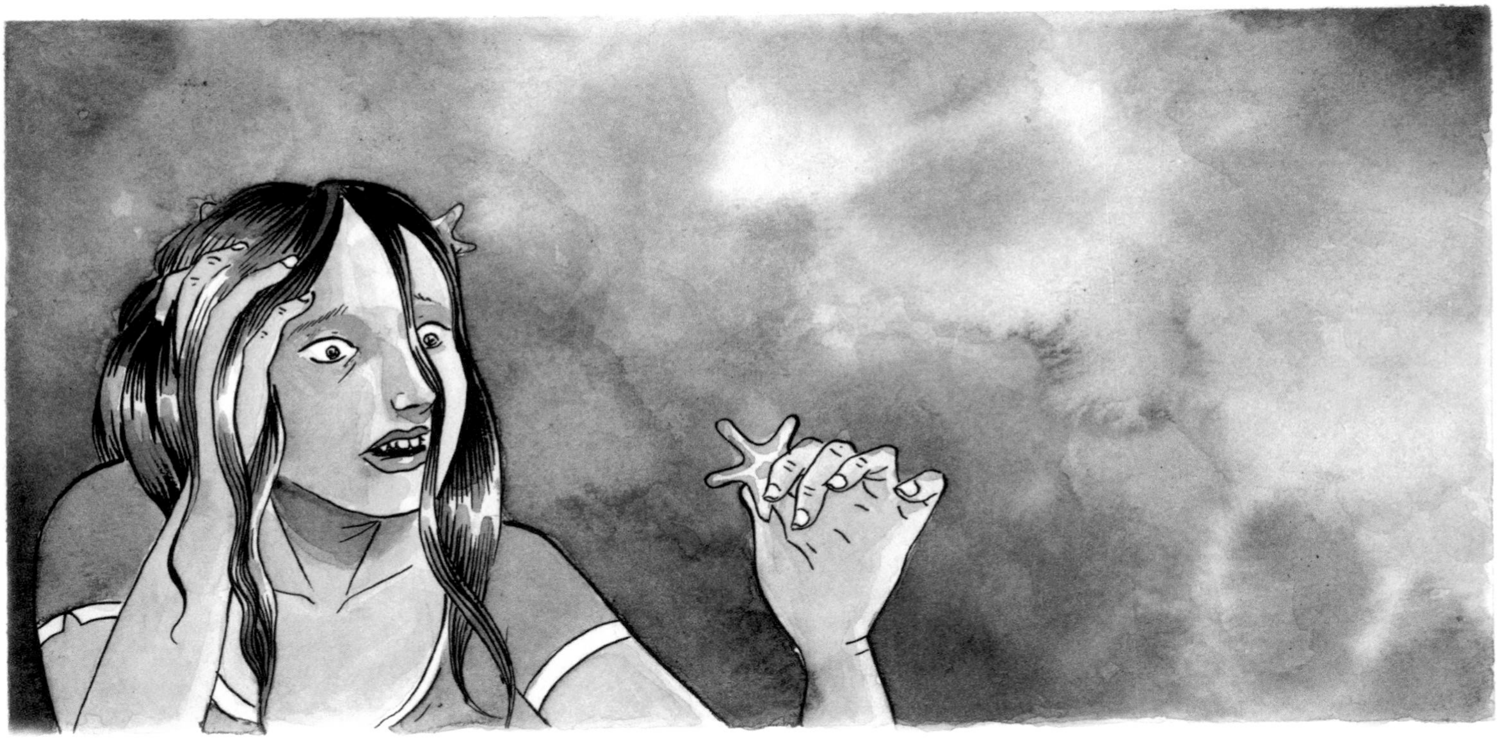

Tonight I want James. In nothing but a leopard-skin loincloth, bounding around the room, jumping on the bed, beating his chest, and declaring his undying love for me.

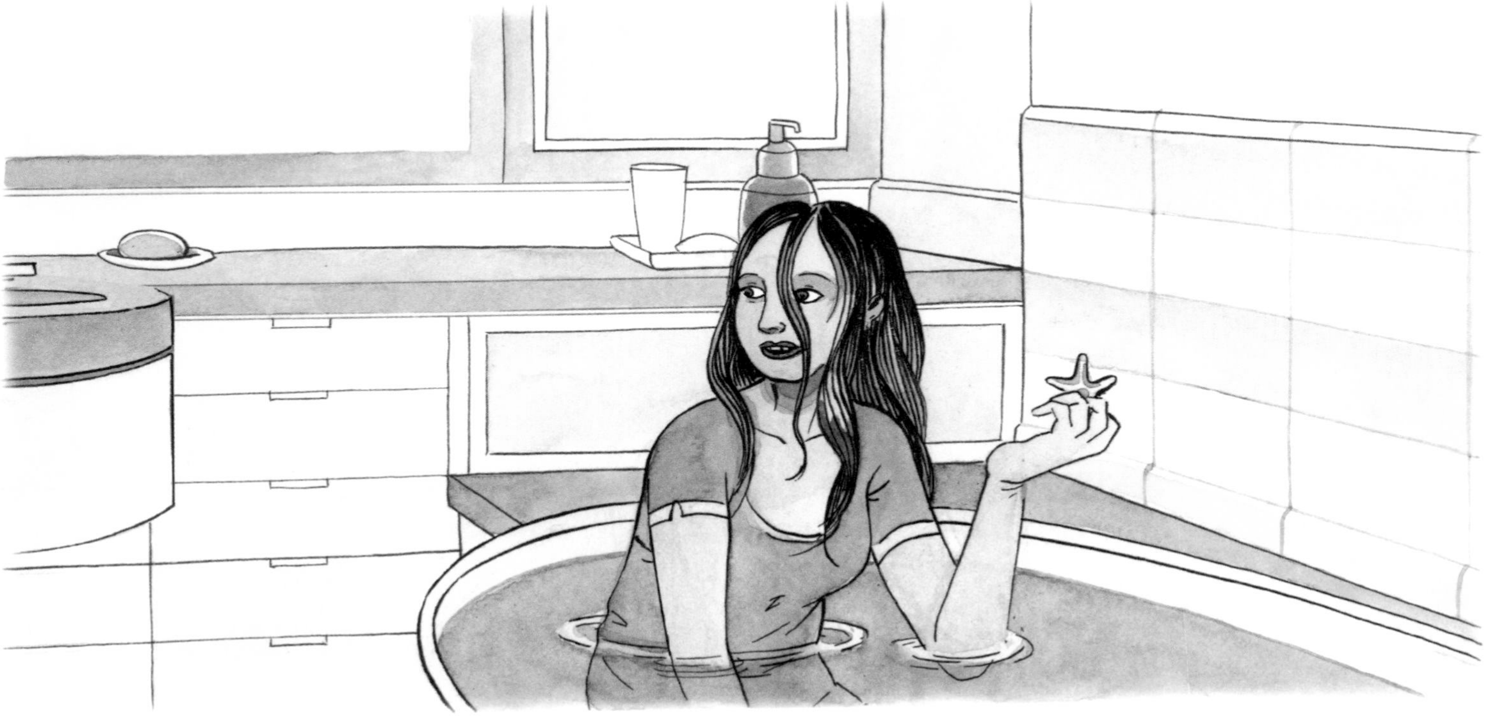

Oh god. Can you imagine that? I love it, ha ha! He'd have to wear a greasy Tarzan wig to complete the effect. Maisie and Gretchen would die laughing.

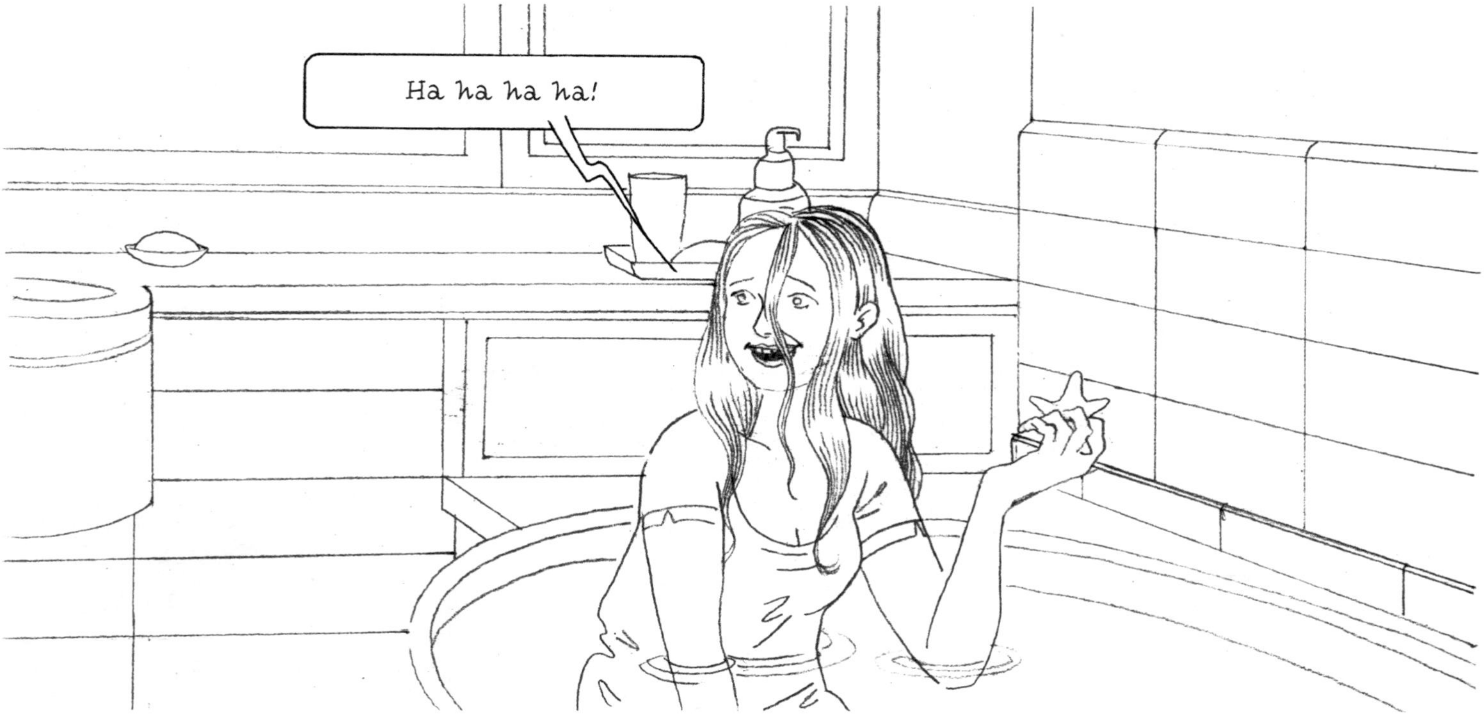
Ha ha ha ha!

Ha ha ha ha!

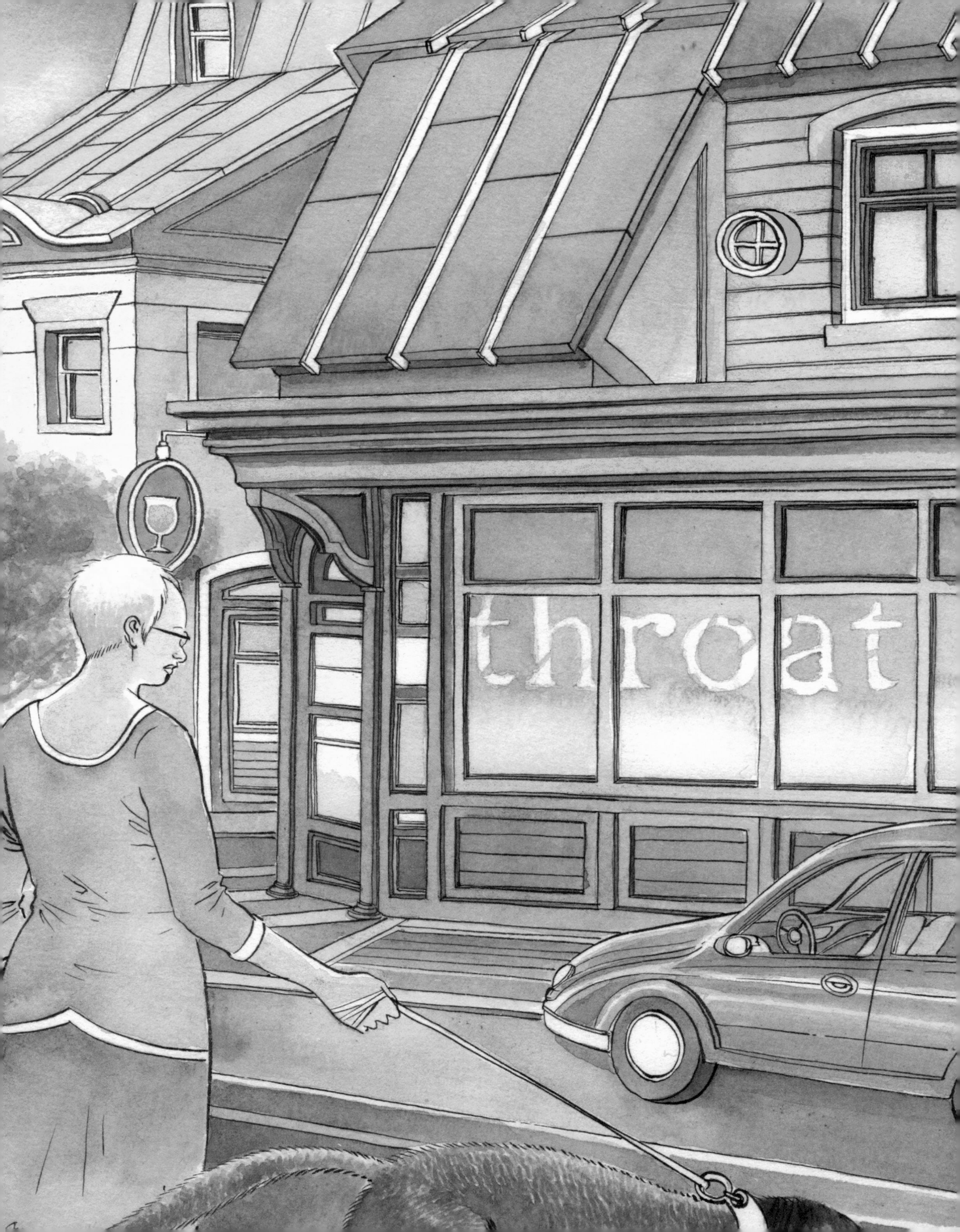
throat

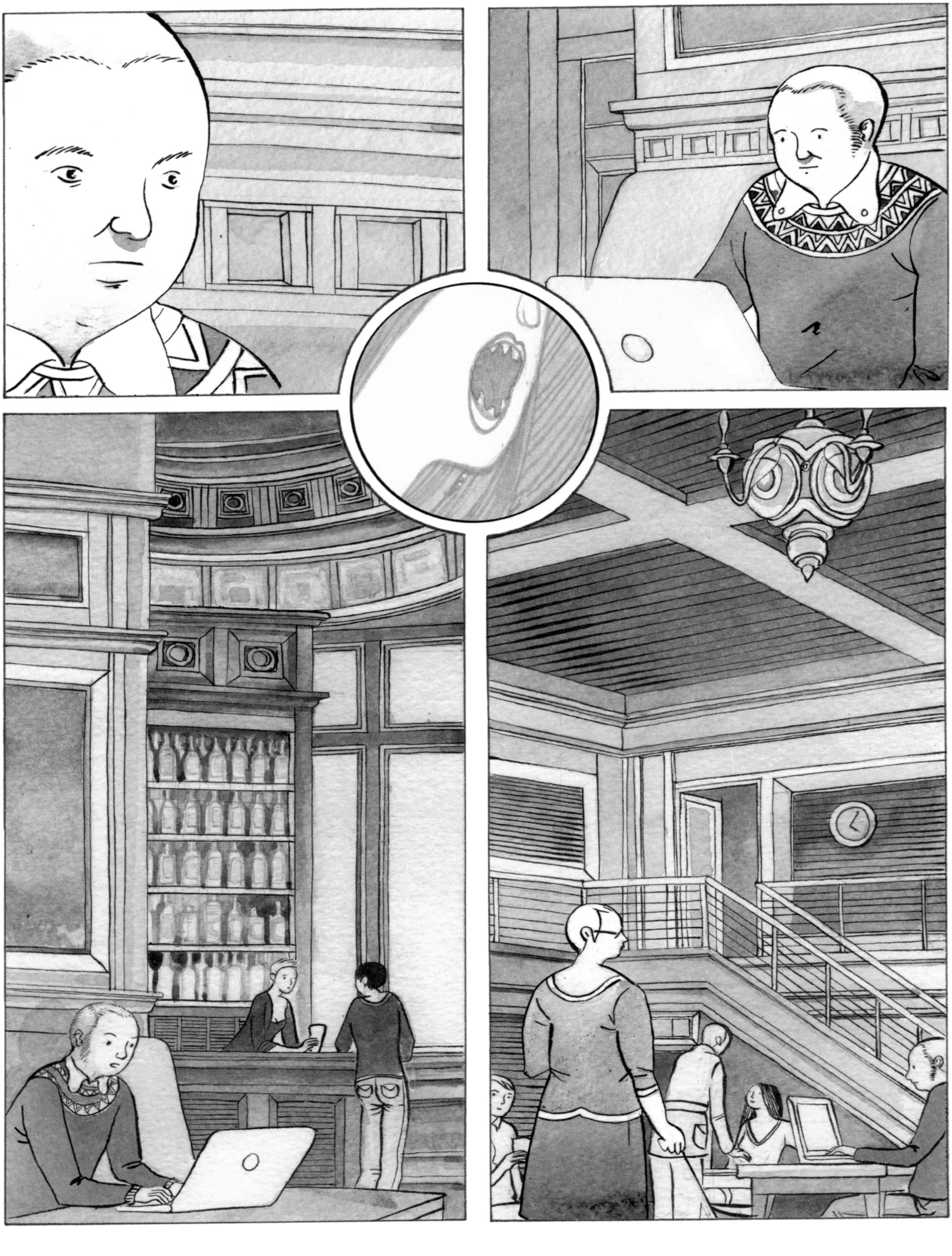

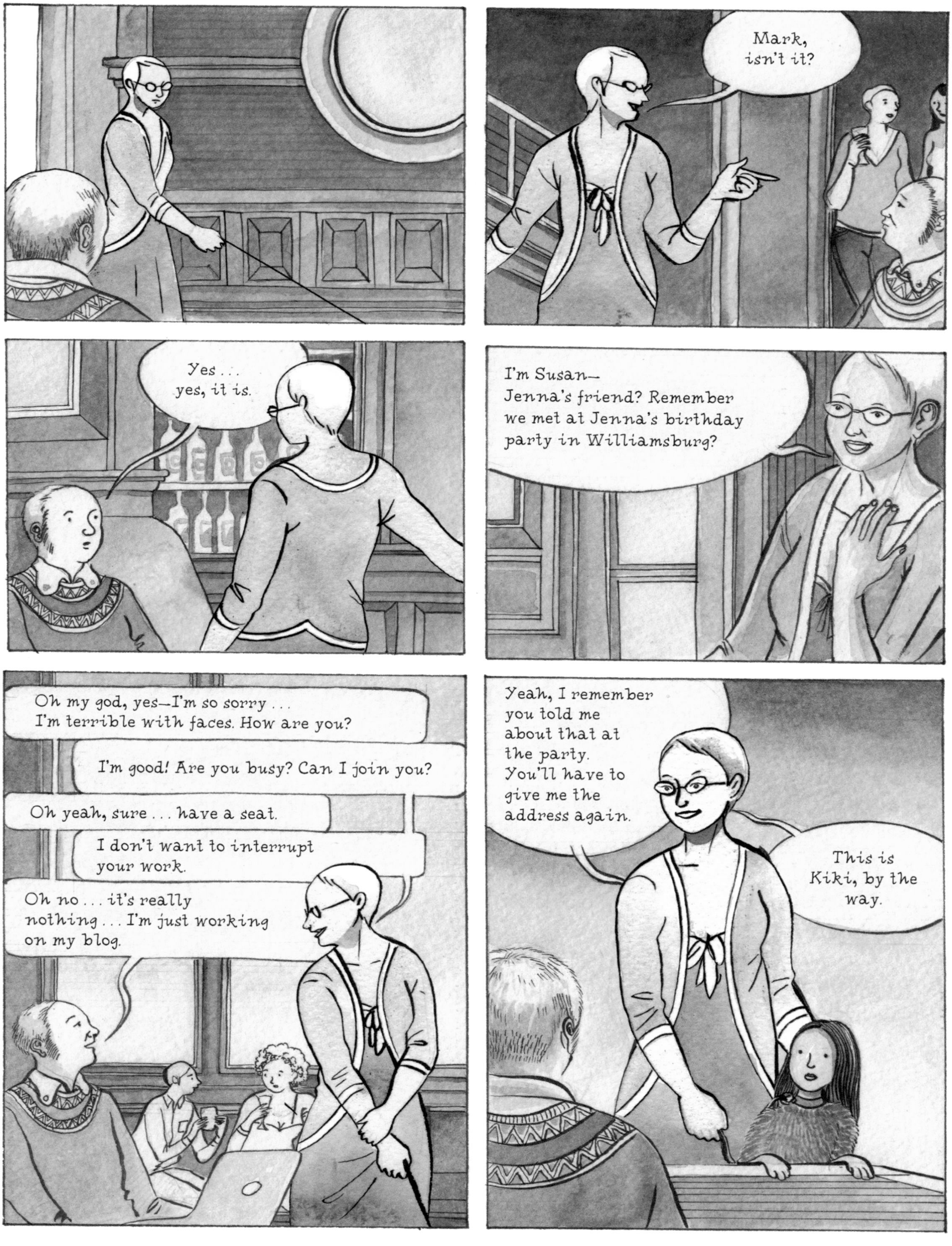
Mark,
isn't it?
Yes . . .
yes, it is.
I'm Susan—
Jenna's friend? Remember
we met at Jenna's birthday
party in Williamsburg?
Oh my god, yes—I'm so sorry . . .
I'm terrible with faces. How are you?
I'm good! Are you busy? Can I join you?
Oh yeah, sure . . . have a seat.
I don't want to interrupt
your work.
Oh no . . . it's really
nothing . . . I'm just working
on my blog.
Yeah, I remember
you told me
about that at
the party.
You'll have to
give me the
address again.
This is
Kiki, by the
way.

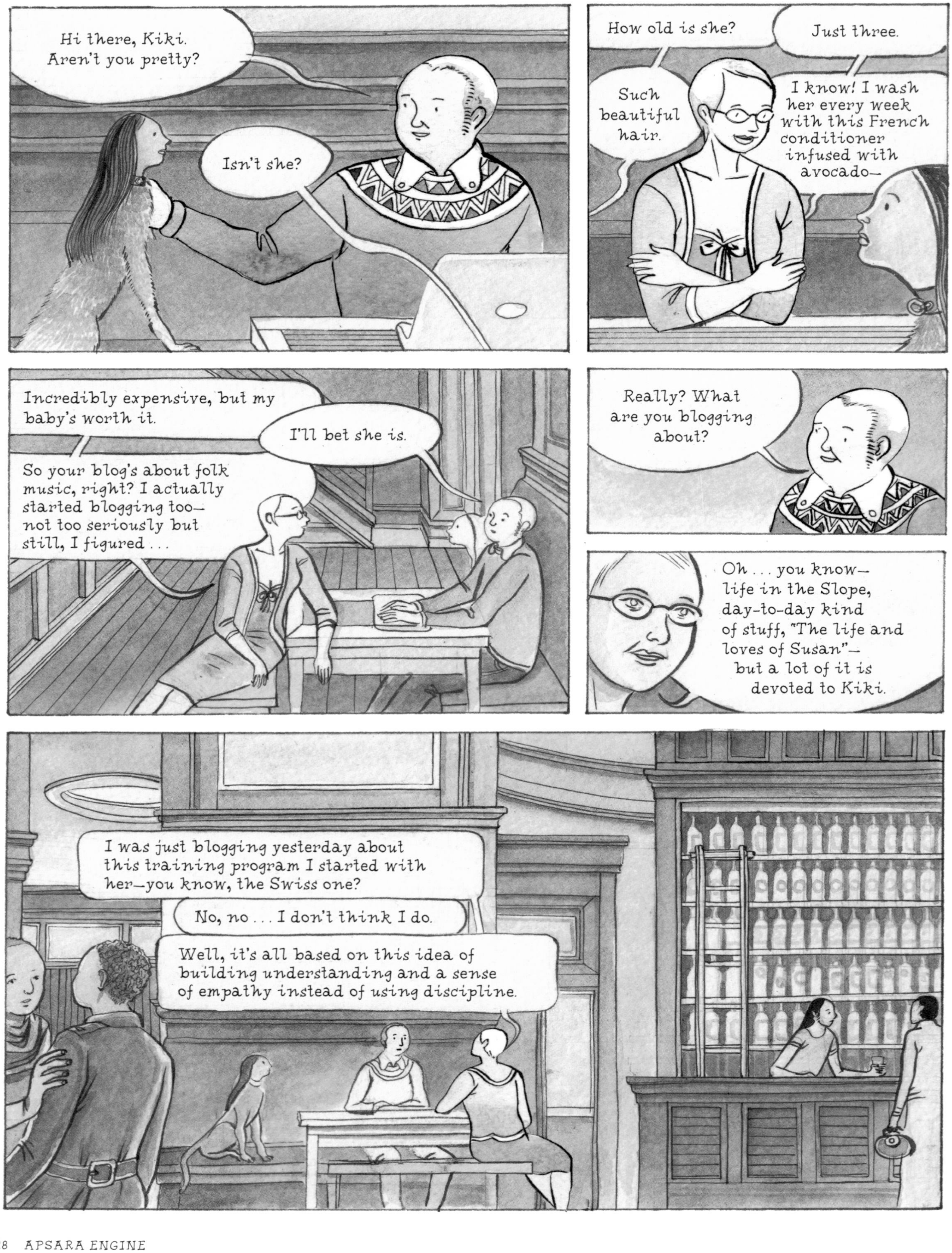
Hi there, Kiki. Aren't you pretty?
Isn't she?
How old is she?
Just three.
Such beautiful hair.
I know! I wash her every week with this French conditioner infused with avocado—
Incredibly expensive, but my baby's worth it.
I'll bet she is.
So your blog's about folk music, right? I actually started blogging too—not too seriously but still, I figured . . .
Really? What are you blogging about?
Oh . . . you know—life in the Slope, day-to-day kind of stuff, "The life and loves of Susan"—but a lot of it is devoted to Kiki.
I was just blogging yesterday about this training program I started with her—you know, the Swiss one?
No, no . . . I don't think I do.
Well, it's all based on this idea of building understanding and a sense of empathy instead of using discipline.

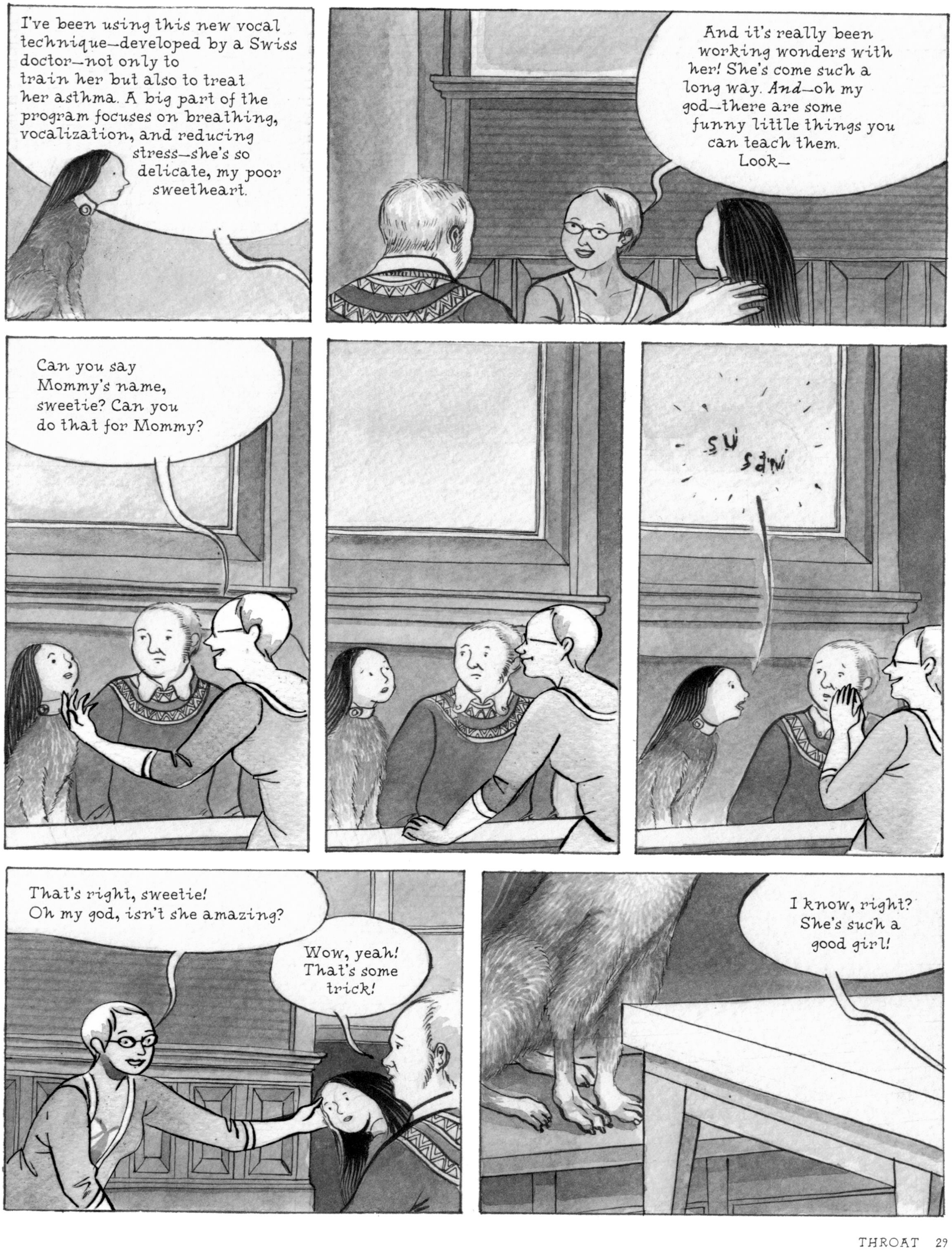
I've been using this new vocal technique—developed by a Swiss doctor—not only to train her but also to treat her asthma. A big part of the program focuses on breathing, vocalization, and reducing stress—she's so delicate, my poor sweetheart.
And it's really been working wonders with her! She's come such a long way. *And*—oh my god—there are some funny little things you can teach them. Look—
Can you say Mommy's name, sweetie? Can you do that for Mommy?
That's right, sweetie! Oh my god, isn't she amazing?
Wow, yeah! That's some trick!
I know, right? She's such a good girl!

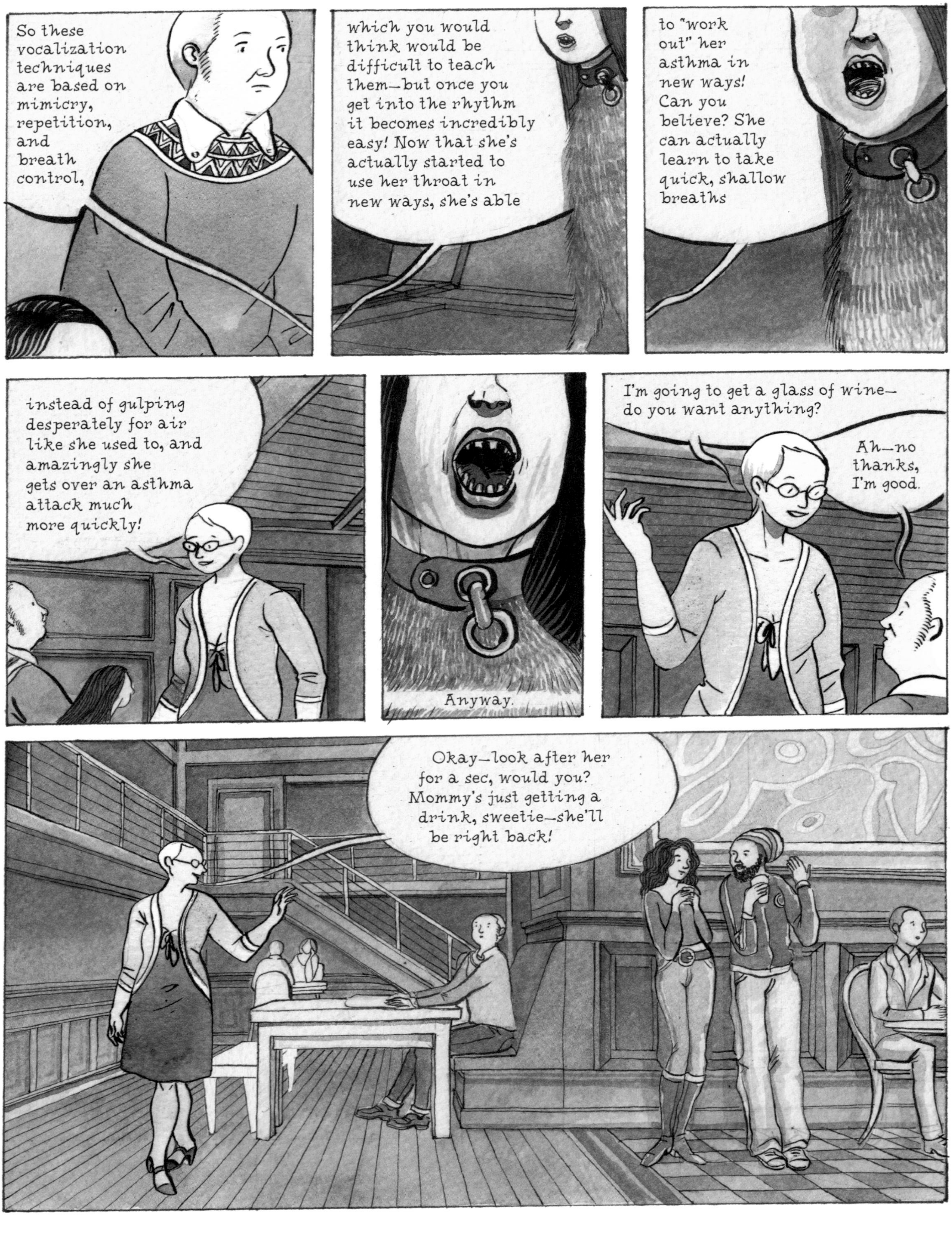
So these vocalization techniques are based on mimicry, repetition, and breath control,
which you would think would be difficult to teach them—but once you get into the rhythm it becomes incredibly easy! Now that she's actually started to use her throat in new ways, she's able
to "work out" her asthma in new ways! Can you believe? She can actually learn to take quick, shallow breaths
instead of gulping desperately for air like she used to, and amazingly she gets over an asthma attack much more quickly!
Anyway.
I'm going to get a glass of wine—do you want anything?
Ah—no thanks, I'm good.
Okay—look after her for a sec, would you? Mommy's just getting a drink, sweetie—she'll be right back!

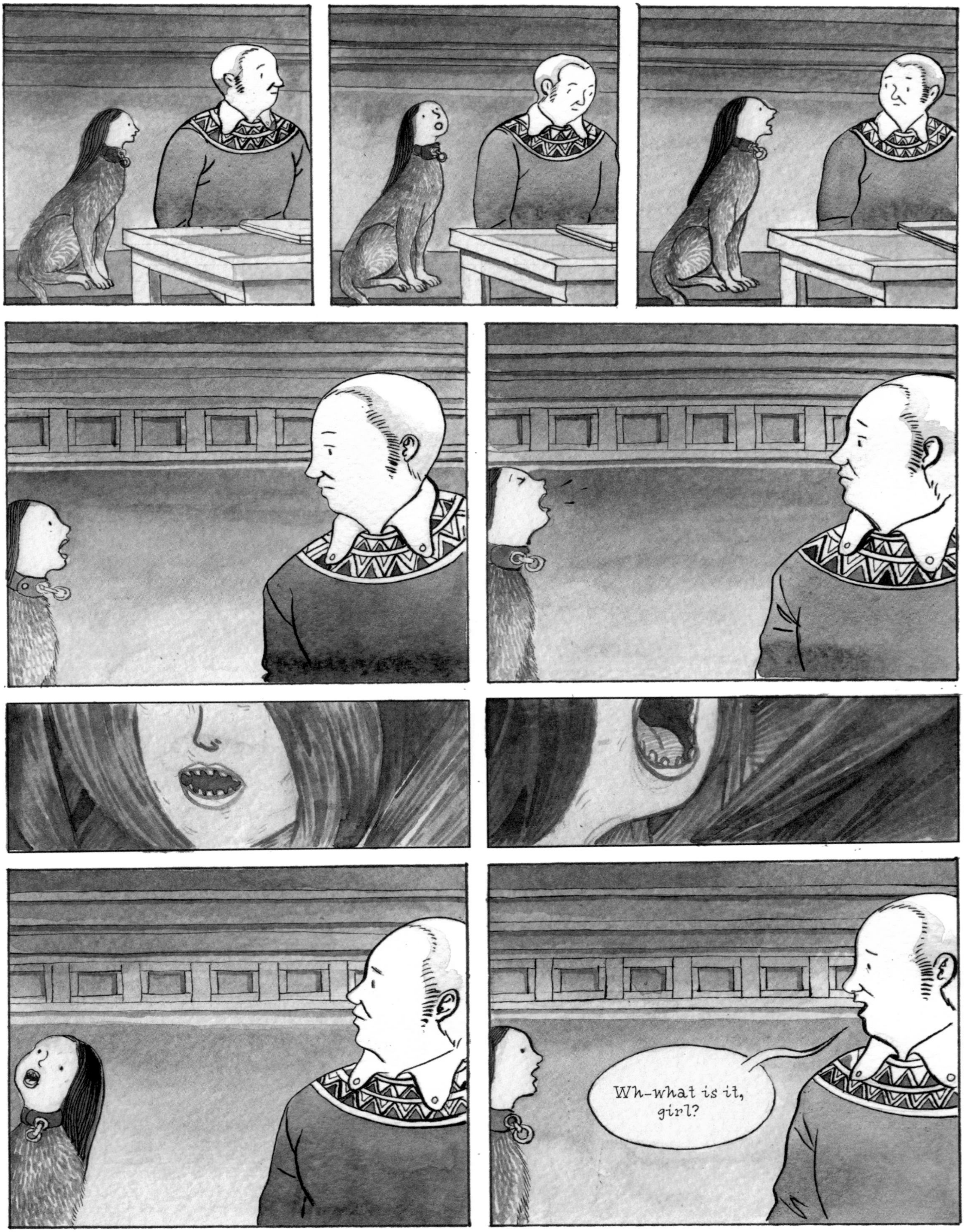
Wh-what is it, girl?

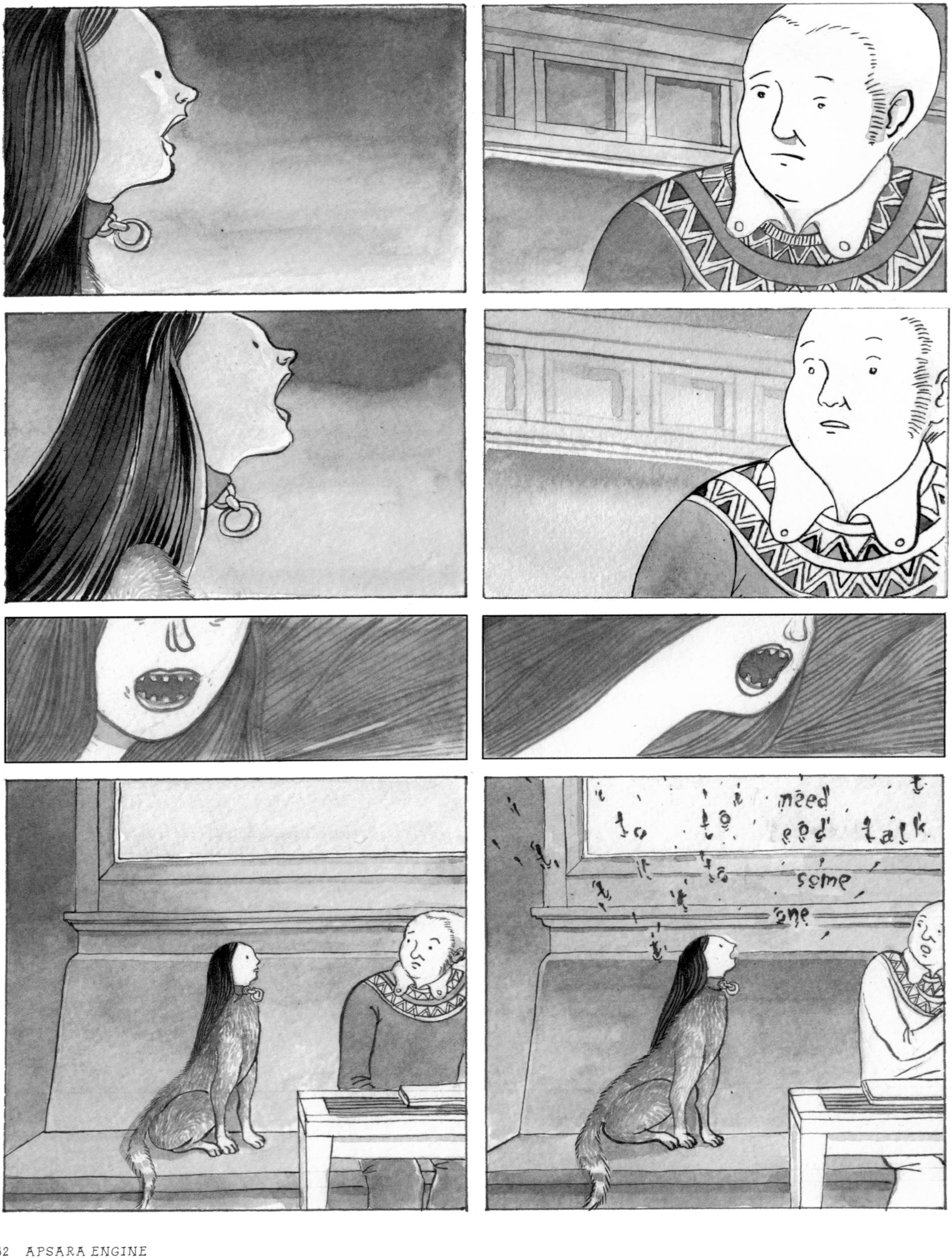
need
talk
some
one

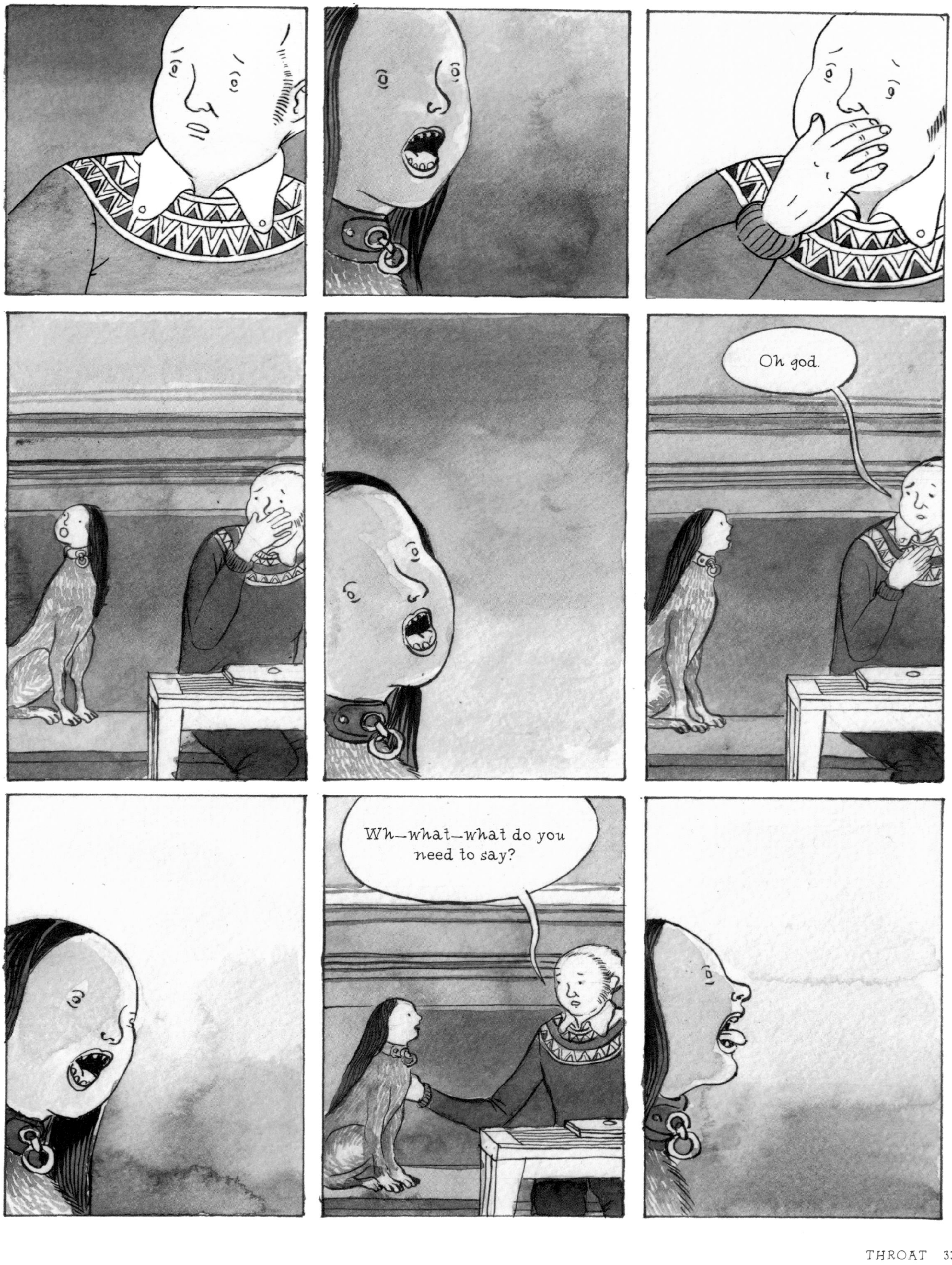
Oh god.
Wh—what—what do you need to say?

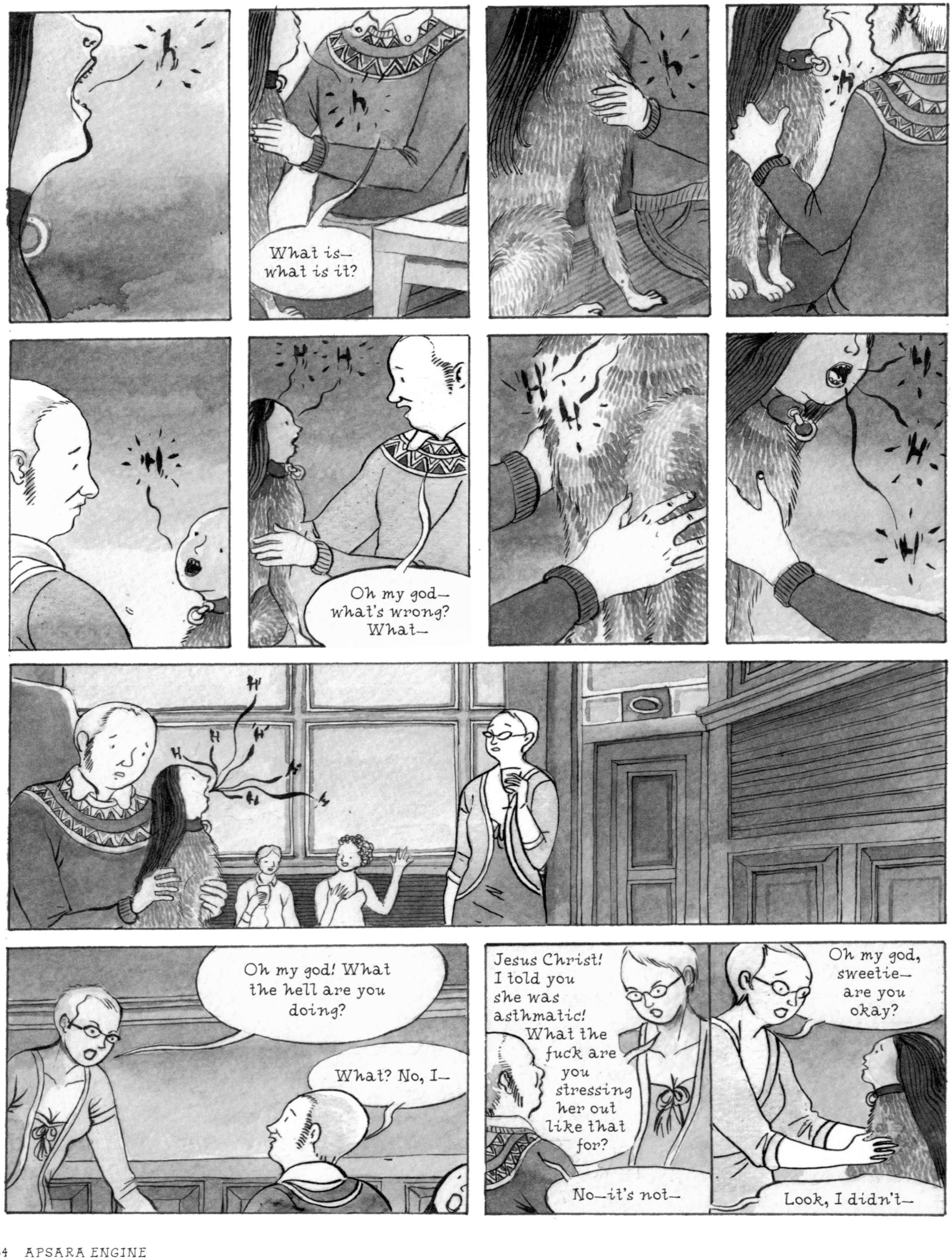
What is—
what is it?
Oh my god—
what's wrong?
What—
Oh my god! What
the hell are you
doing?
What? No, I—
Jesus Christ!
I told you
she was
asthmatic!
What the
fuck are
you
stressing
her out
like that
for?
No—it's not—
Oh my god,
sweetie—
are you
okay?
Look, I didn't—

What is your fucking problem? Where do you get off, manhandling her like that?

Now wait a minute!

She's not having a—

My poor baby! Where's your inhaler?

Here you go, sweetie.

HSSHH—

Is that better?

I seriously don't know what's wrong with you! Being so rough with her when I told you she was delicate! Come on, sweetie.

You don't understand!

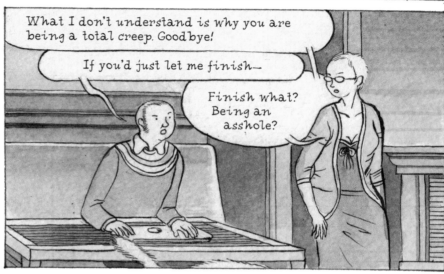

What I don't understand is why you are being a total creep. Goodbye!

If you'd just let me finish—

Finish what? Being an asshole?

Will you listen to me? She wasn't having an asthma attack! She's trying—she's—

She's WHAT?

She's—AWARE!

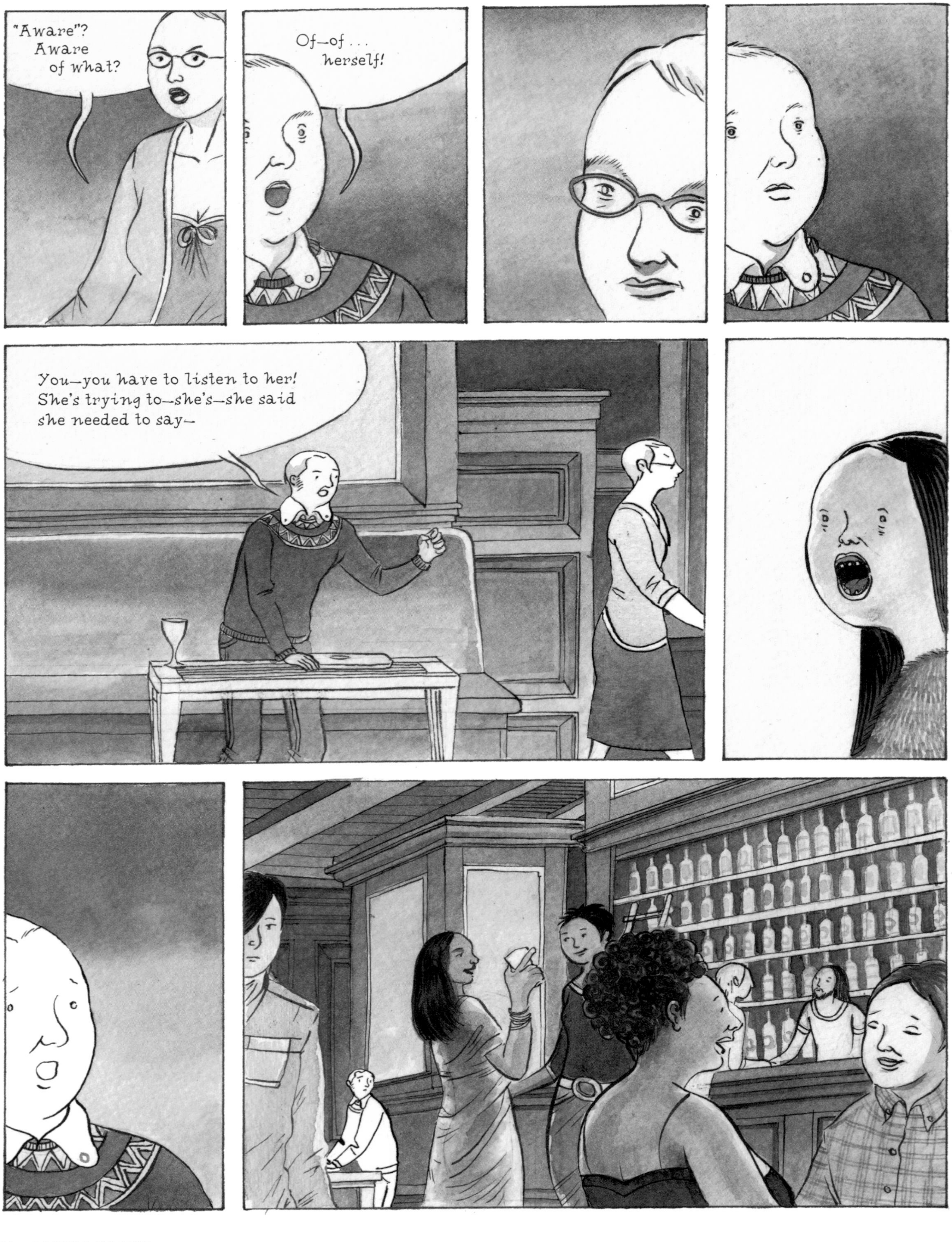
"Aware"? Aware of what?
Of—of . . . herself!
You—you have to listen to her! She's trying to—she's—she said she needed to say—

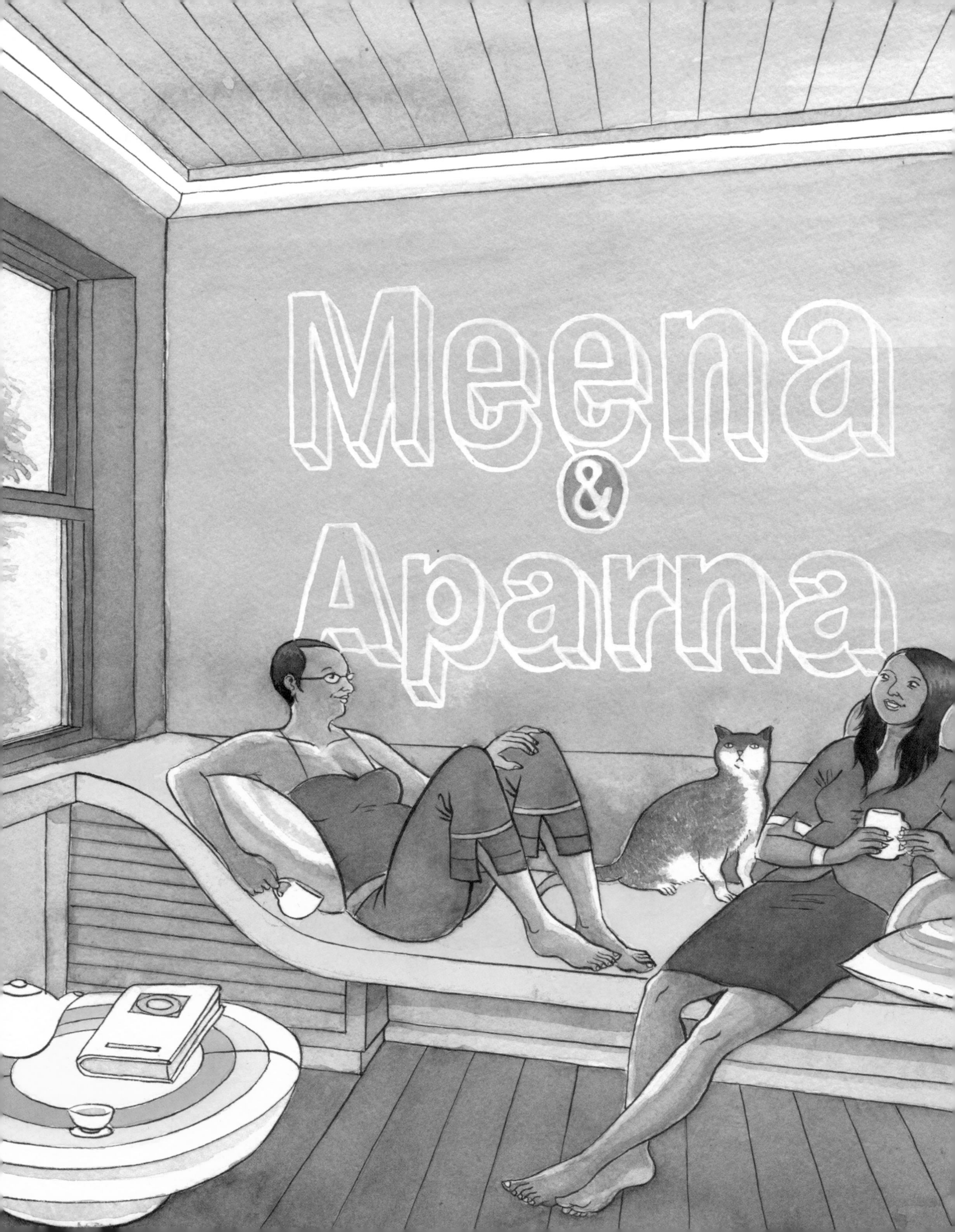
Meena
&
Aparna

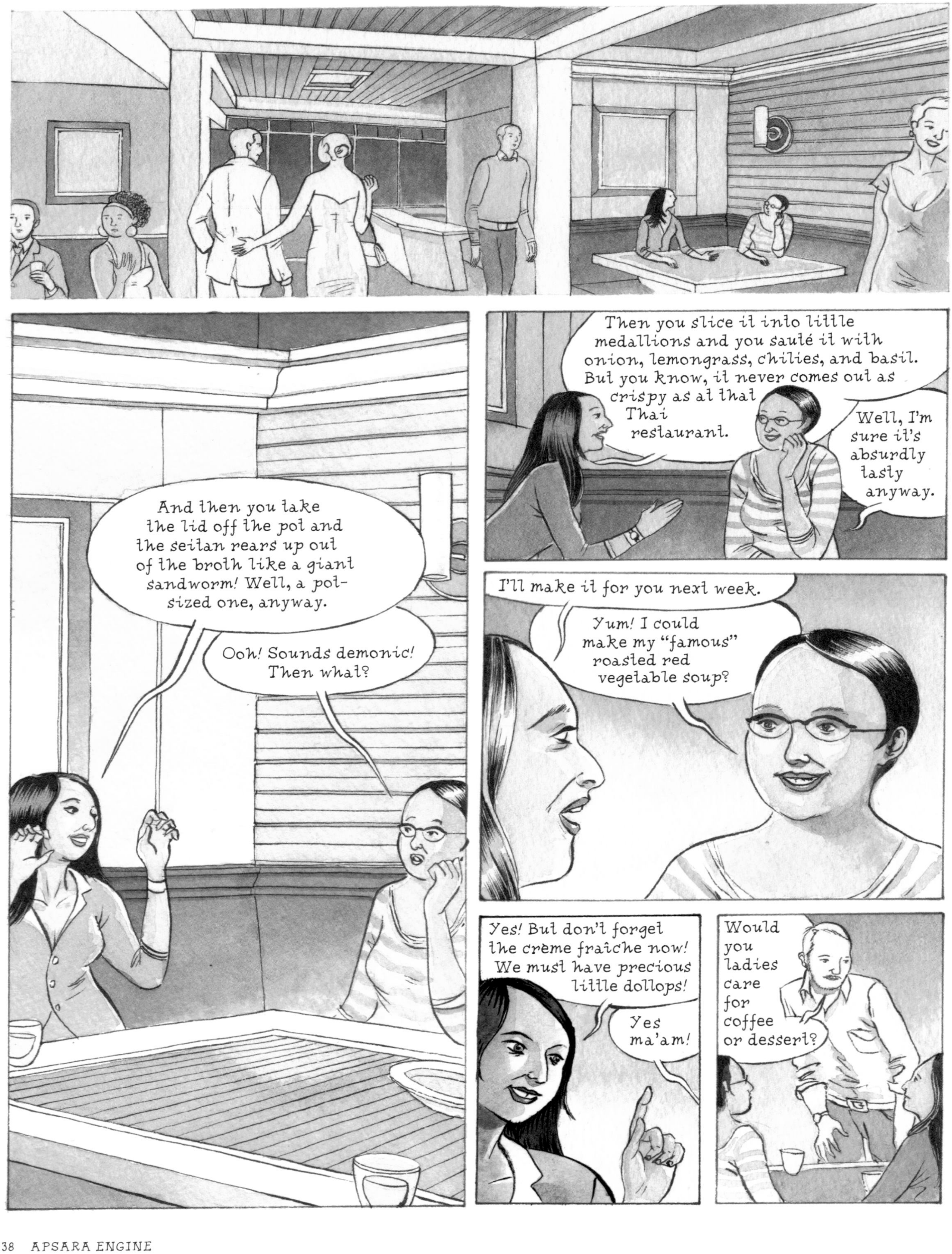
And then you take the lid off the pot and the seitan rears up out of the broth like a giant sandworm! Well, a pot-sized one, anyway.
Ooh! Sounds demonic! Then what?
Then you slice it into little medallions and you sauté it with onion, lemongrass, chilies, and basil. But you know, it never comes out as crispy as at that Thai restaurant.
Well, I'm sure it's absurdly tasty anyway.
I'll make it for you next week.
Yum! I could make my "famous" roasted red vegetable soup?
Yes! But don't forget the creme fraiche now! We must have precious little dollops!
Yes ma'am!
Would you ladies care for coffee or dessert?

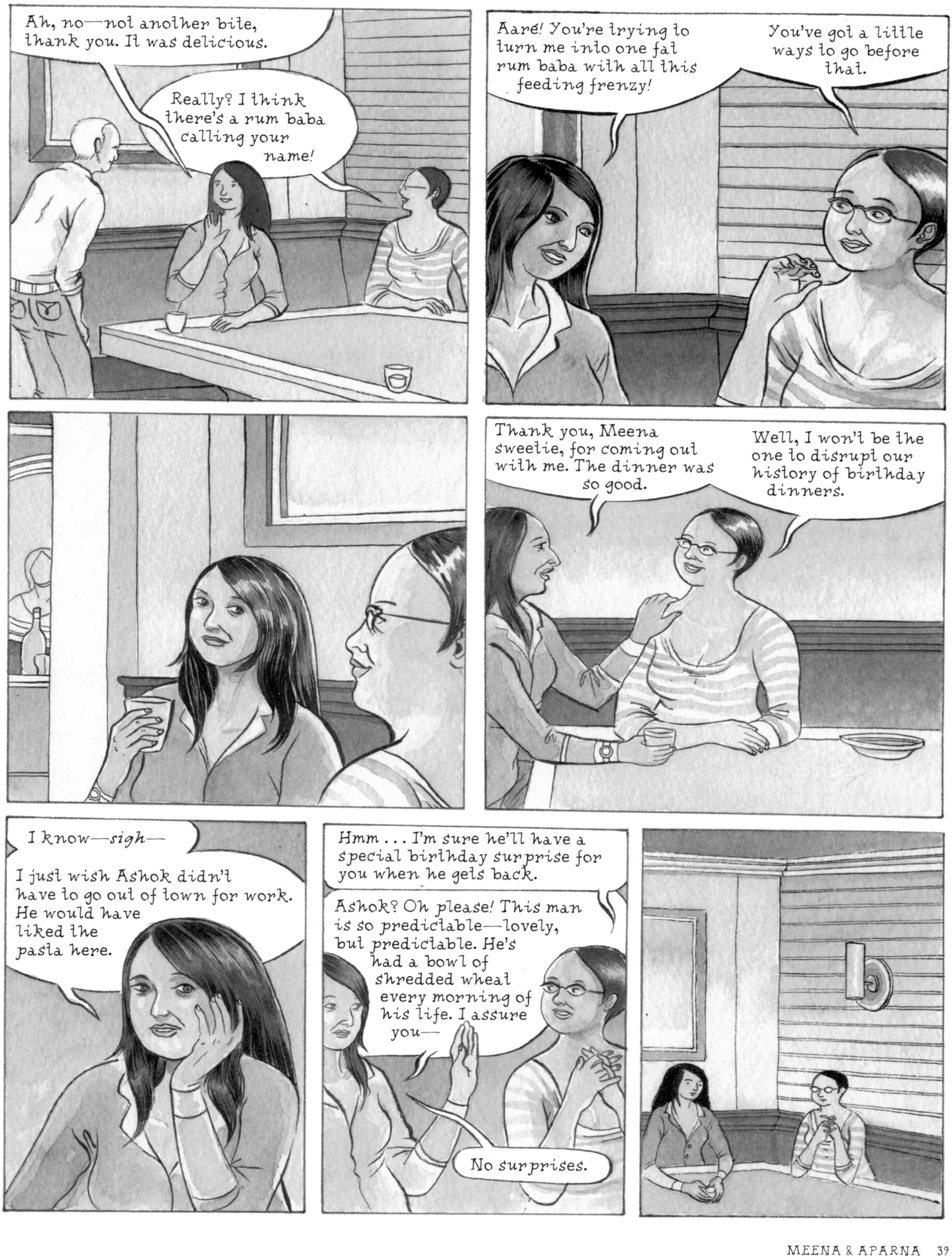
Ah, no—not another bite, thank you. It was delicious.
Really? I think there's a rum baba calling your name!
Aare! You're trying to turn me into one fat rum baba with all this feeding frenzy!
You've got a little ways to go before that.
Thank you, Meena sweetie, for coming out with me. The dinner was so good.
Well, I won't be the one to disrupt our history of birthday dinners.
I know—*sigh*—
I just wish Ashok didn't have to go out of town for work. He would have liked the pasta here.
Hmm . . . I'm sure he'll have a special birthday surprise for you when he gets back.
Ashok? Oh *please!* This man is so *predictable*—lovely, but *predictable.* He's had a bowl of shredded wheat every morning of his life. I assure you—
No surprises.

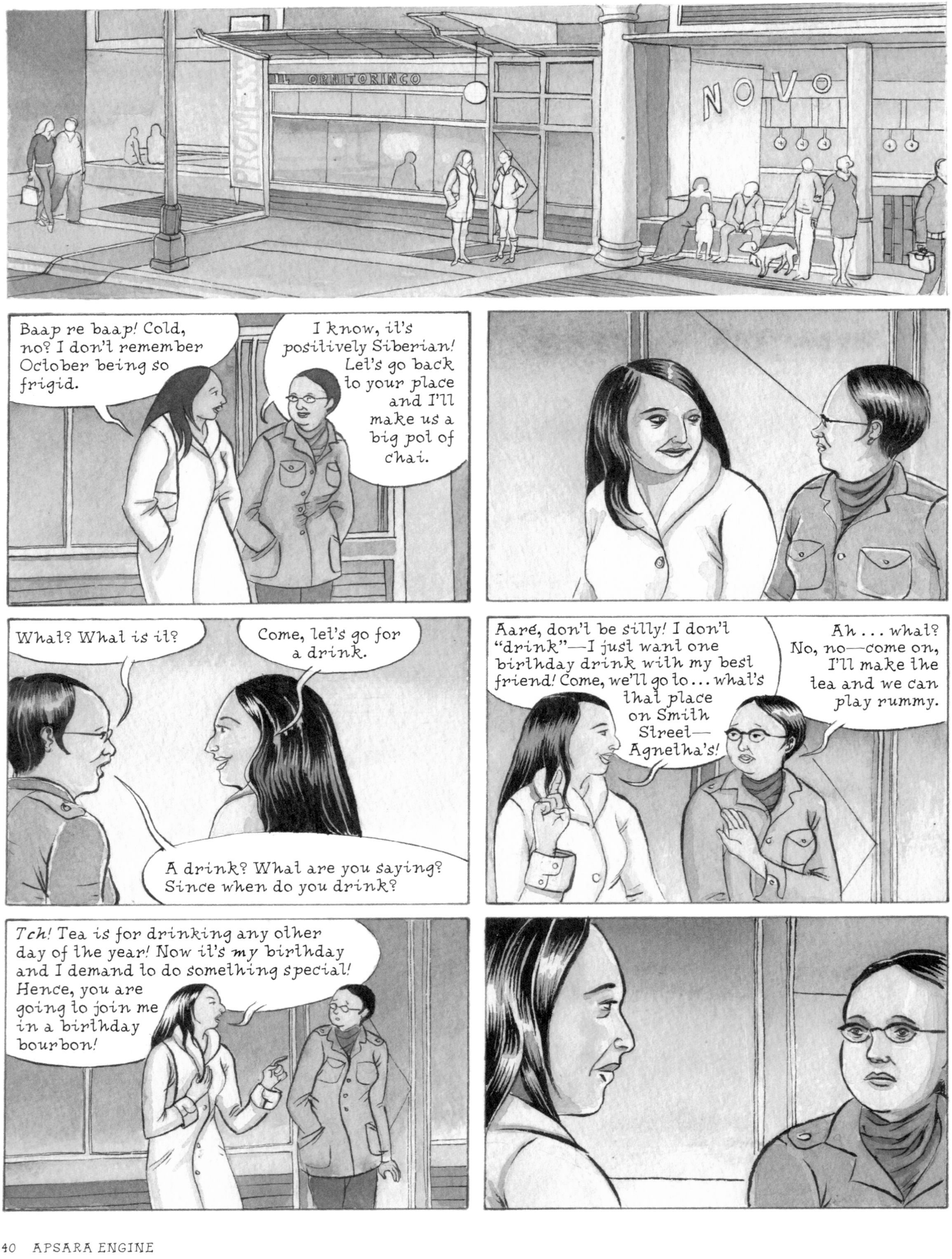

IL ORNITORINCO
NOVO
Baap re baap! Cold, no? I don't remember October being so frigid.
I know, it's positively Siberian! Let's go back to your place and I'll make us a big pot of chai.
What? What is it?
Come, let's go for a drink.
A drink? What are you saying? Since when do you drink?
Aare, don't be silly! I don't "drink"—I just want one birthday drink with my best friend! Come, we'll go to . . . what's that place on Smith Street— Agnetha's!
Ah . . . what? No, no—come on, I'll make the tea and we can play rummy.
Tch! Tea is for drinking any other day of the year! Now it's *my* birthday and I demand to do something special! Hence, you are going to join me in a birthday bourbon!

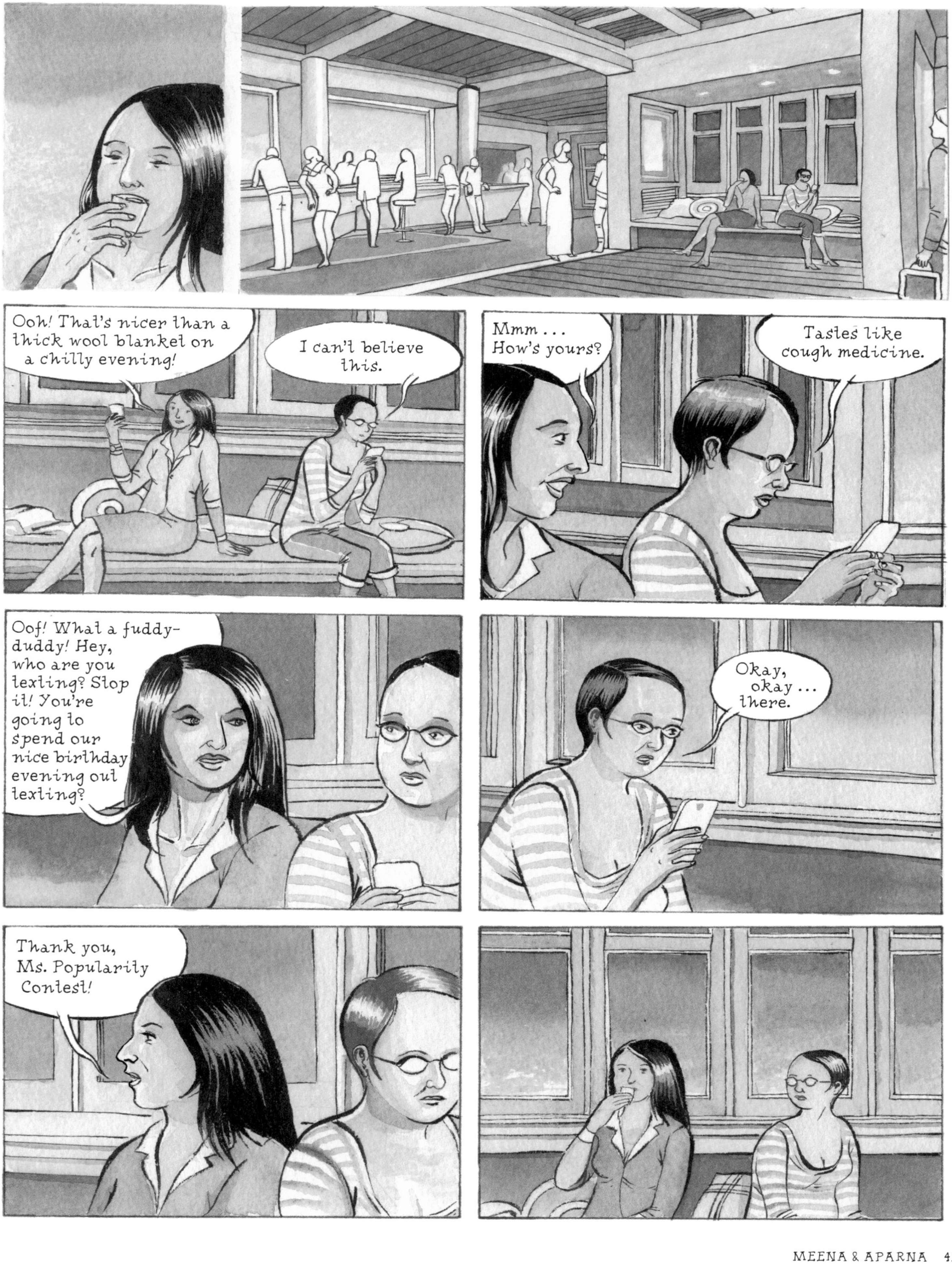
Ooh! That's nicer than a thick wool blanket on a chilly evening!
I can't believe this.
Mmm . . . How's yours?
Tastes like cough medicine.
Oof! What a fuddy-duddy! Hey, who are you texting? Stop it! You're going to spend our nice birthday evening out texting?
Okay, okay . . . there.
Thank you, Ms. Popularity Contest!

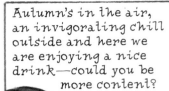

Autumn's in the air, an invigorating chill outside and here we are enjoying a nice drink—could you be more content?

So nice to just sit and talk, no?

Uhh... lovely.

You know, I'm *glad* Ashok is away! If he had been here, I wouldn't be able to talk to you the way we used to, like in college, before all this...this...

This what?

Aare, you know! Wedding-ledding, nuclear family, marital bliss...

I miss the *old* us.

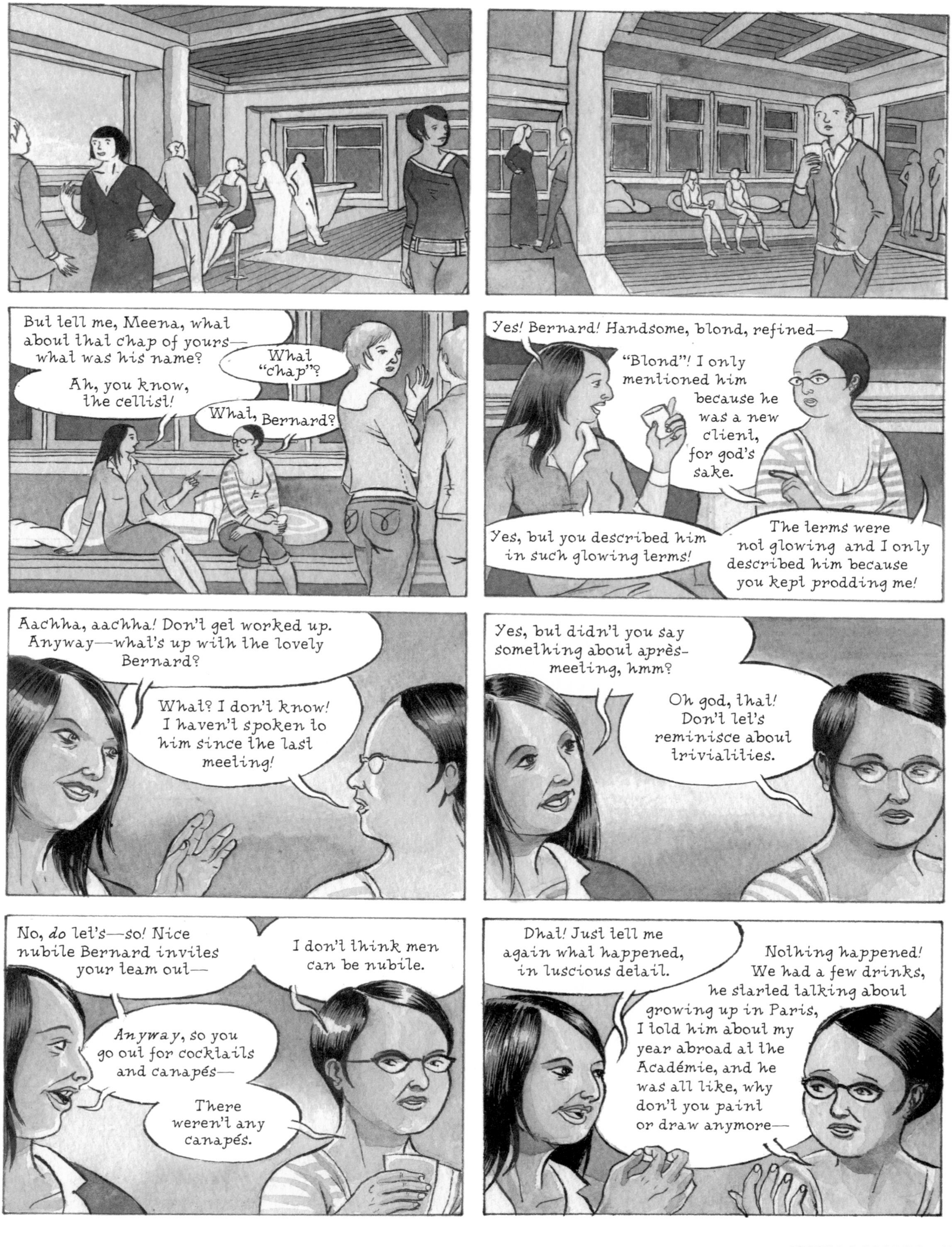

But tell me, Meena, what about that chap of yours—what was his name?
What "chap"?
Ah, you know, the cellist!
What, Bernard?
Yes! Bernard! Handsome, blond, refined—
"Blond"! I only mentioned him because he was a new client, for god's sake.
Yes, but you described him in such glowing terms!
The terms were not glowing and I only described him because you kept prodding me!
Aachha, aachha! Don't get worked up. Anyway—what's up with the lovely Bernard?
What? I don't know! I haven't spoken to him since the last meeting!
Yes, but didn't you say something about après-meeting, hmm?
Oh god, that! Don't let's reminisce about trivialities.
No, *do* let's—so! Nice nubile Bernard invites your team out—
I don't think men can be nubile.
Anyway, so you go out for cocktails and canapés—
There weren't any canapés.
Dhat! Just tell me again what happened, in luscious detail.
Nothing happened! We had a few drinks, he started talking about growing up in Paris, I told him about my year abroad at the Académie, and he was all like, why don't you paint or draw anymore—

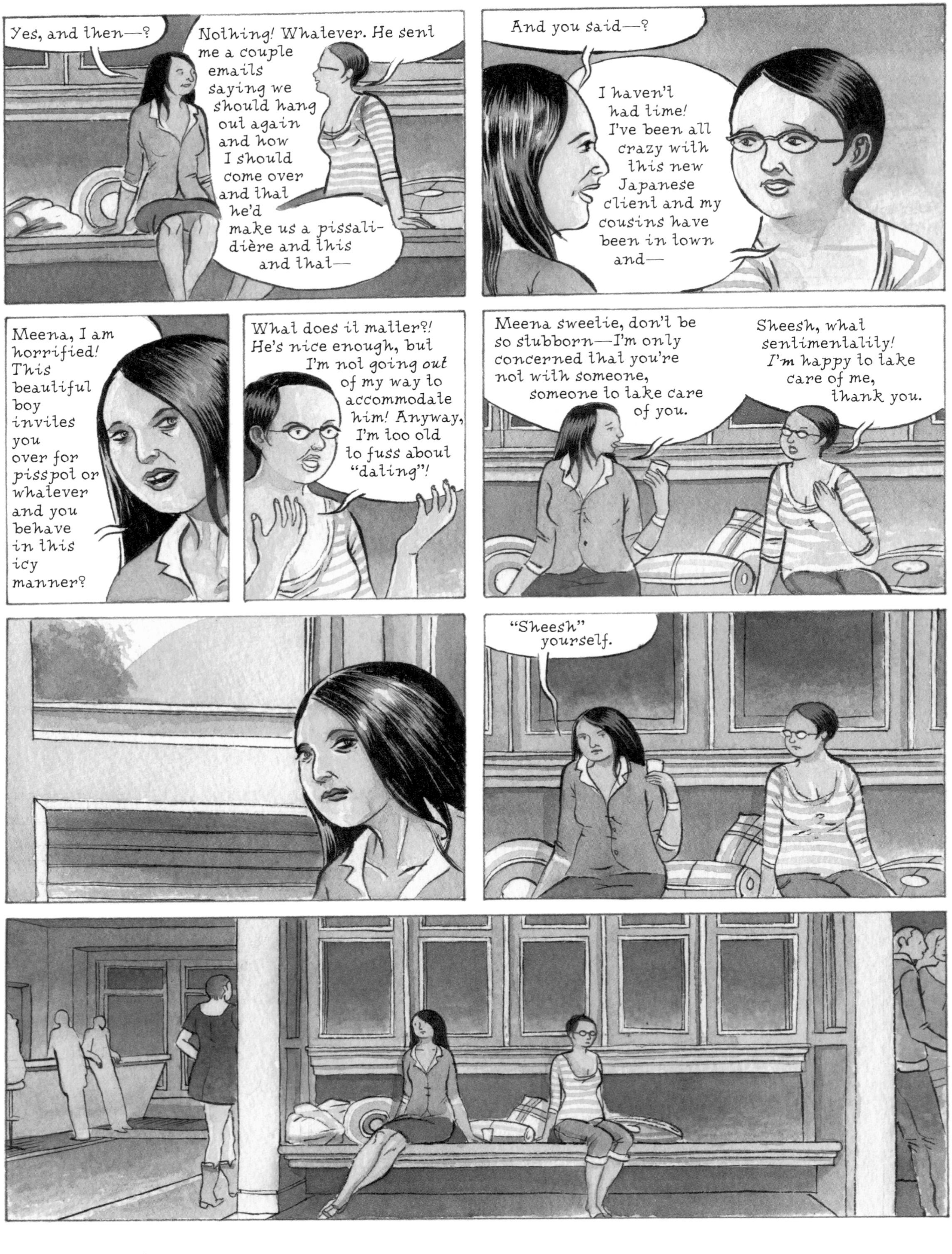
Yes, and then—?
Nothing! Whatever. He sent me a couple emails saying we should hang out again and how I should come over and that he'd make us a *pissalidière* and this and that—
And you said—?
I haven't had time! I've been all crazy with this new Japanese client and my cousins have been in town and—
Meena, I am *horrified!* This beautiful boy invites you over for *pisspot* or whatever and you behave in this icy manner?
What does it matter?! He's *nice* enough, but I'm not going *out* of my way to accommodate him! Anyway, I'm too old to fuss about "dating"!
Meena sweetie, don't be so stubborn—I'm only concerned that you're not with someone, someone to take care of you.
Sheesh, what sentimentality! *I'm* happy to take care of me, thank you.
"Sheesh" yourself.

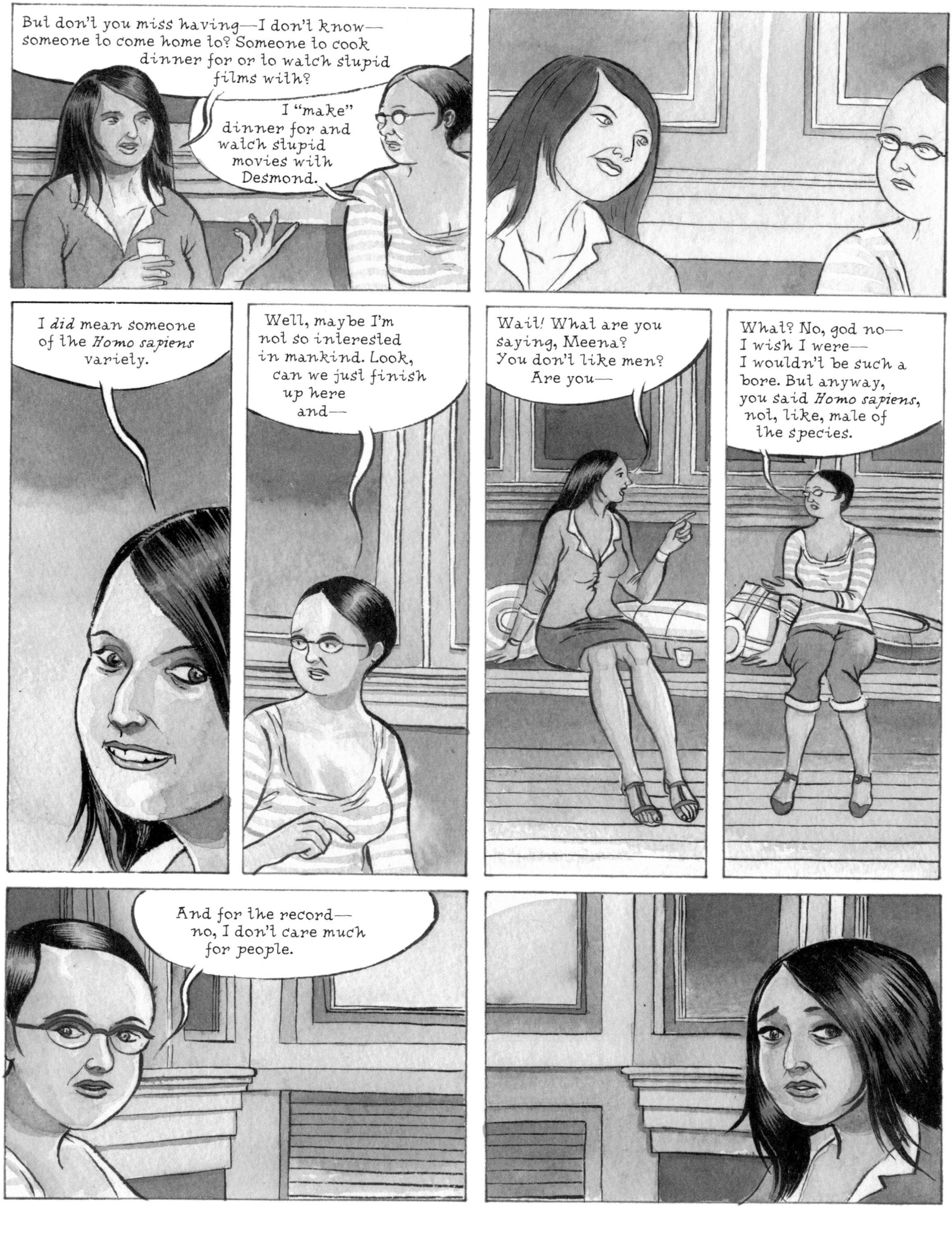
Bul don't you miss having—I don't know—someone to come home to? Someone to cook dinner for or to watch stupid films with?
I "make" dinner for and watch stupid movies with Desmond.
I *did* mean someone of the *Homo sapiens* variety.
Well, maybe I'm not so interested in mankind. Look, can we just finish up here and—
Wait! What are you saying, Meena? You don't like men? Are you—
What? No, god no—I wish I were—I wouldn't be such a bore. But anyway, you said *Homo sapiens*, not, like, male of the species.
And for the record—no, I don't care much for people.

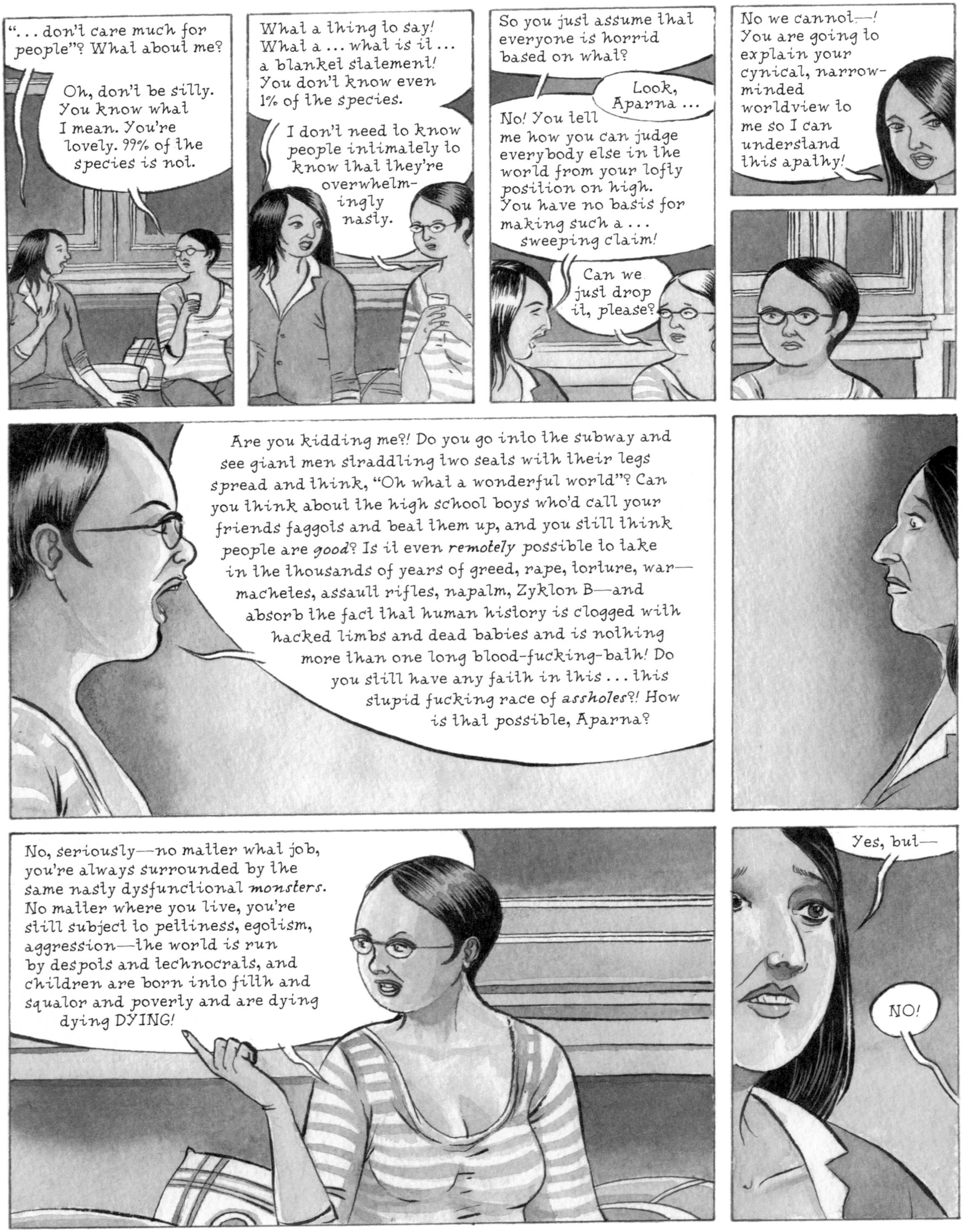
"... don't care much for people"? What about me?
Oh, don't be silly. You know what I mean. You're lovely. 99% of the species is not.
What a thing to say! What a ... what is it ... a blanket statement! You don't know even 1% of the species.
I don't need to know people intimately to know that they're overwhelmingly nasty.
So you just assume that everyone is horrid based on what?
Look, Aparna ...
No! You tell me how you can judge everybody else in the world from your lofty position on high. You have no basis for making such a ... sweeping claim!
Can we just drop it, please?
No we cannot—! You are going to explain your cynical, narrow-minded worldview to me so I can understand this apathy!
Are you kidding me?! Do you go into the subway and see giant men straddling two seats with their legs spread and think, "Oh what a wonderful world"? Can you think about the high school boys who'd call your friends faggots and beat them up, and you still think people are *good*? Is it even *remotely* possible to take in the thousands of years of greed, rape, torture, war—machetes, assault rifles, napalm, Zyklon B—and absorb the fact that human history is clogged with hacked limbs and dead babies and is nothing more than one long blood-fucking-bath! Do you still have any faith in this ... this stupid fucking race of *assholes*?! How is that possible, Aparna?
No, seriously—no matter what job, you're always surrounded by the same nasty dysfunctional *monsters*. No matter where you live, you're still subject to pettiness, egotism, aggression—the world is run by despots and technocrats, and children are born into filth and squalor and poverty and are dying dying DYING!
Yes, but—
NO!

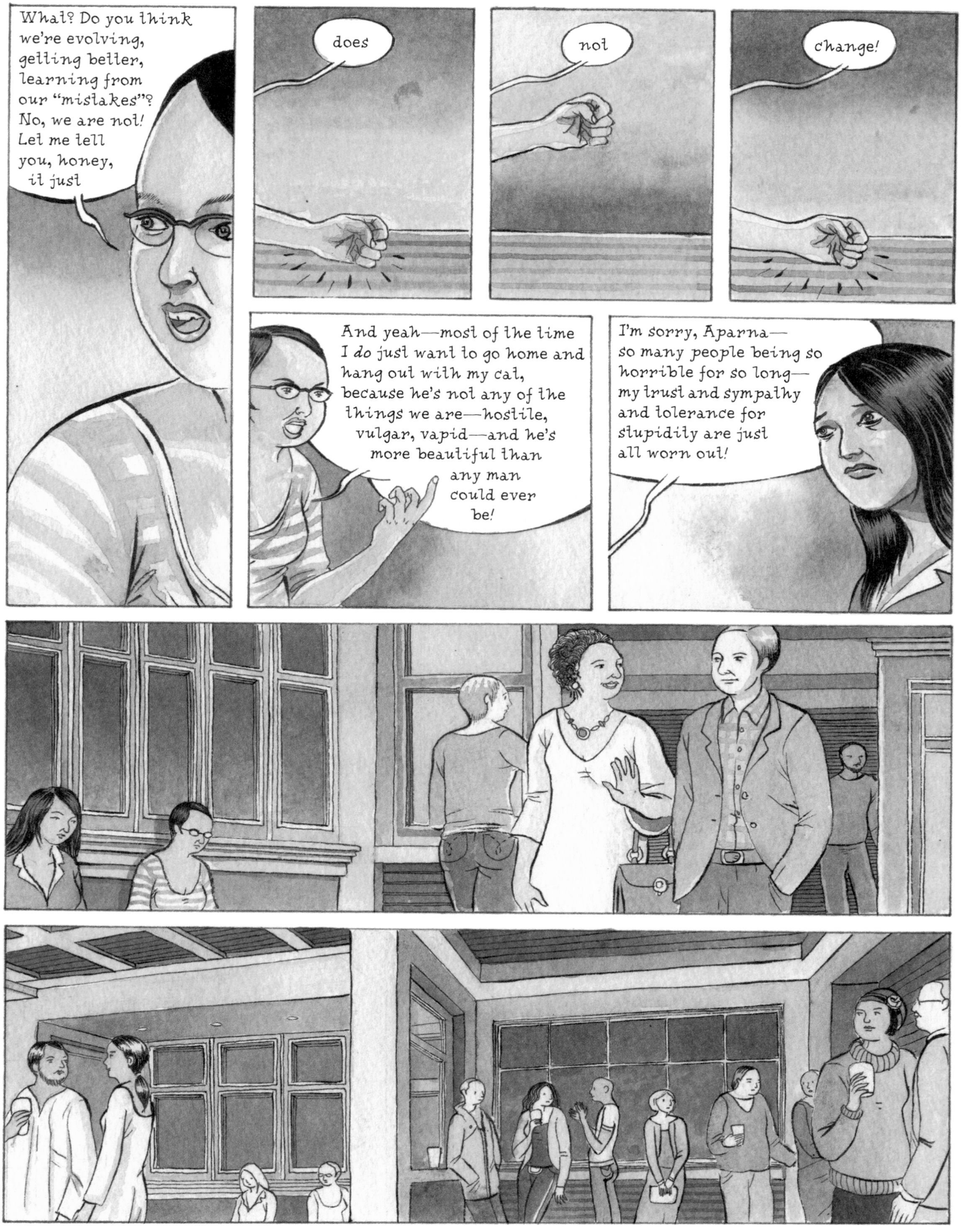
What? Do you think we're evolving, getting better, learning from our "mistakes"? No, we are not! Let me tell you, honey, it just
does
not
change!
And yeah—most of the time I do just want to go home and hang out with my cat, because he's not any of the things we are—hostile, vulgar, vapid—and he's more beautiful than any man could ever be!
I'm sorry, Aparna— so many people being so horrible for so long— my trust and sympathy and tolerance for stupidity are just all worn out!

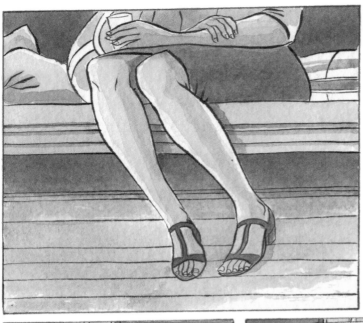
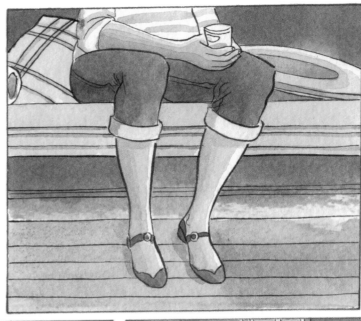

You needn't be so pedantic.

How do you manage to go on from day to day?

I get by.

I'm sorry. It's your birthday. That was all really inappropriate.

Oh, you think so?!

Chhi chhi! What a misanthrope you've become! At least in college you were balancing out your bad attitude with tomfoolery.

I know. Don't think I don't know. And now I'm a cynical old bore, right?

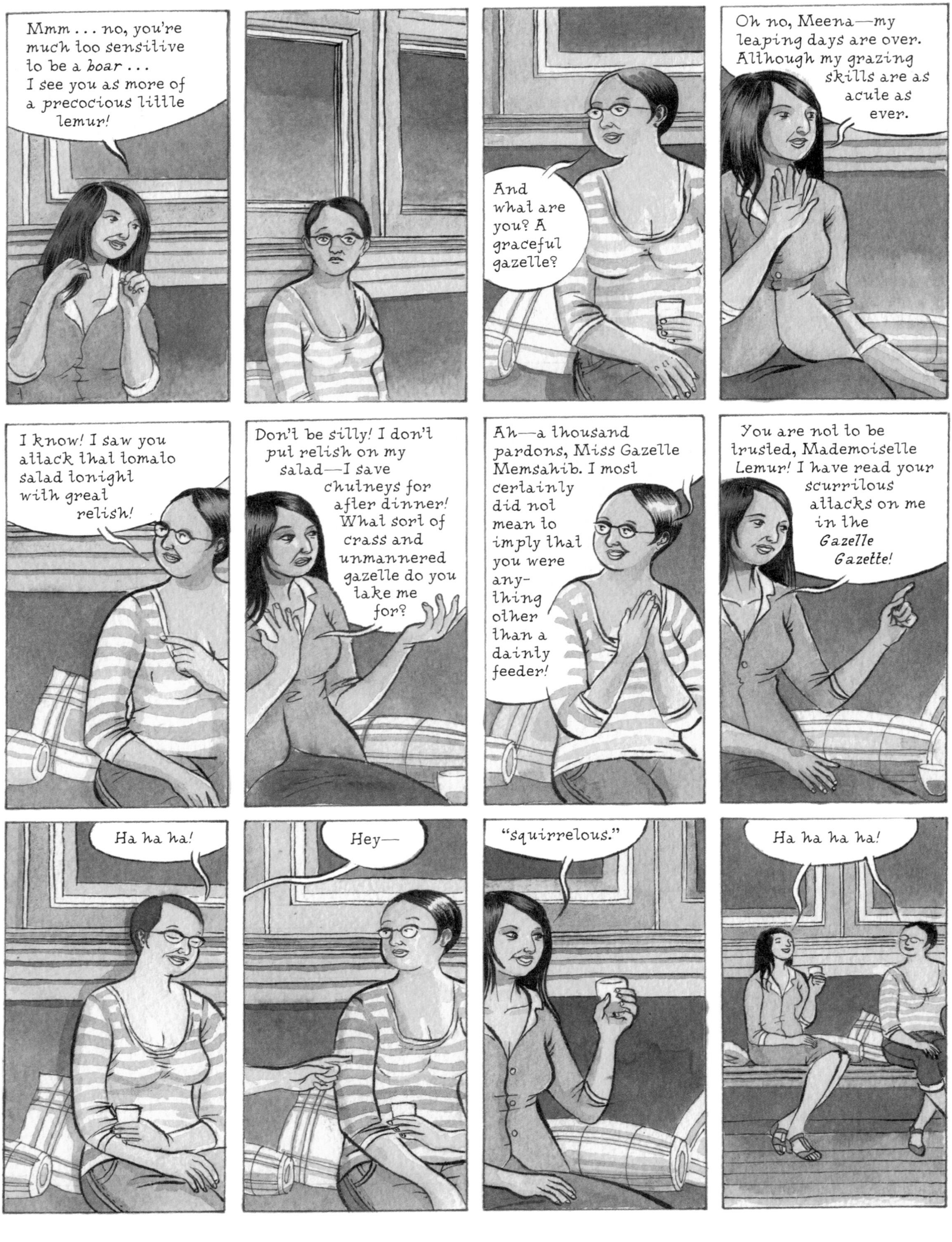
Mmm . . . no, you're much too sensitive to be a *boar* . . . I see you as more of a *precocious* little lemur!
And what are you? A graceful gazelle?
Oh no, Meena—my leaping days are over. Although my grazing skills are as acute as ever.
I know! I saw you attack that tomato salad tonight with great relish!
Don't be silly! I don't put relish on my salad—I save chutneys for after dinner! What sort of crass and unmannered gazelle do you take me for?
Ah—a thousand pardons, Miss Gazelle Memsahib. I most certainly did not mean to imply that you were any-thing other than a dainty feeder!
You are not to be trusted, Mademoiselle Lemur! I have read your scurrilous attacks on me in the *Gazelle Gazette!*
Ha ha ha!
Hey—
"squirrelous."
Ha ha ha ha!

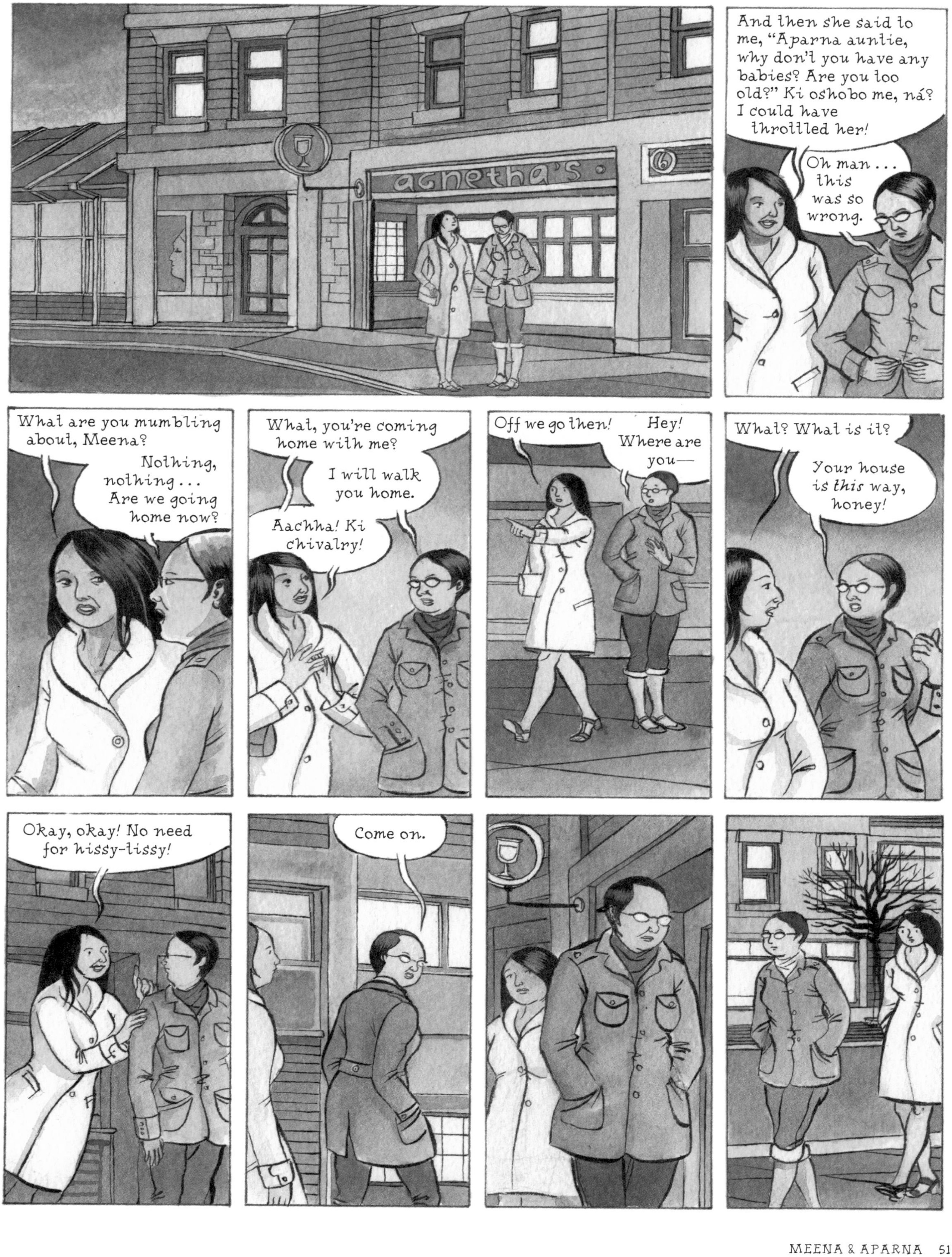
agnetha's
And then she said to me, "Aparna auntie, why don't you have any babies? Are you too old?" Ki oshobo me, ná? I could have throttled her!
Oh man . . . this was so wrong.
What are you mumbling about, Meena?
Nothing, nothing . . . Are we going home now?
What, you're coming home with me?
I will walk you home.
Aachha! Ki chivalry!
Off we go then!
Hey! Where are you—
What? What is it?
Your house is *this* way, honey!
Okay, okay! No need for hissy-lissy!
Come on.

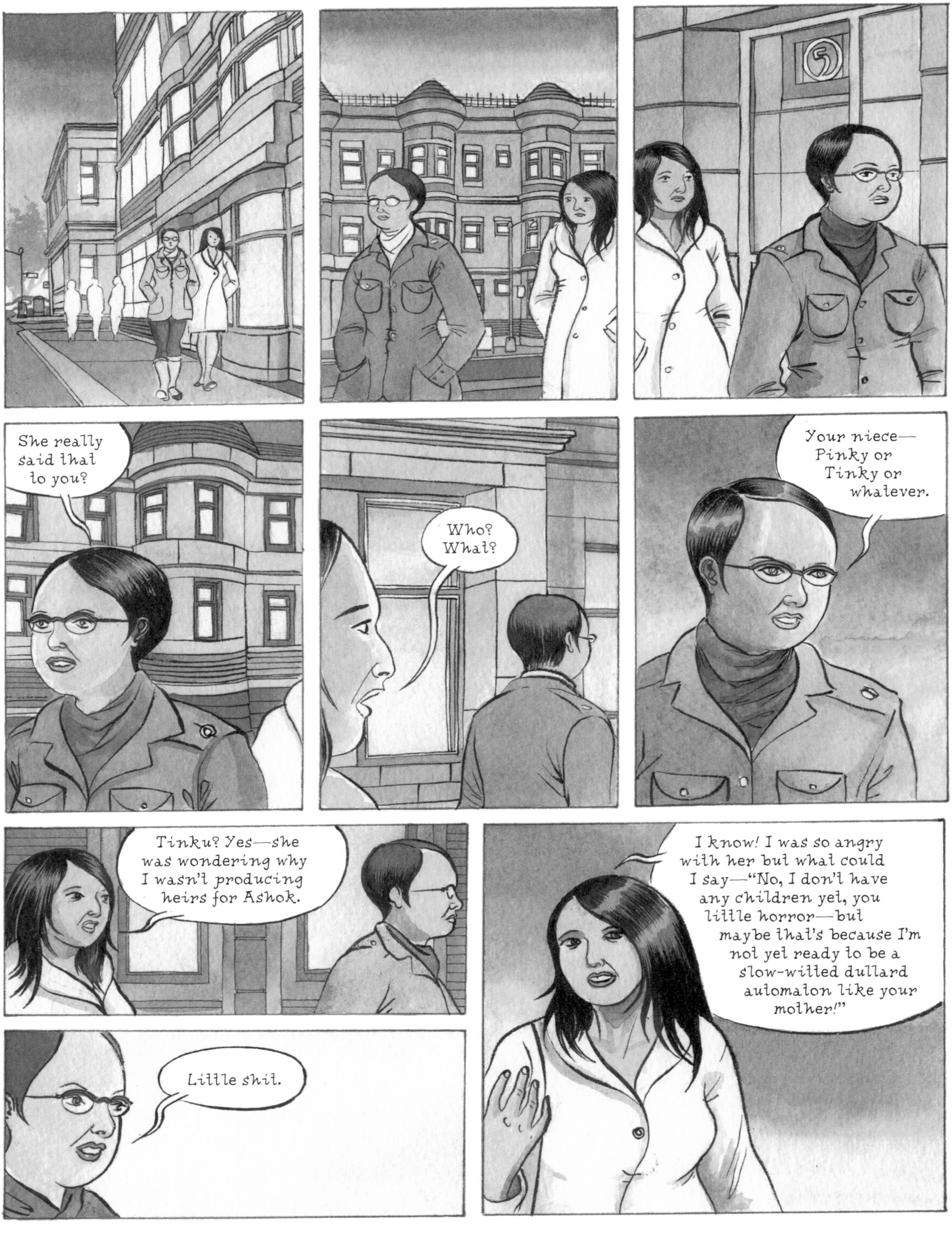
She really said that to you?
Who? What?
Your niece—Pinky or Tinky or whatever.
Tinku? Yes—she was wondering why I wasn't producing heirs for Ashok.
I know! I was so angry with her but what could I say—"No, I don't have any children yet, you little horror—but maybe that's because I'm not yet ready to be a slow-witted dullard automaton like your mother!"
Little shit.

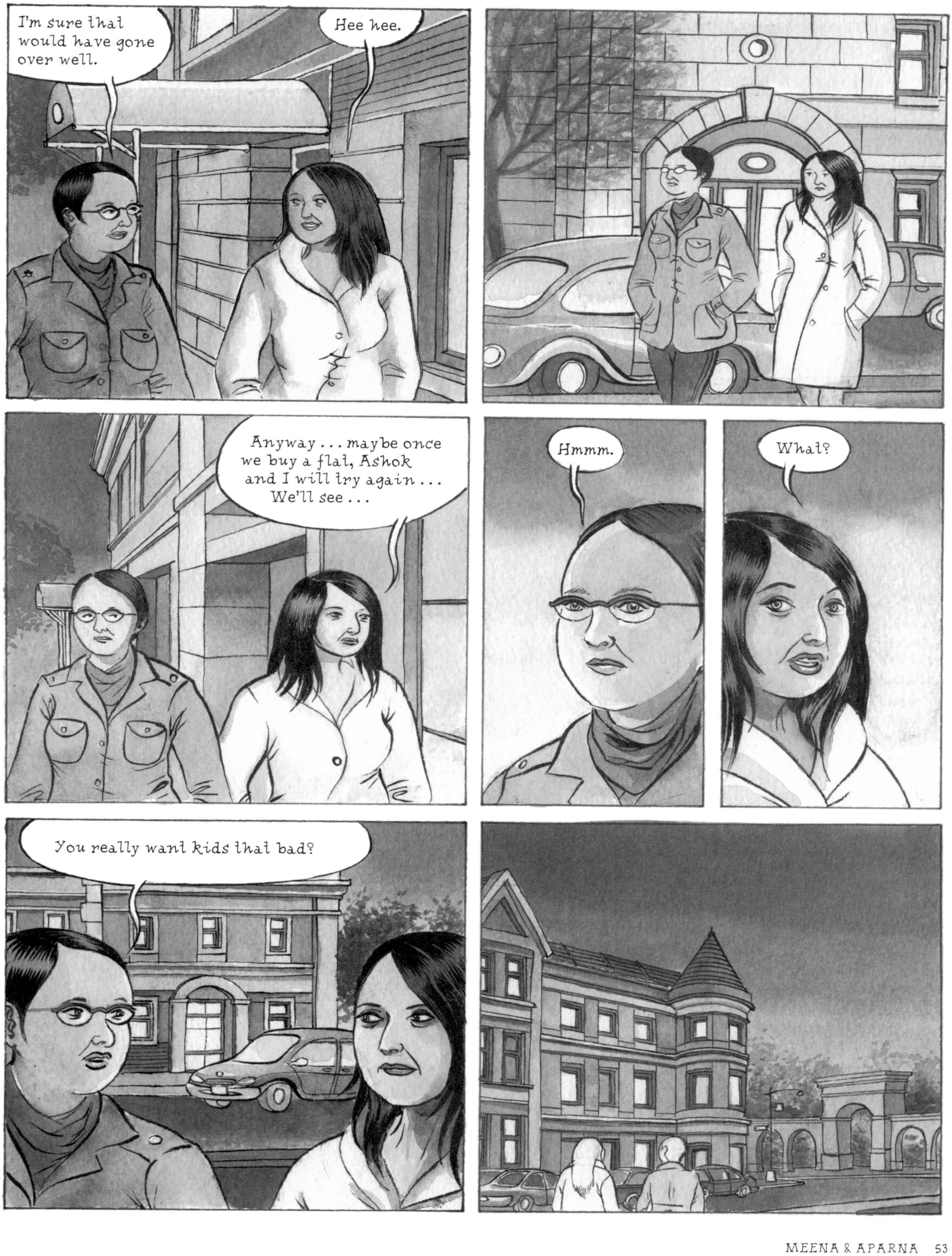
I'm sure that would have gone over well.
Hee hee.
Anyway . . . maybe once we buy a flat, Ashok and I will try again . . . We'll see . . .
Hmmm.
What?
You really want kids that bad?

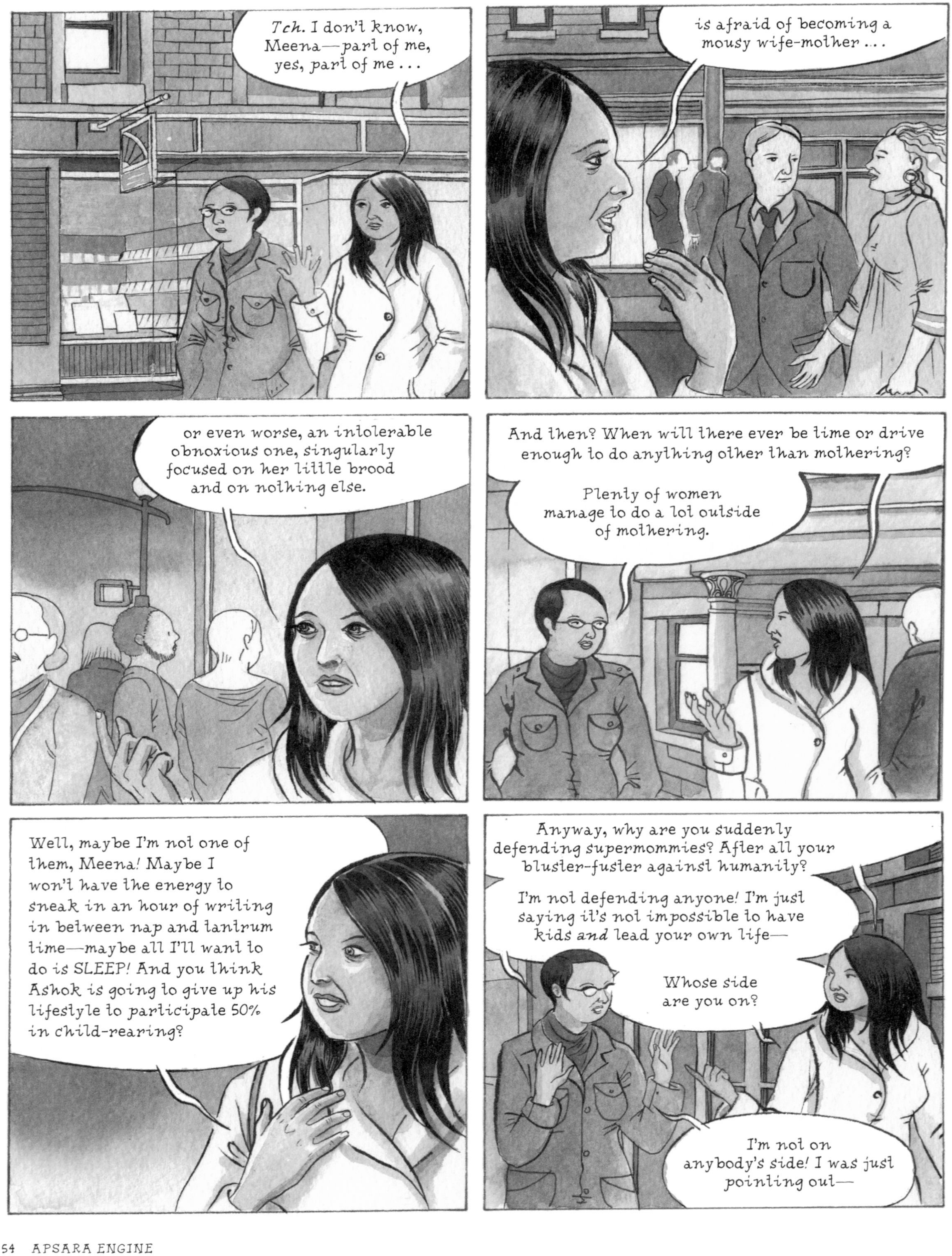
Tch. I don't know, Meena—part of me, yes, part of me . . .
is afraid of becoming a mousy wife-mother . . .
or even worse, an intolerable obnoxious one, singularly focused on her little brood and on nothing else.
And then? When will there ever be time or drive enough to do anything other than mothering?
Plenty of women manage to do a lot outside of mothering.
Well, maybe I'm not one of them, Meena! Maybe I won't have the energy to sneak in an hour of writing in between nap and tantrum time—maybe all I'll want to do is SLEEP! And you think Ashok is going to give up his lifestyle to participate 50% in child-rearing?
Anyway, why are you suddenly defending supermommies? After all your bluster-fuster against humanity?
I'm not defending anyone! I'm just saying it's not impossible to have kids *and* lead your own life—
Whose side are you on?
I'm not on anybody's side! I was just pointing out—

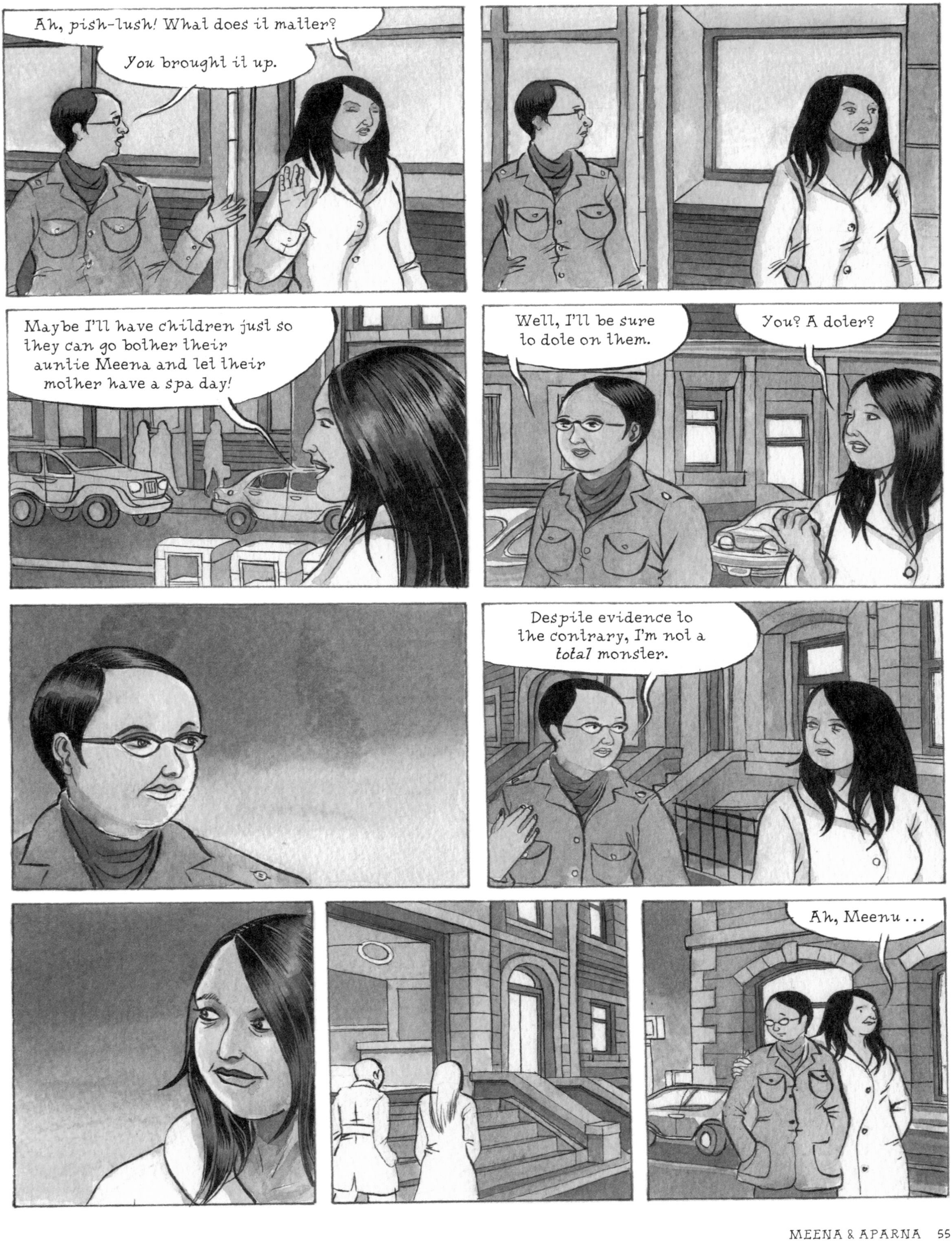
Ah, pish-tush! What does it matter?
You brought it up.
Maybe I'll have children just so they can go bother their auntie Meena and let their mother have a spa day!
Well, I'll be sure to dote on them.
You? A doter?
Despite evidence to the contrary, I'm not a *total* monster.
Ah, Meenu . . .

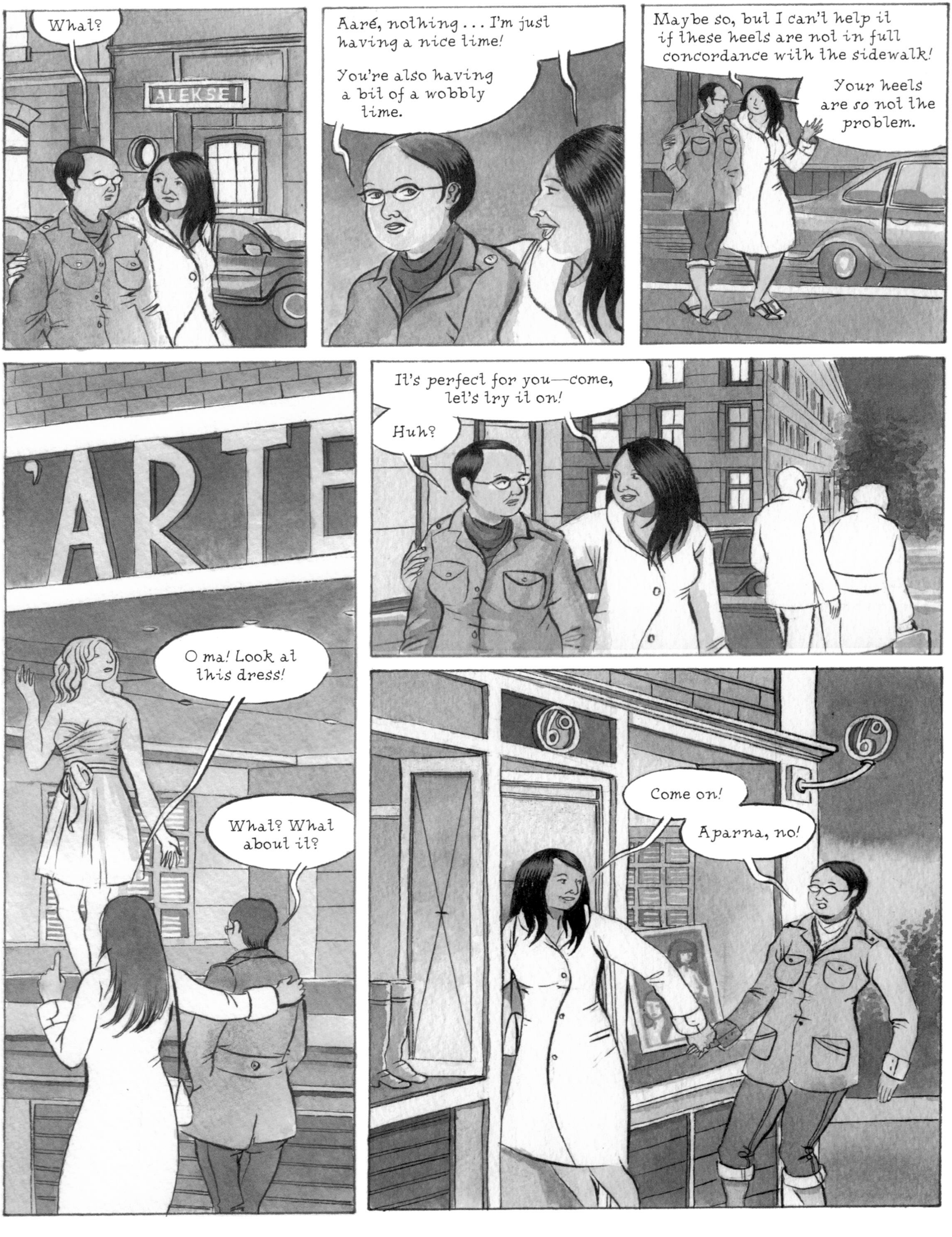
What?
ALEKSEI
Aaré, nothing . . . I'm just having a nice time!
You're also having a bit of a wobbly time.
Maybe so, but I can't help it if these heels are not in full concordance with the sidewalk!
Your heels are so not the problem.
'ARTE
O ma! Look at this dress!
What? What about it?
It's perfect for you—come, let's try it on!
Huh?
Come on!
Aparna, no!

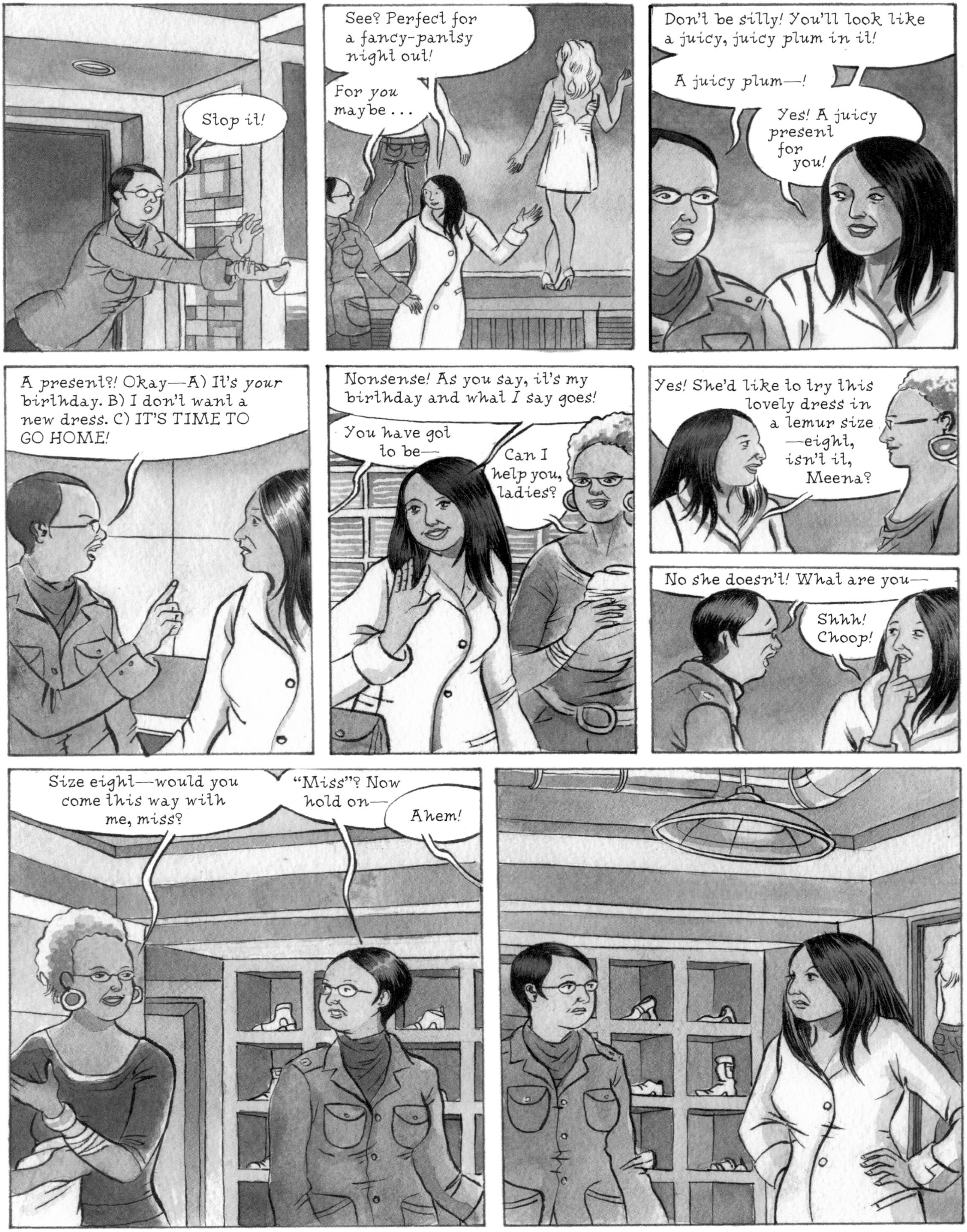
Stop it!
See? Perfect for a fancy-pantsy night out!
For you maybe . . .
Don't be silly! You'll look like a juicy, juicy plum in it!
A juicy plum—!
Yes! A juicy present for you!
A present?! Okay—A) It's your birthday. B) I don't want a new dress. C) IT'S TIME TO GO HOME!
Nonsense! As you say, it's my birthday and what I say goes!
You have got to be—
Can I help you, ladies?
Yes! She'd like to try this lovely dress in a lemur size —eight, isn't it, Meena?
No she doesn't! What are you—
Shhh! Choop!
Size eight—would you come this way with me, miss?
"Miss"? Now hold on—
Ahem!

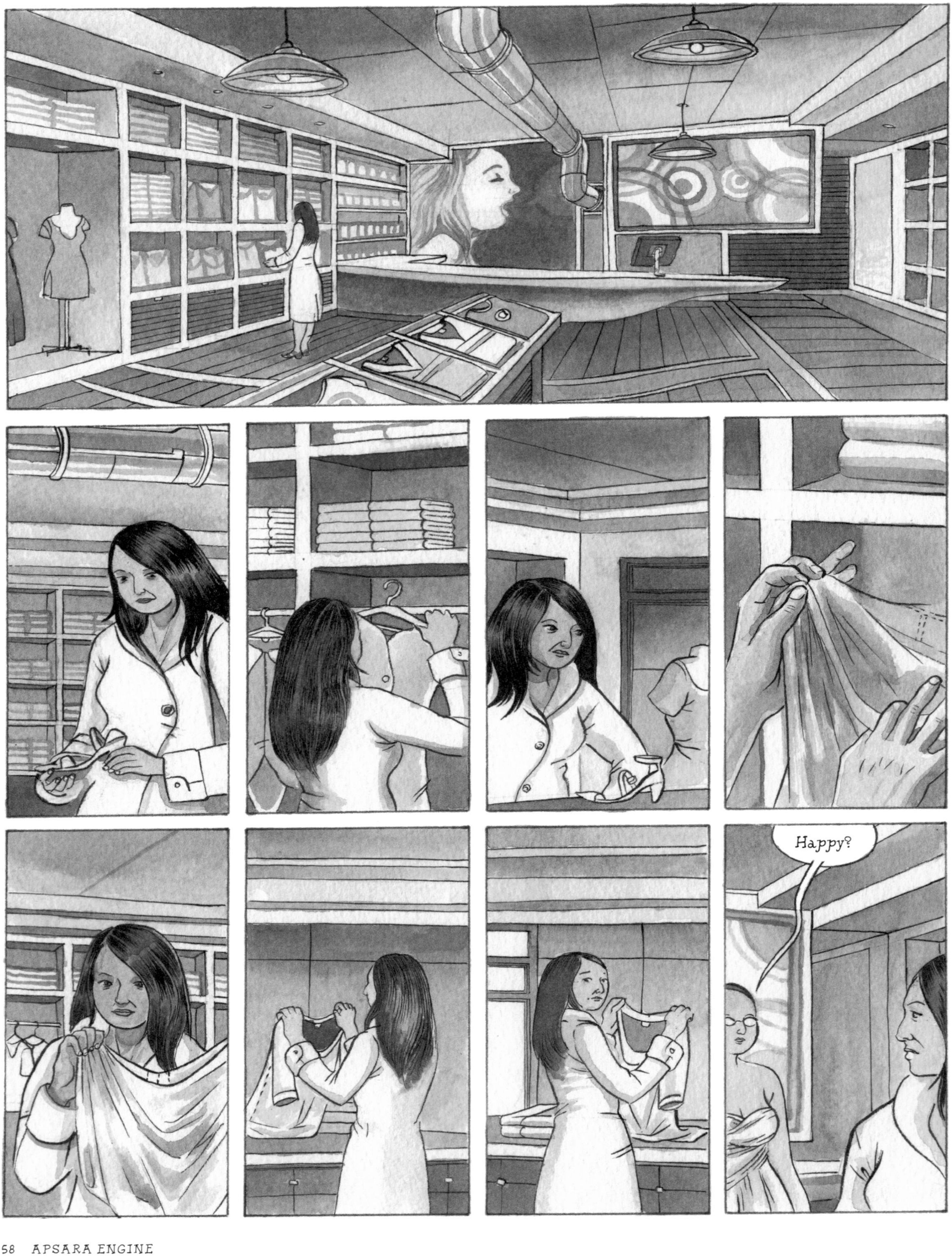
Happy?

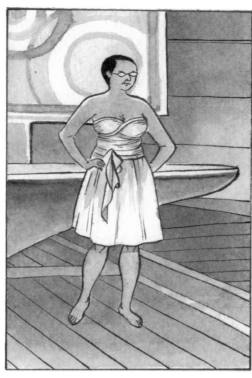

Very.

Well, I'm glad.

Now what?

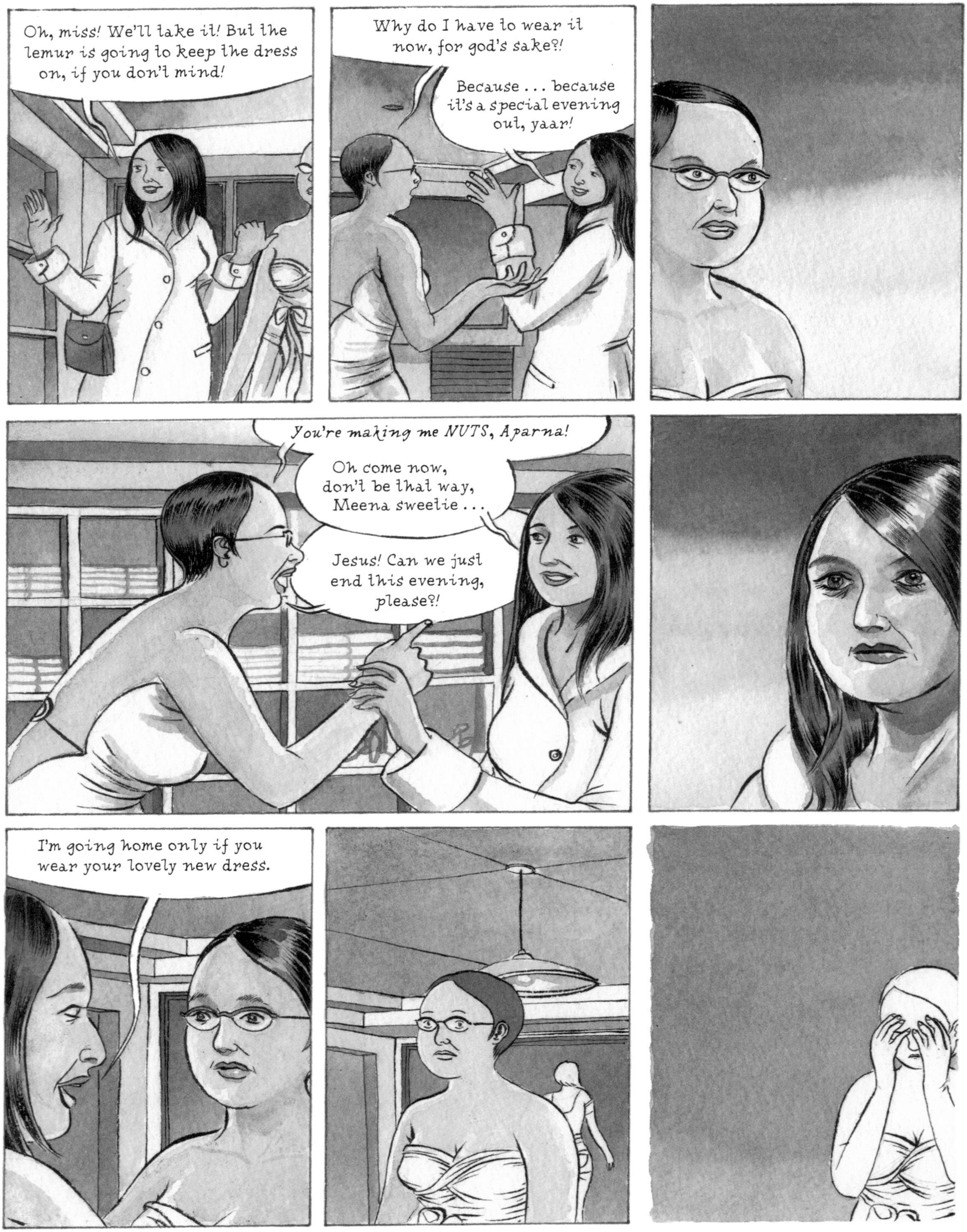

Oh, miss! We'll take it! But the lemur is going to keep the dress on, if you don't mind!
Why do I have to wear it now, for god's sake?!
Because . . . because it's a special evening out, yaar!
You're making me NUTS, Aparna!
Oh come now, don't be that way, Meena sweetie . . .
Jesus! Can we just end this evening, please?!
I'm going home only if you wear your lovely new dress.

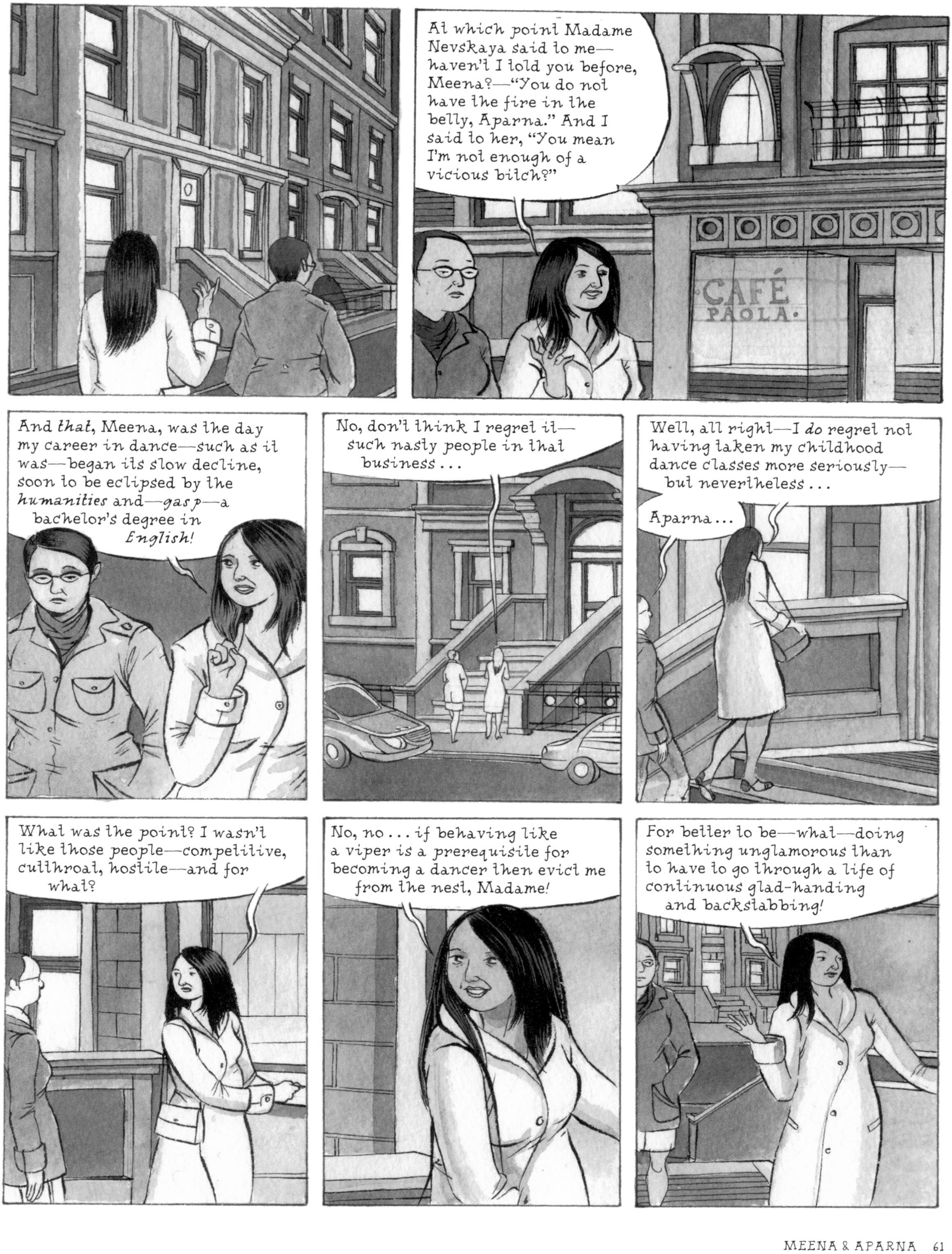
At which point Madame Nevskaya said to me—haven't I told you before, Meena?—"You do not have the fire in the belly, Aparna." And I said to her, "You mean I'm not enough of a vicious bitch?"
CAFÉ PAOLA
And *that*, Meena, was the day my career in dance—such as it was—began its slow decline, soon to be eclipsed by the *humanities* and—*gasp*—a bachelor's degree in *English*!
No, don't think I regret it—such nasty people in that business . . .
Well, all right—I *do* regret not having taken my childhood dance classes more seriously—but nevertheless . . .
Aparna . . .
What was the point? I wasn't like those people—competitive, cutthroat, hostile—and for what?
No, no . . . if behaving like a viper is a prerequisite for becoming a dancer then evict me from the nest, Madame!
For better to be—what—doing something unglamorous than to have to go through a life of continuous glad-handing and backslabbing!

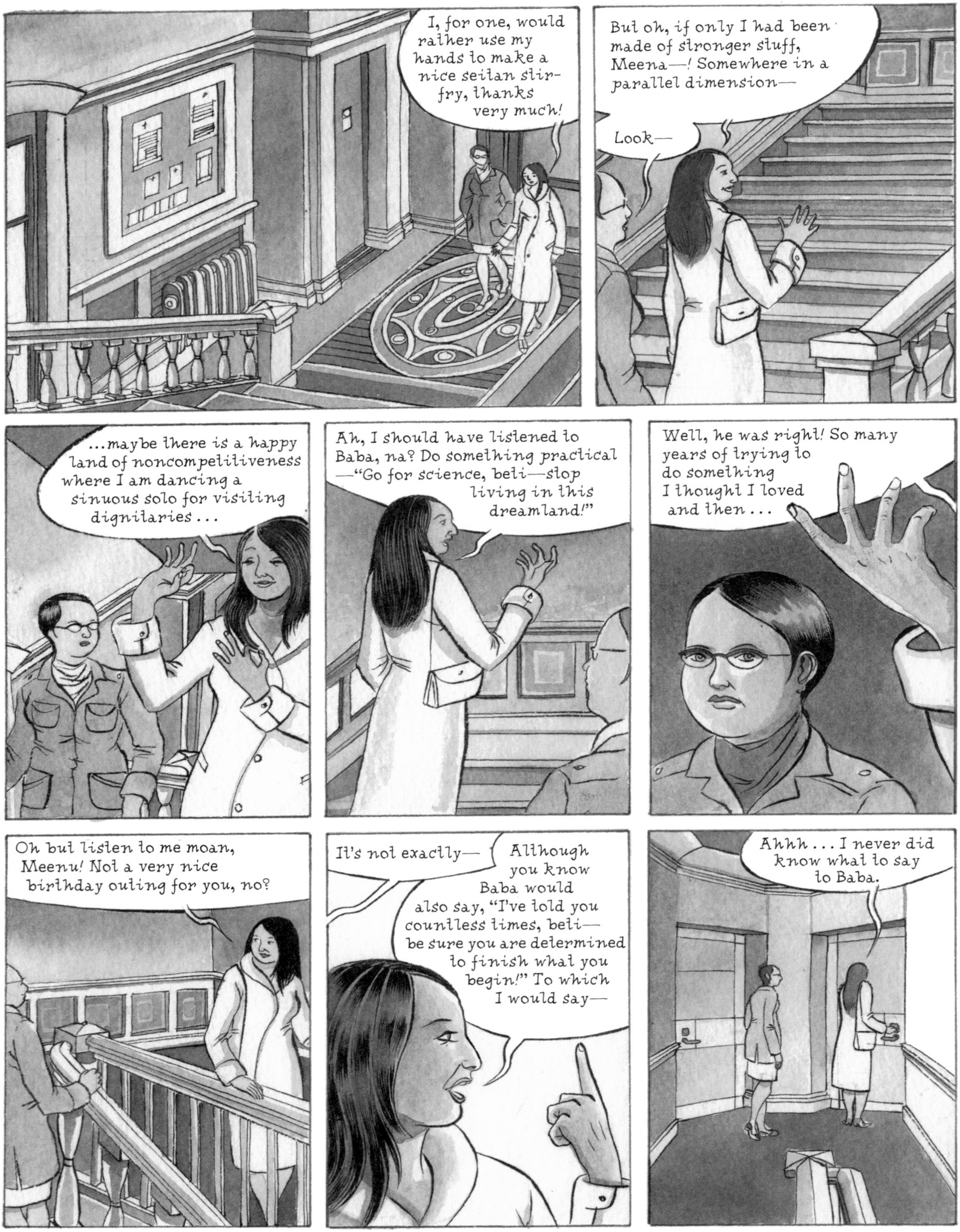
I, for one, would rather use my hands to make a nice seitan stir-fry, thanks very much!
But oh, if only I had been made of stronger stuff, Meena—! Somewhere in a parallel dimension—
Look—
...maybe there is a happy land of noncompetitiveness where I am dancing a sinuous solo for visiting dignitaries...
Ah, I should have listened to Baba, na? Do something practical —"Go for science, beti—stop living in this dreamland!"
Well, he was right! So many years of trying to do something I thought I loved and then...
Oh but listen to me moan, Meenu! Not a very nice birthday outing for you, no?
It's not exactly—
Although you know Baba would also say, "I've told you countless times, beti— be sure you are determined to finish what you begin!" To which I would say—
Ahhh... I never did know what to say to Baba.

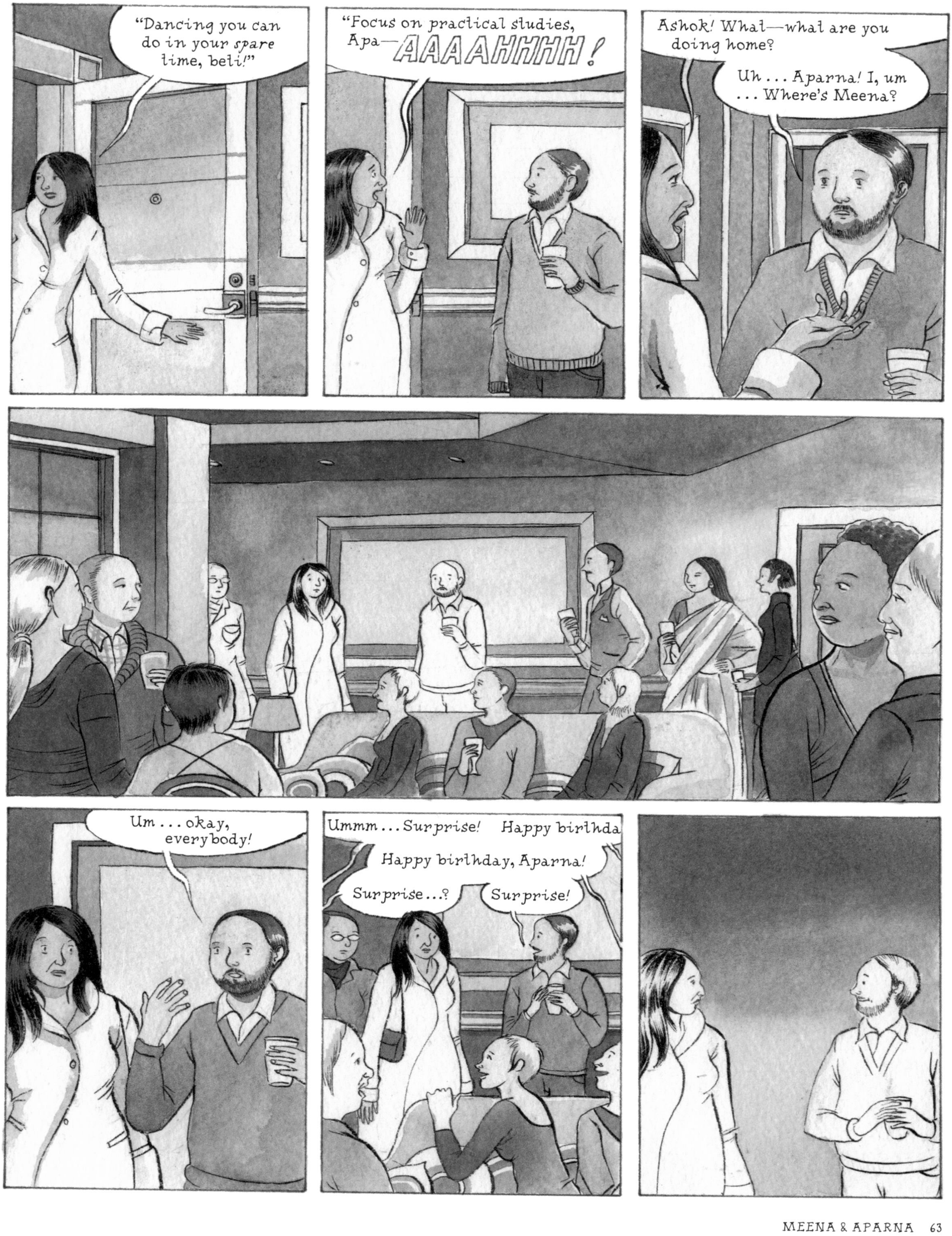
"Dancing you can do in your *spare* time, beti!"
"Focus on practical studies, Apa—AAAAHHHH!
Ashok! What—what are you doing home?
Uh . . . Aparna! I, um . . . Where's Meena?
Um . . . okay, everybody!
Ummm . . . Surprise!
Happy birthda
Happy birthday, Aparna!
Surprise . . .?
Surprise!

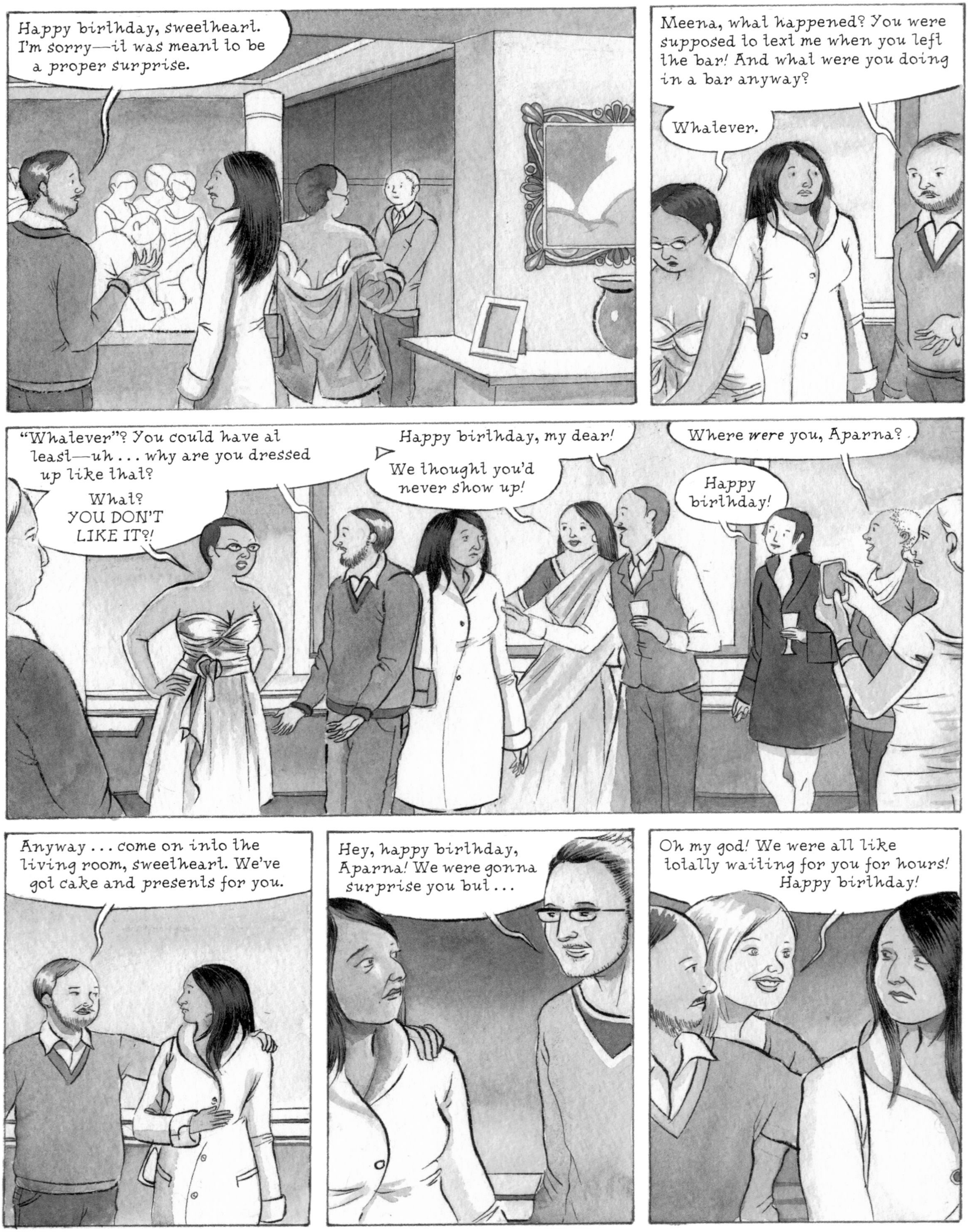
Happy birthday, sweetheart. I'm sorry—it was meant to be a *proper surprise*.
Meena, what happened? You were *supposed* to text me when you left the bar! And what were you doing in a bar anyway?
Whatever.
"Whatever"? You could have at least—uh . . . why are you dressed up like that?
What? YOU DON'T LIKE IT?!
Happy birthday, my dear!
We thought you'd never show up!
Where *were* you, Aparna?
Happy birthday!
Anyway . . . come on into the living room, sweetheart. We've got cake and *presents* for you.
Hey, happy birthday, Aparna! We were gonna *surprise* you but . . .
Oh my god! We were all like totally waiting for you for hours! Happy birthday!

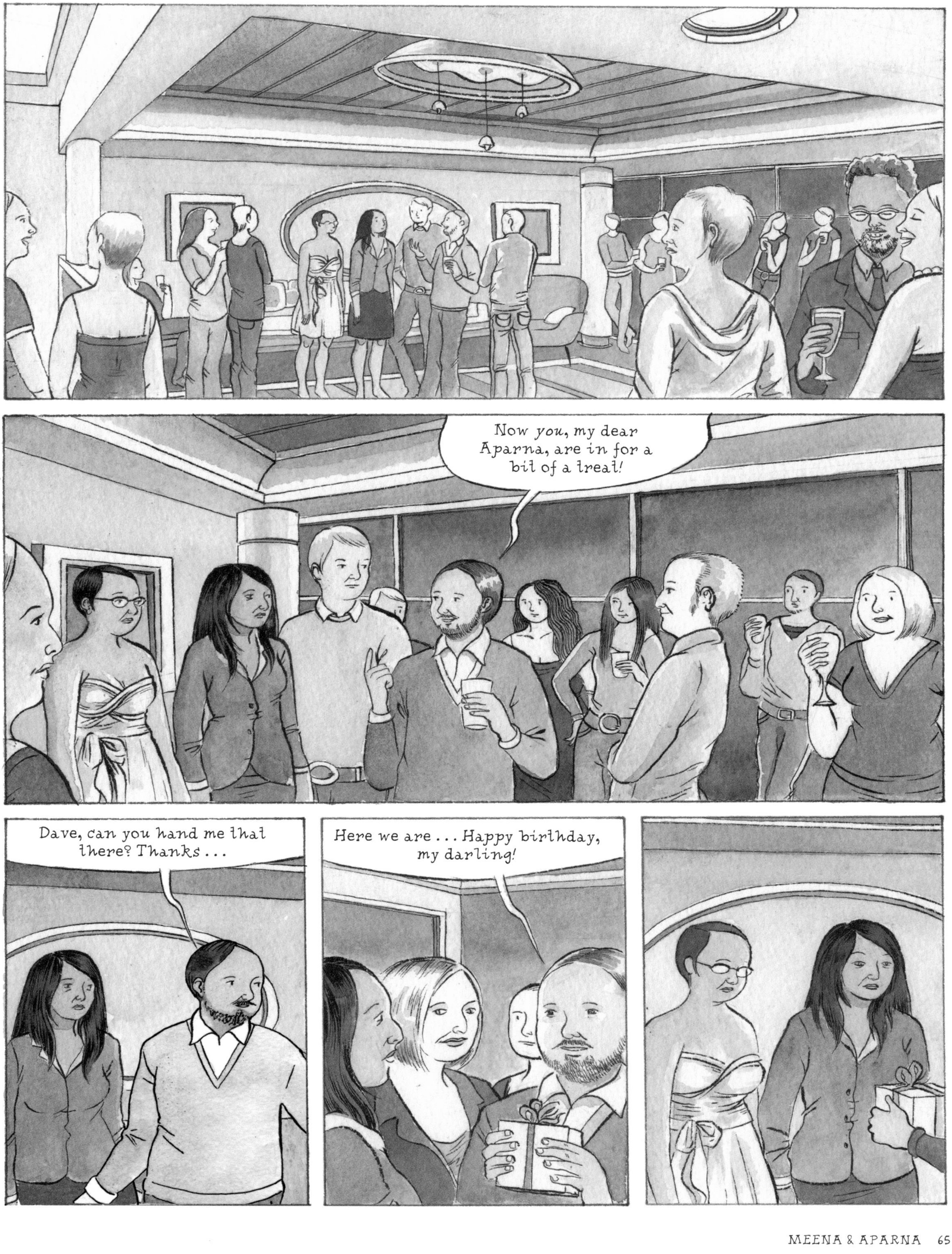
Now *you*, my dear Aparna, are in for a bit of a treat!
Dave, can you hand me that there? Thanks . . .
Here we are . . . Happy birthday, my darling!

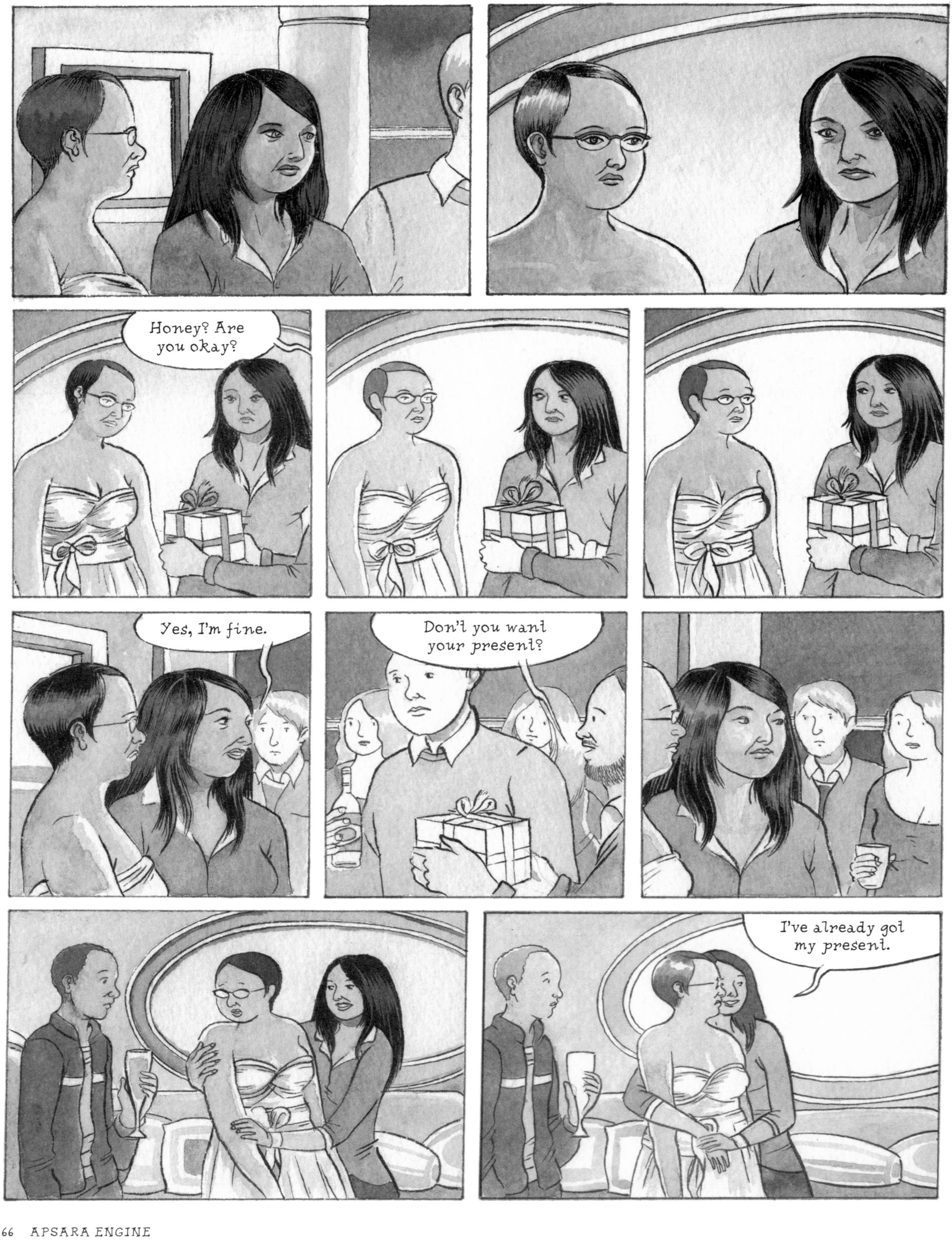
Honey? Are you okay?
Yes, I'm fine.
Don't you want your present?
I've already got my present.

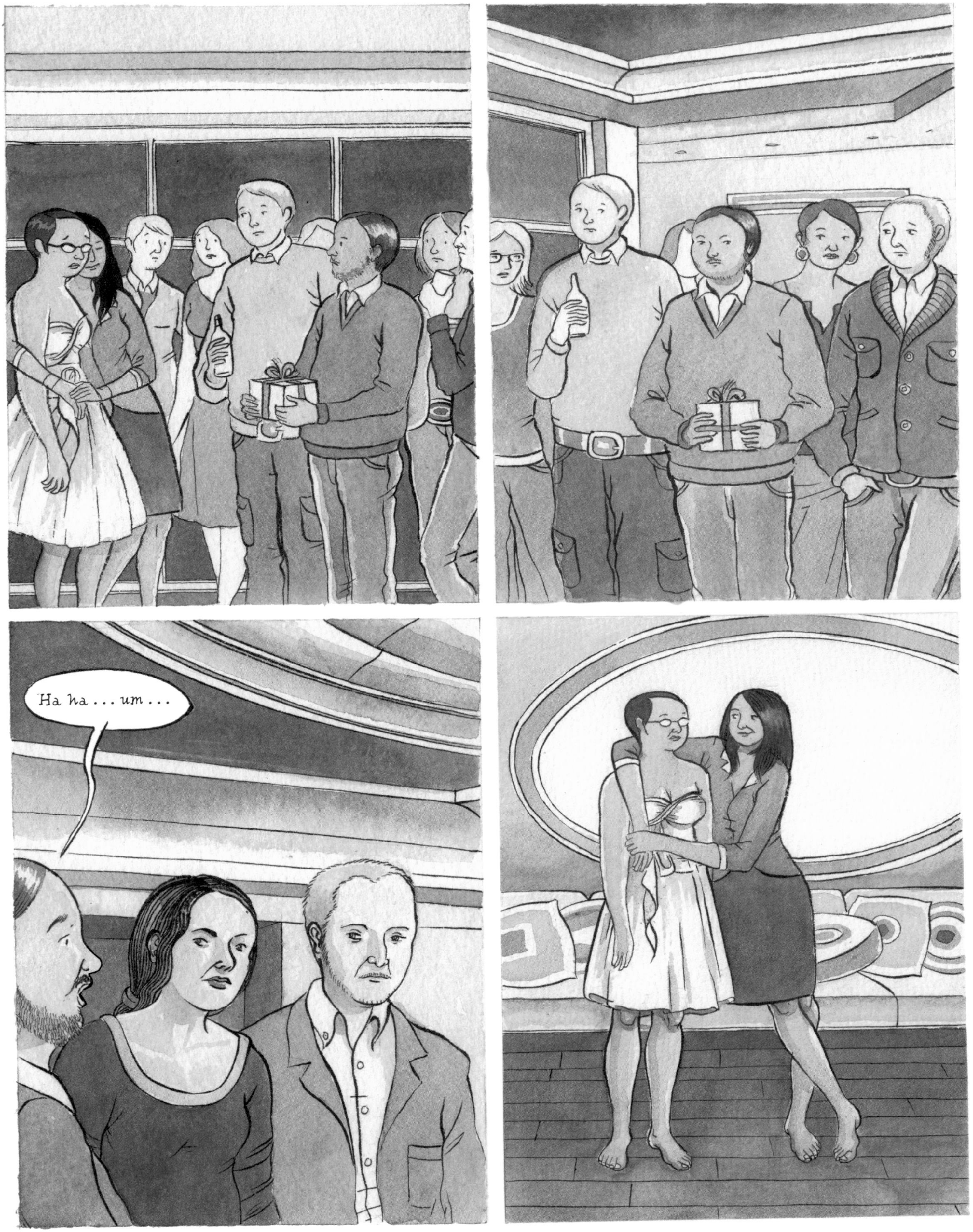
Ha ha . . . um . . .

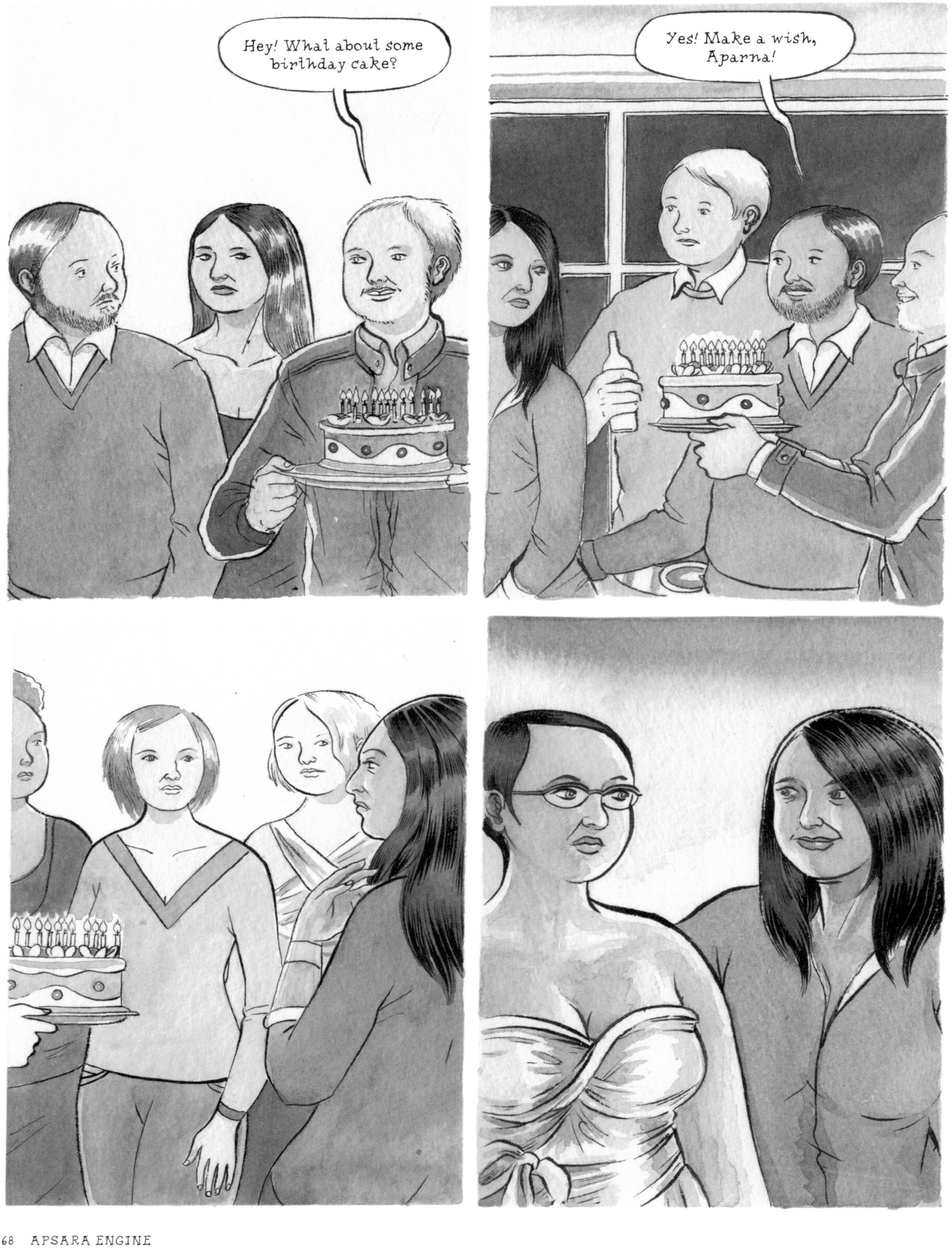
Hey! What about some birthday cake?
Yes! Make a wish, Aparna!

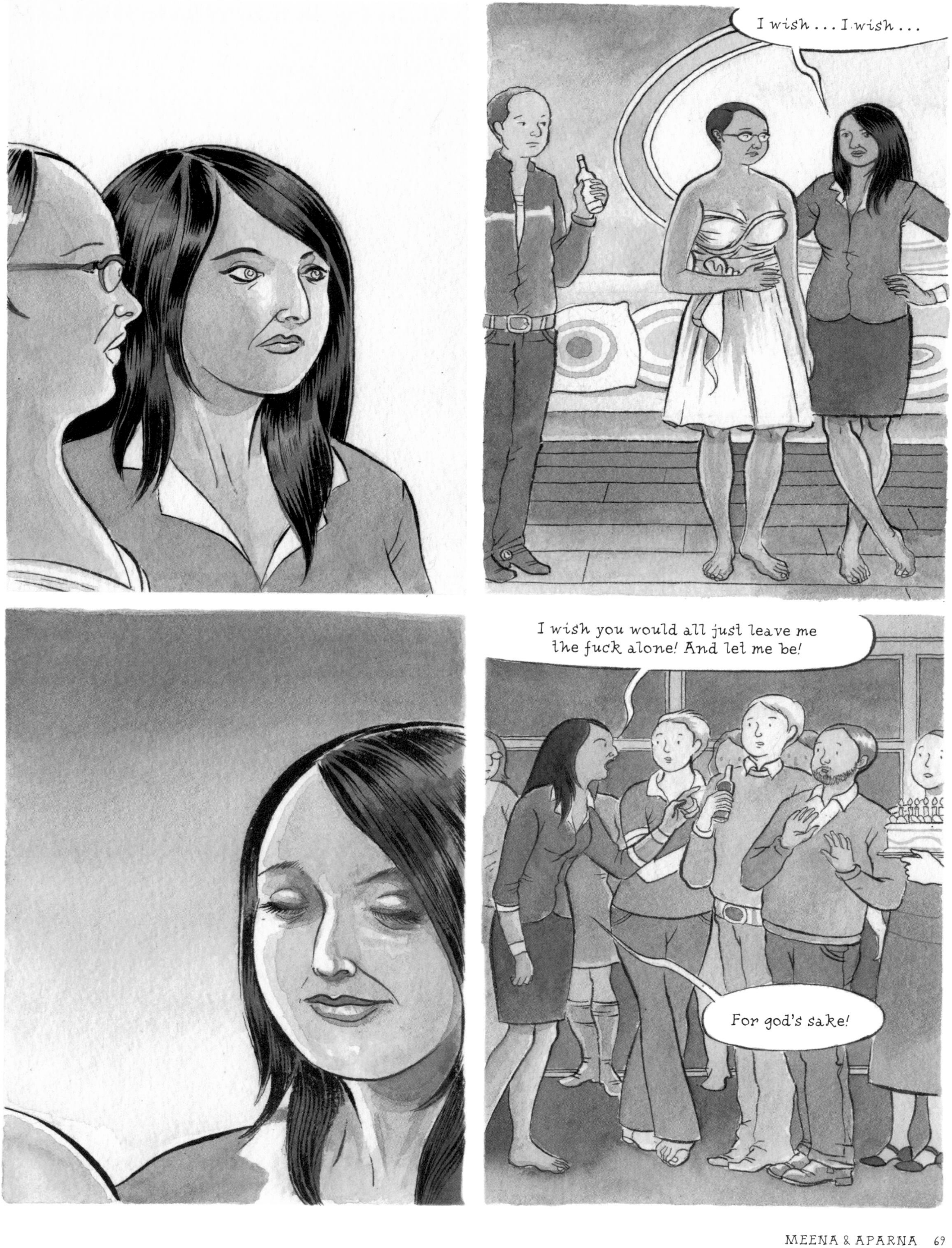
I wish . . . I wish . . .
I wish you would all just leave me the fuck alone! And let me be!
For god's sake!

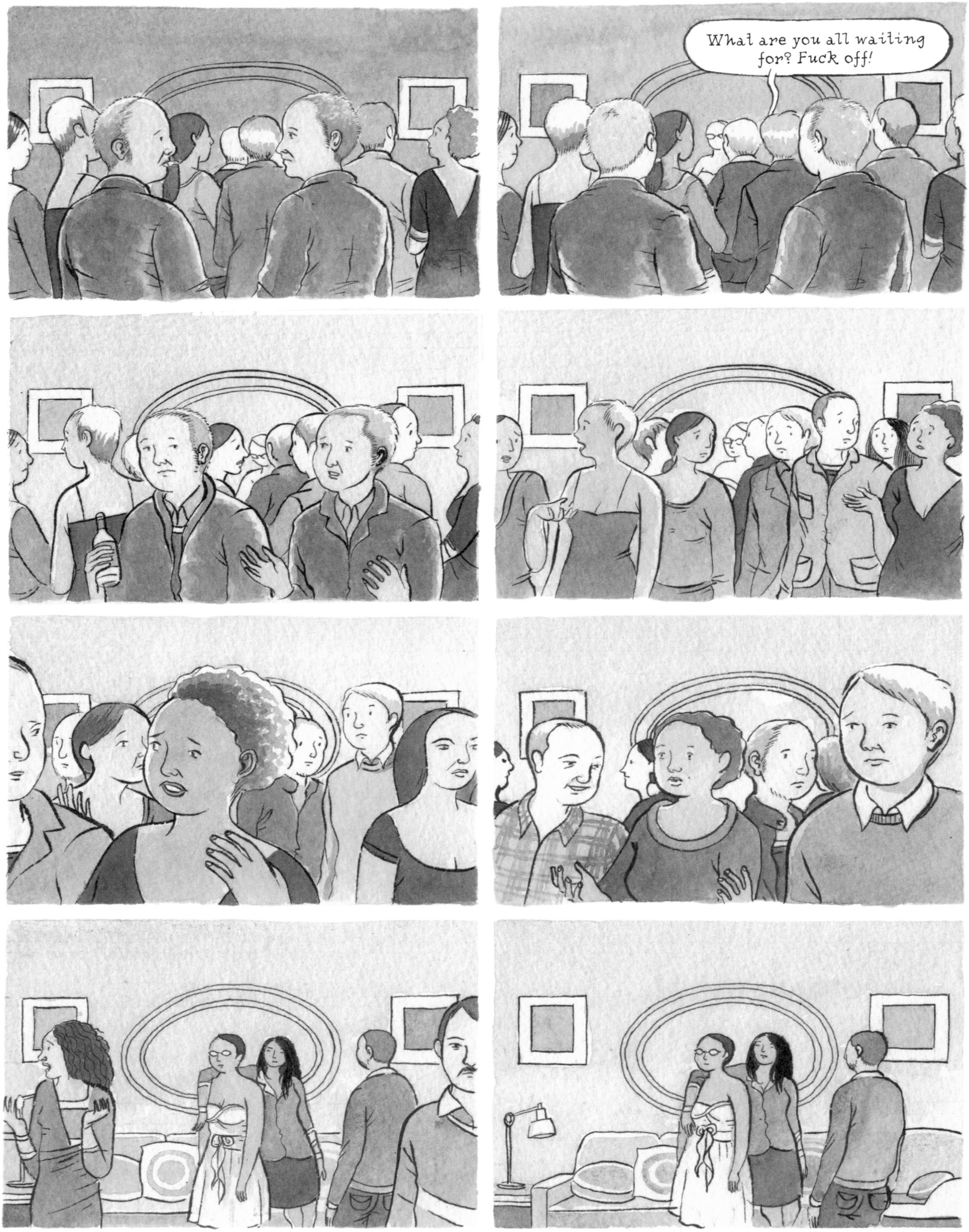
What are you all waiting for? Fuck off!

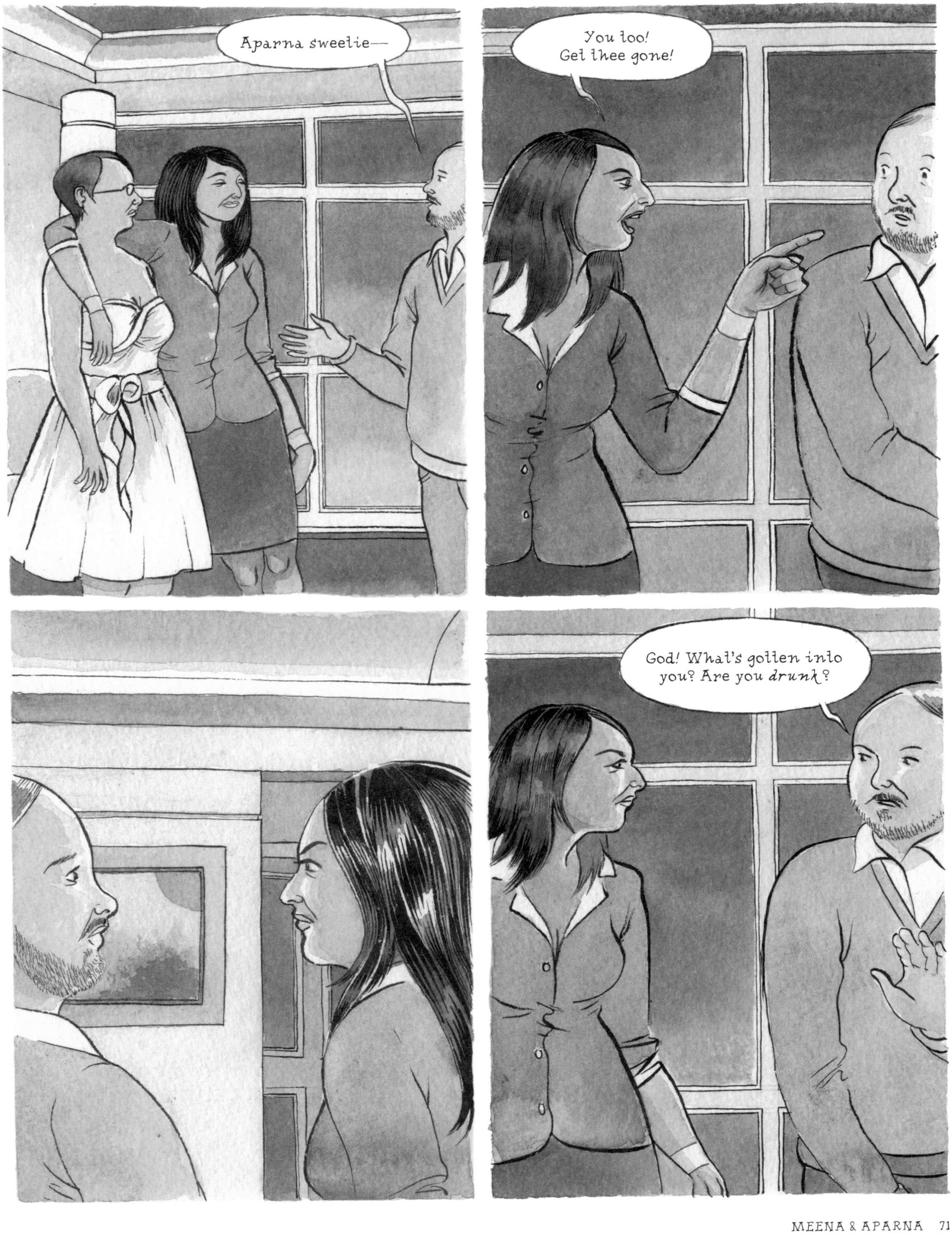
Aparna sweetie—
You too! Get thee gone!
God! What's gotten into you? Are you *drunk*?

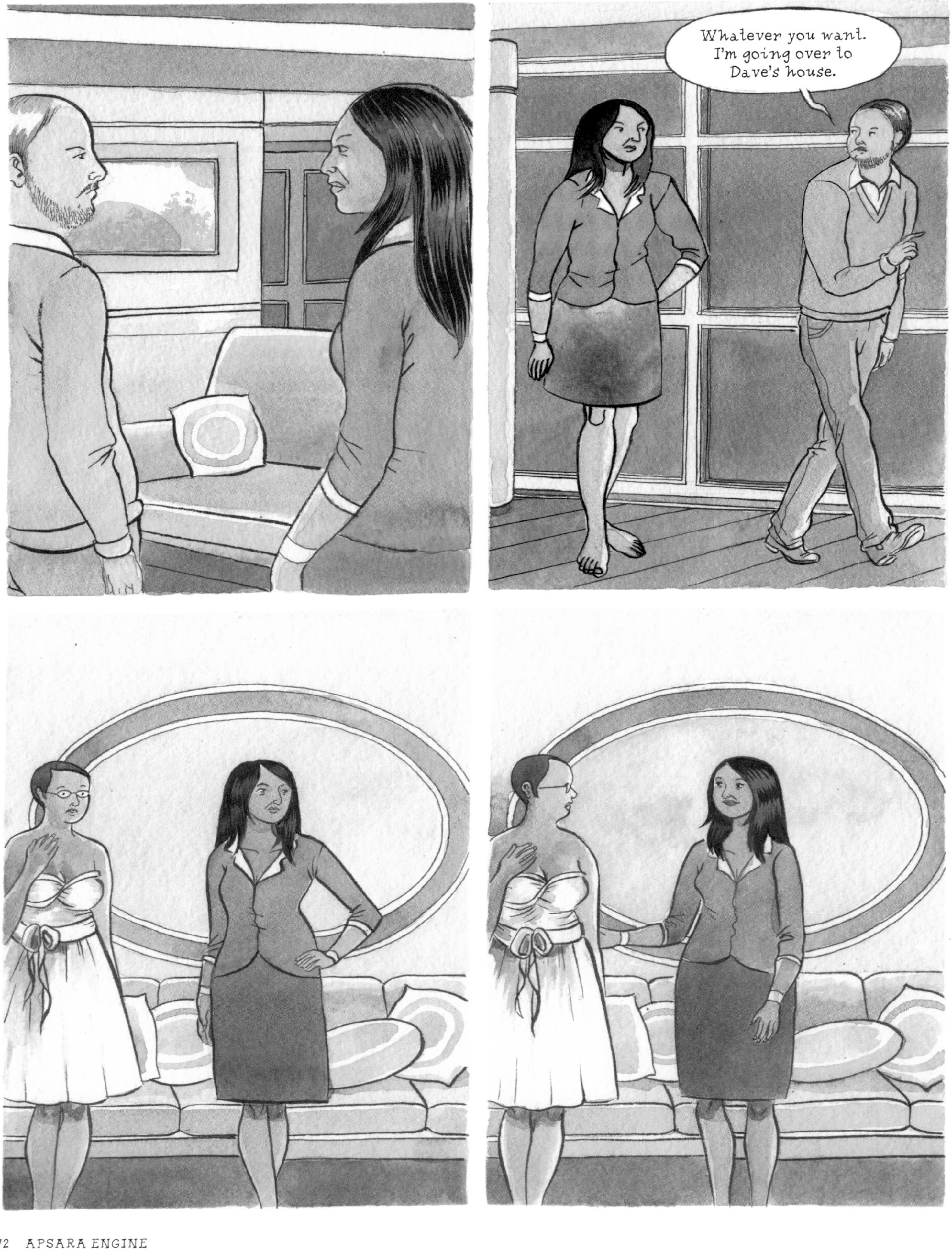
Whatever you want.
I'm going over to
Dave's house.

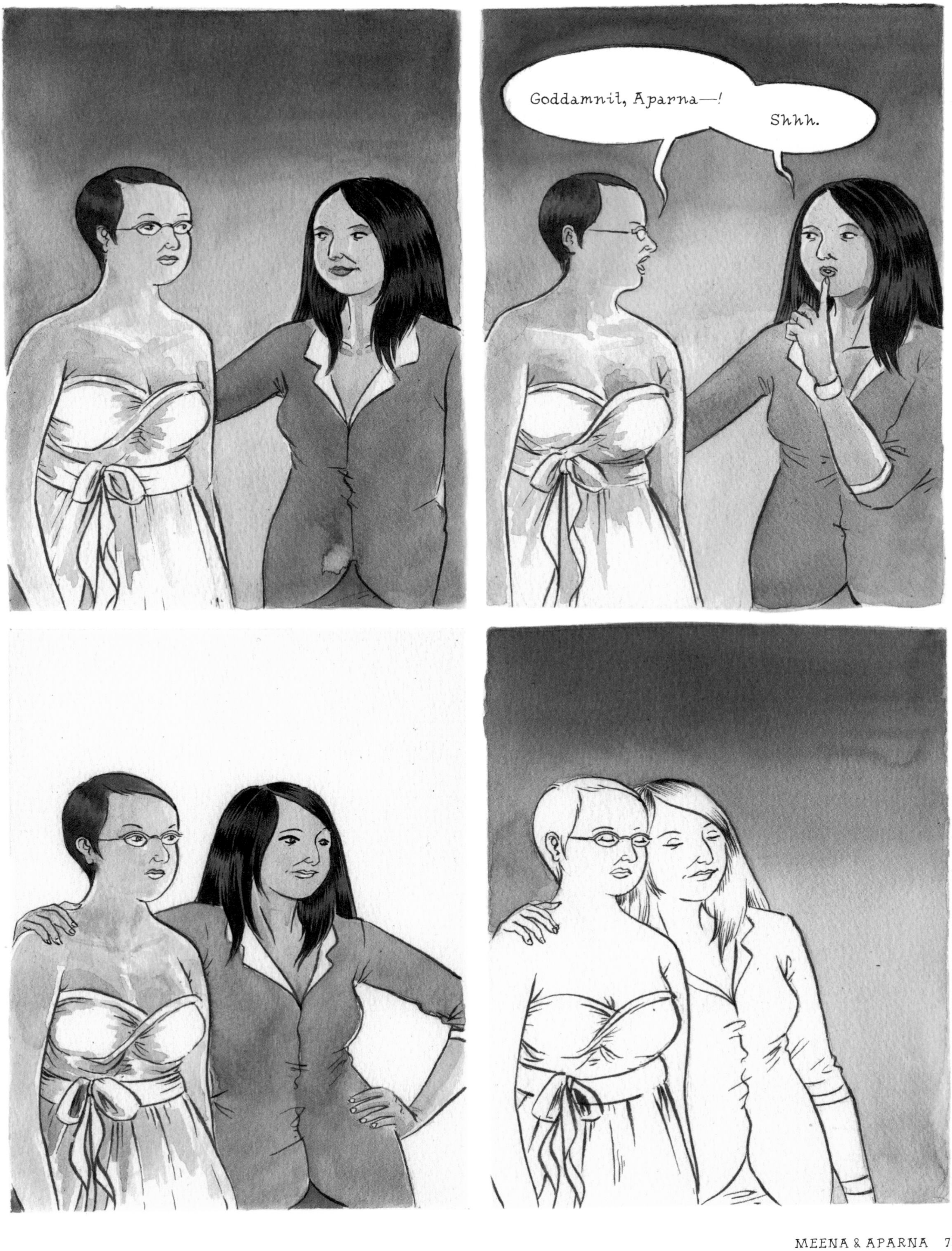
Goddamnit, Aparna—!
Shhh.

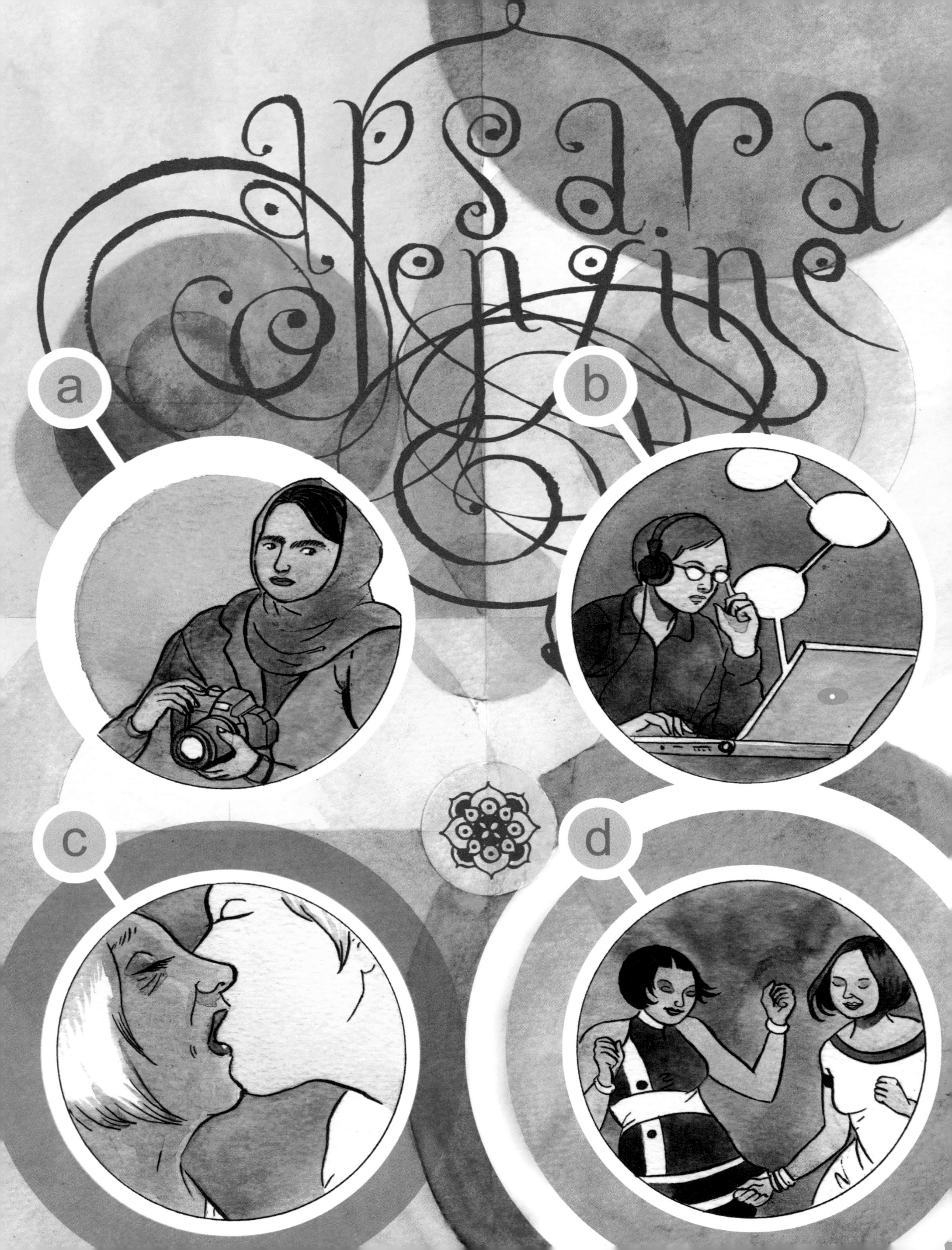
apsara engine
a
b
c
d

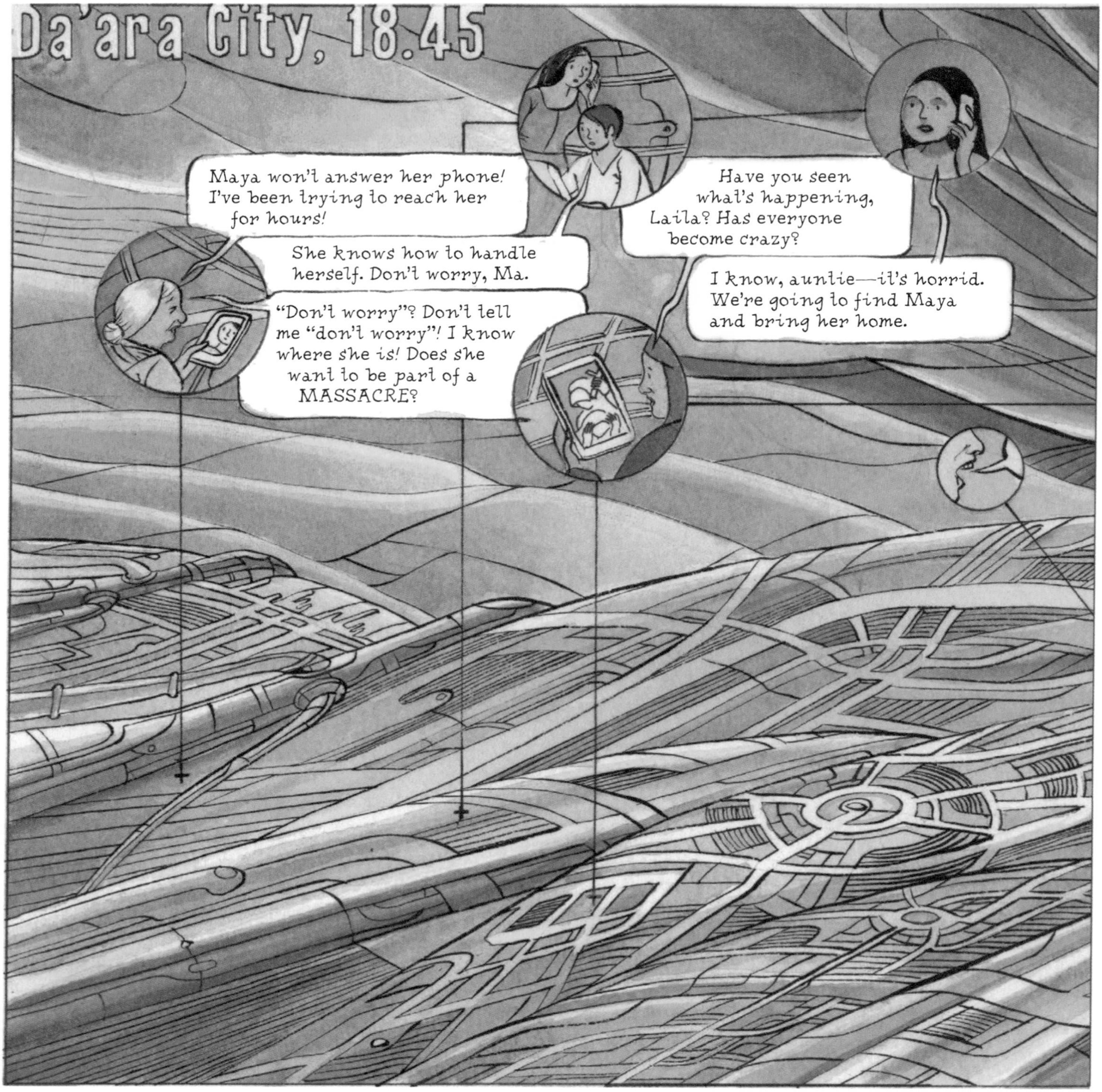
Da'ara City, 18.45
Maya won't answer her phone! I've been trying to reach her for hours!
She knows how to handle herself. Don't worry, Ma.
"Don't worry"? Don't tell me "don't worry"! I know where she is! Does she want to be part of a MASSACRE?
Have you seen what's happening, Laila? Has everyone become crazy?
I know, auntie—it's horrid. We're going to find Maya and bring her home.

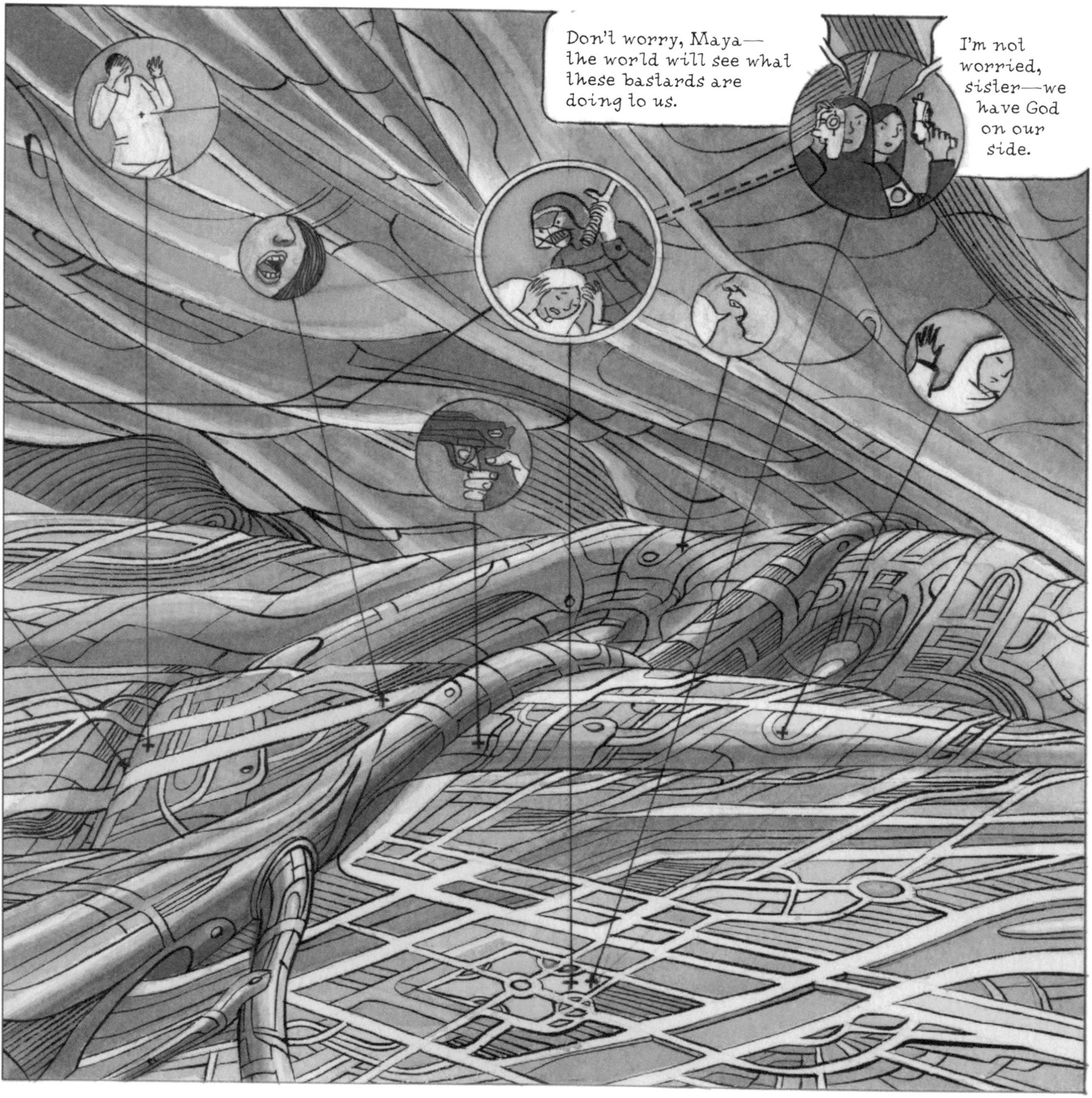
Don't worry, Maya—the world will see what these bastards are doing to us.
I'm not worried, sister—we have God on our side.

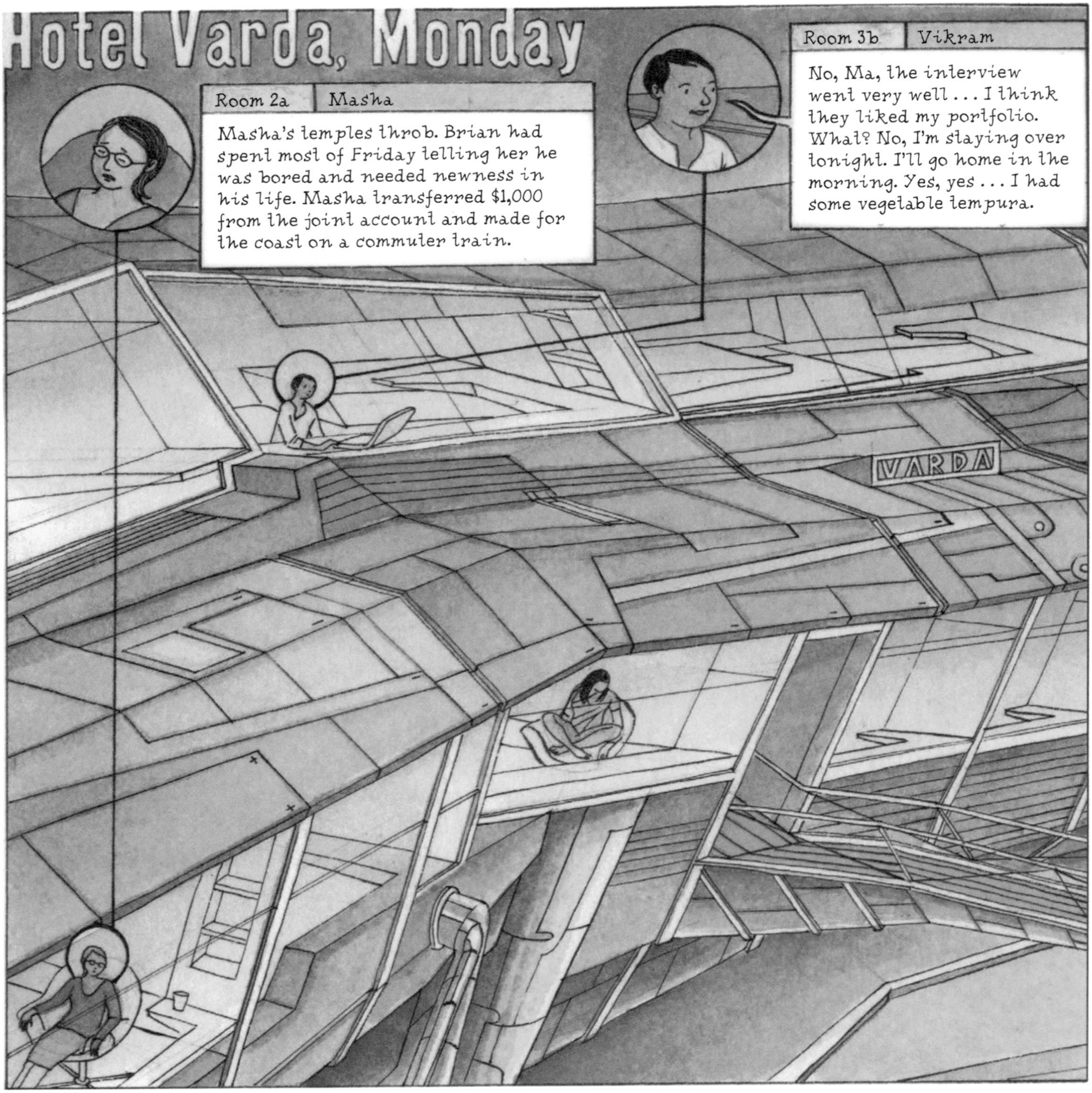
Hotel Varda, Monday
Room 2a
Masha
Masha's temples throb. Brian had spent most of Friday telling her he was bored and needed newness in his life. Masha transferred $1,000 from the joint account and made for the coast on a commuter train.
Room 3b
Vikram
No, Ma, the interview went very well . . . I think they liked my portfolio. What? No, I'm staying over tonight. I'll go home in the morning. Yes, yes . . . I had some vegetable tempura.
VARDA

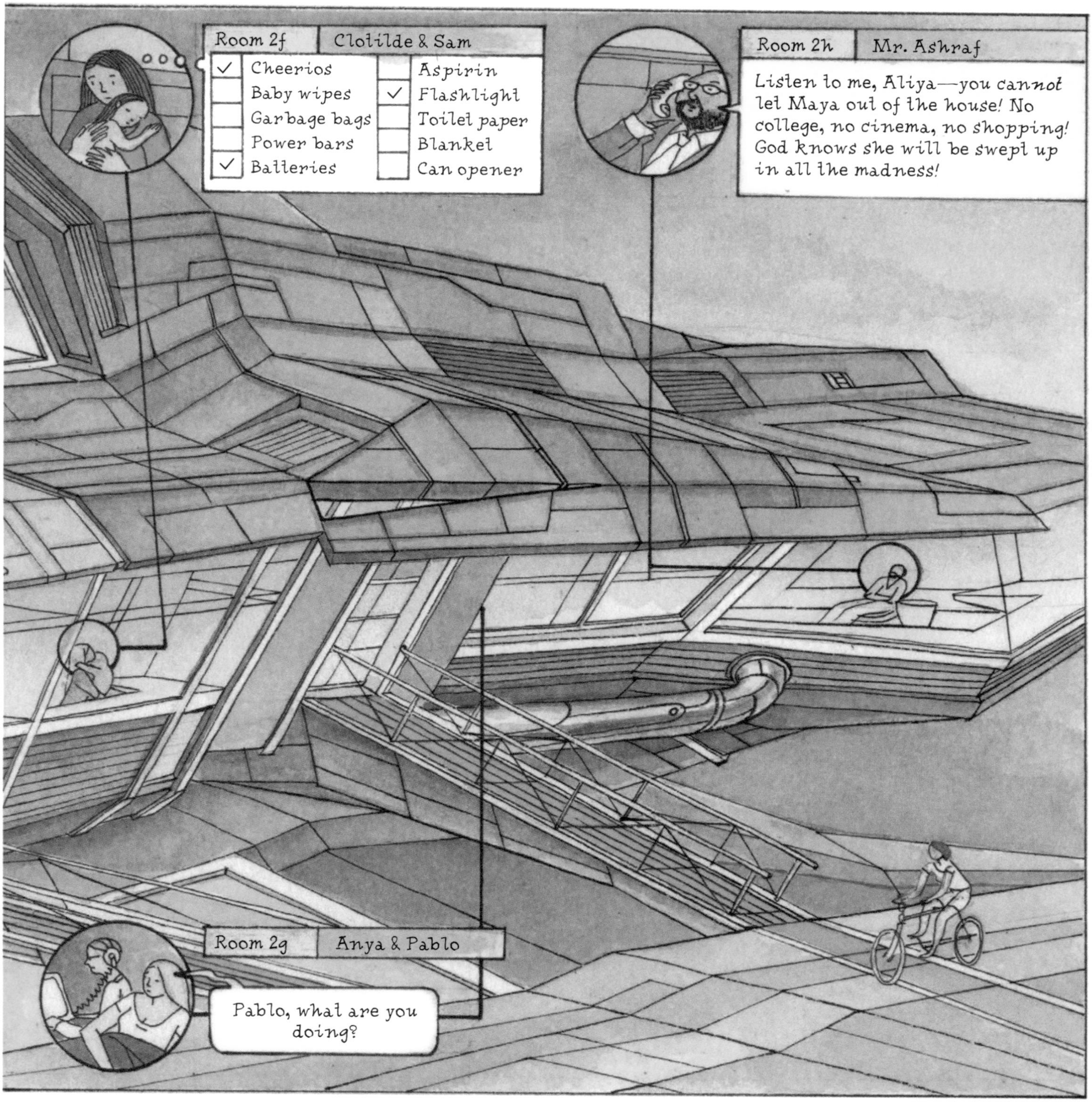
Room 2f
Clotilde & Sam
Cheerios
Baby wipes
Garbage bags
Power bars
Batteries
Aspirin
Flashlight
Toilet paper
Blanket
Can opener
Room 2h
Mr. Ashraf
Listen to me, Aliya—you can*not* let Maya out of the house! No college, no cinema, no shopping! God knows she will be swept up in all the madness!
Room 2g
Anya & Pablo
Pablo, what are you doing?

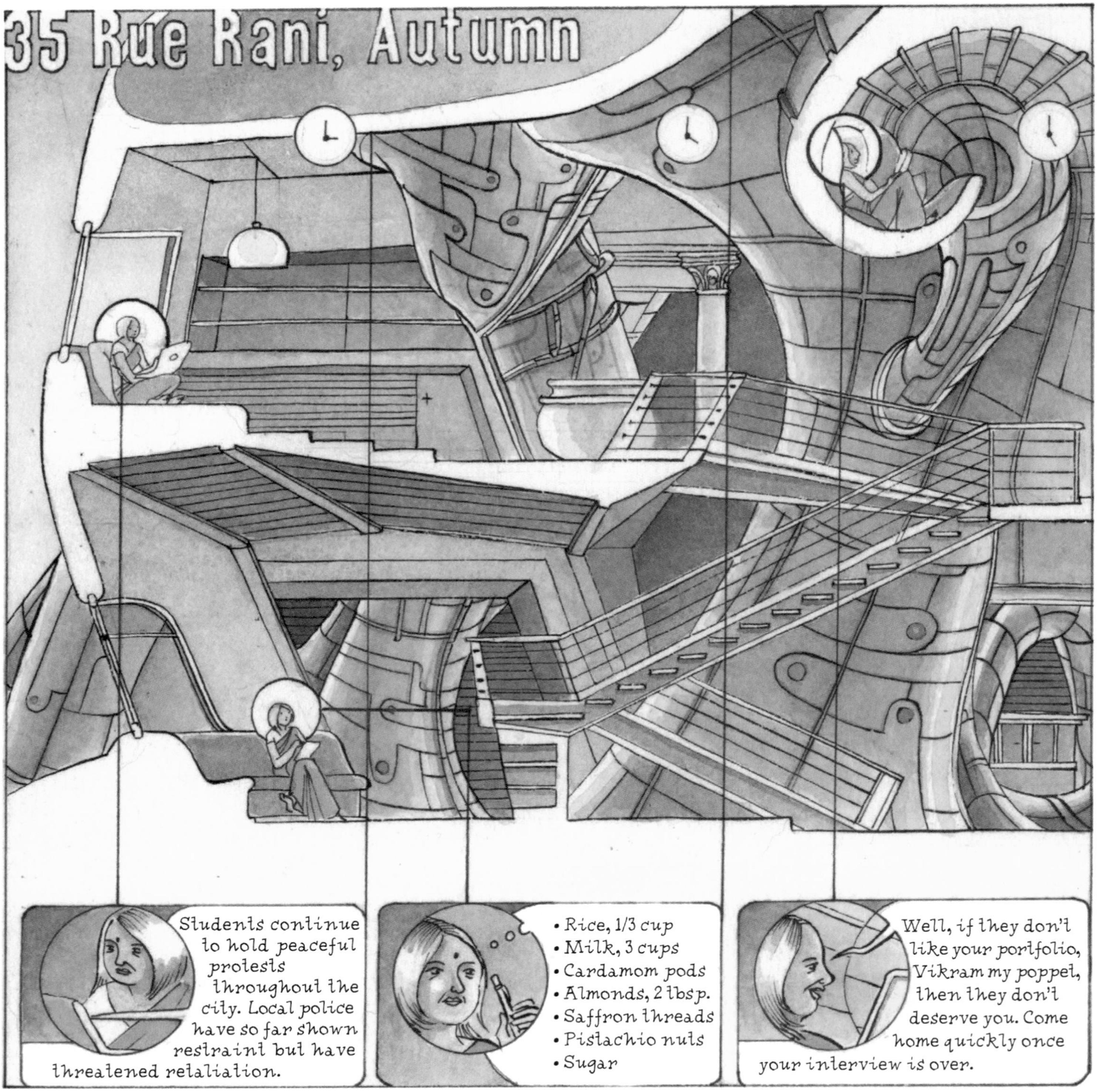
35 Rue Rani, Autumn
Students continue to hold peaceful protests throughout the city. Local police have so far shown restraint but have threatened retaliation.
• Rice, 1/3 cup
• Milk, 3 cups
• Cardamom pods
• Almonds, 2 tbsp.
• Saffron threads
• Pistachio nuts
• Sugar
Well, if they don't like your portfolio, Vikram my poppet, then they don't deserve you. Come home quickly once your interview is over.

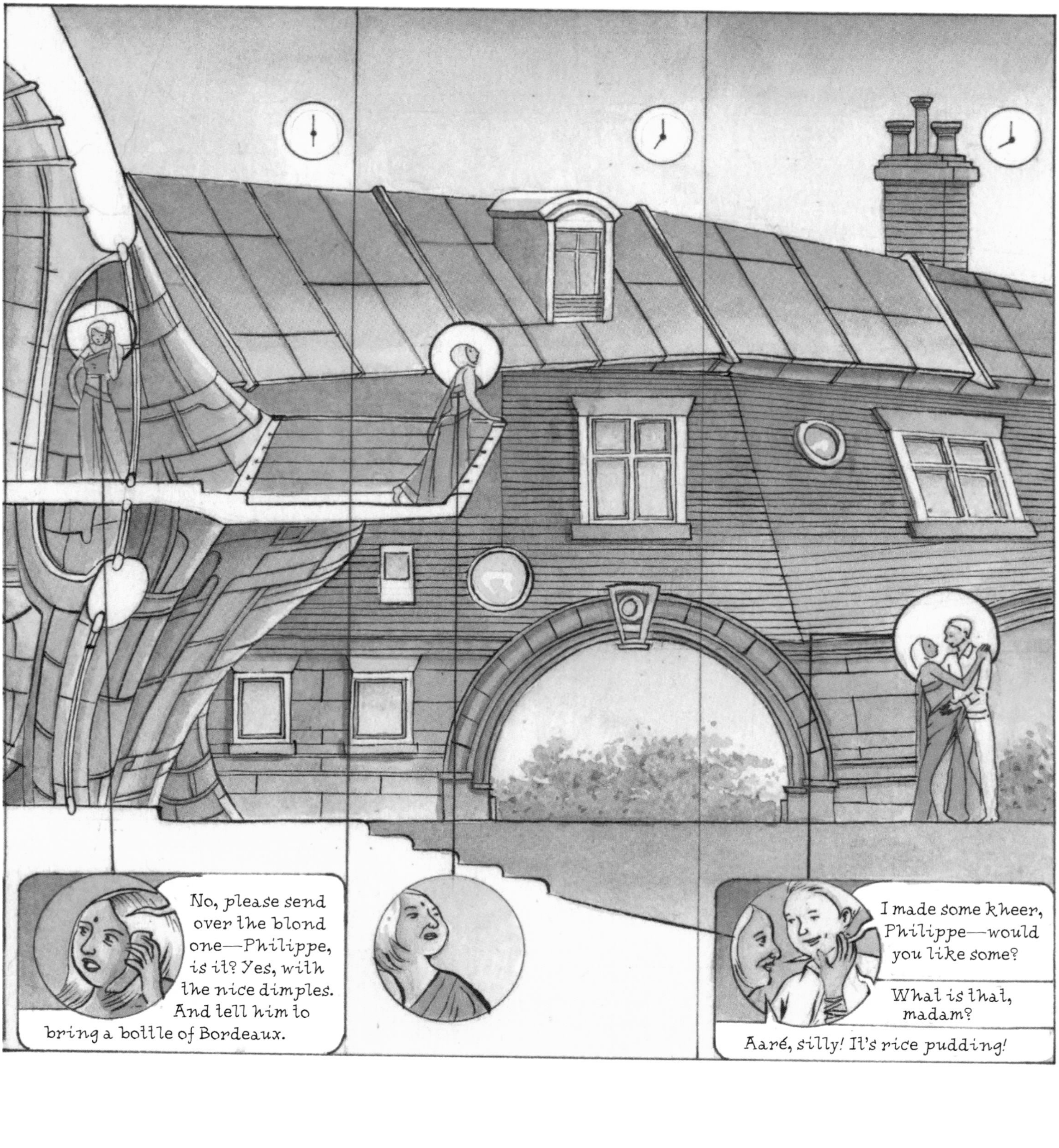
No, please send over the blond one—Philippe, is it? Yes, with the nice dimples. And tell him to bring a bottle of Bordeaux.
I made some kheer, Philippe—would you like some?
What is that, madam?
Aaré, silly! It's rice pudding!

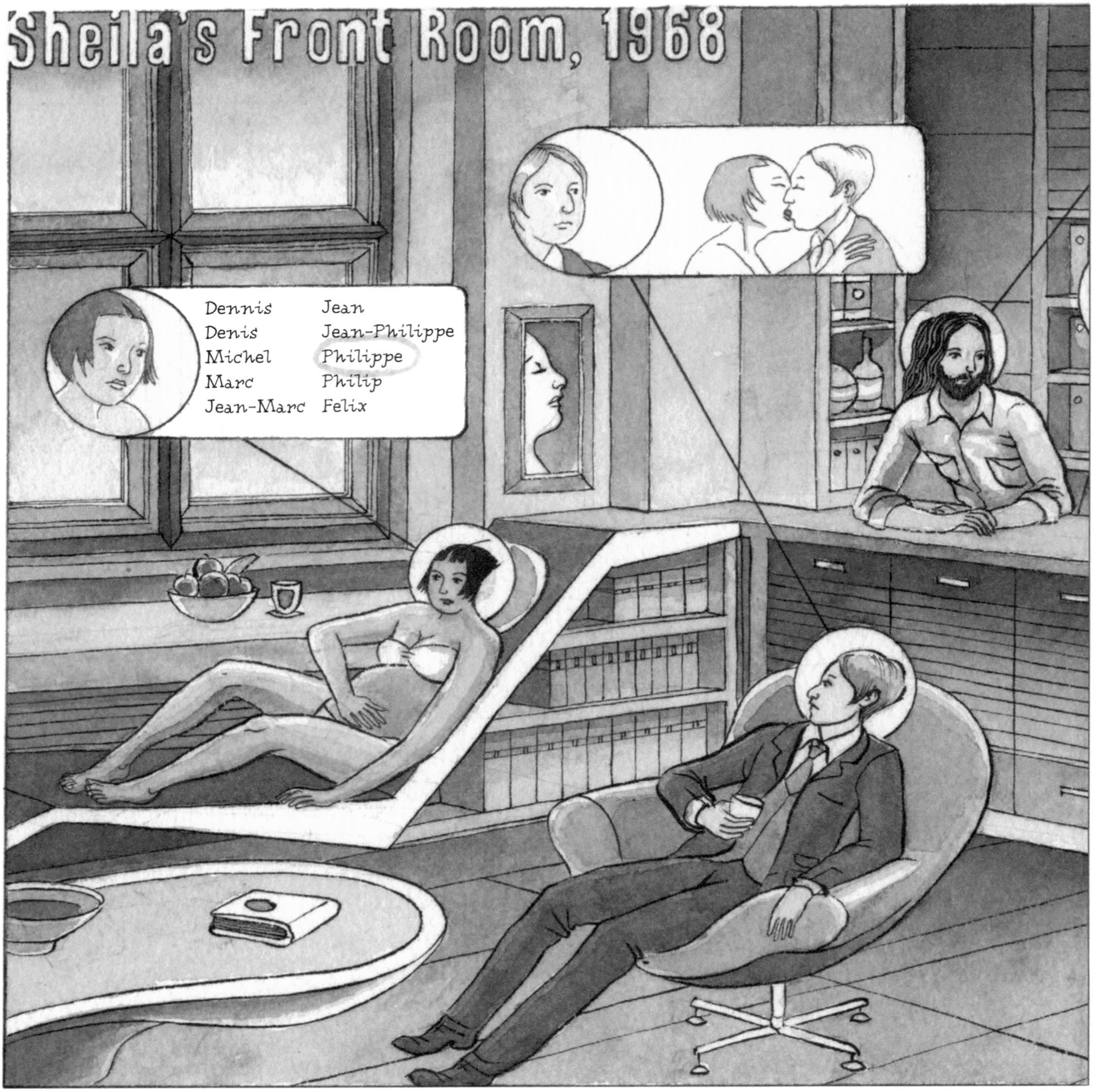
Sheila's Front Room, 1968
Dennis
Denis
Michel
Marc
Jean-Marc
Jean
Jean-Philippe
Philippe
Philip
Felix

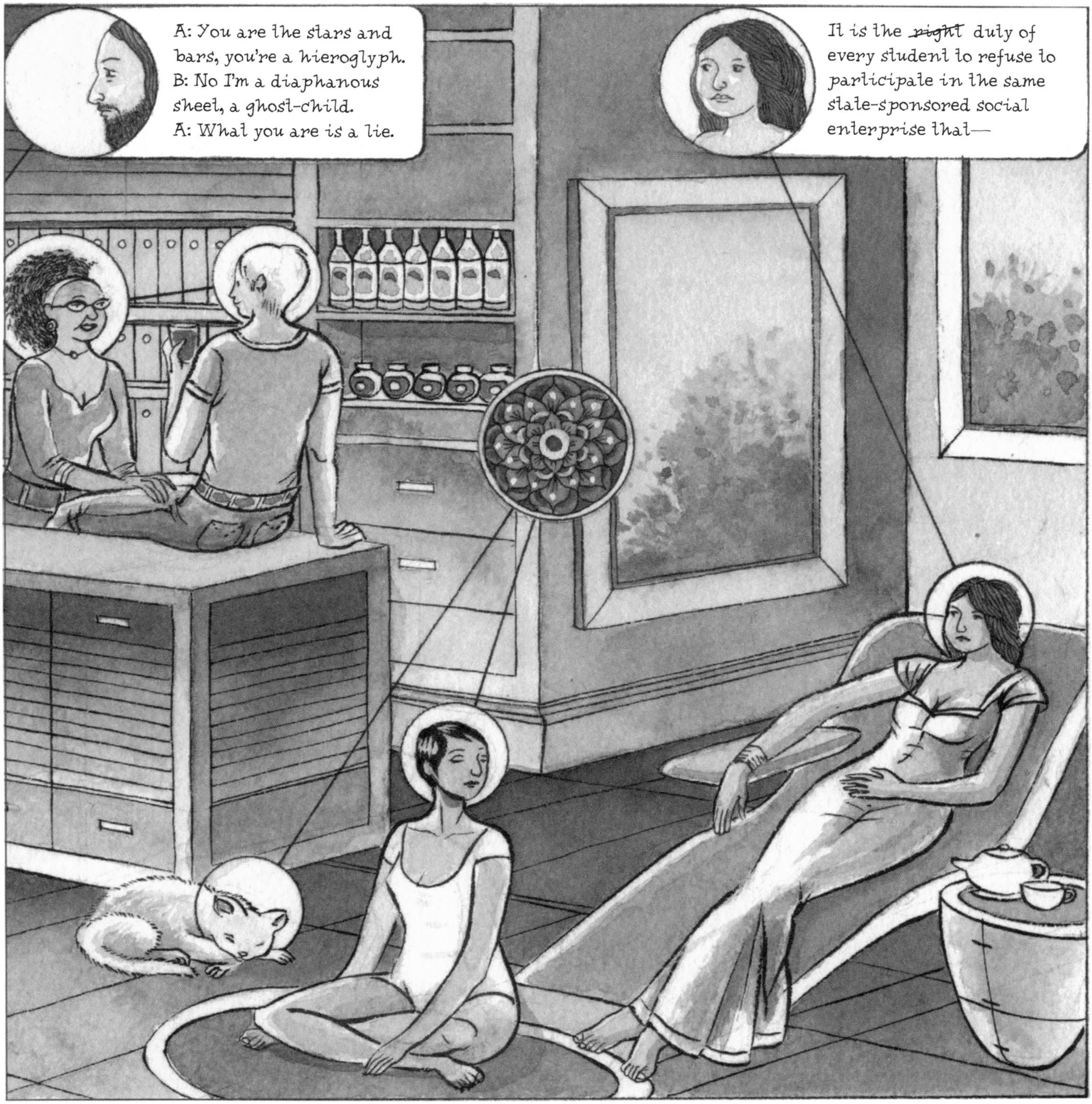
A: You are the stars and bars, you're a hieroglyph. B: No I'm a diaphanous sheet, a ghost-child. A: What you are is a lie.
It is the ~~right~~ duty of every student to refuse to participate in the same state-sponsored social enterprise that—

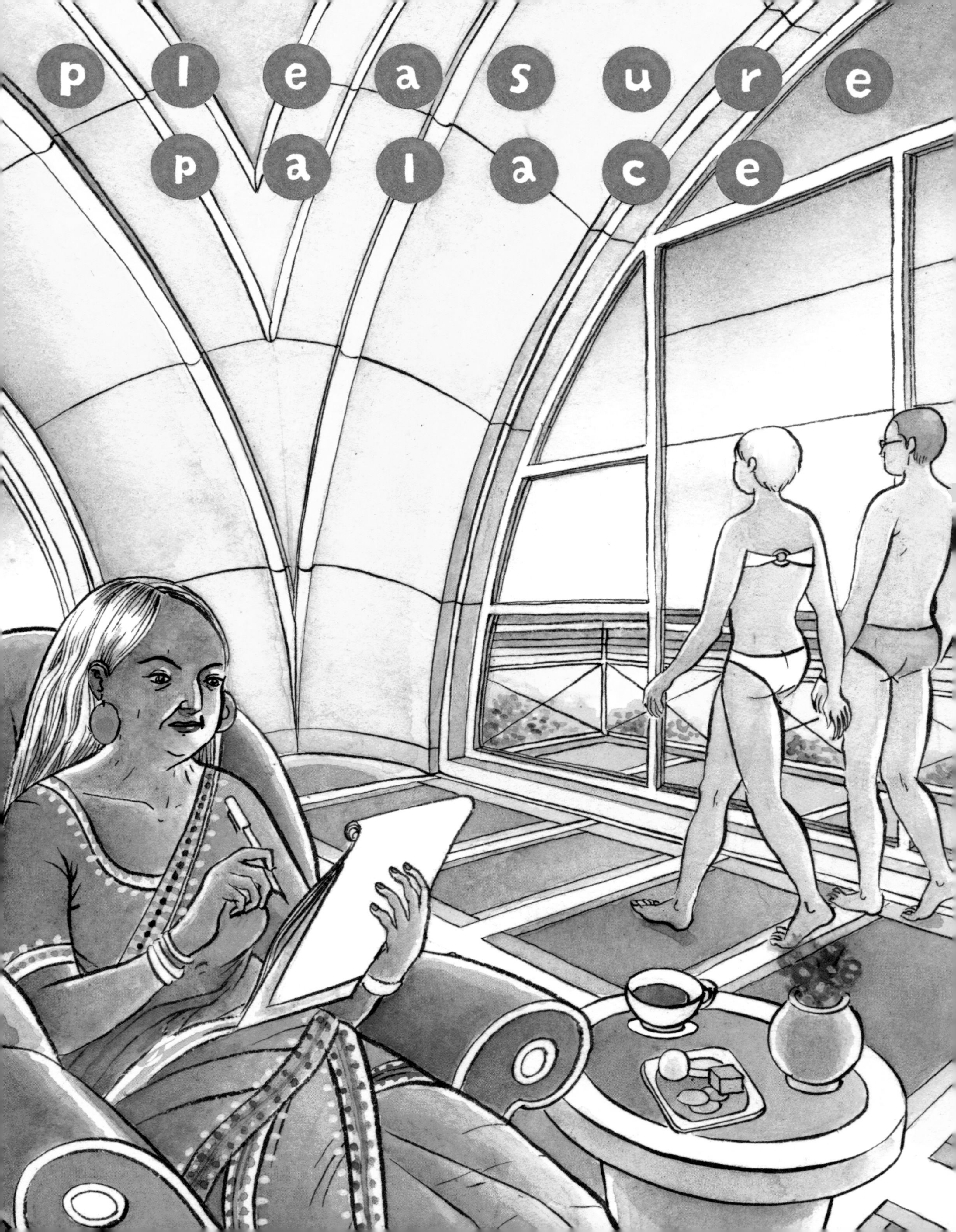
pleasure
palace

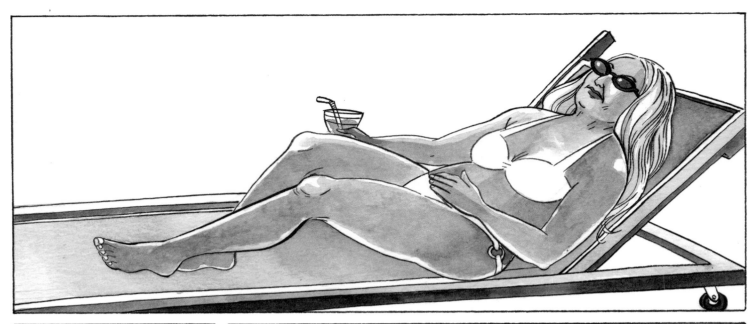

My dearest Laila,

you were right, as always.

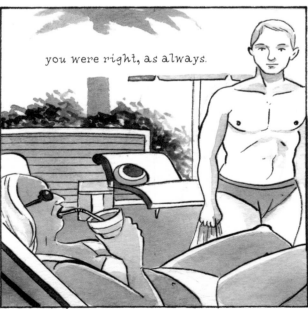

I needed to go away.

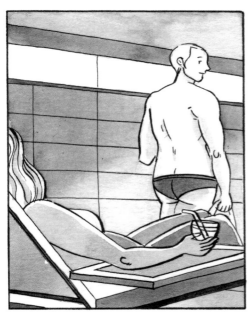

For a long time, forever—yes. But also for just a spell. Just long enough to be someone else for a while, to forget who I am and what I was. And, I confess, to forget you, if only for some moments. But that, my dear, will never happen.

What an extraordinarily silly place this is, Laila. You would have turned tail the first day.

But I never minded silly as much as you did. And for once, it suits me nicely.

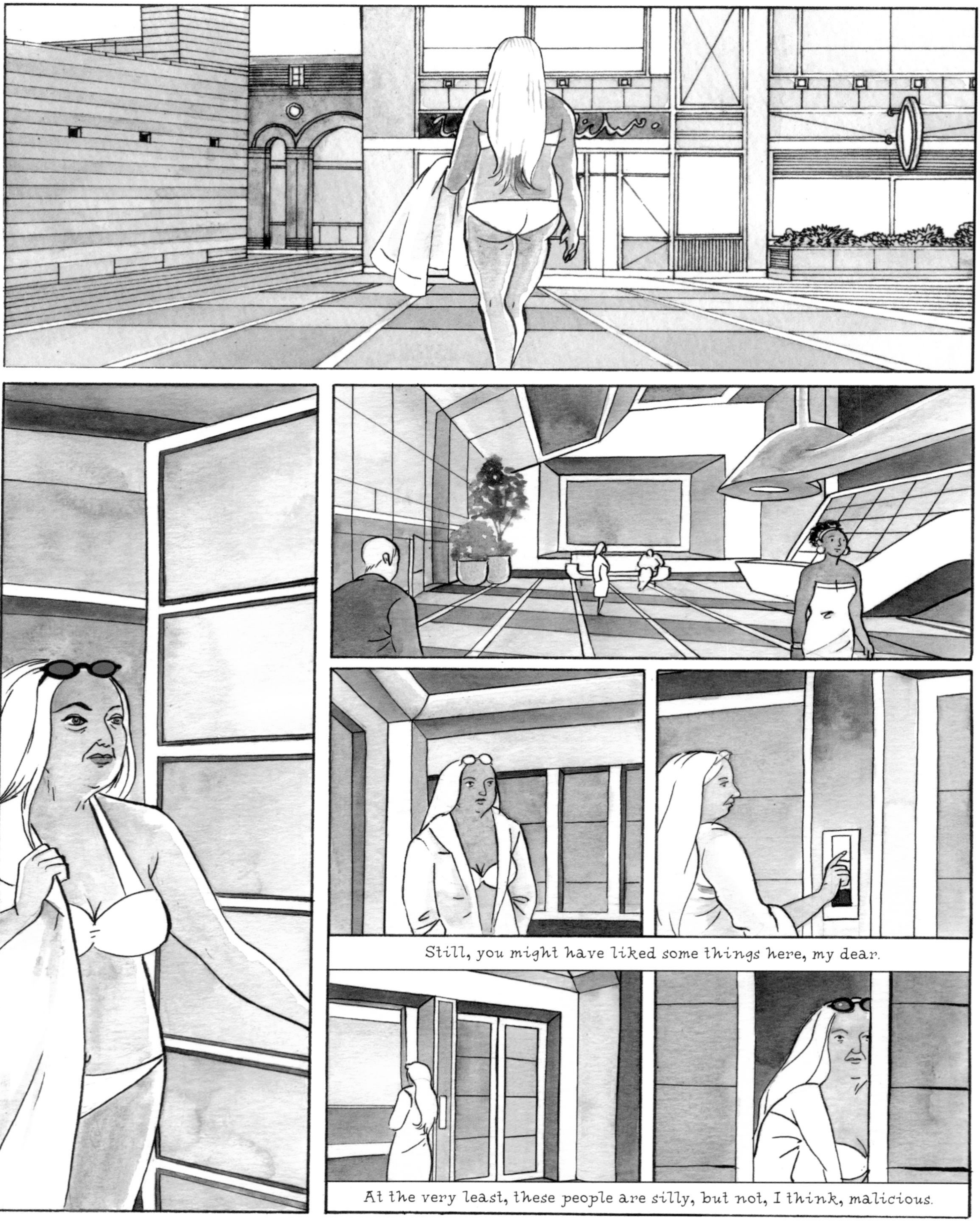
Still, you might have liked some things here, my dear.
At the very least, these people are silly, but not, I think, malicious.

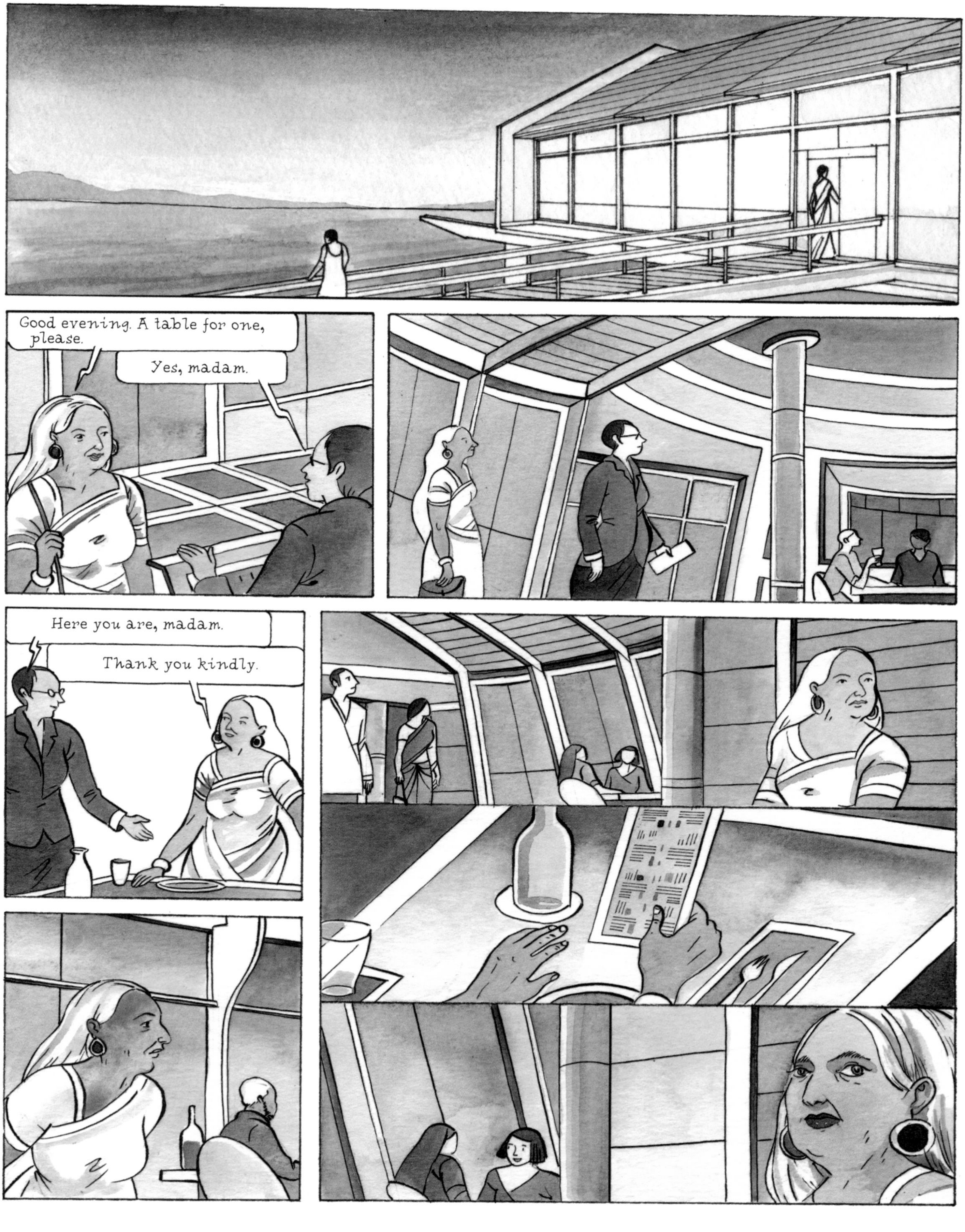
Good evening. A table for one, please.
Yes, madam.
Here you are, madam.
Thank you kindly.

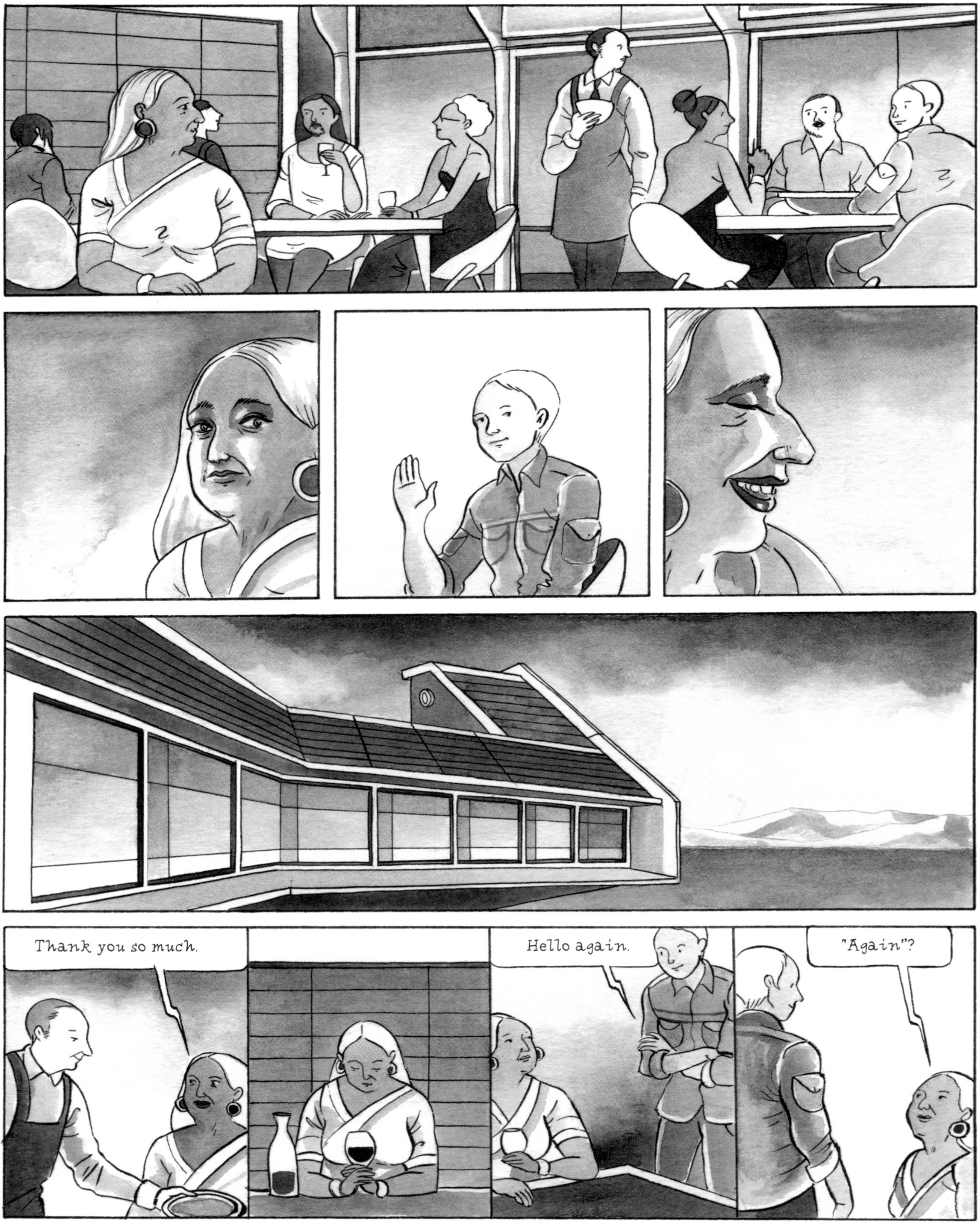
Thank you so much.
Hello again.
"Again"?

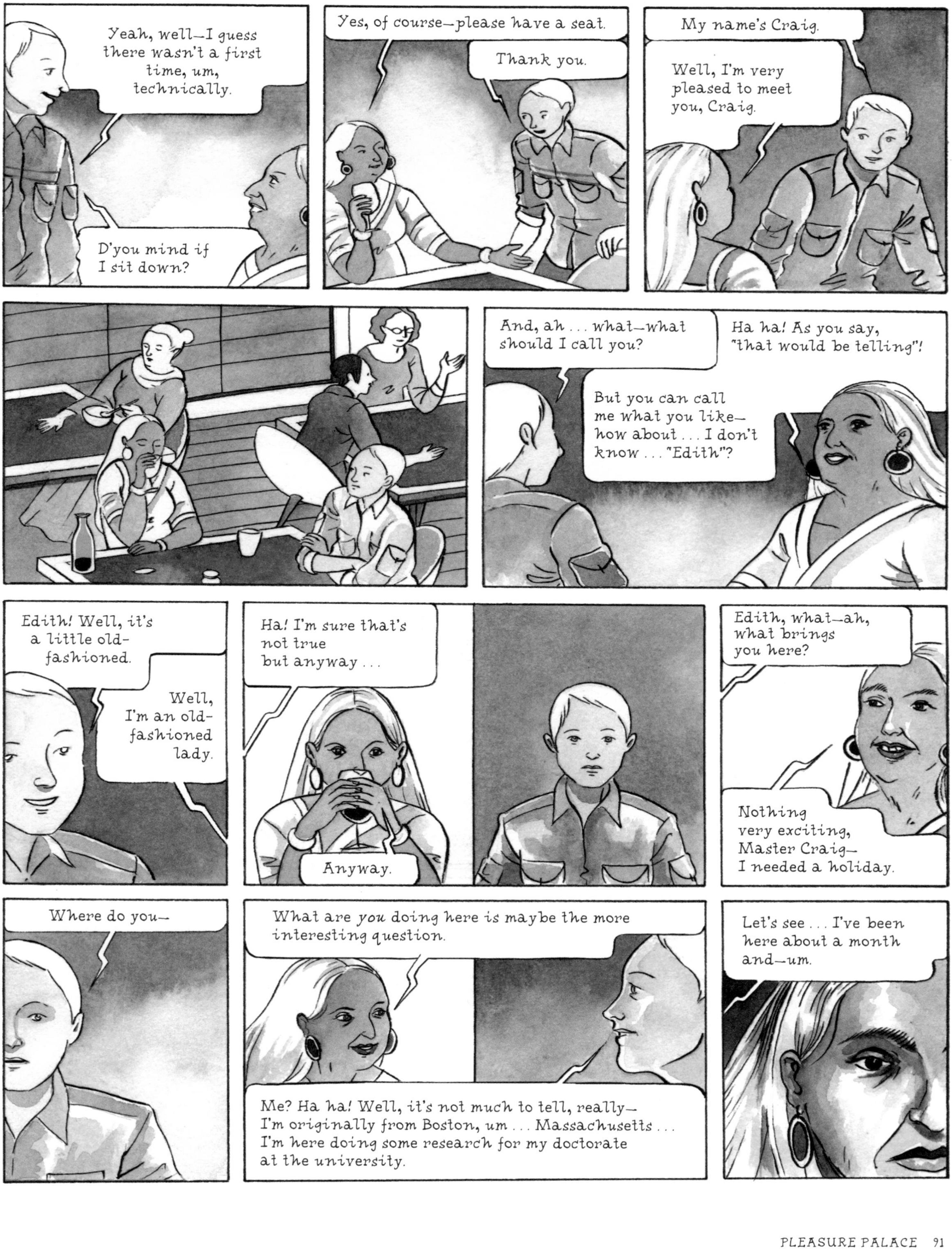
Yeah, well—I guess there wasn't a first time, um, technically.
D'you mind if I sit down?
Yes, of course—please have a seat.
Thank you.
My name's Craig.
Well, I'm very pleased to meet you, Craig.
And, ah . . . what—what should I call you?
Ha ha! As you say, "that would be telling"!
But you can call me what you like—how about . . . I don't know . . . "Edith"?
Edith! Well, it's a little old-fashioned.
Well, I'm an old-fashioned lady.
Ha! I'm sure that's not true but anyway . . .
Anyway.
Edith, what—ah, what brings you here?
Nothing very exciting, Master Craig—I needed a holiday.
Where do you—
What are *you* doing here is maybe the more interesting question.
Me? Ha ha! Well, it's not much to tell, really—I'm originally from Boston, um . . . Massachusetts . . . I'm here doing some research for my doctorate at the university.
Let's see . . . I've been here about a month and—um.

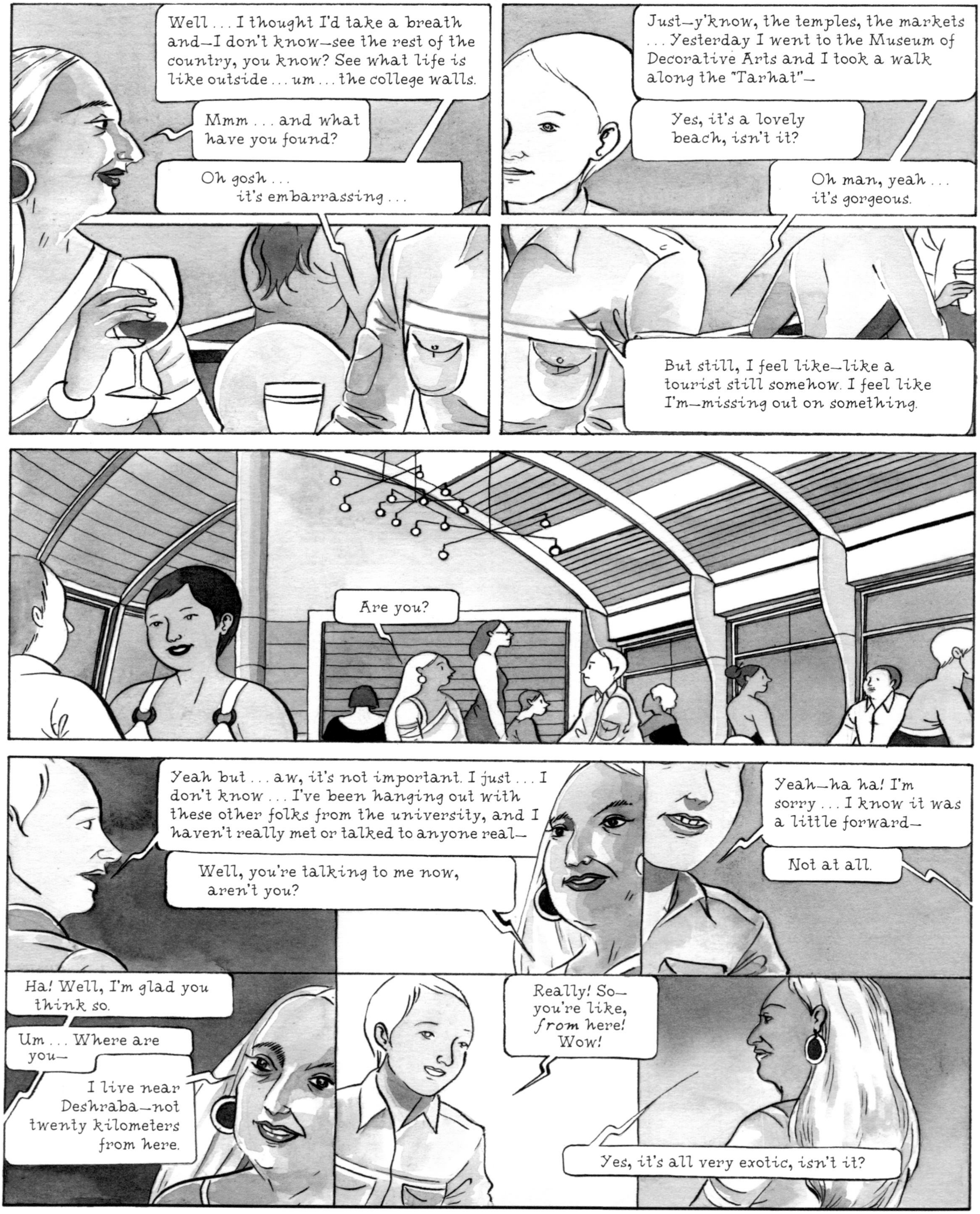

Well . . . I thought I'd take a breath and—I don't know—see the rest of the country, you know? See what life is like outside . . . um . . . the college walls.
Mmm . . . and what have you found?
Oh gosh . . . it's embarrassing . . .
Just—y'know, the temples, the markets . . . Yesterday I went to the Museum of Decorative Arts and I took a walk along the "Tarhat"—
Yes, it's a lovely beach, isn't it?
Oh man, yeah . . . it's gorgeous.
But still, I feel like—like a tourist still somehow. I feel like I'm—missing out on something.
Are you?
Yeah but . . . aw, it's not important. I just . . . I don't know . . . I've been hanging out with these other folks from the university, and I haven't really met or talked to anyone real—
Well, you're talking to me now, aren't you?
Yeah—ha ha! I'm sorry . . . I know it was a little forward—
Not at all.
Ha! Well, I'm glad you think so.
Um . . . Where are you—
I live near Deshraba—not twenty kilometers from here.
Really! So— you're like, *from* here! Wow!
Yes, it's all very exotic, isn't it?

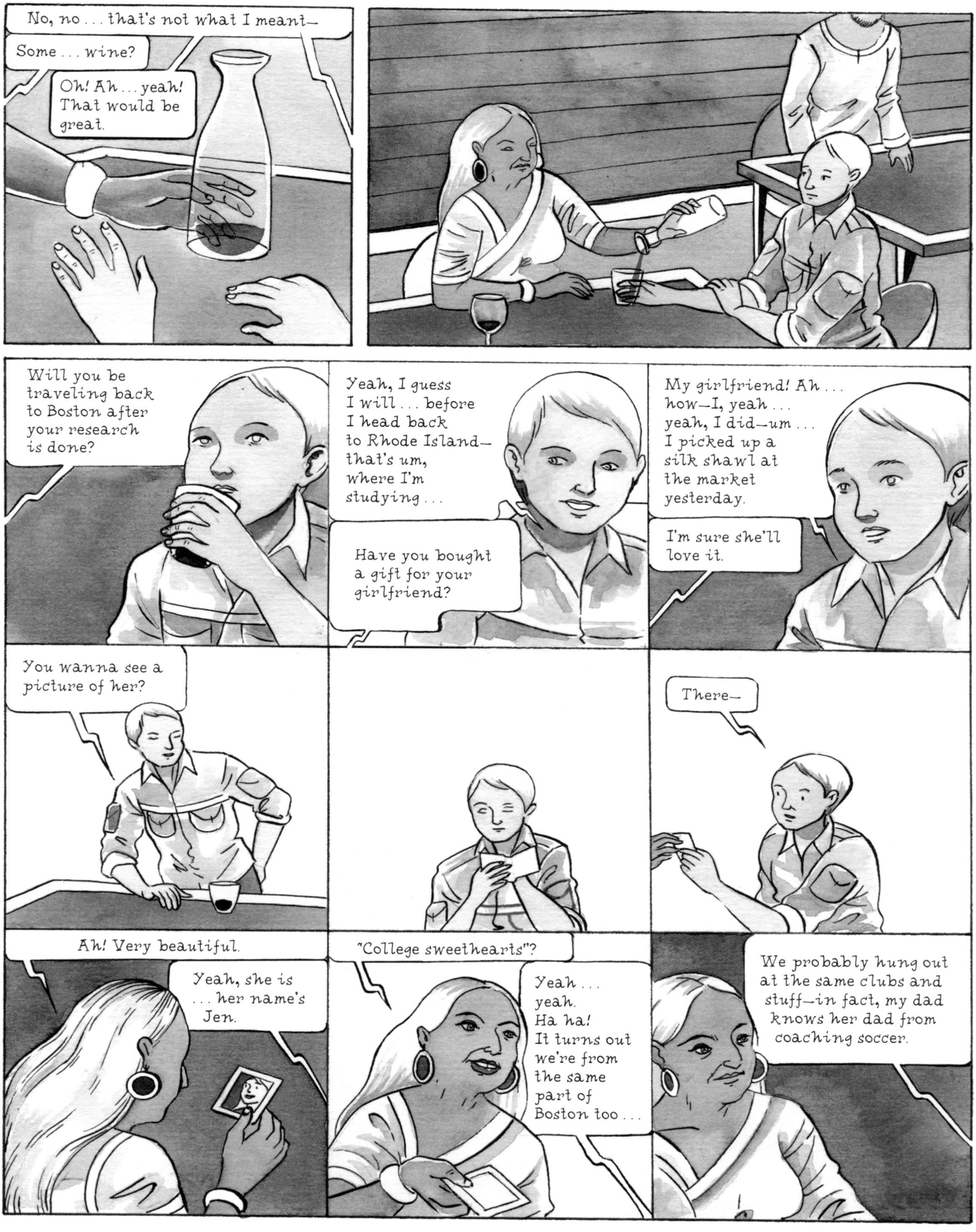
No, no . . . that's not what I meant—
Some . . . wine?
Oh! Ah . . . yeah! That would be great.
Will you be traveling back to Boston after your research is done?
Yeah, I guess I will . . . before I head back to Rhode Island— that's um, where I'm studying . . .
Have you bought a gift for your girlfriend?
My girlfriend! Ah . . . how—I, yeah . . . yeah, I did—um . . . I picked up a silk shawl at the market yesterday.
I'm sure she'll love it.
You wanna see a picture of her?
There—
Ah! Very beautiful.
Yeah, she is . . . her name's Jen.
"College sweethearts"?
Yeah . . . yeah. Ha ha! It turns out we're from the same part of Boston too . . .
We probably hung out at the same clubs and stuff—in fact, my dad knows her dad from coaching soccer.

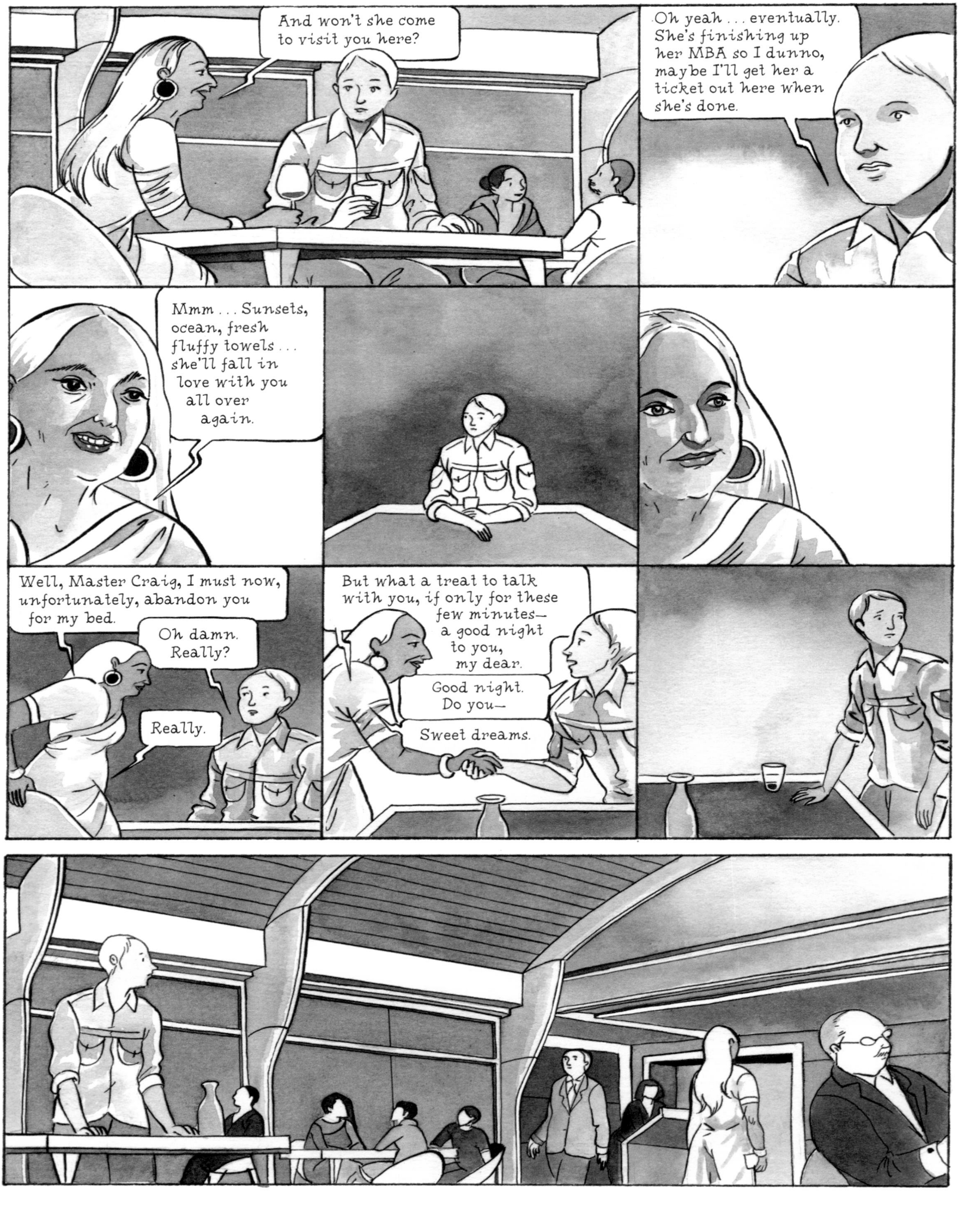
And won't she come to visit you here?
Oh yeah . . . eventually. She's finishing up her MBA so I dunno, maybe I'll get her a ticket out here when she's done.
Mmm . . . Sunsets, ocean, fresh fluffy towels . . . she'll fall in love with you all over again.
Well, Master Craig, I must now, unfortunately, abandon you for my bed.
Oh damn. Really?
Really.
But what a treat to talk with you, if only for these few minutes— a good night to you, my dear.
Good night. Do you—
Sweet dreams.

My dear Laila—my room overlooks the gulf. Though the warm eastern winds might lull me to sleep, I've decided to soak in the air-conditioning instead.

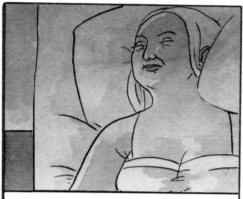

The bedsheets are—no, not silk—

but made of cotton and boast some astonishing thread count,

I'm assured. They have outfitted the television with—

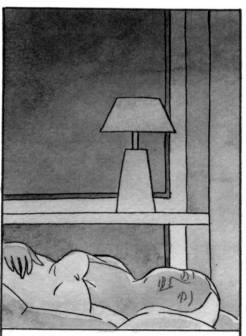

can you believe—150 channels! Iranian soap operas, Russian quiz shows, Spanish

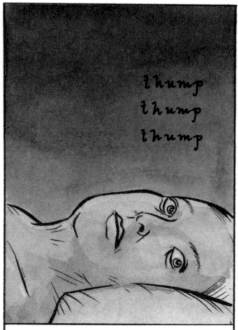

thump
thump
thump

cooking instruction. I watched —no, don't mock— a documentary about sea turtles

older than I am.

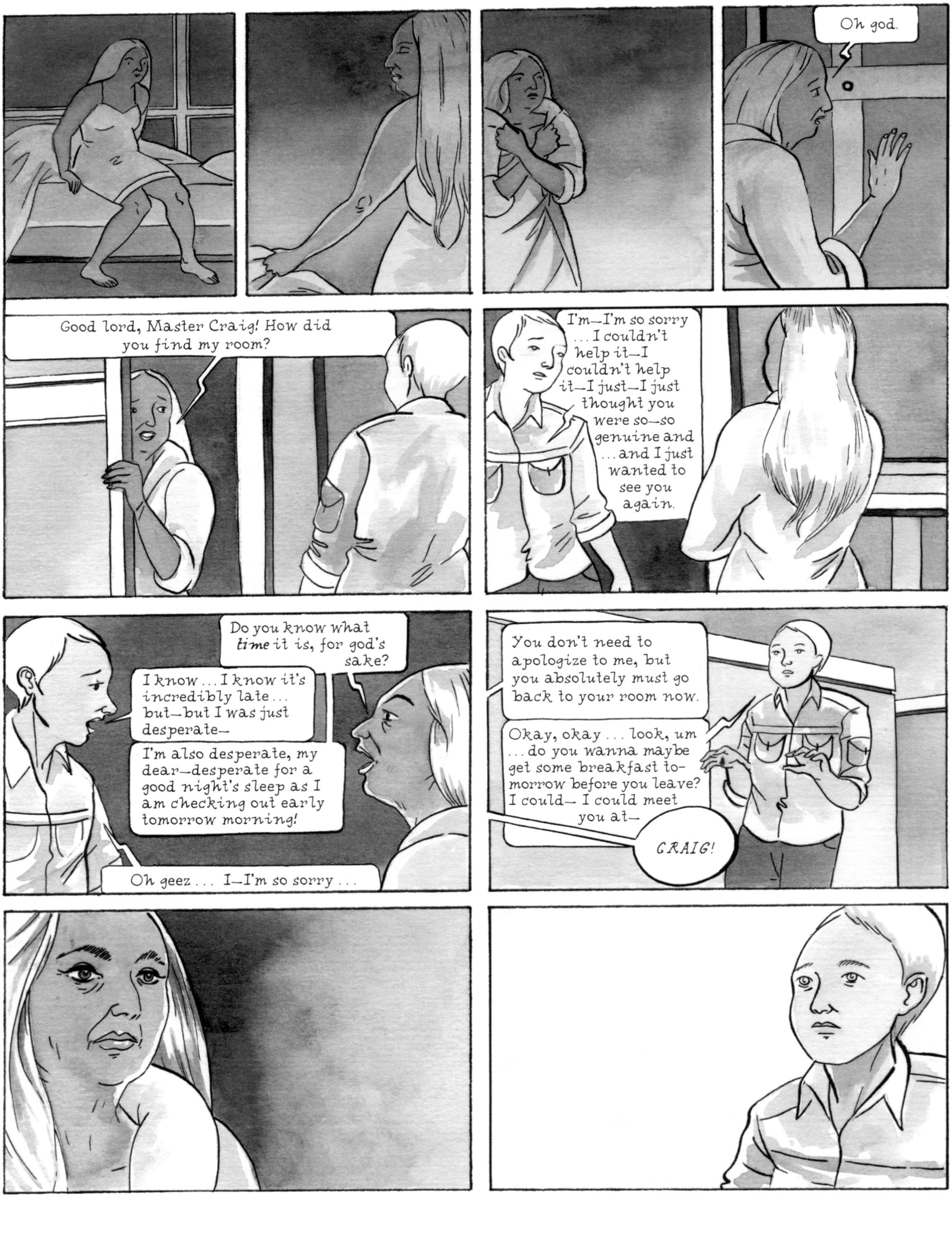
Oh god.
Good lord, Master Craig! How did you find my room?
I'm—I'm so sorry ... I couldn't help it—I couldn't help it—I just—I just thought you were so—so genuine and ... and I just wanted to see you again.
Do you know what *time* it is, for god's sake?
I know ... I know it's incredibly late ... but—but I was just desperate—
I'm also desperate, my dear—desperate for a good night's sleep as I am checking out early tomorrow morning!
Oh geez ... I—I'm so sorry ...
You don't need to apologize to me, but you absolutely must go back to your room now.
Okay, okay ... look, um ... do you wanna maybe get some breakfast tomorrow before you leave? I could— I could meet you at—
CRAIG!

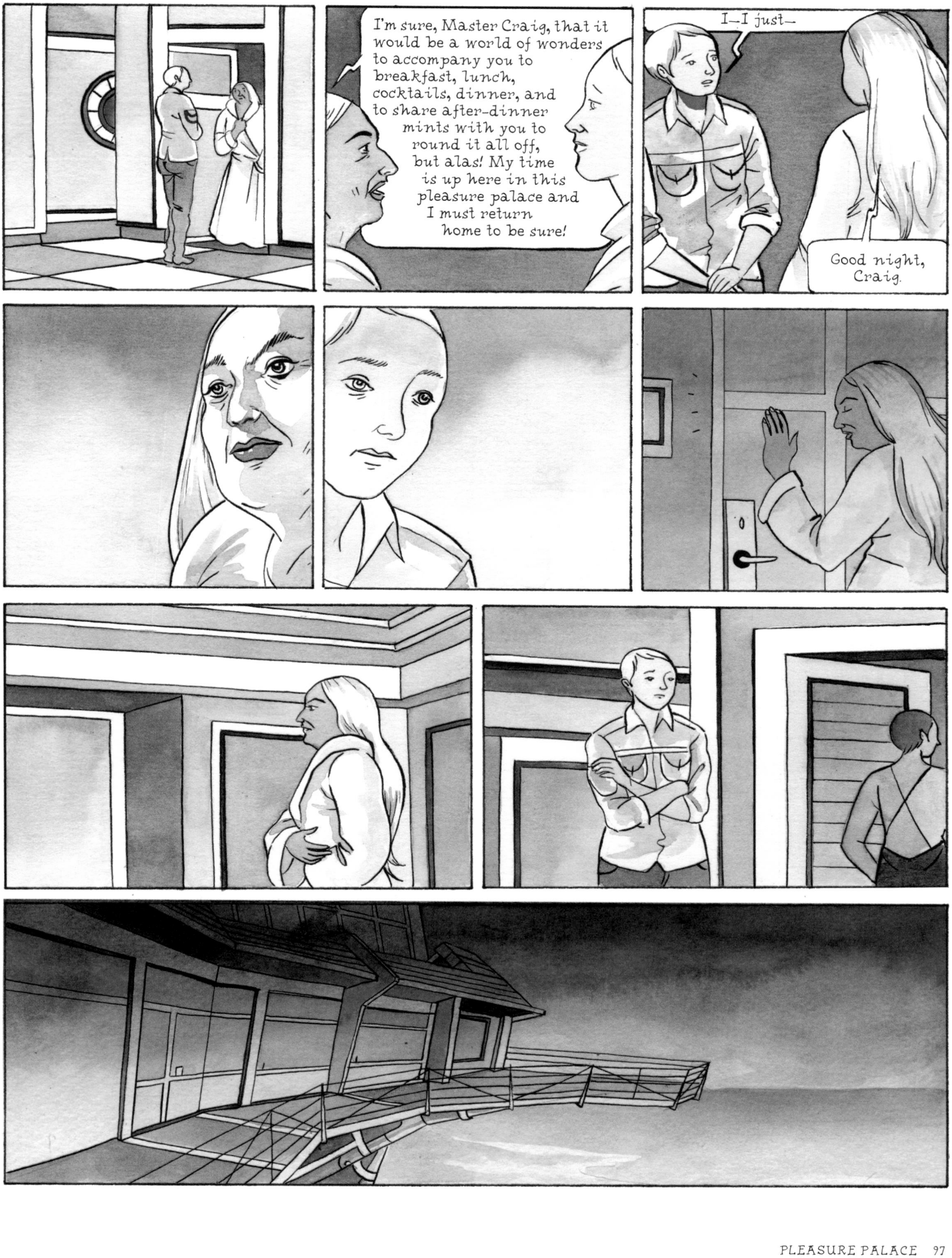
I'm sure, Master Craig, that it would be a world of wonders to accompany you to breakfast, lunch, cocktails, dinner, and to share after-dinner mints with you to round it all off, but alas! My time is up here in this pleasure palace and I must return home to be sure!
I—I just—
Good night, Craig.

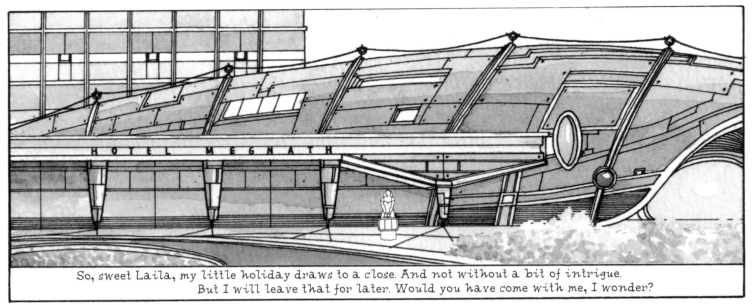

So, sweet Laila, my little holiday draws to a close. And not without a bit of intrigue. But I will leave that for later. Would you have come with me, I wonder?

I think you may have relented eventually—"Why can't we just go to the mountains?" would have given way with a sigh.

Good morning, sister.

Hello, Anuradha.

Let me get your bags, sister.

Thank you.

Edith?

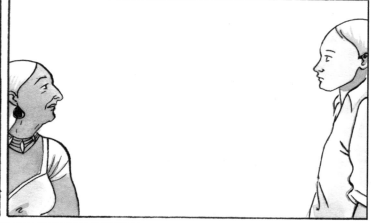

Master Craig, you are ubiquitous.

I know. Listen— I'm so sorry. I— I was a complete ass last night— I don't know what to say—I'm just . . . horrified at myself . . . I don't know how to tell you—

It's really okay.

Well, it's decent of you to still be civil to me.

Not at all.

No, I mean it—I just hope you don't think I'm a total jerk . . . I don't know what I was thinking.

It's perfectly all right.

Hmm.

What is it?

I am a total jerk.

Sigh. No, you are not, thank goodness.

I am.

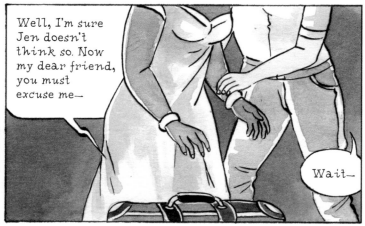

Well, I'm sure Jen doesn't think so. Now my dear friend, you must excuse me—

Wait—

Please.

Ei bador ke bari niye chalo, Anuradha.

Would you be interested in taking a drive? You'll see more of the land—you could even visit my home if you like.

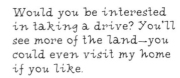

Really? I'd love to!

Good. Please step in.

Chalo, Anuradha.

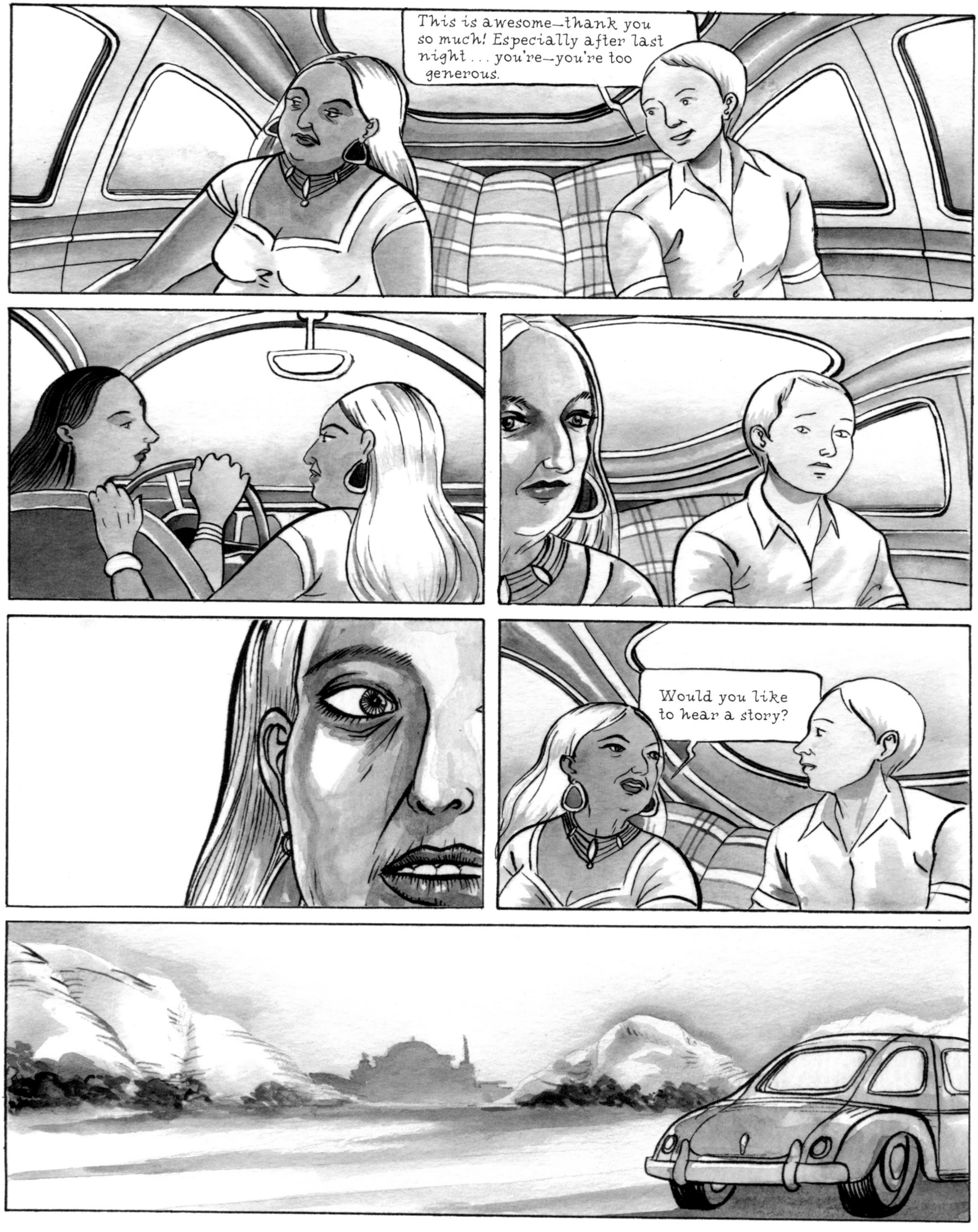
This is awesome—thank you so much! Especially after last night . . . you're—you're too generous.
Would you like to hear a story?

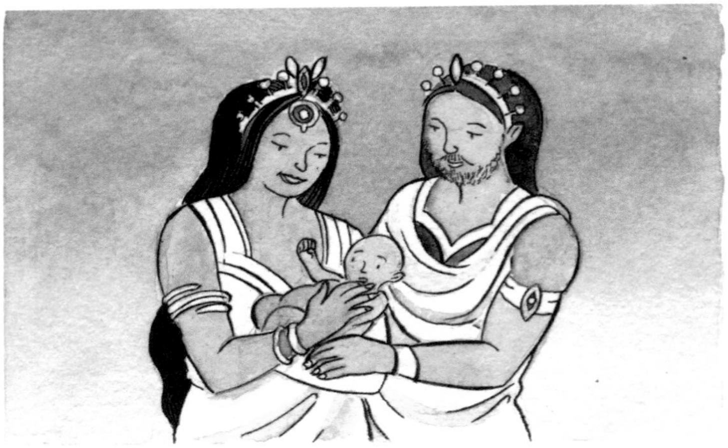

There was born to a king and queen a beautiful baby daughter who quickly became the darling of her people and the royal court.

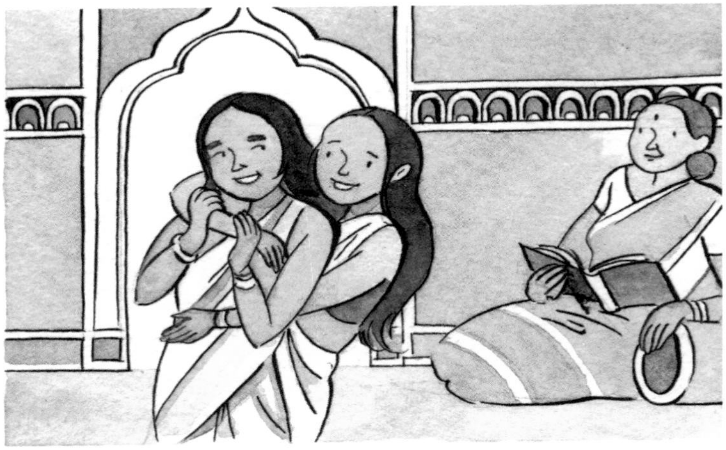

The princess was brought up alongside the nanny's daughter Maya, who became her dearest companion. The two girls spent their childhoods together.

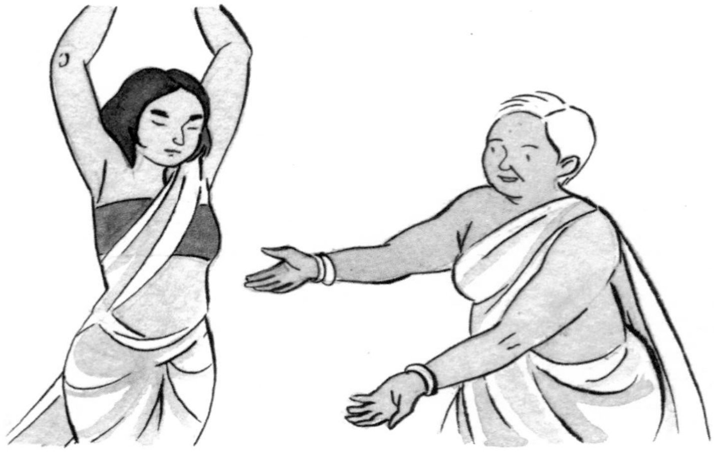

As the two grew older, each was drawn to her own calling—Maya studied the art of dance while the princess proved to be a skillful painter.

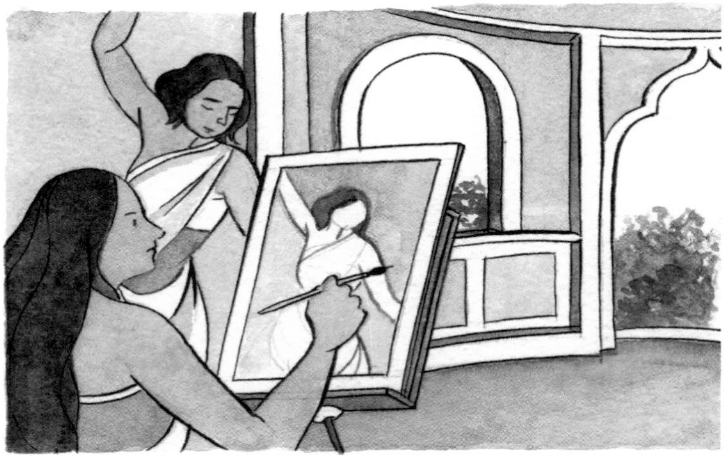

Maya would rehearse in front of the princess, who would lovingly render her movements in line and color.

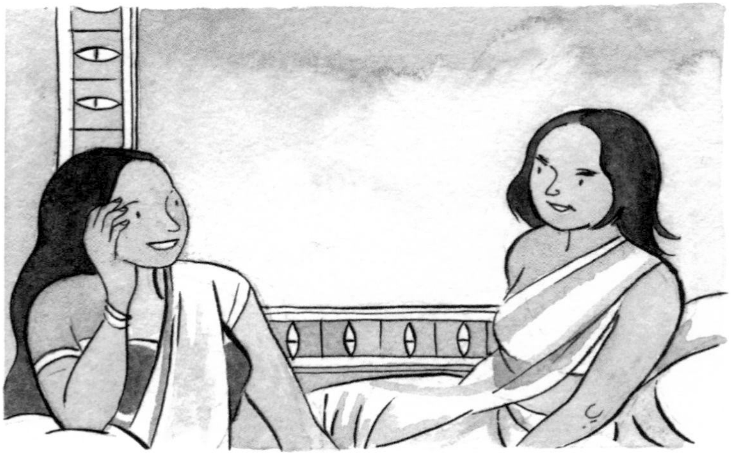

Several years passed—Maya and the princess grew up to be strong, fine women. They still spent their hours and days together and could not be separated.

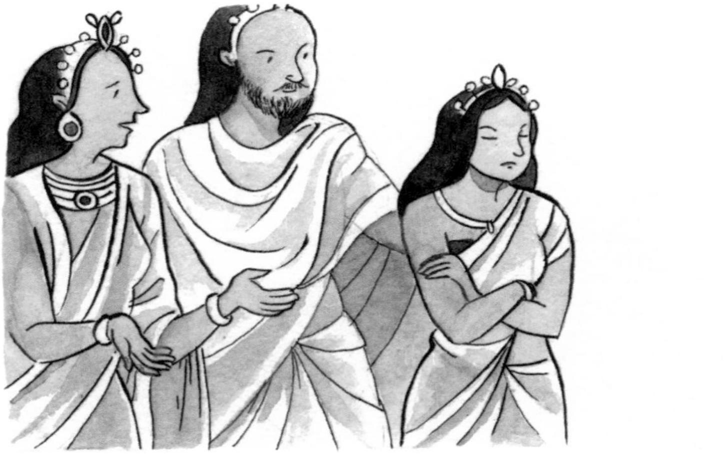

One day the king and queen proposed that they should search for a suitable husband. "You can do as you wish," the princess said, "but I will refuse them all. What need have I of a husband when I have Maya?"

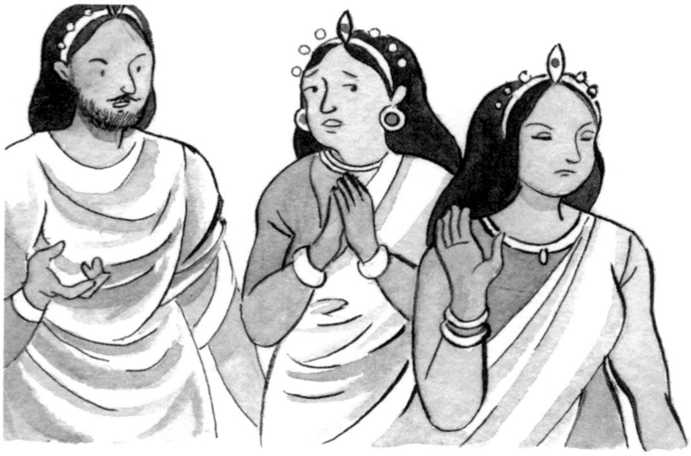

"Please," the queen pleaded. "Never," said the princess.

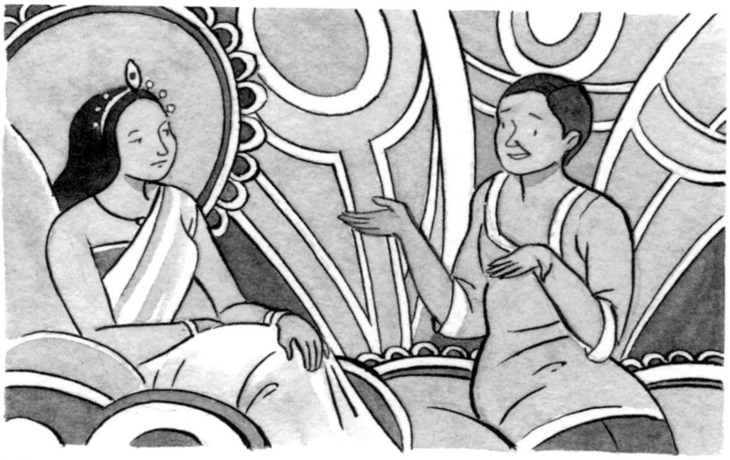

Nevertheless, the search began. A handsome young man from a neighboring southern kingdom was introduced to the princess. The two seemed to get along very well, for the prince was quick-witted, gentle, and kind.

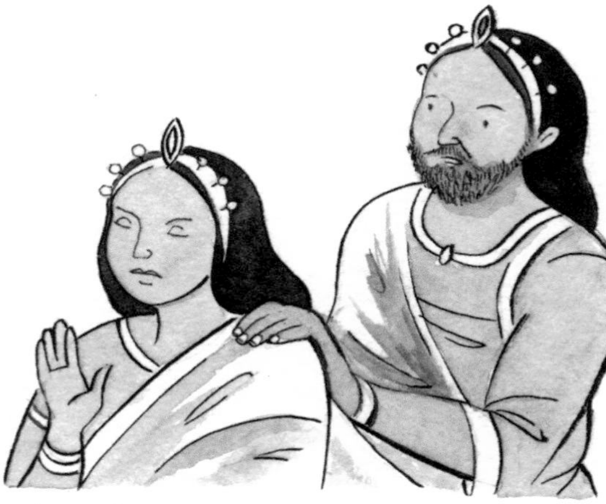

But when the king and queen asked the princess if she should like to wed the young prince, she replied, "Never."

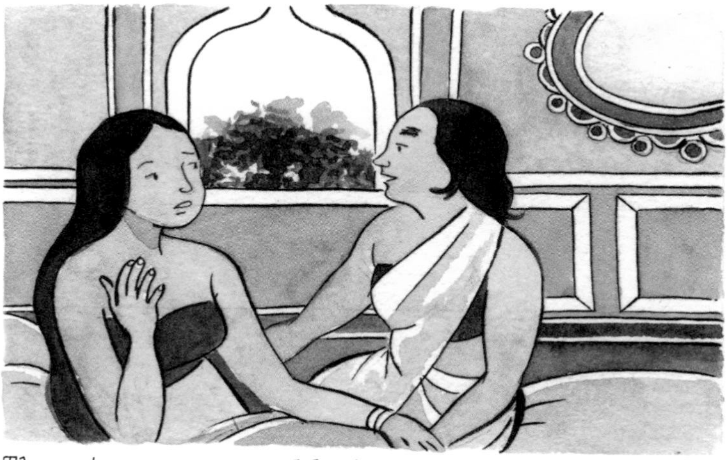

The princess, unnerved by her parents' insistence, shared her fear and confusion with Maya. "Why?" asked the princess. "Why do they want to force me into this?"

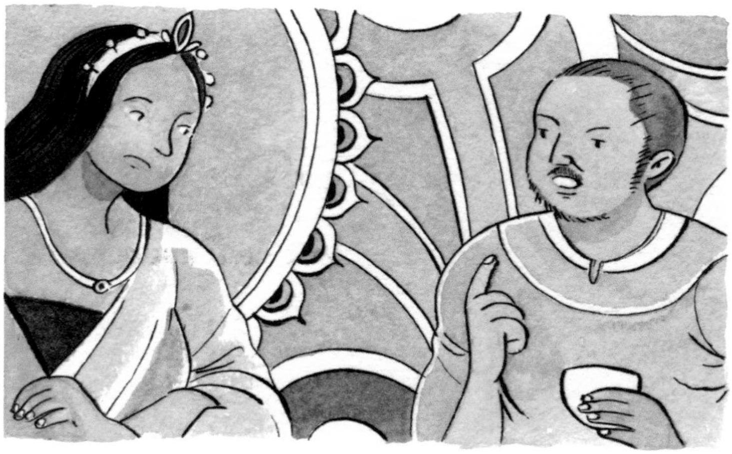

Then a young prince from a northern kingdom was invited to court—he was as strong as a horse, bold as a tiger, and wise as a sage.

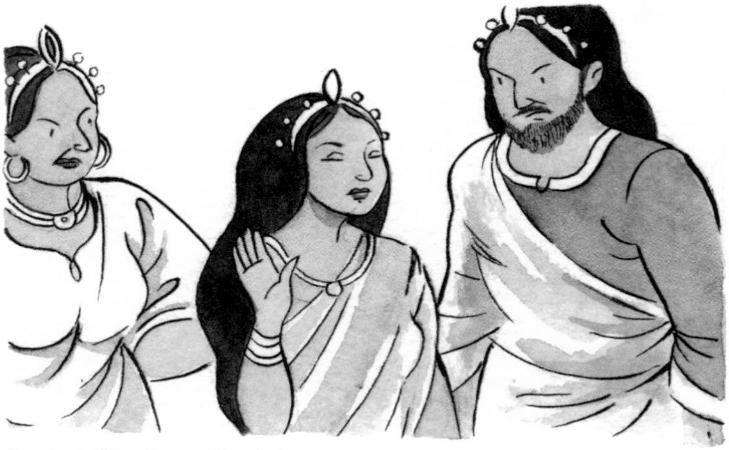

And still when the king and queen confronted their daughter afterward, her reply was again the same—"Never."

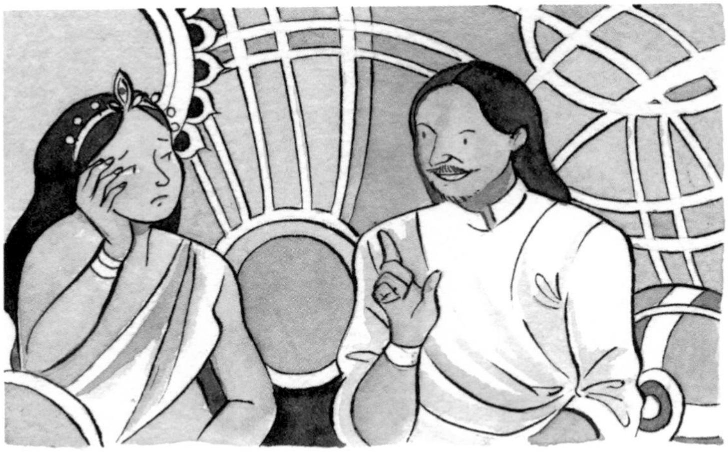

Then a prince from the east was brought to the court—he was tall, athletic, and full of laughter and merriment.

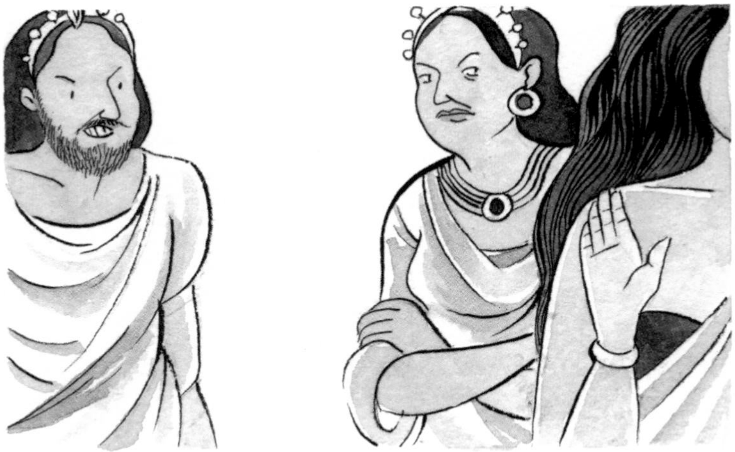

Still the princess's reply did not change—"Never," she said, more solemnly than ever before.

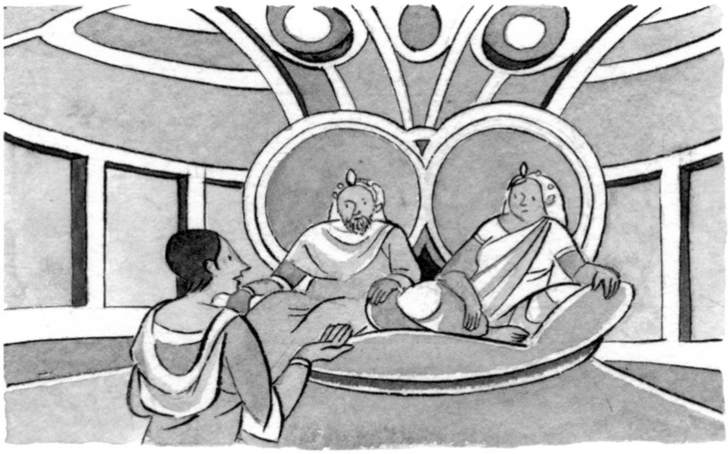

And so it went until there were no more princes to be found. The king and queen were frustrated, but the princess displayed no interest in any of her suitors, preferring as ever the company of Maya.

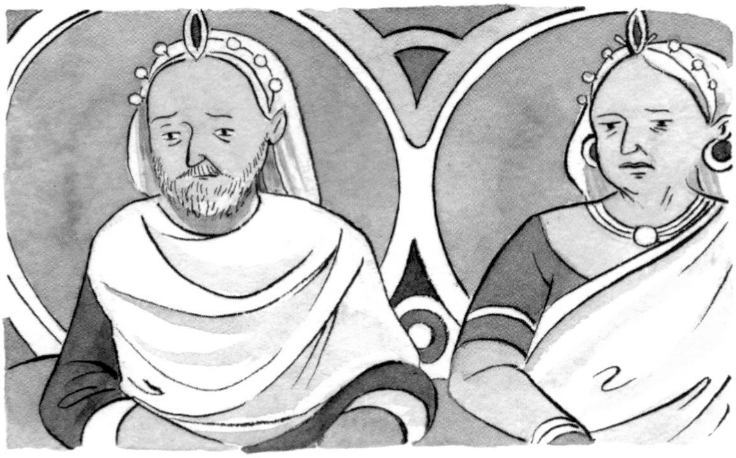

The king and queen entered their twilight years heartbroken that their daughter was unmarried. The people of the kingdom also longed for stability and reacted bitterly to the princess's stubbornness.

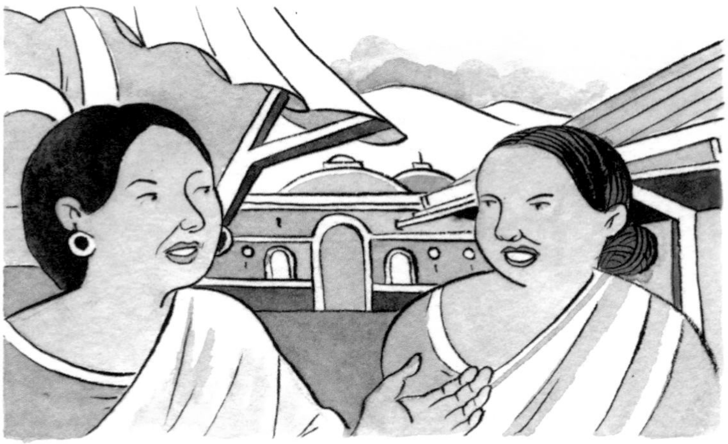

They blamed Maya for the princess's refusal to marry. In the market square, they said Maya and the princess should have long outgrown their childhood friendship, and wasn't it unhealthy for two girls to be unmarried at their age?

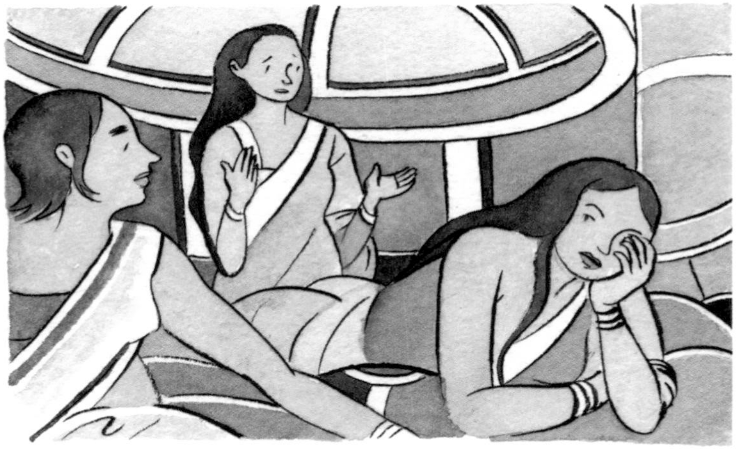

These mutterings were carried to the princess's ears by her attendants. The princess, saddened as she was by the people's disquiet, did not relent.

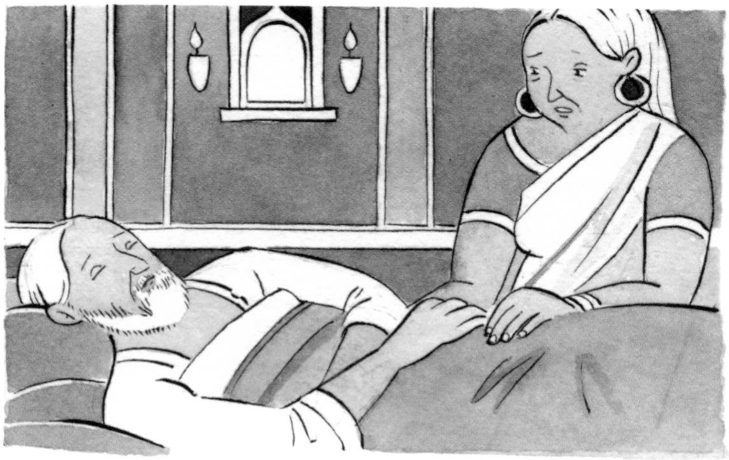

Soon the king fell ill and lay in his bed for months before he finally lost the strength to live.

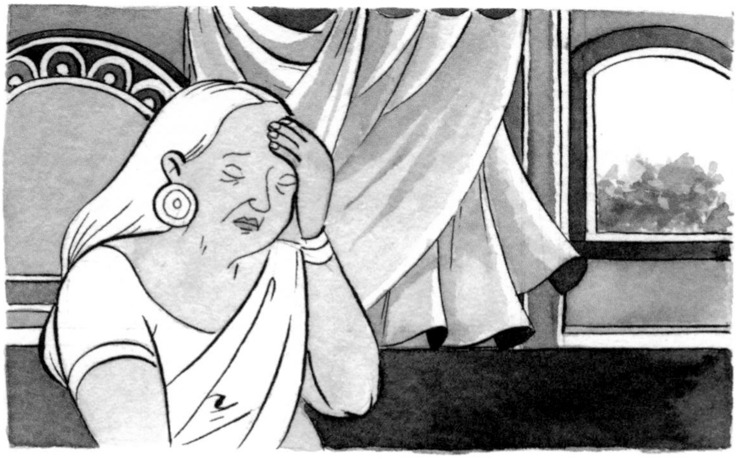

The queen, now doubly heartbroken, retreated into a melancholy that laid her so low that she did not move from her bed. She died soon thereafter.

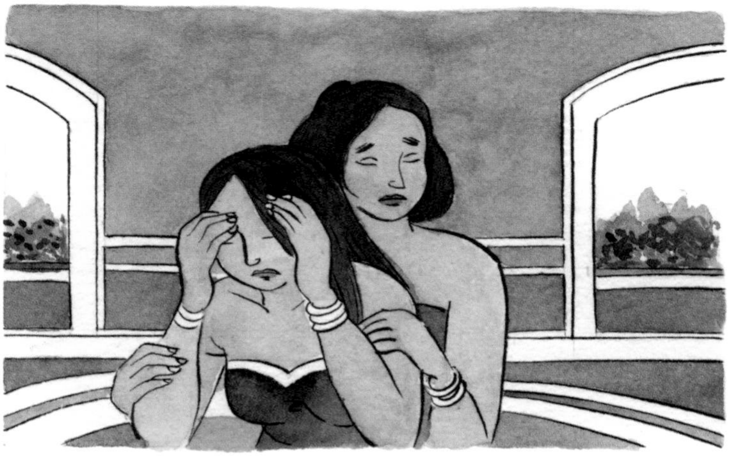

The princess was shattered and aggrieved but took solace in Maya's company.

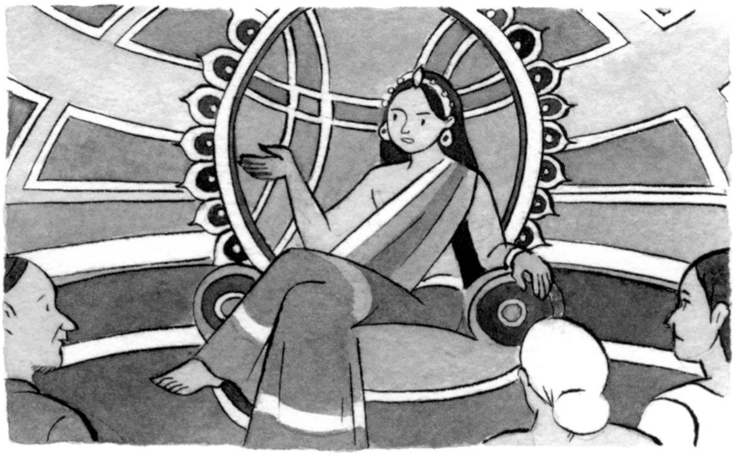

The princess ascended the throne. She took on her queenly duties with strength and grace.

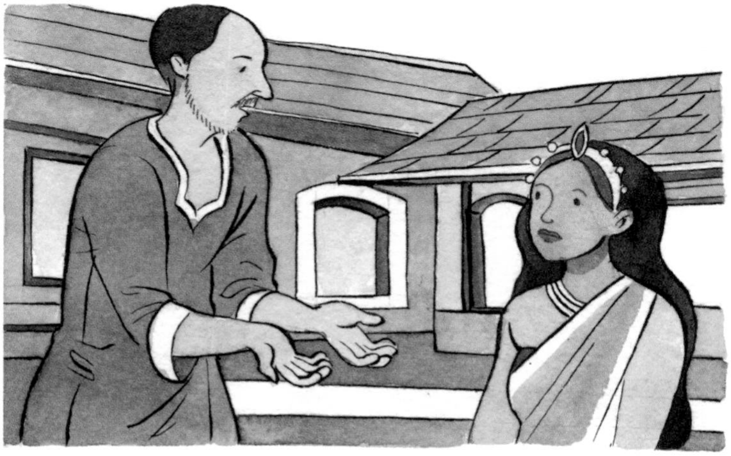

She came to know her subjects more intimately and did everything she could to better their lot in life, much to the chagrin of the royal court—who thought it beneath a queen's dignity to mix with the masses.

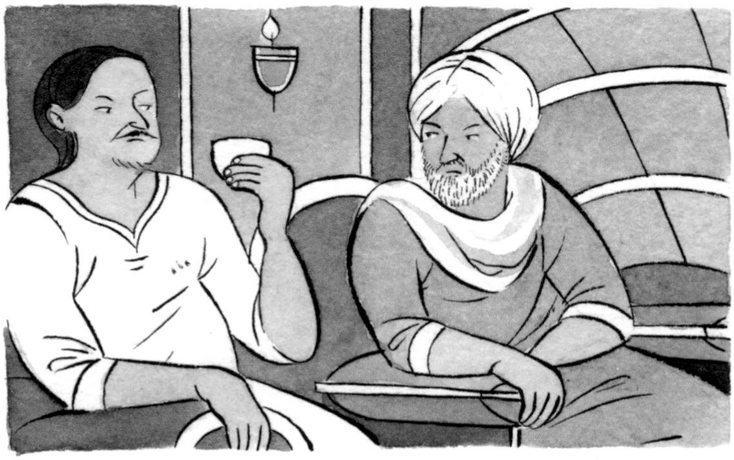

Members of the royal court thought that things could not go on this way.

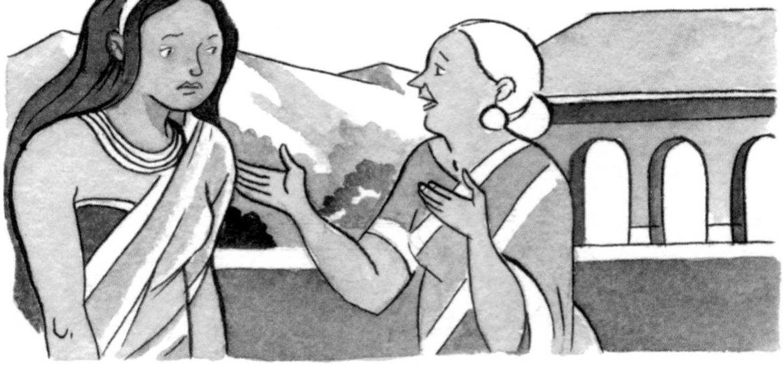

The people of the kingdom grumbled that they were the only kingdom with an unmarried queen. They were anxious and accosted the queen, begging her to find a husband and continue the bloodline.

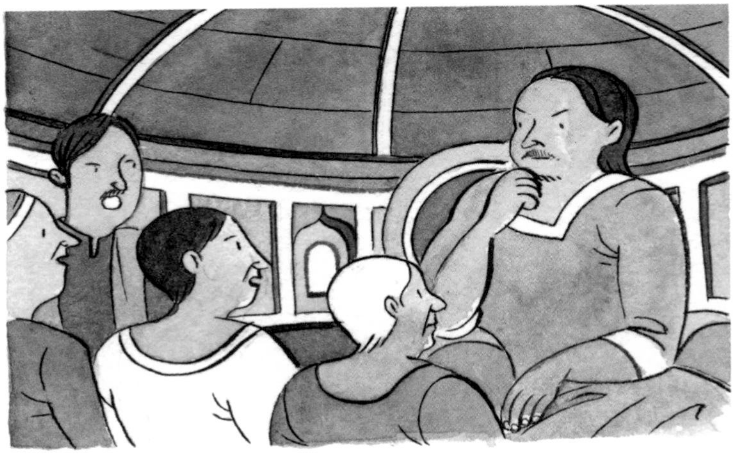

But because the queen could not satisfy their hunger for an answer, a group of townspeople approached the royal vizier of the court with their concerns.

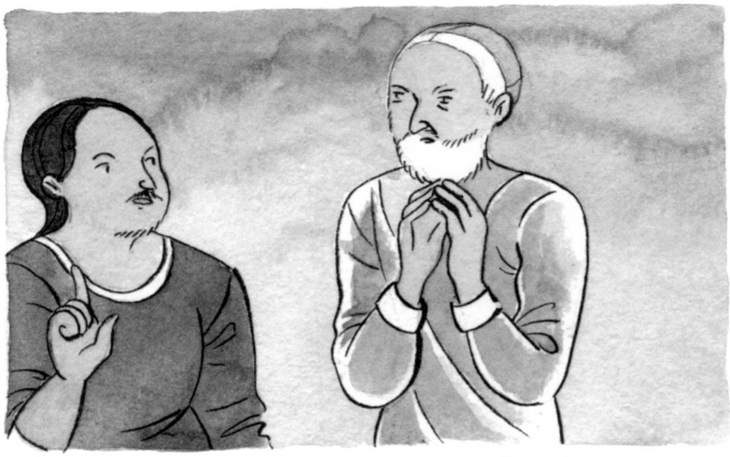

The royal vizier and court sages fretted and were very anxious too. But they soon devised a scheme.

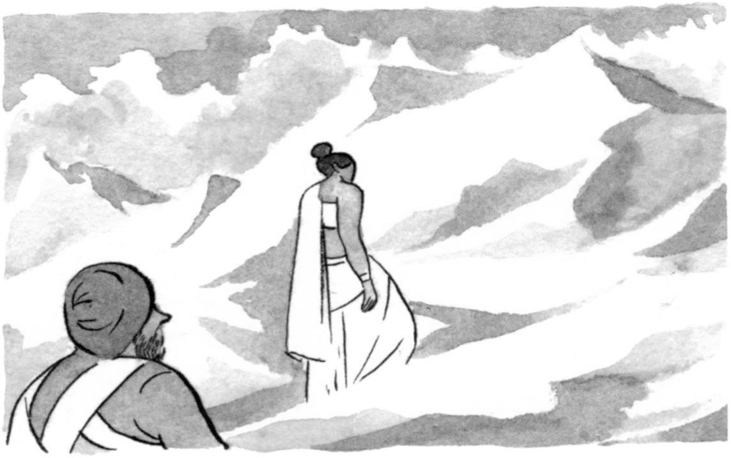

On her twenty-first birthday, the queen was obliged, as was the custom, to make a weeklong pilgrimage to the holiest site in the kingdom, a grotto nestled in the side of the tallest mountain in the land.

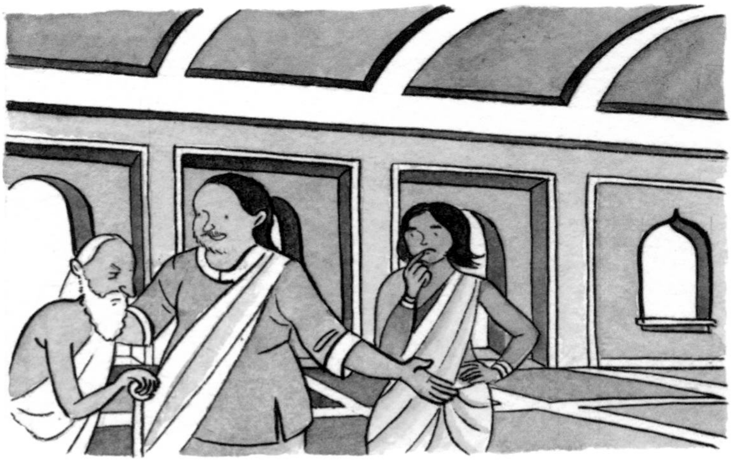

During that time, the royal vizier invited a great sage to court. The holiest man in the kingdom was also an avid patron of the arts, especially of dance. The vizier asked Maya to perform for the sage—something she could not refuse.

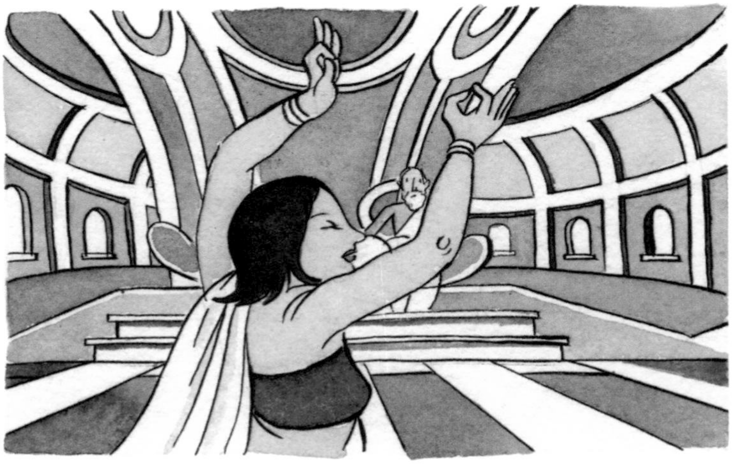

Maya appeared before the sage and the court and performed for them a great, demanding, and daring dance of the ancients.

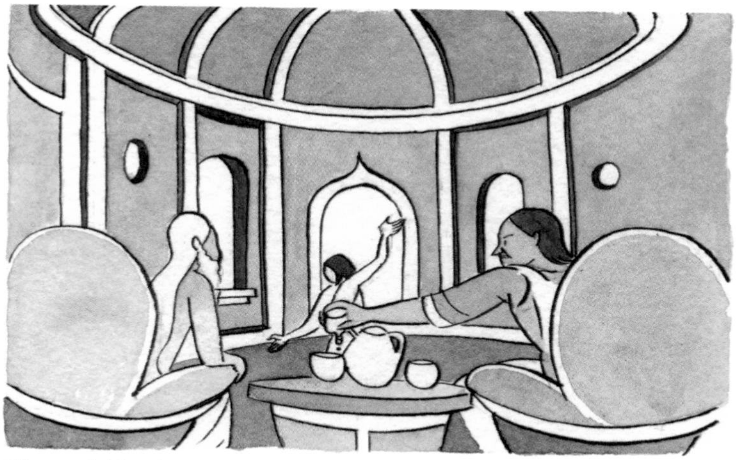

Now while the great sage was soaking in Maya's skillful display, the vizier slipped into the sage's tea a drug that amplified his appetite for sensory pleasures.

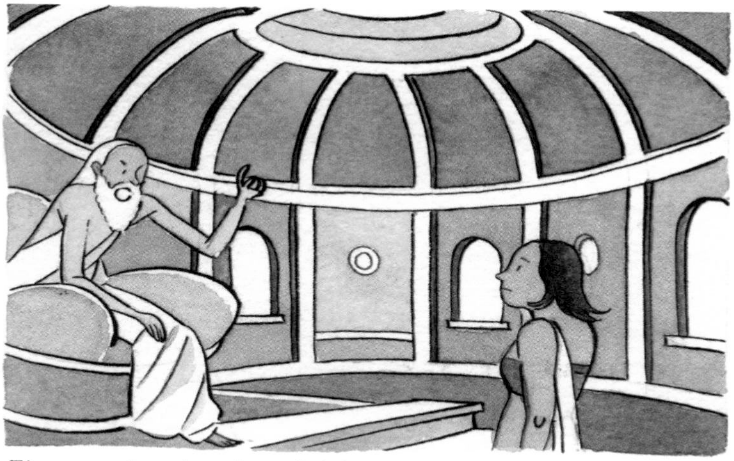

The sage, having drunk his tea, was spellbound both by the vizier's drug as well as Maya's dance, and asked her to perform another.

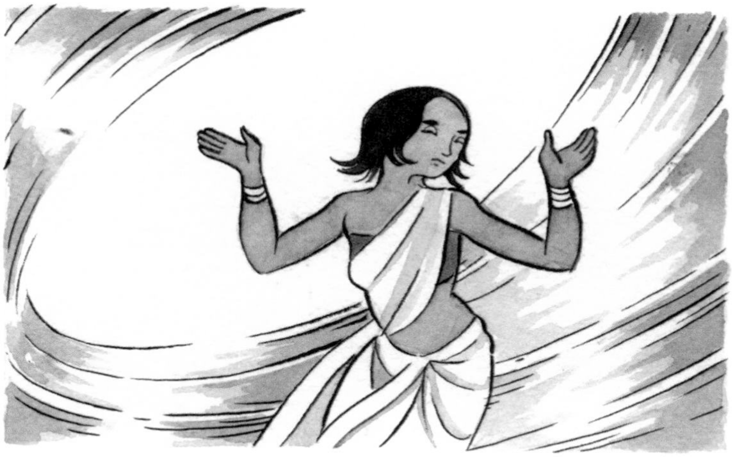

Though she was exhausted, Maya mastered her strength and performed a complex contemporary work, more sensual and beguiling than the last.

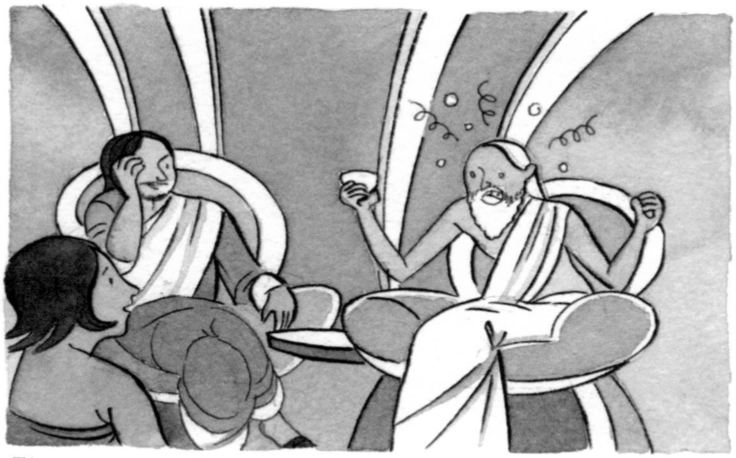

The sage, now fully entranced, demanded more tea and yet another dance. Maya by this time was ready to drop, but still she could not say no to this most holy of men.

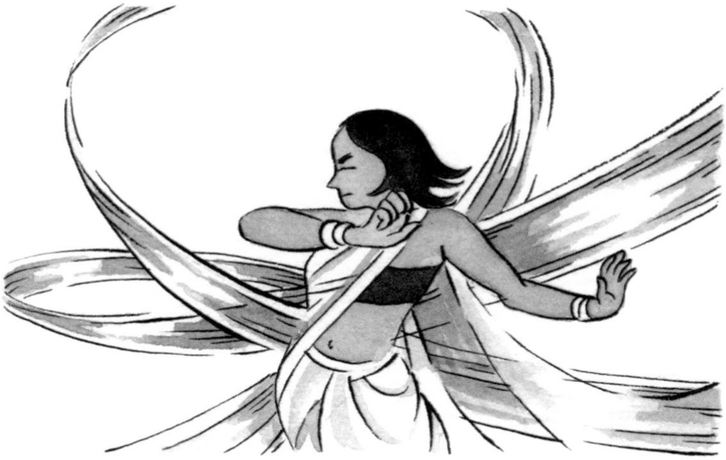

So she performed yet another dance of exquisite grace and beauty.

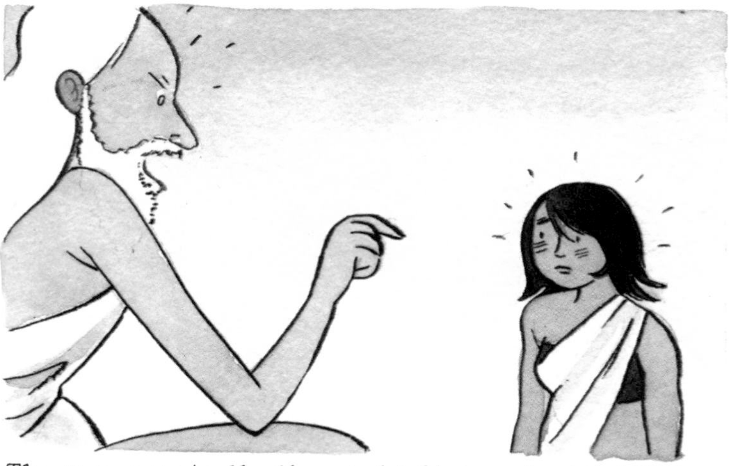

The sage, now in the throes of delirium, insisted that Maya continue to perform.

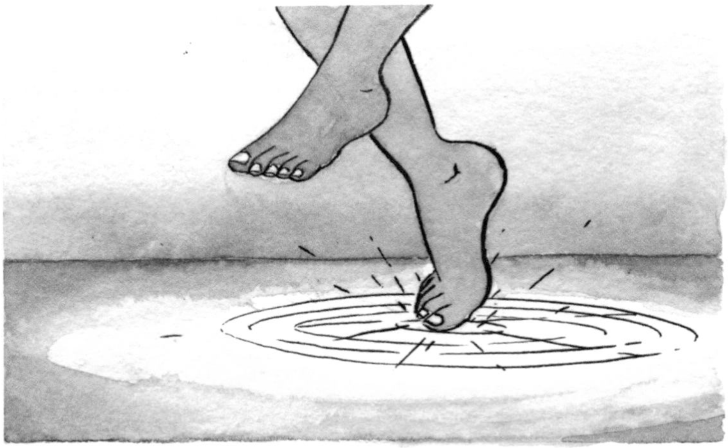

Though her feet were raw and her muscles shot through with pain, Maya danced yet again.

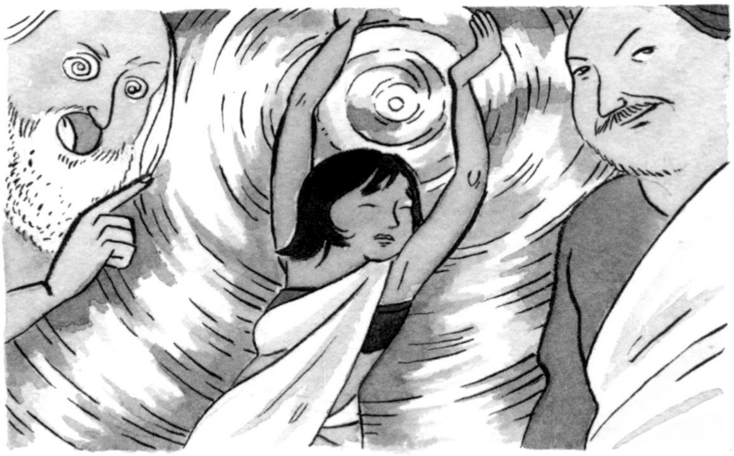

And so it went until the next day, the sage wild-eyed and transfixed, exclaiming at the end of each dance that the performance must not stop.

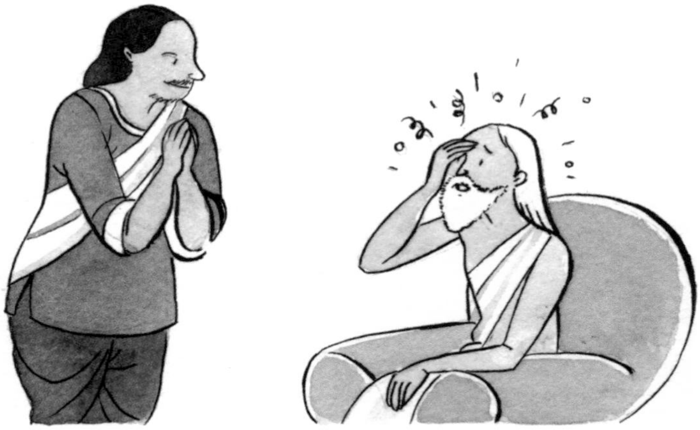

Eventually the vizier's drug wore off,

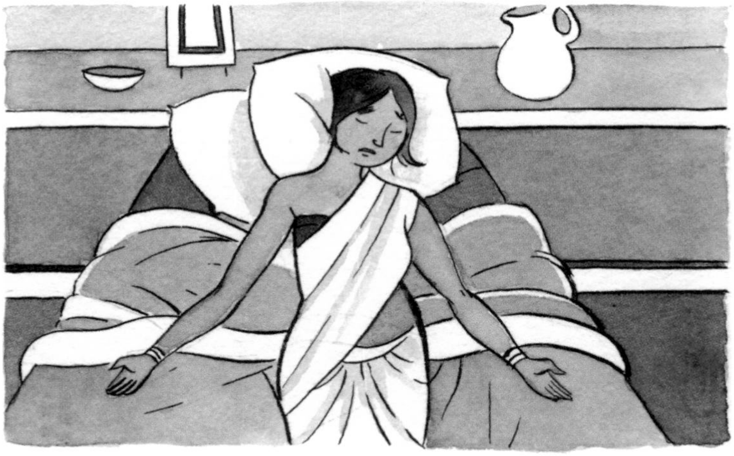

and Maya took to her chamber, spent and bloody, and there collapsed from exhaustion and pain.

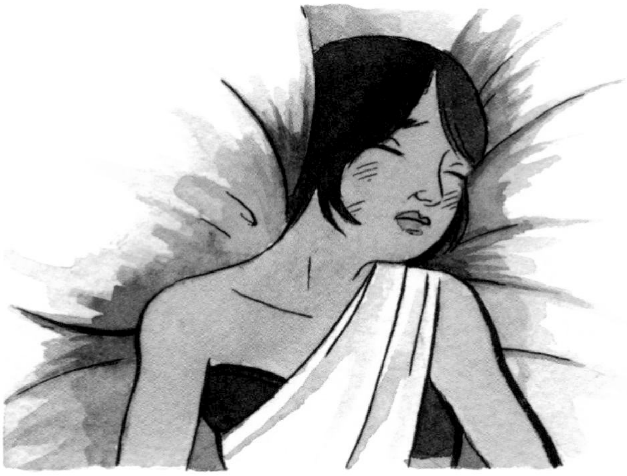

She did not awaken again.

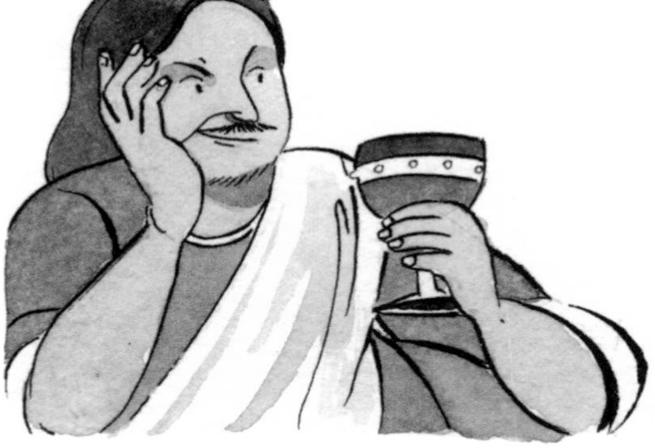

Now, thought the royal vizier, there is nothing to stand in the way of a royal marriage. Once the queen accepts her loss, she must give in to the need for companionship and will certainly marry.

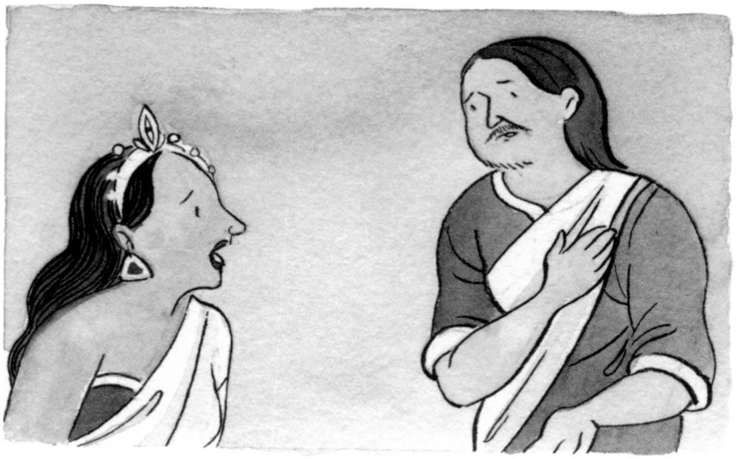

When the queen returned from her pilgrimage, the vizier relayed to her the sad news of Maya's demise.

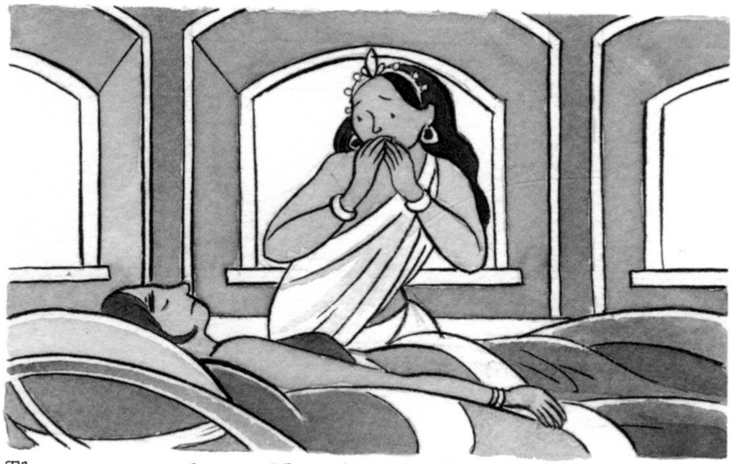

The queen wept over Maya's body. She was shocked to discover her bruised, bloody feet.

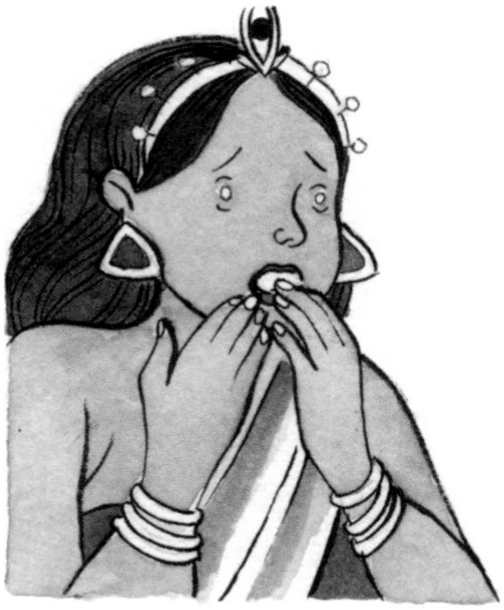

She asked the vizier what had happened, and he said, "The great sage demanded that Maya dance. The poor girl performed admirably but was overwhelmed by the sage's continued requests. It is indeed a shame."

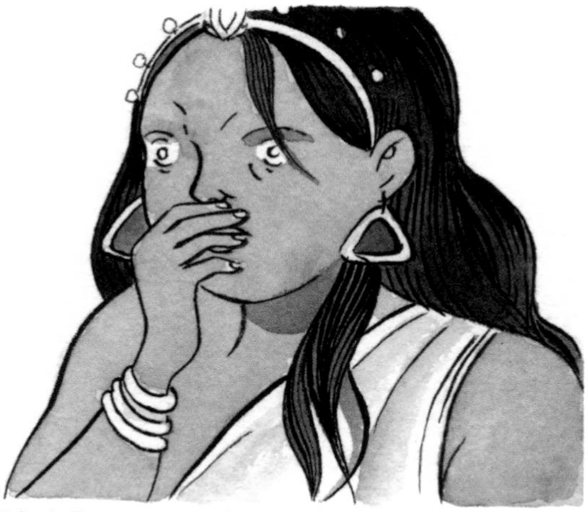

The queen immediately sensed the vizier's deception. She saw in the faces of the vizier, the court attendants, and the people, the truth—that they, who she had loved as a ruler, rejoiced at Maya's death because they blamed her for the queen's refusal to marry.

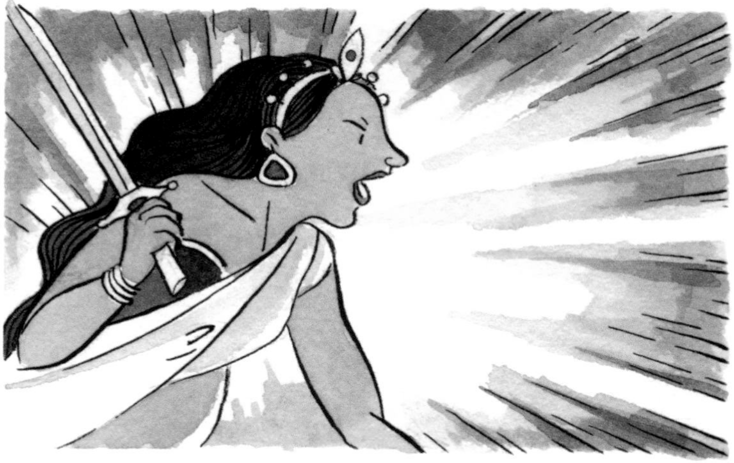

And so she flew into a rage.

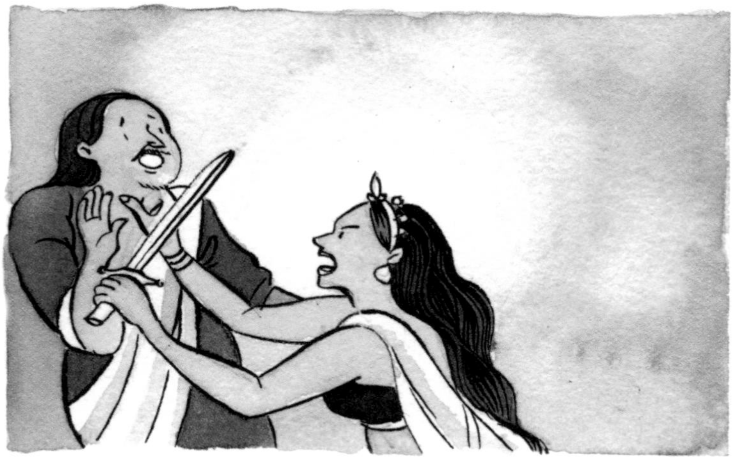

She unsheathed her sword from its scabbard, grabbed the vizier by the neck, held him aloft, and threatened to slit his throat in front of her subjects.

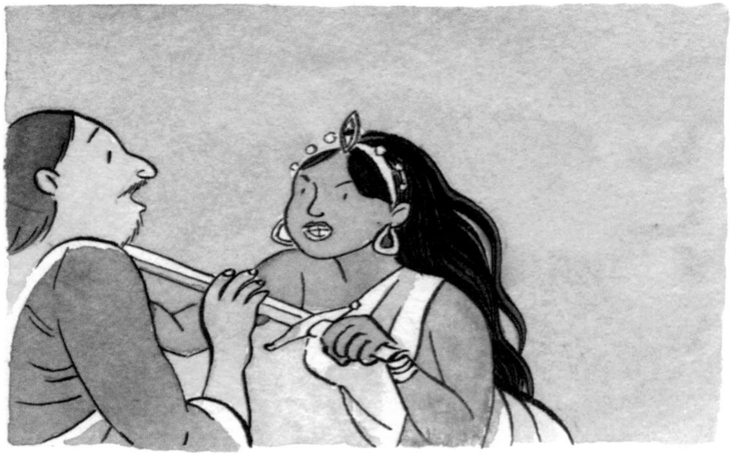

But she held herself. The vizier was only carrying out the people's wishes. And if the people wished for murder, for the destruction of love, how could she still love them and rule over them as their queen?

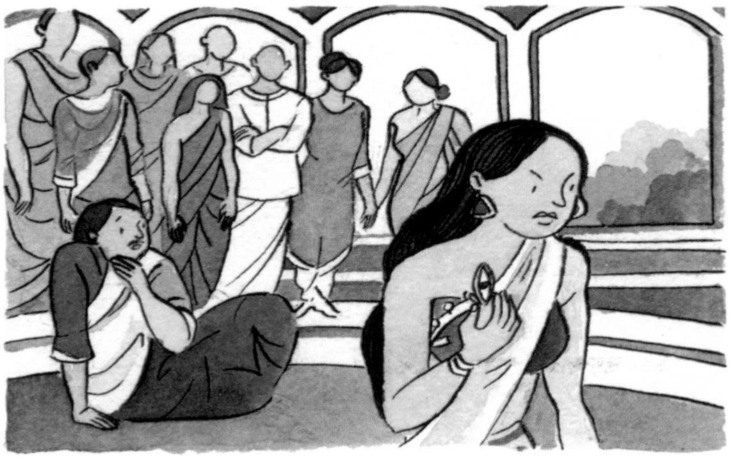

She let the vizier, gasping for breath, down on the marble floor of the grand hall. The queen then retired to her bedchamber.

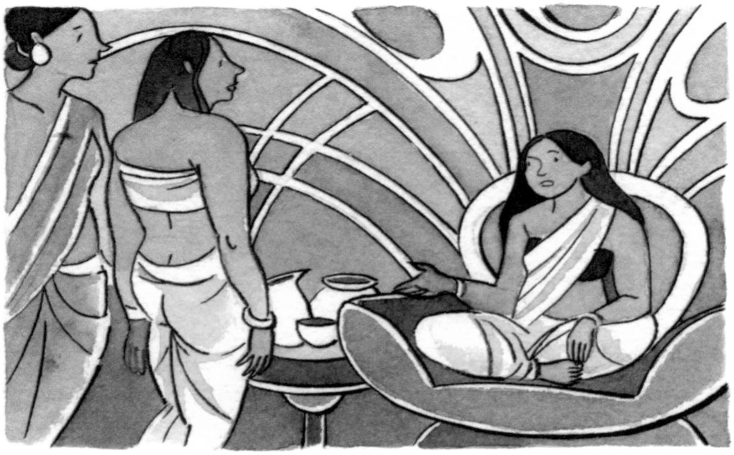

The next day the queen gathered her closest attendants and told them to pack all their belongings.

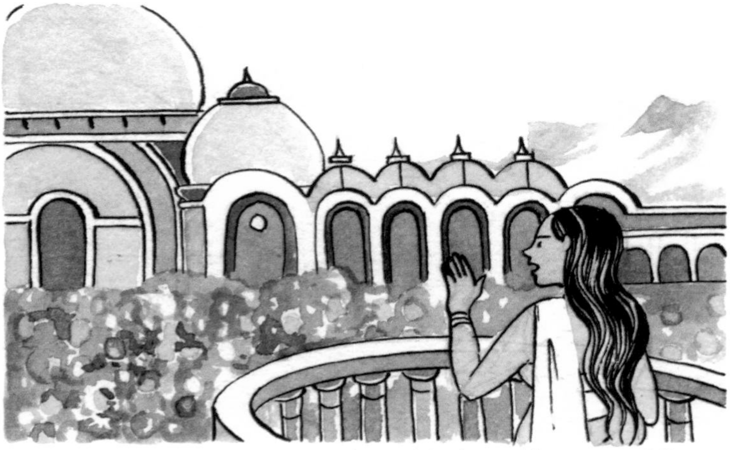

At the noonday address, she told them, "I am unable to guide you as a queen must. There exists between us a vast canyon that cannot be bridged. I therefore abdicate my title as queen and take my leave of you."

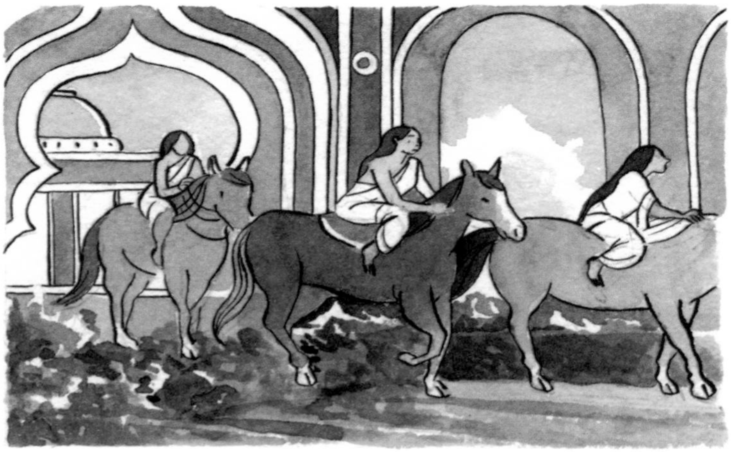

With that, she, along with a band of her maids-in-waiting, formed a caravan and made for the farthest northern reaches of the kingdom, where they found a home in exile.

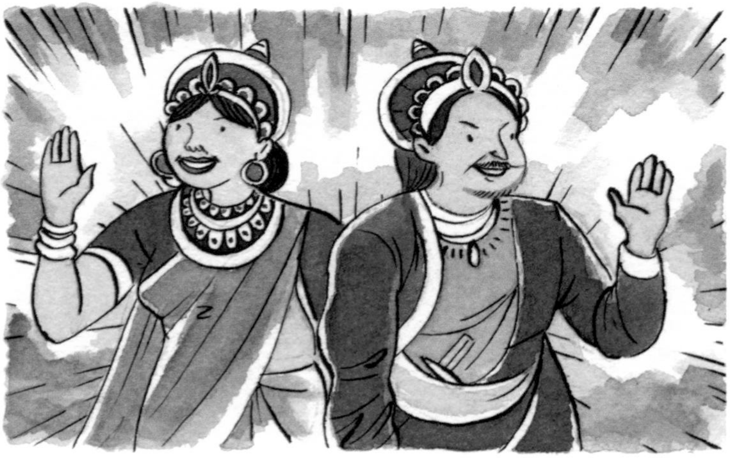

The grand vizier proclaimed himself king, married a princess from the east, and ruled the kingdom for decades.

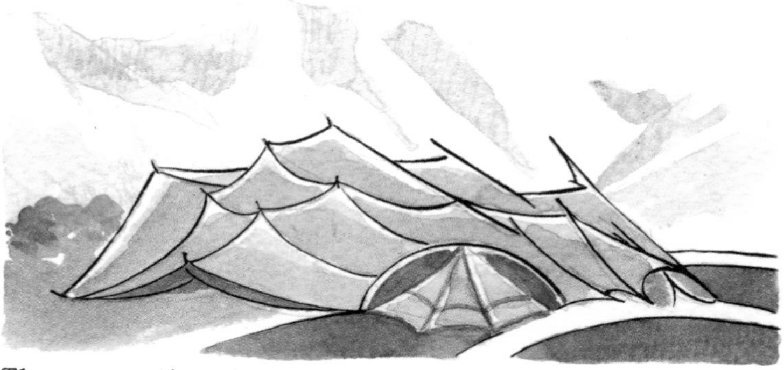

The queen, though torn by disillusionment and grief, lived for many years with her entourage,

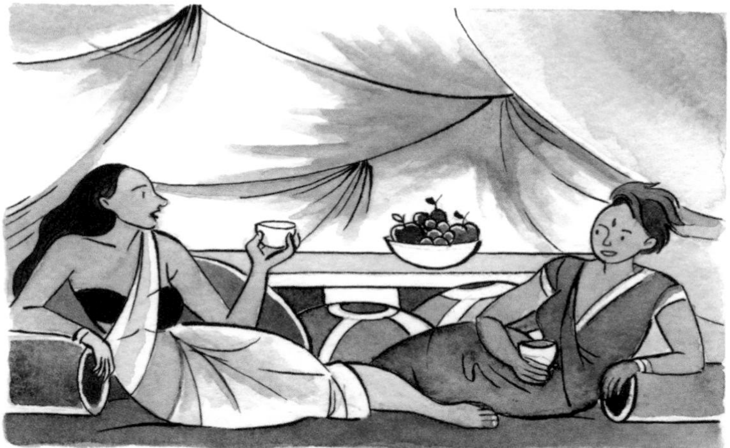

happy in the familiarity and security of the company of those she loved and trusted the most.

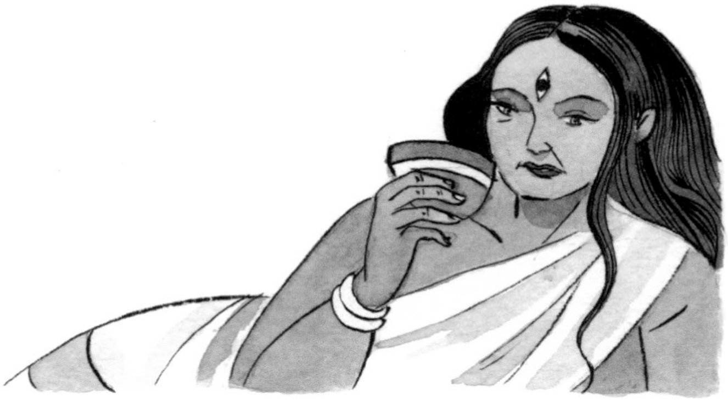

She sometimes thought to herself, in idle moments, over a cup of sun-brewed tea,

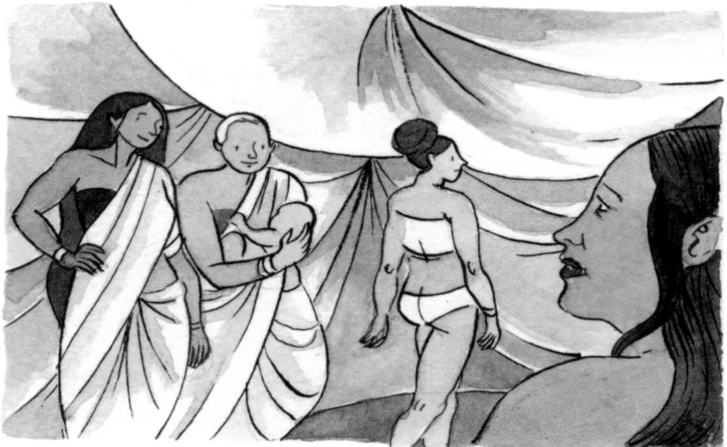

that she might wrest power back from the vizier and rule over her people again.

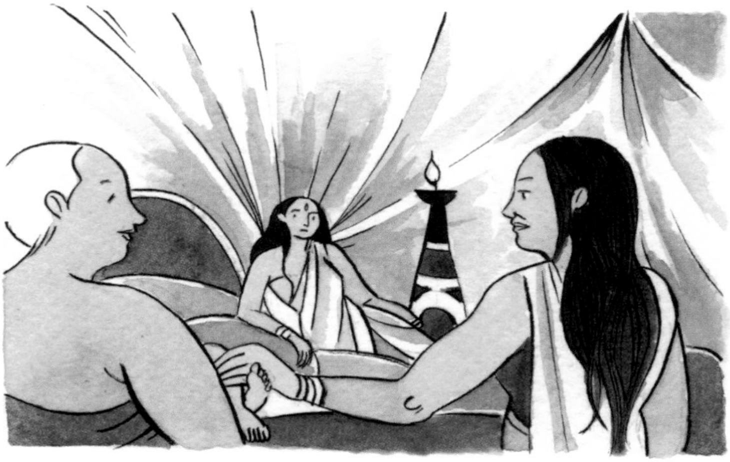

She would then remember

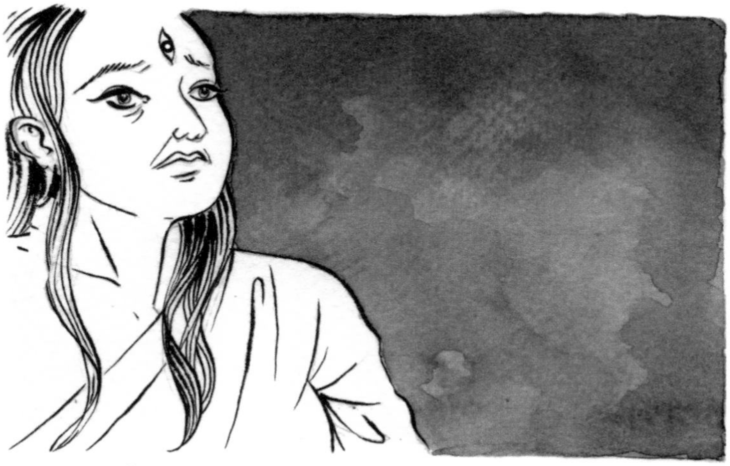

that her people did not want her back.

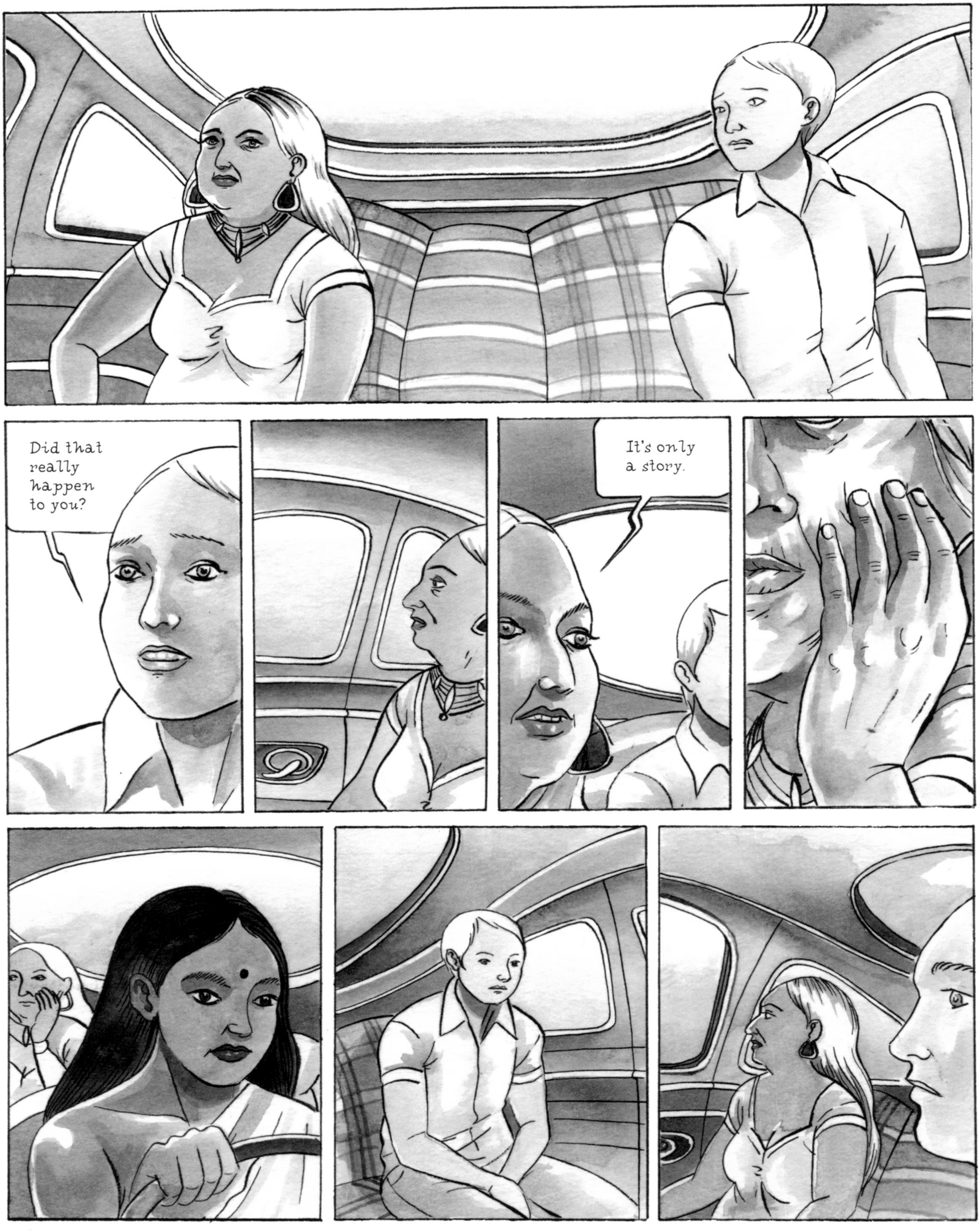
Did that really happen to you?
It's only a story.

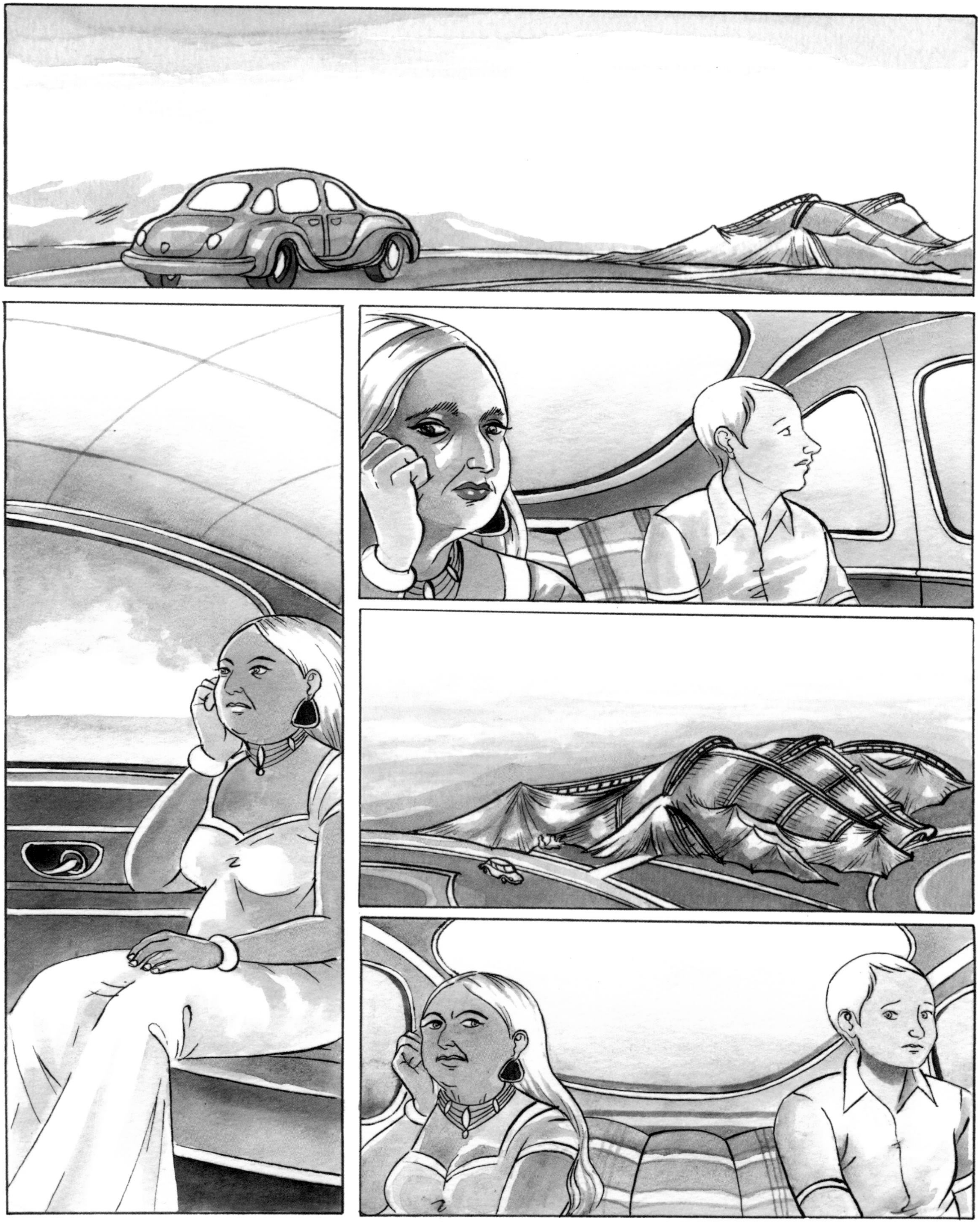

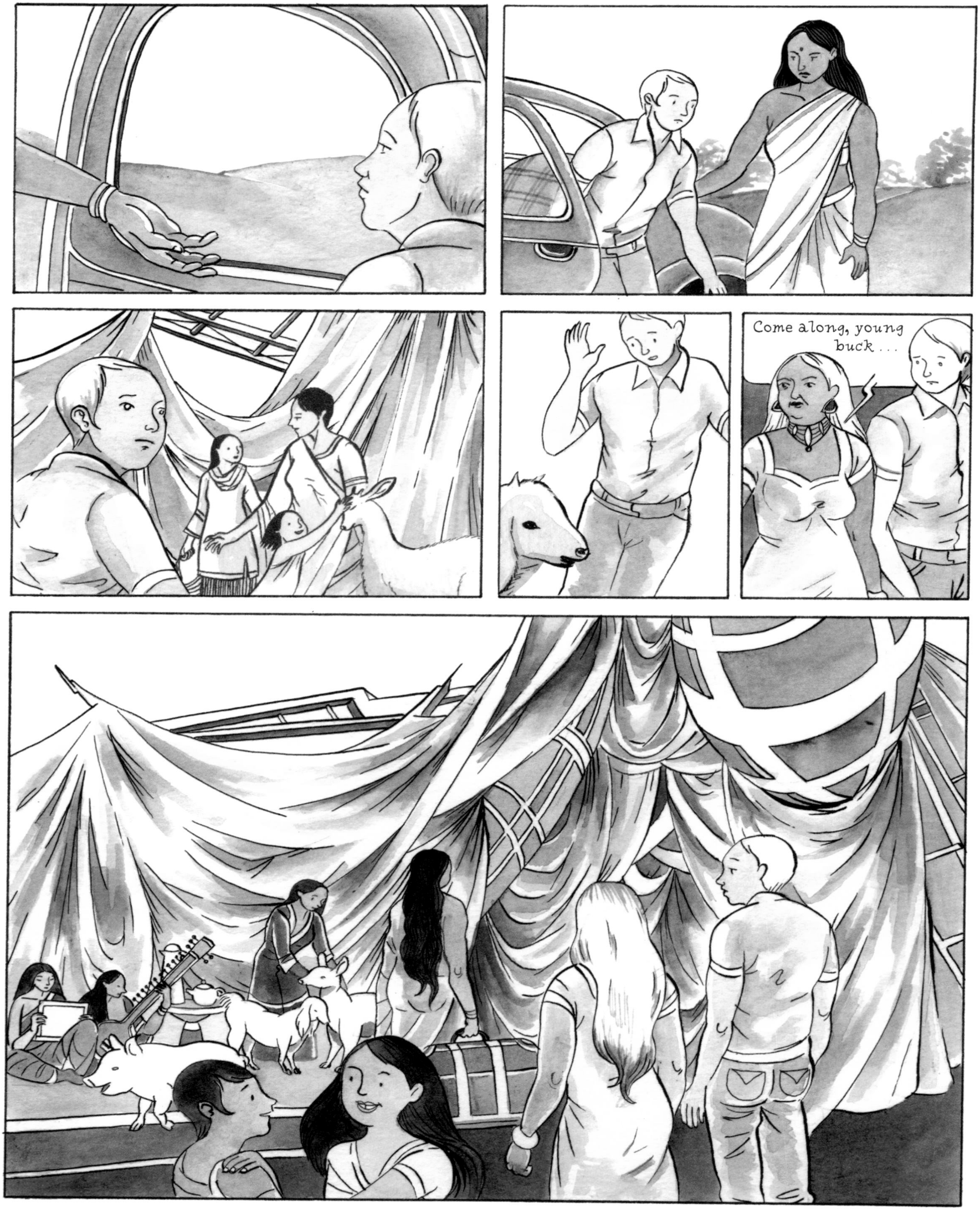
Come along, young buck . . .

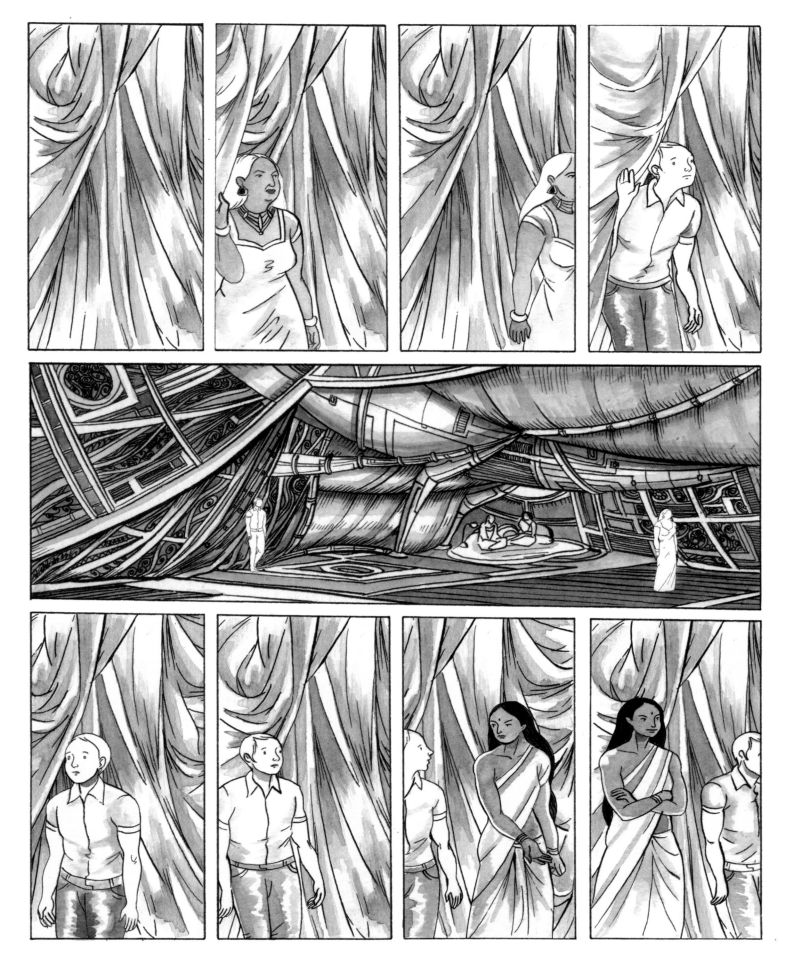

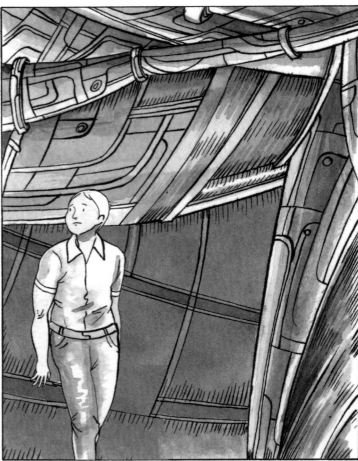

Now then, young pup—you must know, having studied the local ways, about Bhavatiya?

No ... no, I don't know about that. What is it?

Bhavatiya is an old custom amongst our people—it decrees that if one is invited into the home of another, one must undress to show that he has nothing to hide from his host. Of course, back then, our ancestors were concerned primarily with spies and assassins—still, the custom survives to this day despite the absence of such intrigue.

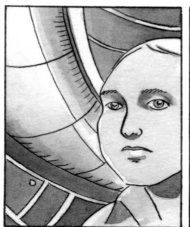

You—you want me to take my clothes off?

Good lord—far be it from me to impose such an admittedly strange custom on you—but these are our ways.

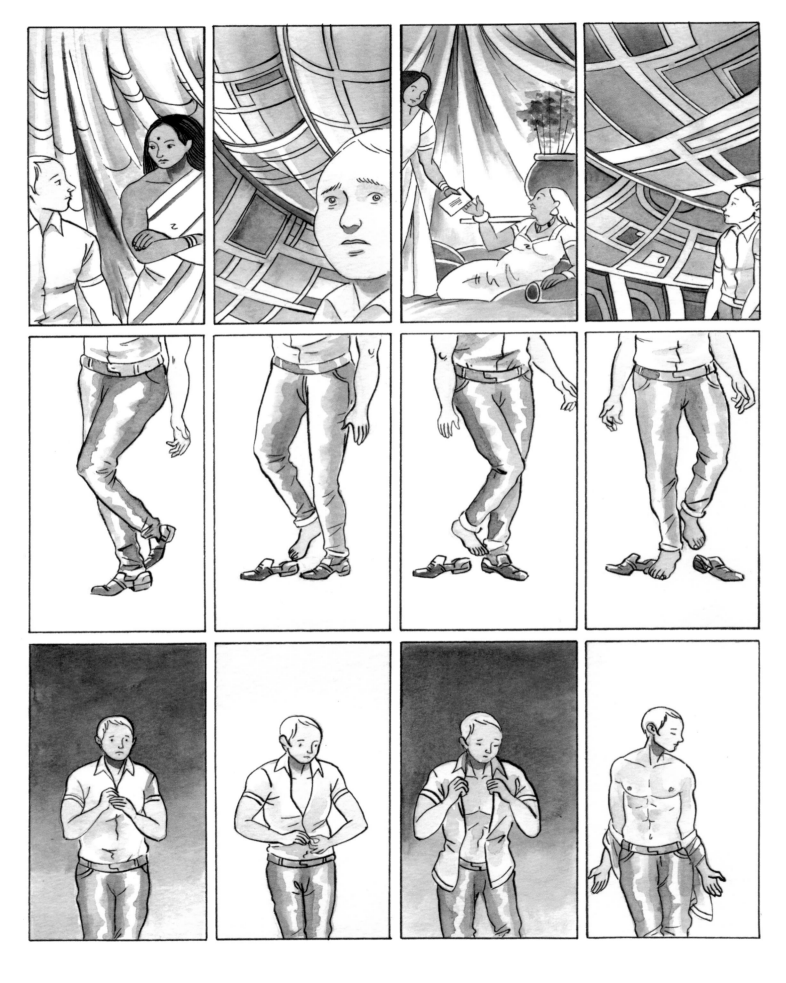

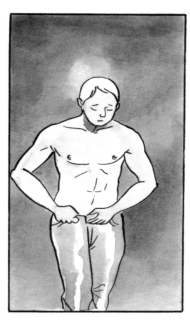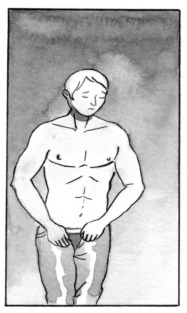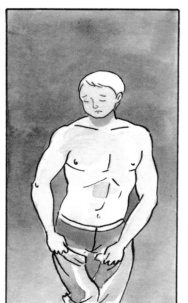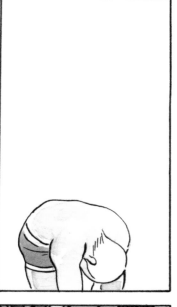

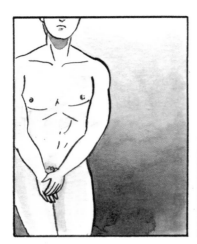

Now before I can offer you anything, there is the second part of Bhavatiya, which decrees that the guest must honor the host with a brief song or entertainment.

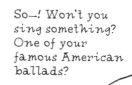

So—! Won't you sing something? One of your famous American ballads?

Or a little dance, perhaps?

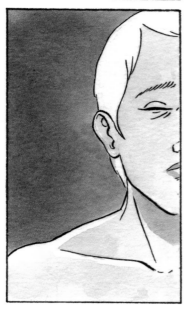

I just want to go home.

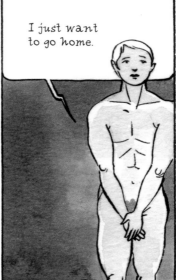

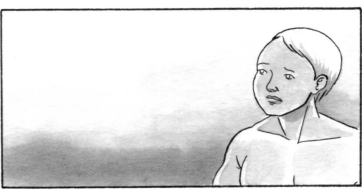

Well! You're no prisoner here, Master Craig. And while we can't take you home, I'm sure Anuradha will be happy to drive you back to the hotel.

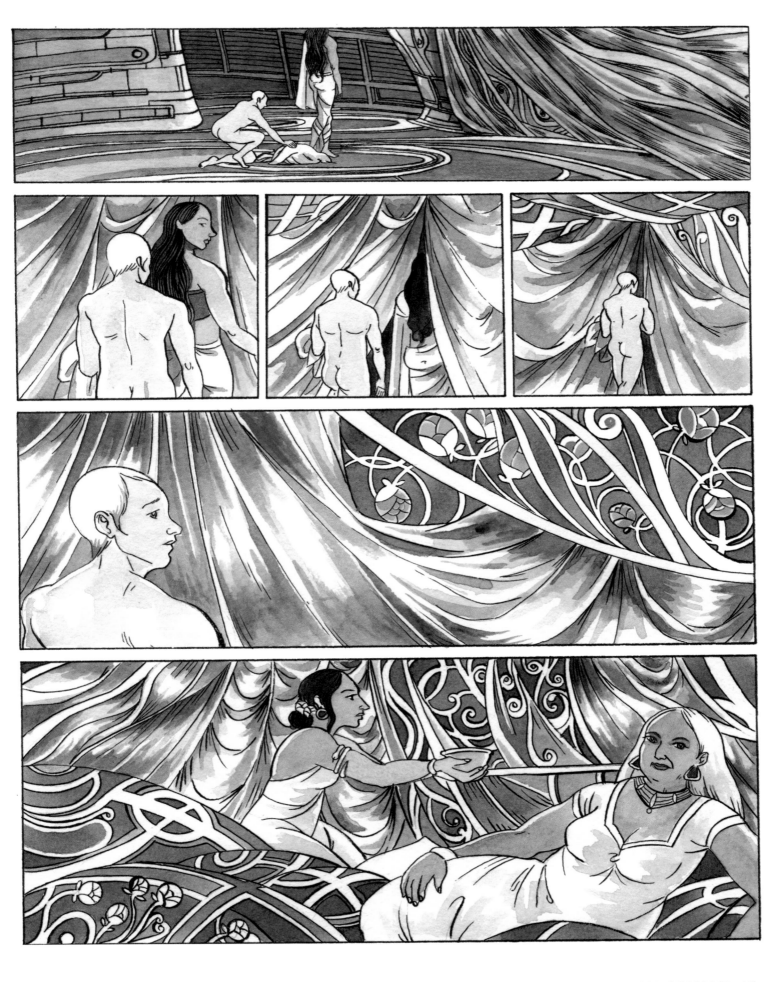

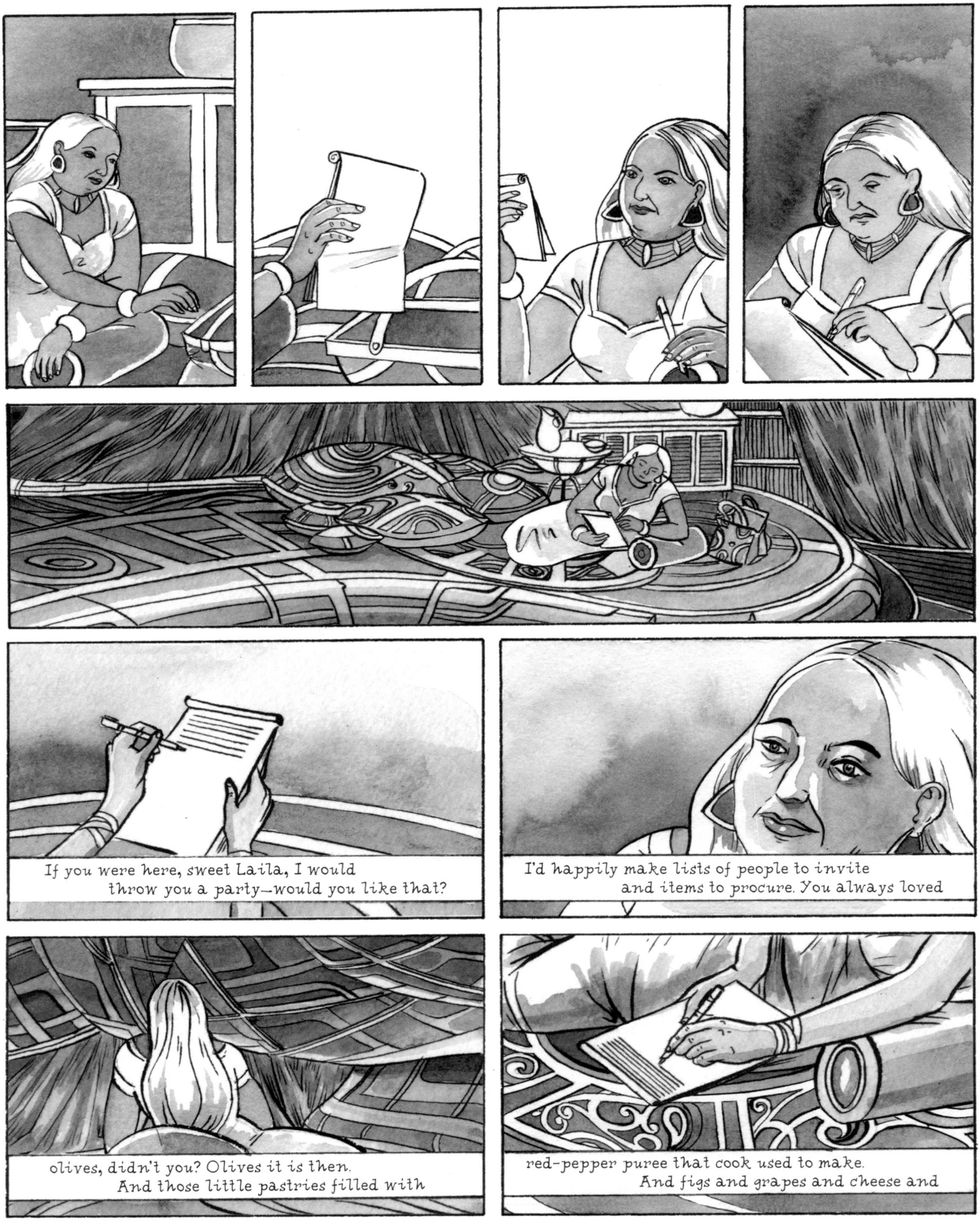
If you were here, sweet Laila, I would throw you a party—would you like that?
I'd happily make lists of people to invite and items to procure. You always loved
olives, didn't you? Olives it is then. And those little pastries filled with
red-pepper puree that cook used to make. And figs and grapes and cheese and

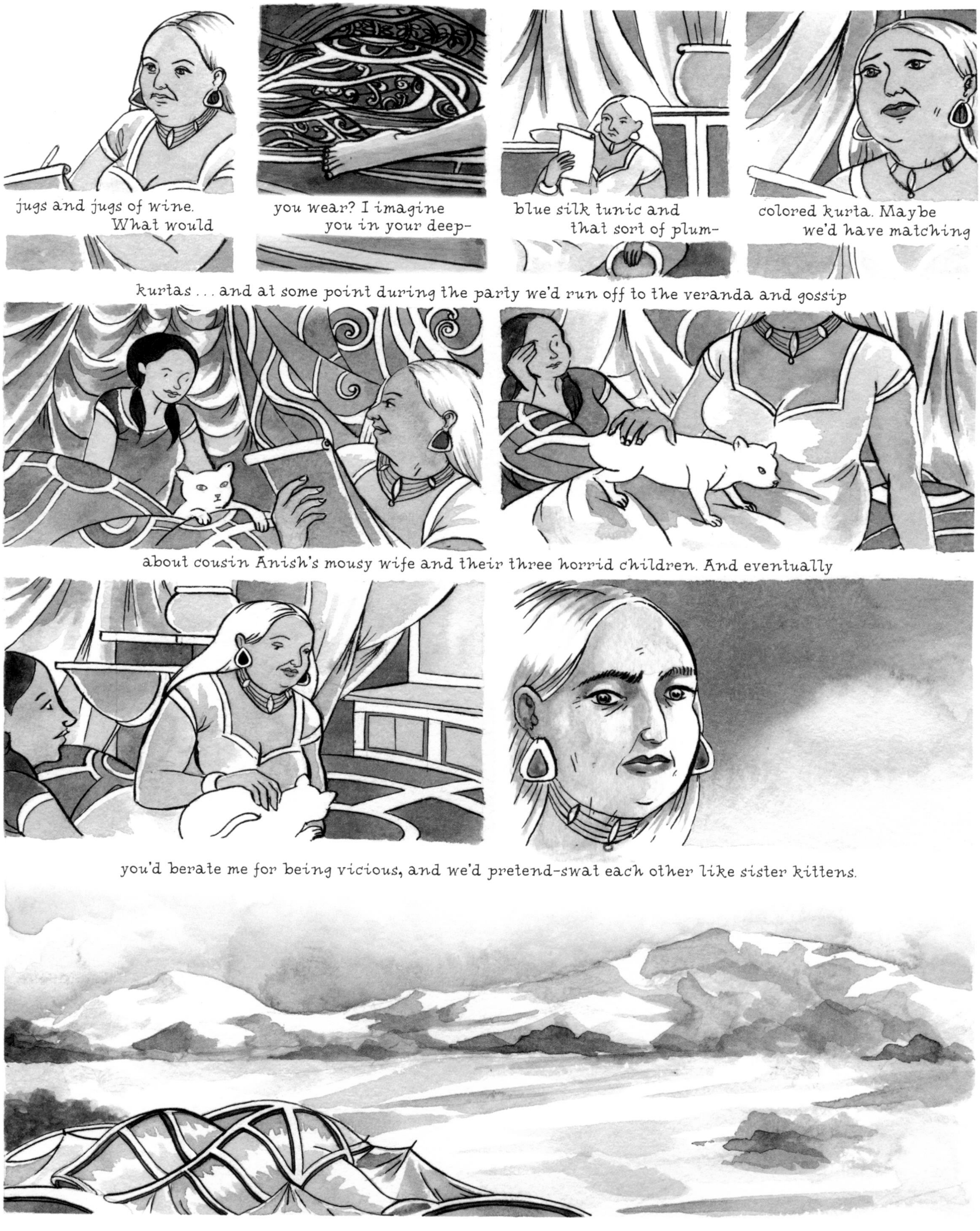
jugs and jugs of wine. What would
you wear? I imagine you in your deep-
blue silk tunic and that sort of plum-
colored kurta. Maybe we'd have matching
kurtas . . . and at some point during the party we'd run off to the veranda and gossip
about cousin Anish's mousy wife and their three horrid children. And eventually
you'd berate me for being vicious, and we'd pretend-swat each other like sister kittens.

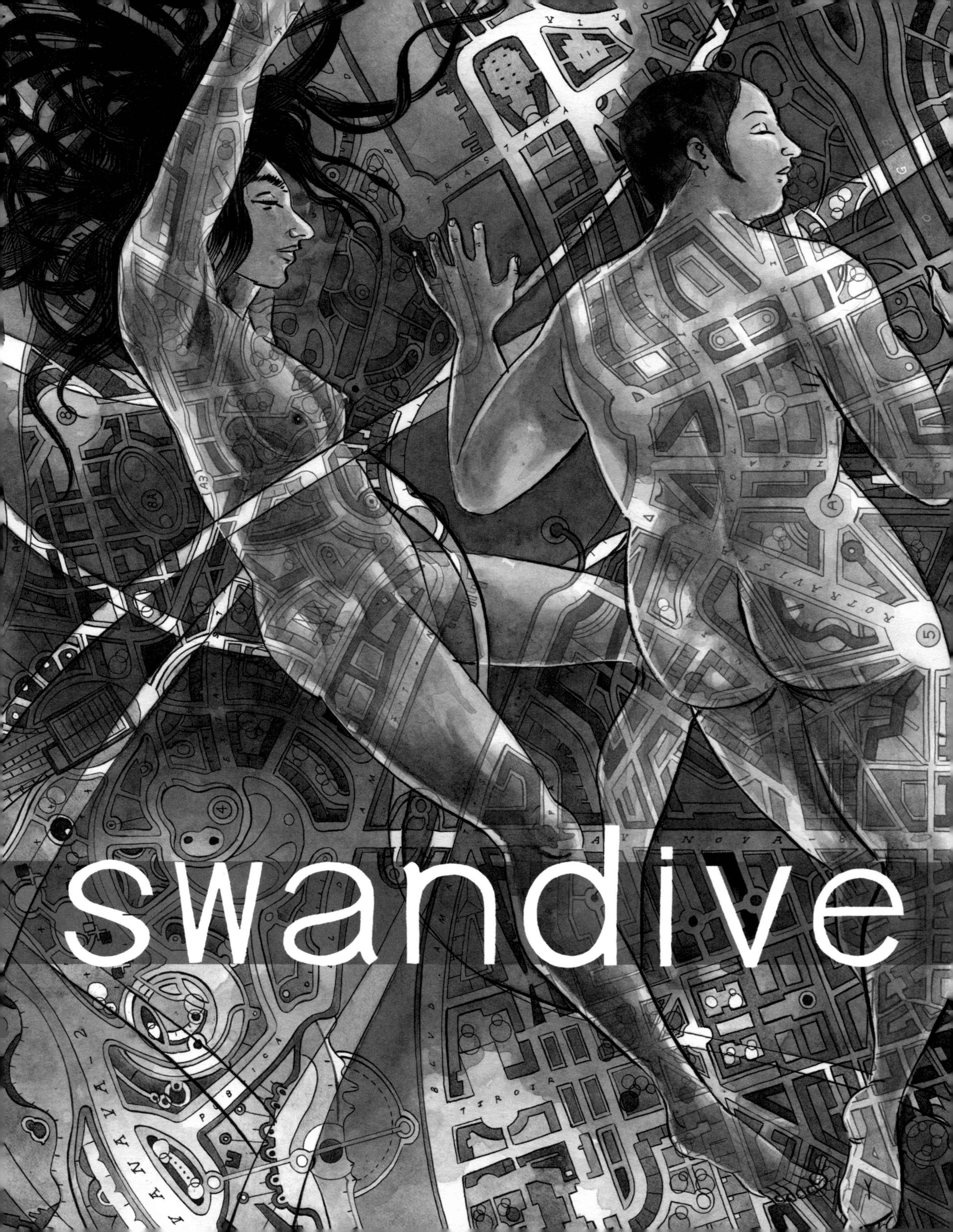
swandive

... maps can circumscribe and set boundaries but can also lay the groundwork for an infinite number of itineraries, of infinite play within and despite boundaries.

You can think of a river as a gap, a chasm, or as a channel, as movement.

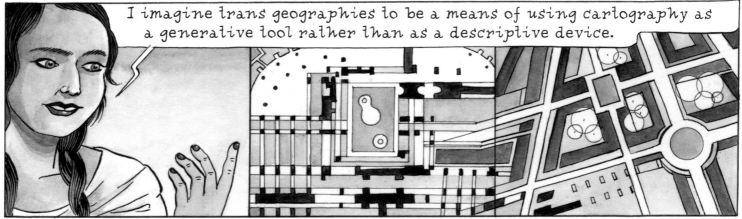

I imagine trans geographies to be a means of using cartography as a generative tool rather than as a descriptive device.

A way to chart possibilities, ways of being that have yet to manifest themselves.

I imagine that trans bodies contain within them the capability to unlock potentialities as well.

ALIVA   HANT

6

HANSA   PIROU

IXILA

8

PEROL

2   ROV

PRIS

AIX   VIZ

VAVA 2

And that trans imaginations can realize new forms, new bodies, entire worlds—radical and novel psychic, social, economic, and political modes.
Cartographies engender more expansive, connected, interdependent conceptions of this world, of possible worlds. If I tell you, "Meet me at the café across the way from the gasworks," you'll know the way even if you have never been there before because you have a map—a document that charts new territories.
DOPPEL
LAXMIBAI
AYA
I imagine trans geographies as maps of a multiplicity of unknown destinations, each unlocking access to a further myriad of open nodes, a kaleidoscope of addresses—
FEB 02
Sab-Rev
a churning constellation of whereabouts.
LUMINA
Thanks so much.

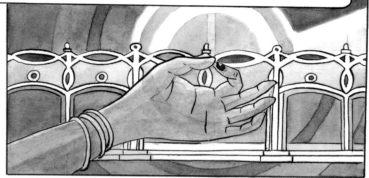

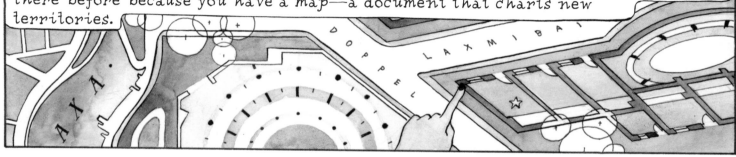

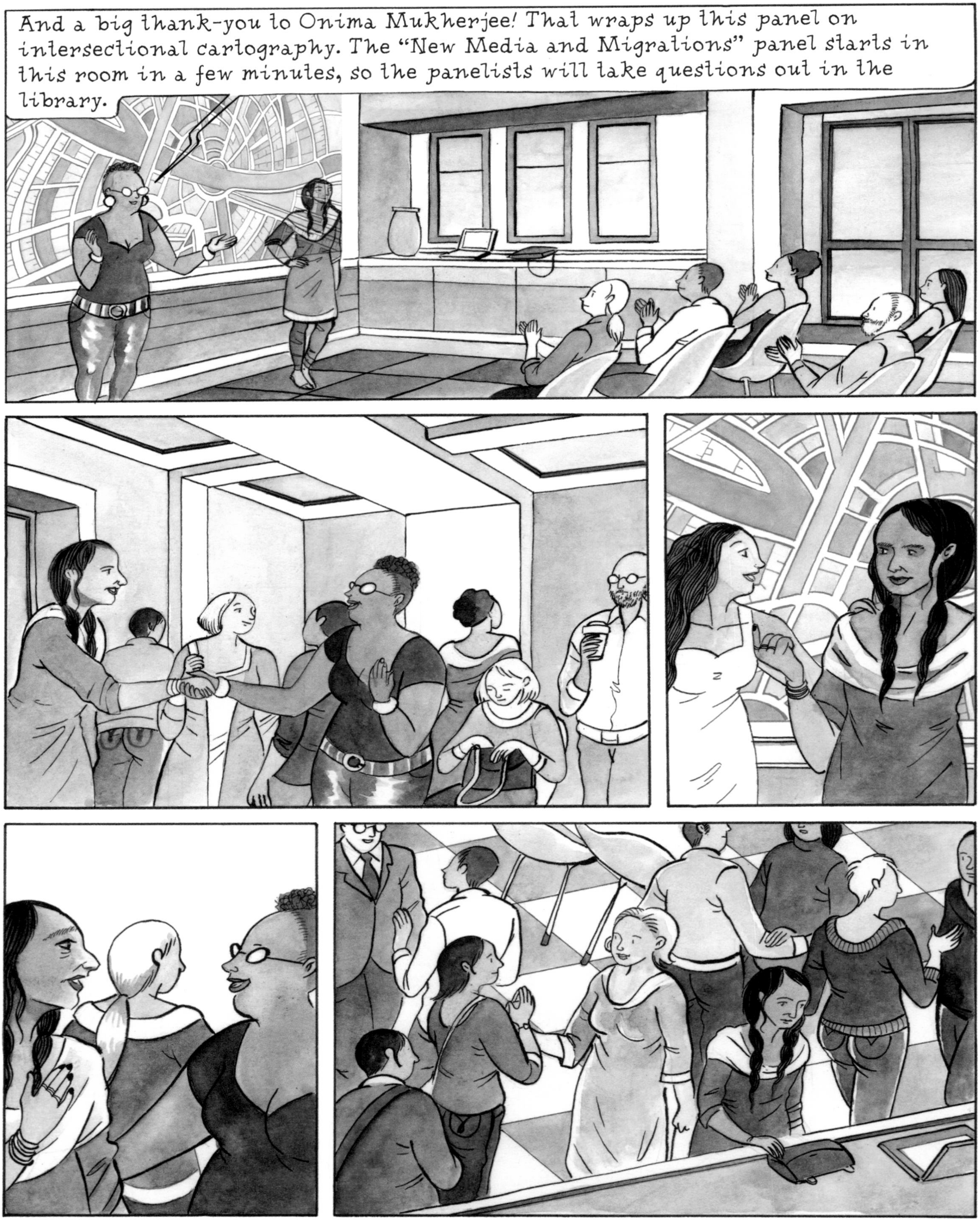
And a big thank-you to Onima Mukherjee! That wraps up this panel on intersectional cartography. The "New Media and Migrations" panel starts in this room in a few minutes, so the panelists will take questions out in the library.

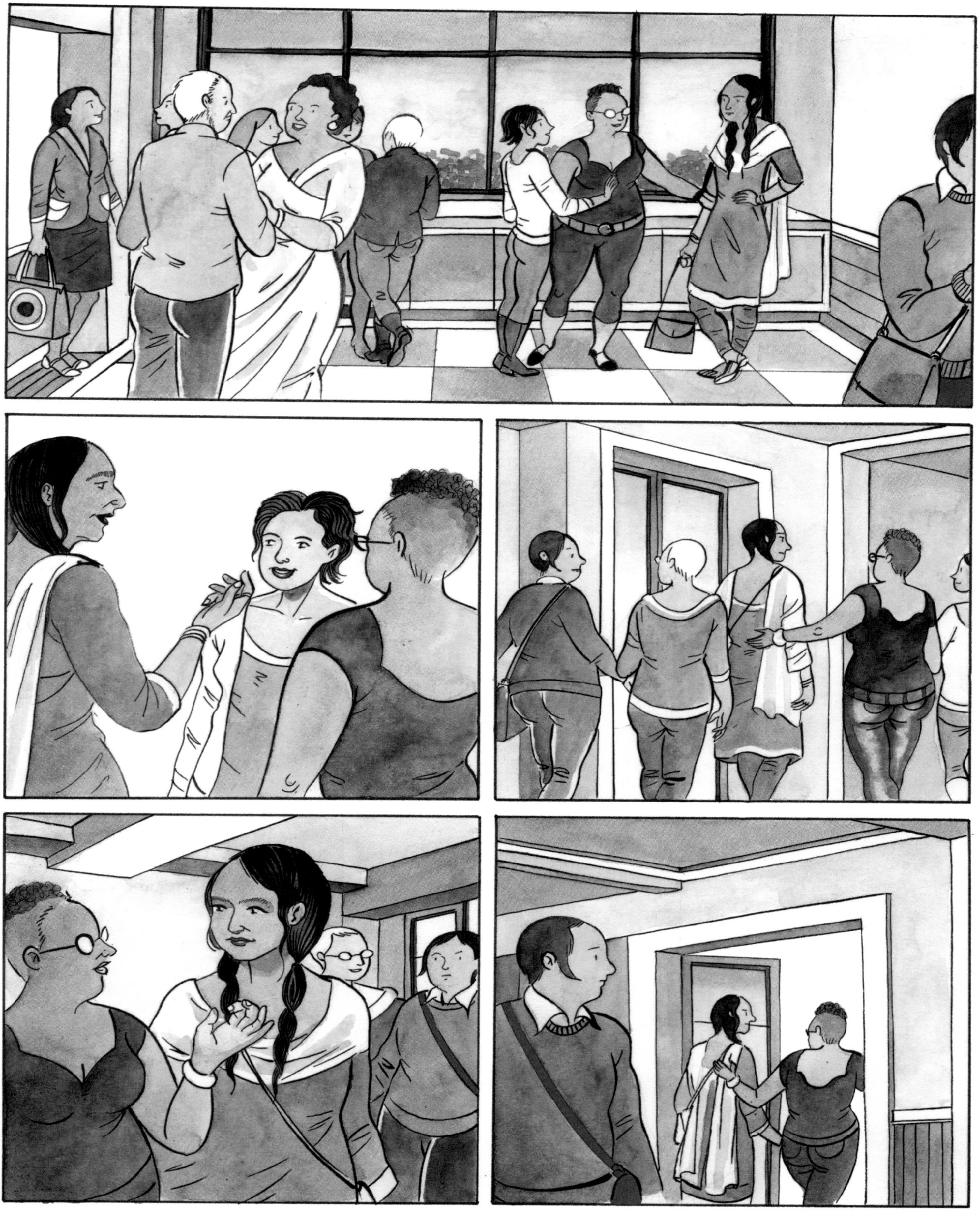

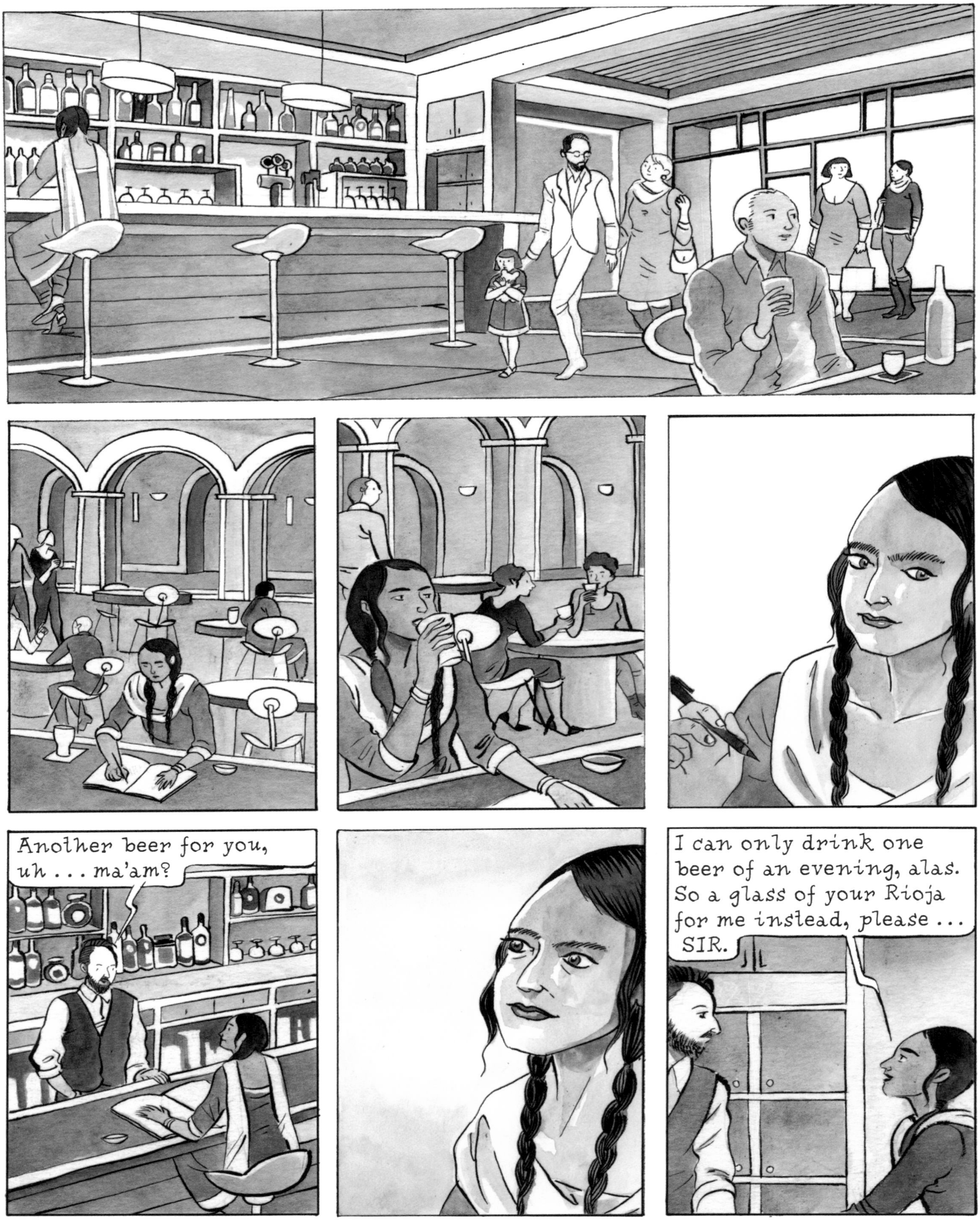
Another beer for you, uh . . . ma'am?
I can only drink one beer of an evening, alas. So a glass of your Rioja for me instead, please . . . SIR.

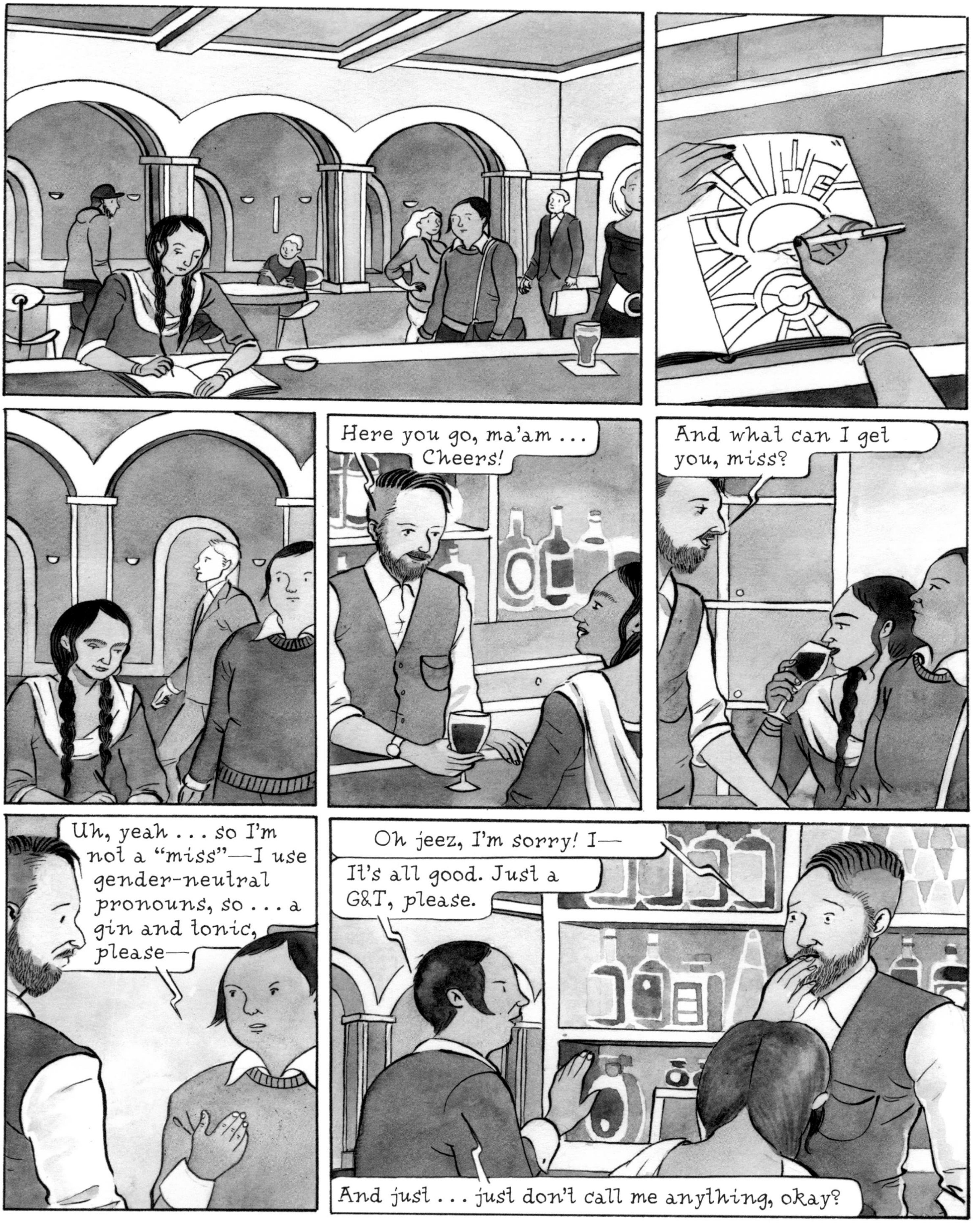
Here you go, ma'am . . . Cheers!
And what can I get you, miss?
Uh, yeah . . . so I'm not a "miss"—I use gender-neutral pronouns, so . . . a gin and tonic, please—
Oh jeez, I'm sorry! I—
It's all good. Just a G&T, please.
And just . . . just don't call me anything, okay?

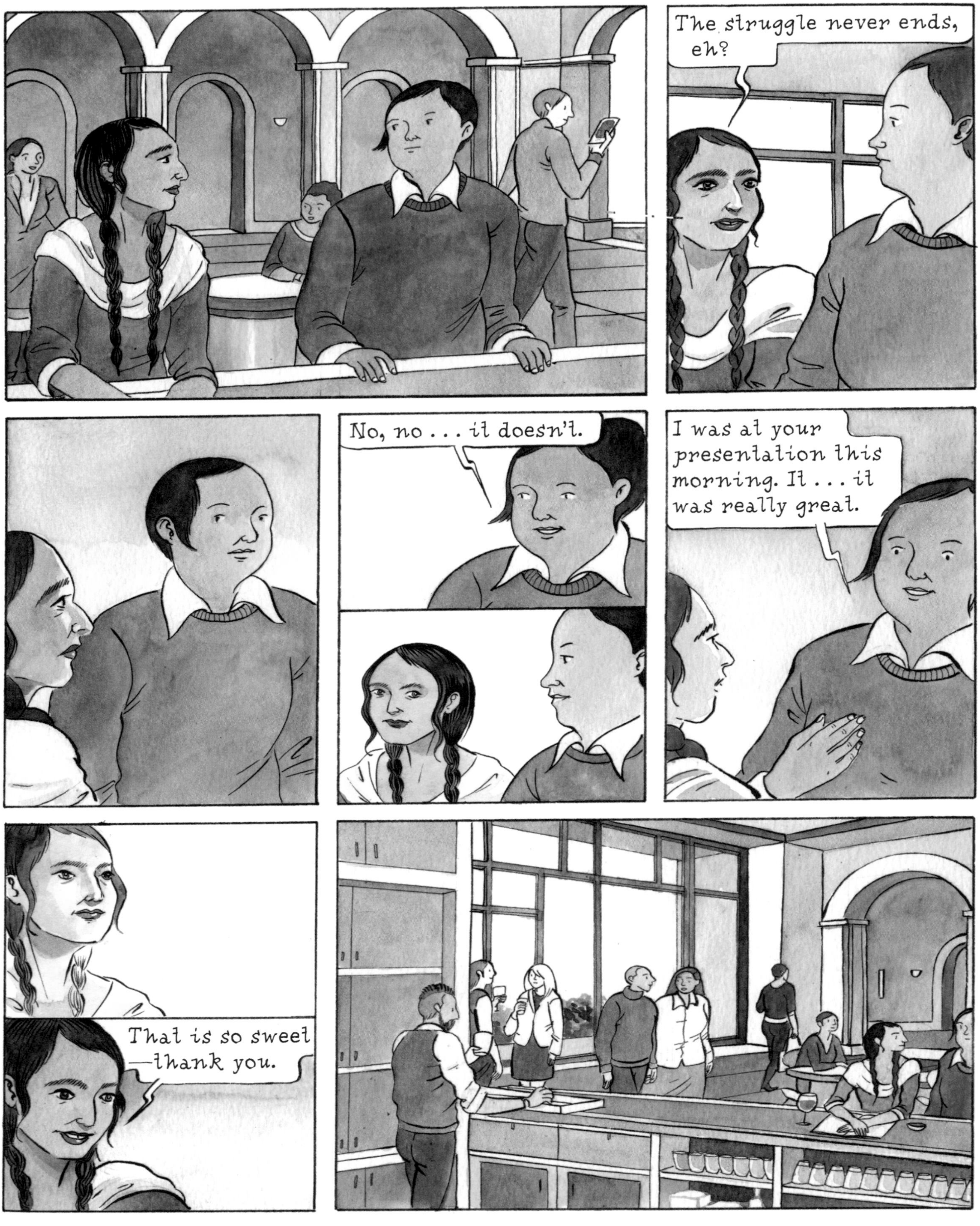
The struggle never ends, eh?
No, no . . . it doesn't.
I was at your presentation this morning. It . . . it was really great.
That is so sweet—thank you.

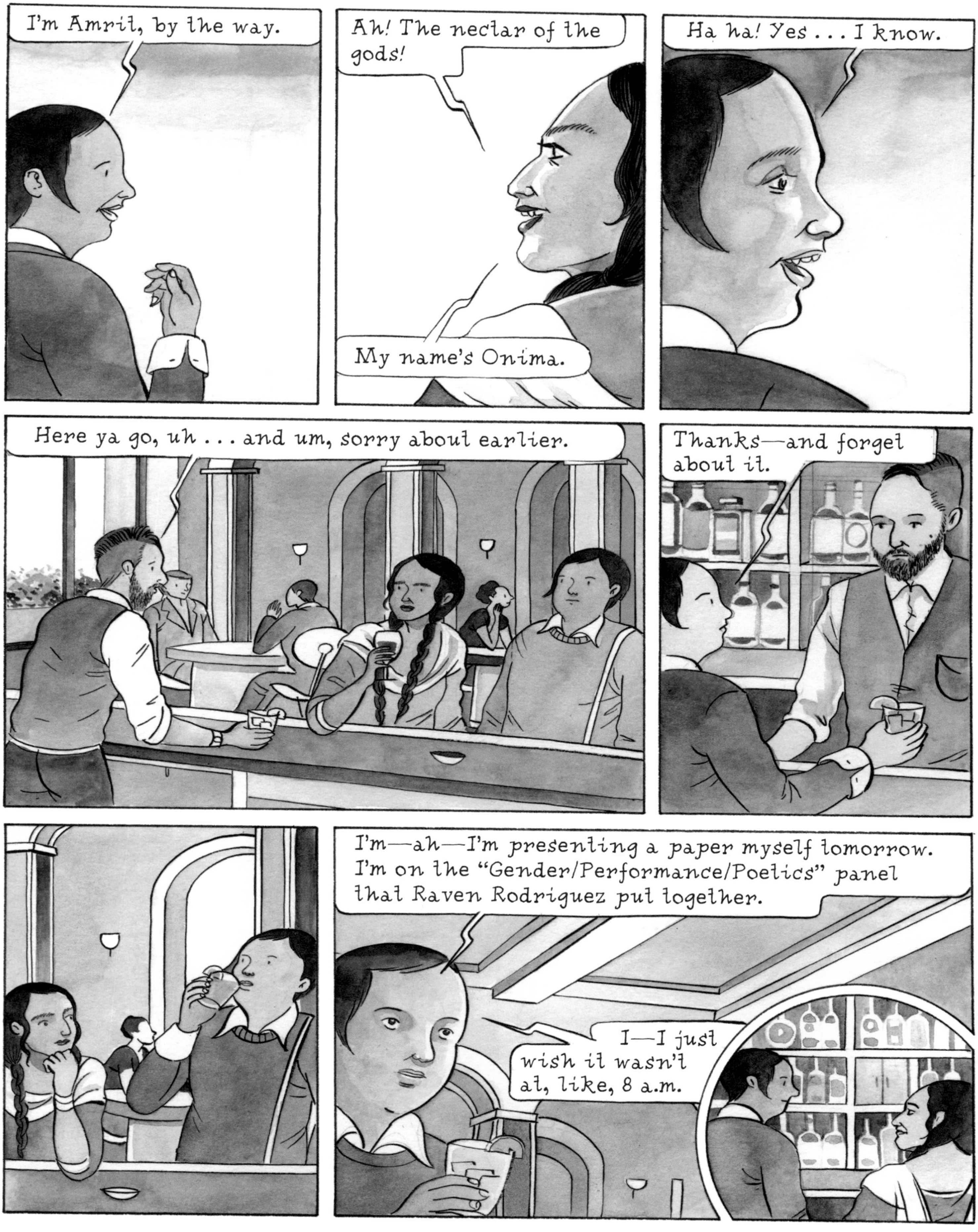
I'm Amril, by the way.
Ah! The nectar of the gods!
My name's Onima.
Ha ha! Yes . . . I know.
Here ya go, uh . . . and um, sorry about earlier.
Thanks—and forget about it.
I'm—ah—I'm presenting a paper myself tomorrow. I'm on the "Gender/Performance/Poetics" panel that Raven Rodriguez put together.
I—I just wish it wasn't at, like, 8 a.m.

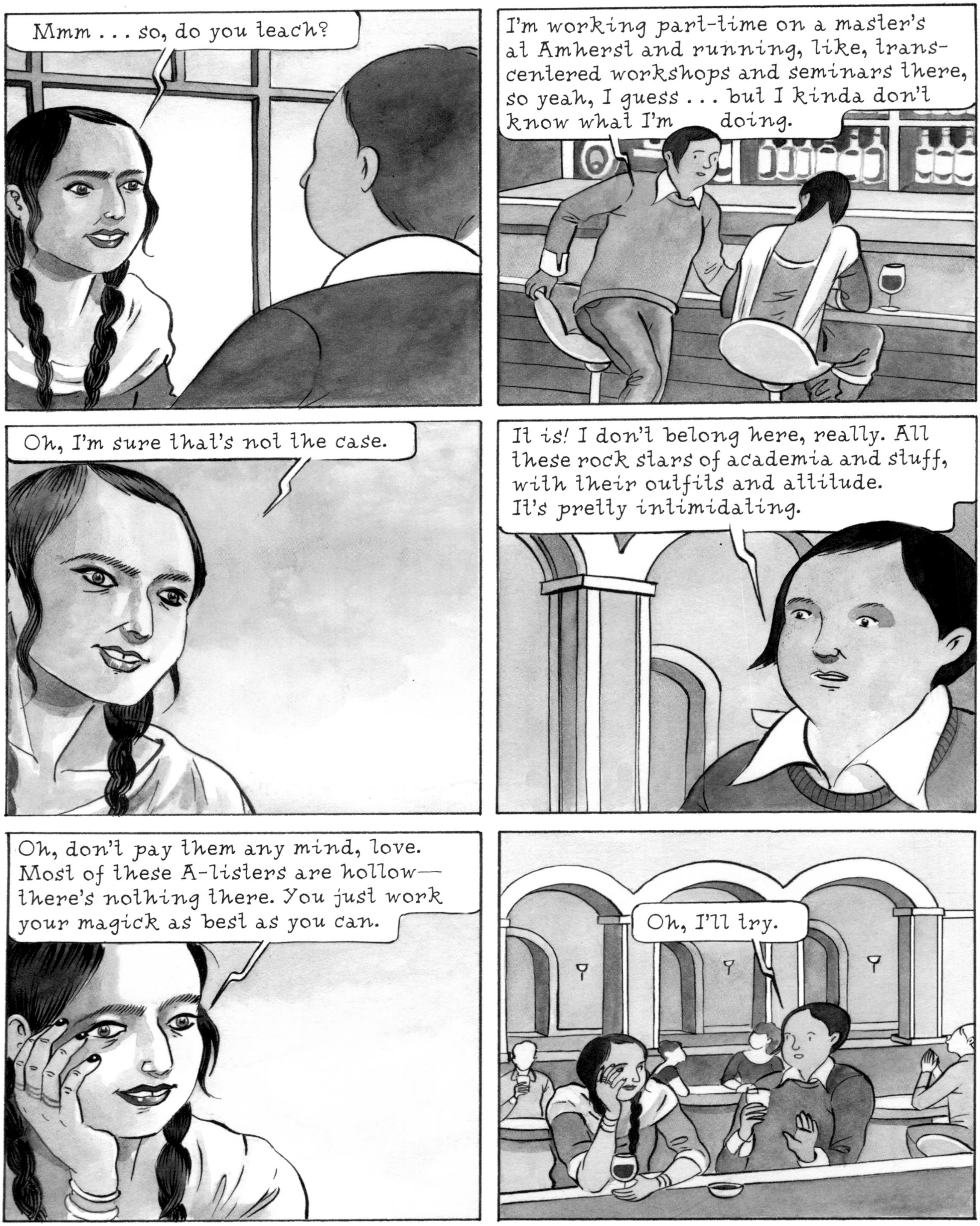
Mmm . . . so, do you teach?
I'm working part-time on a master's at Amherst and running, like, trans-centered workshops and seminars there, so yeah, I guess . . . but I kinda don't know what I'm doing.
Oh, I'm sure that's not the case.
It is! I don't belong here, really. All these rock stars of academia and stuff, with their outfits and attitude. It's pretty intimidating.
Oh, don't pay them any mind, love. Most of these A-listers are hollow— there's nothing there. You just work your magick as best as you can.
Oh, I'll try.

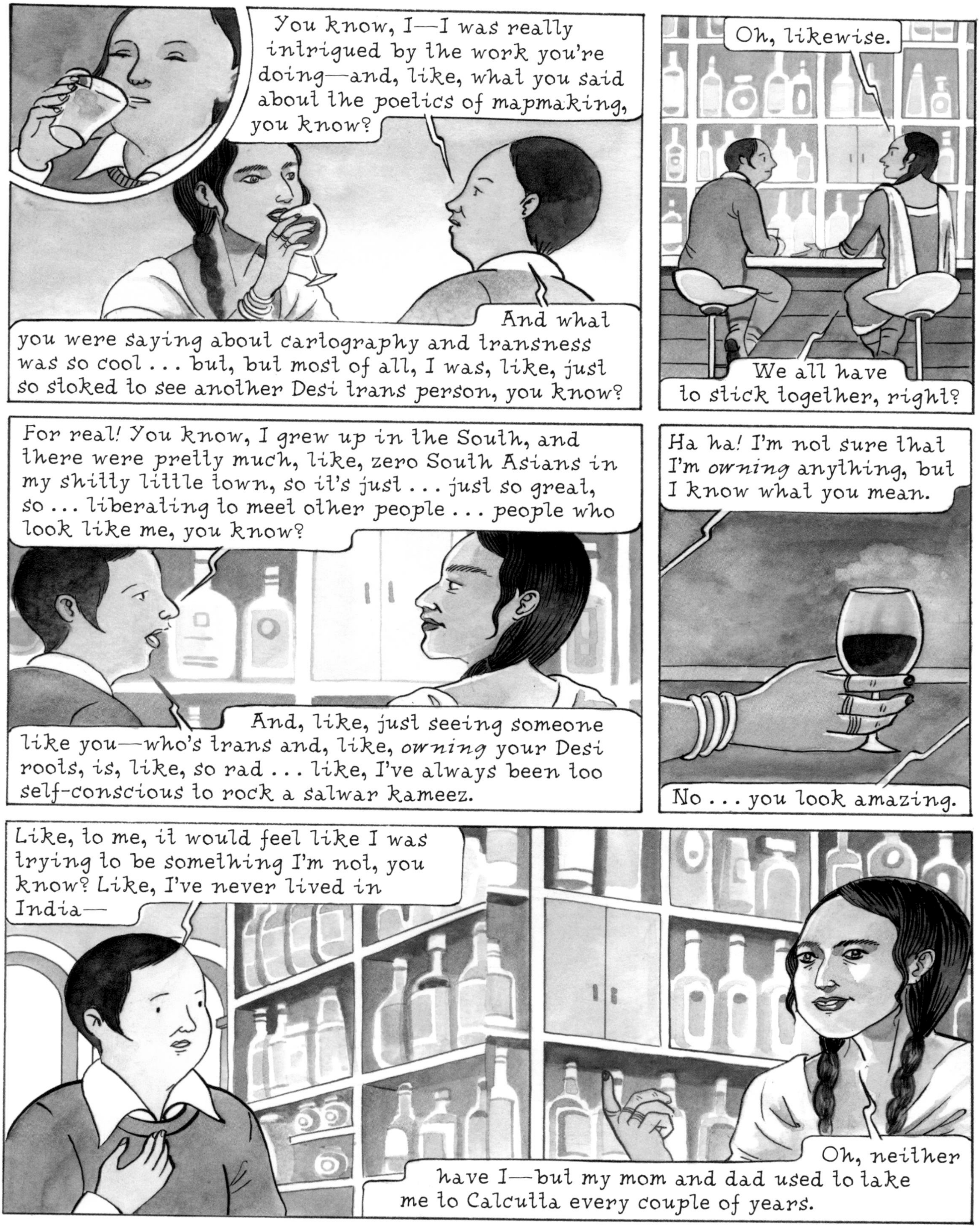
You know, I—I was really intrigued by the work you're doing—and, like, what you said about the poetics of mapmaking, you know?
And what you were saying about cartography and transness was so cool . . . but, but most of all, I was, like, just so stoked to see another Desi trans person, you know?
Oh, likewise.
We all have to stick together, right?
For real! You know, I grew up in the South, and there were pretty much, like, zero South Asians in my shitty little town, so it's just . . . just so great, so . . . liberating to meet other people . . . people who look like me, you know?
And, like, just seeing someone like you—who's trans and, like, *owning* your Desi roots, is, like, so rad . . . like, I've always been too self-conscious to rock a salwar kameez.
Ha ha! I'm not sure that I'm *owning* anything, but I know what you mean.
No . . . you look amazing.
Like, to me, it would feel like I was trying to be something I'm not, you know? Like, I've never lived in India—
Oh, neither have I—but my mom and dad used to take me to Calcutta every couple of years.

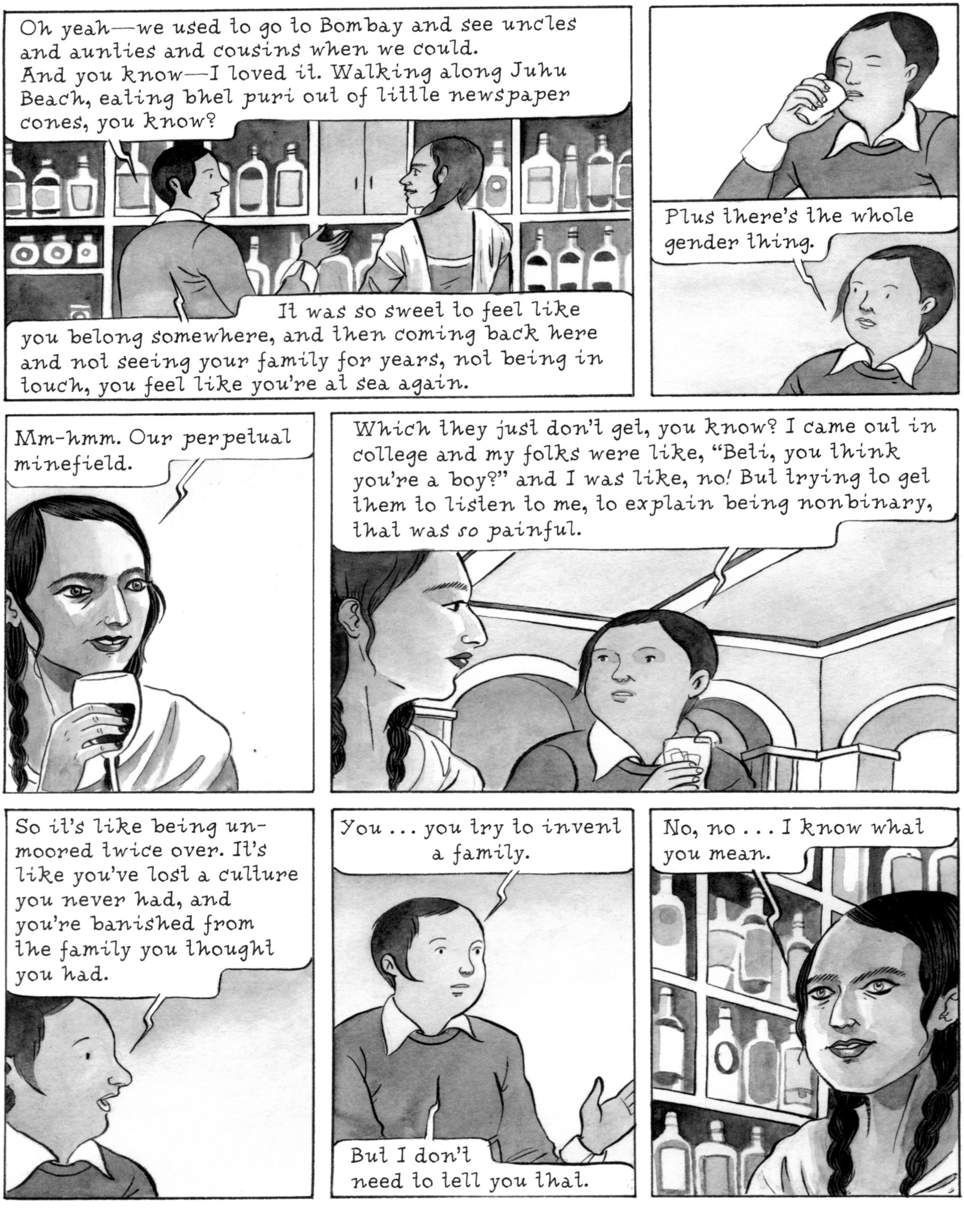
Oh yeah—we used to go to Bombay and see uncles and aunties and cousins when we could. And you know—I loved it. Walking along Juhu Beach, eating bhel *puri* out of little newspaper cones, you know?
It was so sweet to feel like you belong somewhere, and then coming back here and not seeing your family for years, not being in touch, you feel like you're at sea again.
Plus there's the whole gender thing.
Mm-hmm. Our perpetual minefield.
Which they just don't get, you know? I came out in college and my folks were like, "Beti, you think you're a boy?" and I was like, no! But trying to get them to listen to me, to explain being nonbinary, that was so painful.
So it's like being unmoored twice over. It's like you've lost a culture you never had, and you're banished from the family you thought you had.
You ... you try to invent a family.
But I don't need to tell you that.
No, no . . . I know what you mean.

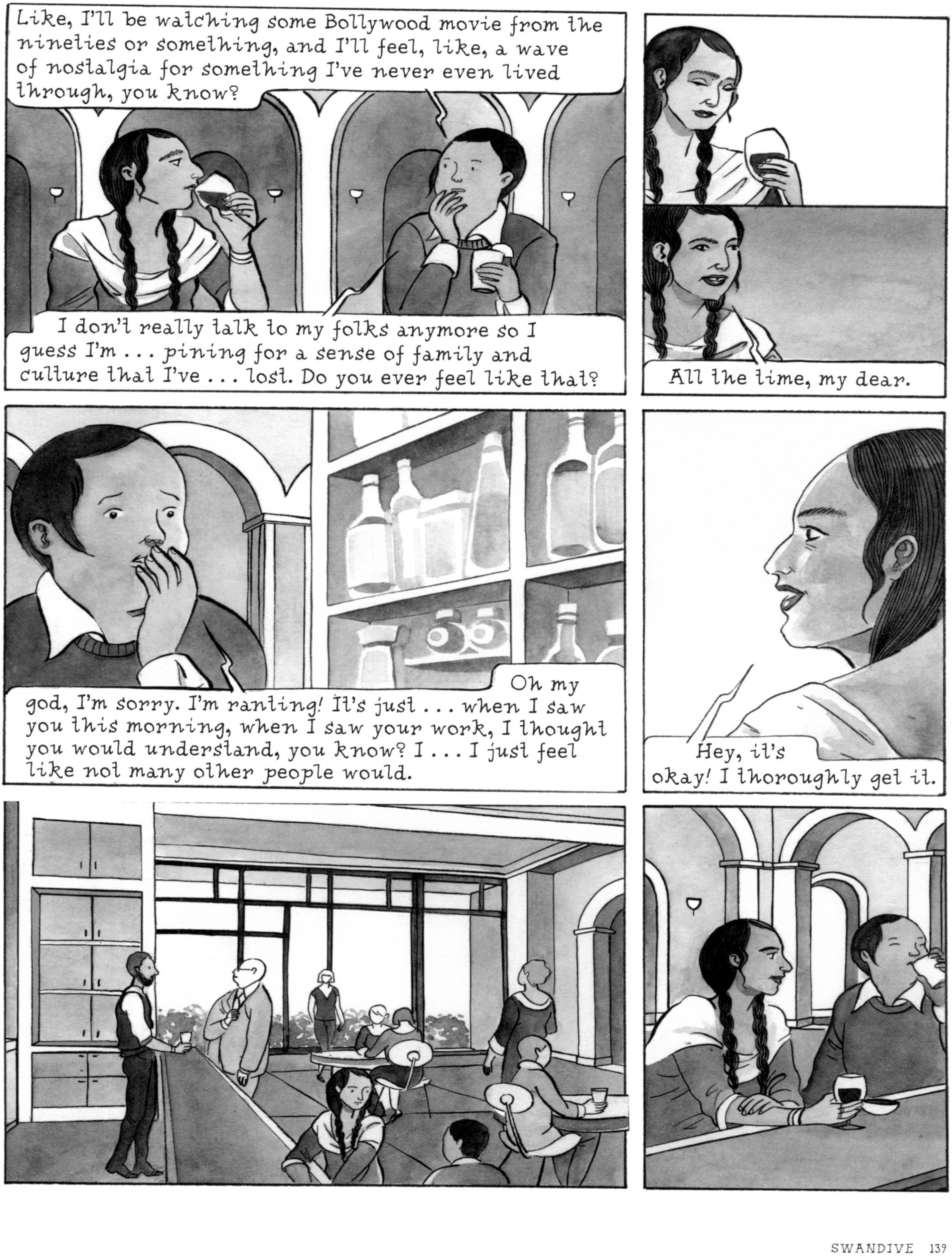
Like, I'll be watching some Bollywood movie from the nineties or something, and I'll feel, like, a wave of nostalgia for something I've never even lived through, you know?
I don't really talk to my folks anymore so I guess I'm . . . pining for a sense of family and culture that I've . . . lost. Do you ever feel like that?
All the time, my dear.
Oh my god, I'm sorry. I'm ranting! It's just . . . when I saw you this morning, when I saw your work, I thought you would understand, you know? I . . . I just feel like not many other people would.
Hey, it's okay! I thoroughly get it.

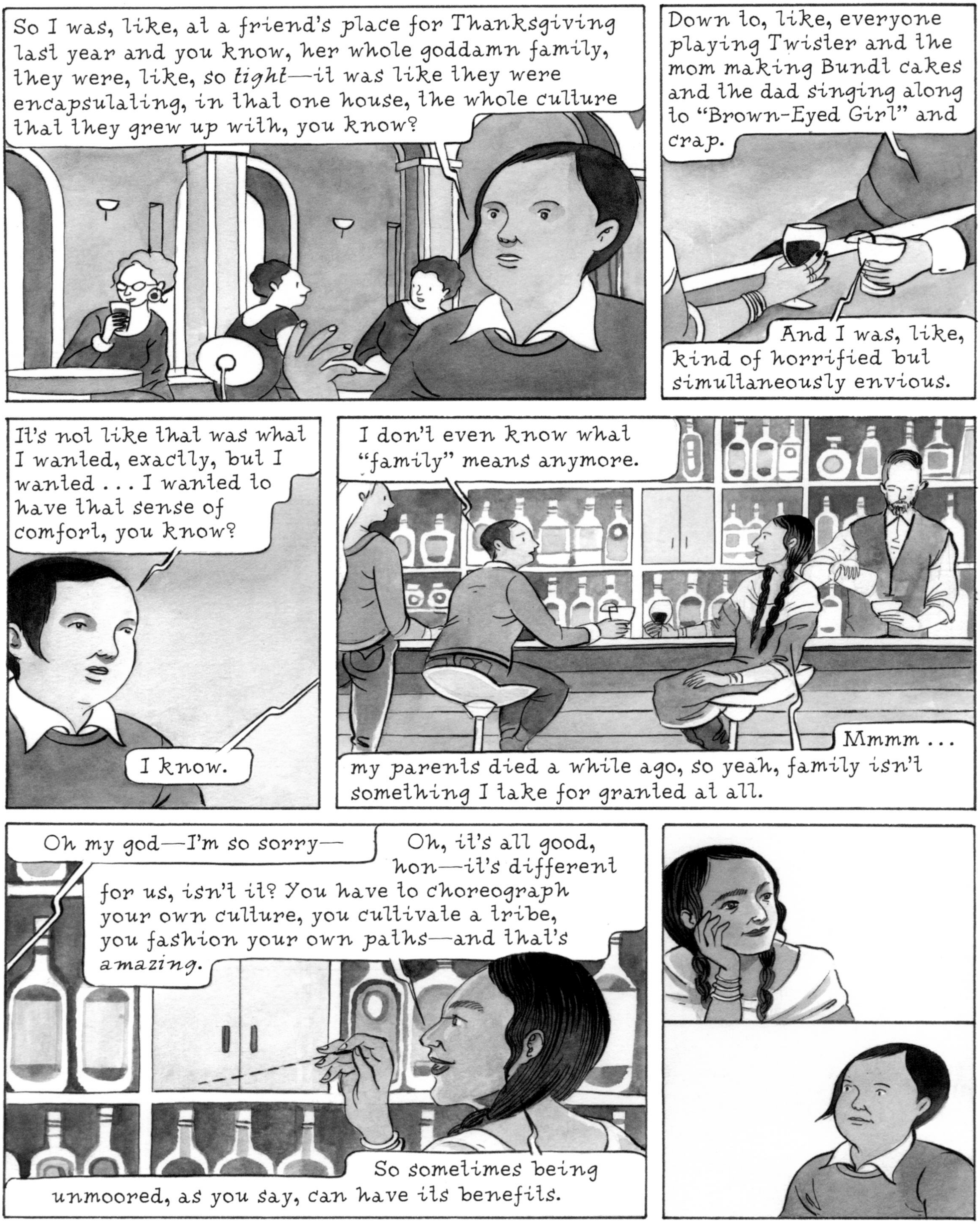
So I was, like, at a friend's place for Thanksgiving last year and you know, her whole goddamn family, they were, like, so *tight*—it was like they were encapsulating, in that one house, the whole culture that they grew up with, you know?
Down to, like, everyone playing Twister and the mom making Bundt cakes and the dad singing along to "Brown-Eyed Girl" and crap.
And I was, like, kind of horrified but simultaneously envious.
It's not like that was what I wanted, exactly, but I wanted . . . I wanted to have that sense of comfort, you know?
I know.
I don't even know what "family" means anymore.
Mmmm . . .
my parents died a while ago, so yeah, family isn't something I take for granted at all.
Oh my god—I'm so sorry—
Oh, it's all good, hon—it's different for us, isn't it? You have to choreograph your own culture, you cultivate a tribe, you fashion your own paths—and that's *amazing*.
So sometimes being unmoored, as you say, can have its benefits.

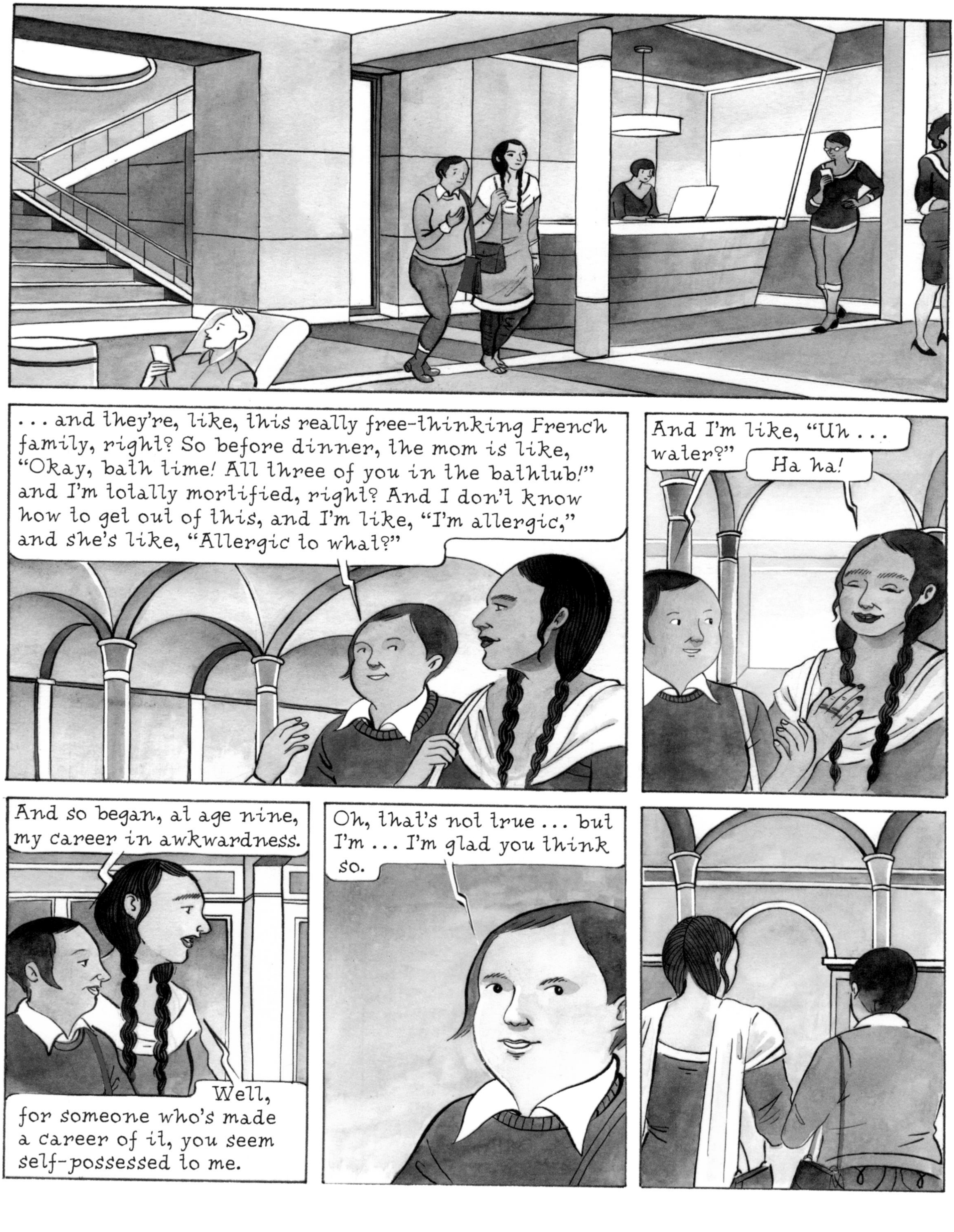
. . . and they're, like, this really free-thinking French family, right? So before dinner, the mom is like, "Okay, bath time! All three of you in the bathtub!" and I'm totally mortified, right? And I don't know how to get out of this, and I'm like, "I'm allergic," and she's like, "Allergic to what?"
And I'm like, "Uh . . . water?"
Ha ha!
And so began, at age nine, my career in awkwardness.
Well, for someone who's made a career of it, you seem self-possessed to me.
Oh, that's not true . . . but I'm . . . I'm glad you think so.

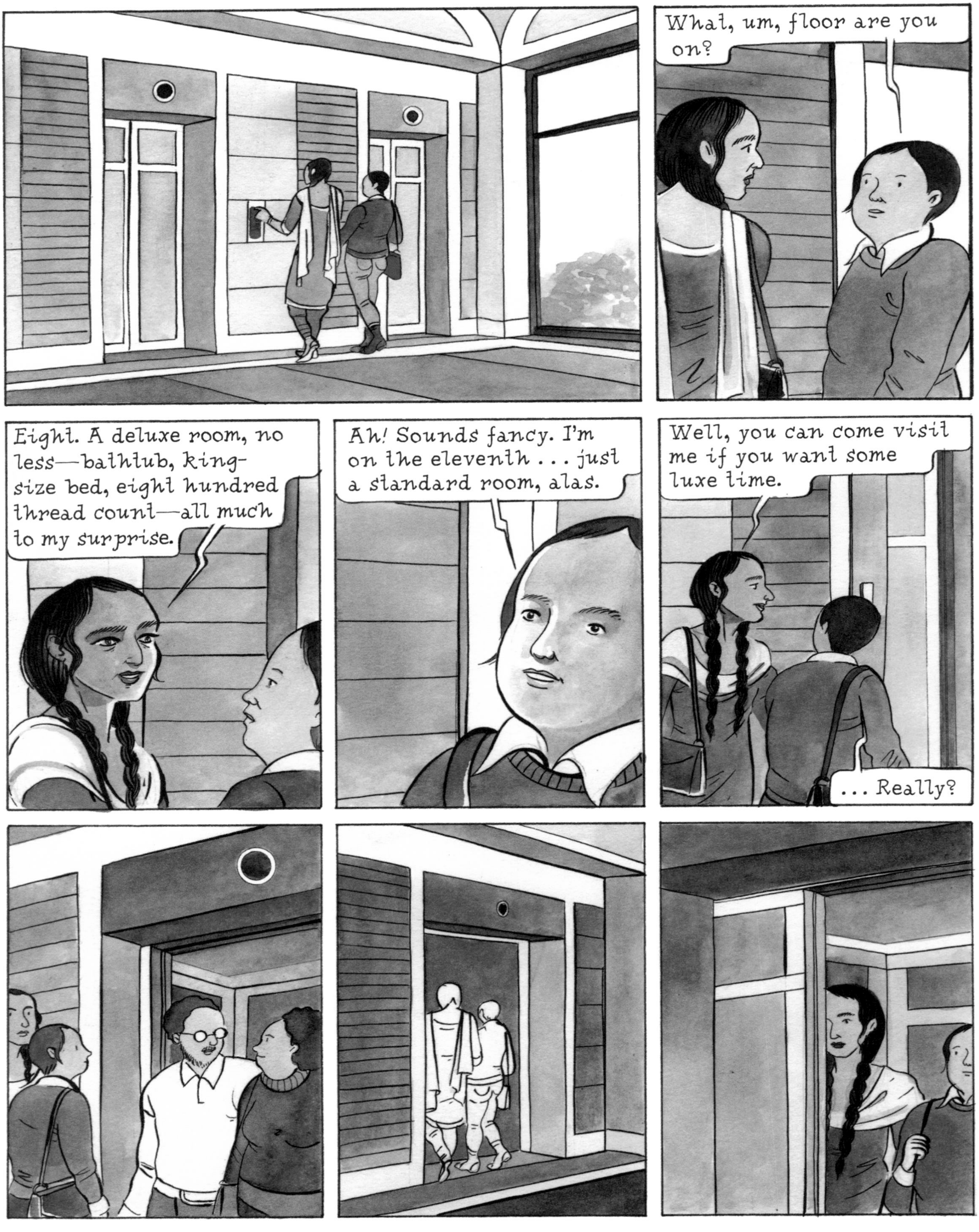
What, um, floor are you on?
Eight. A deluxe room, no less—bathtub, king-size bed, eight hundred thread count—all much to my surprise.
Ah! Sounds fancy. I'm on the eleventh . . . just a standard room, alas.
Well, you can come visit me if you want some luxe time.
. . . Really?

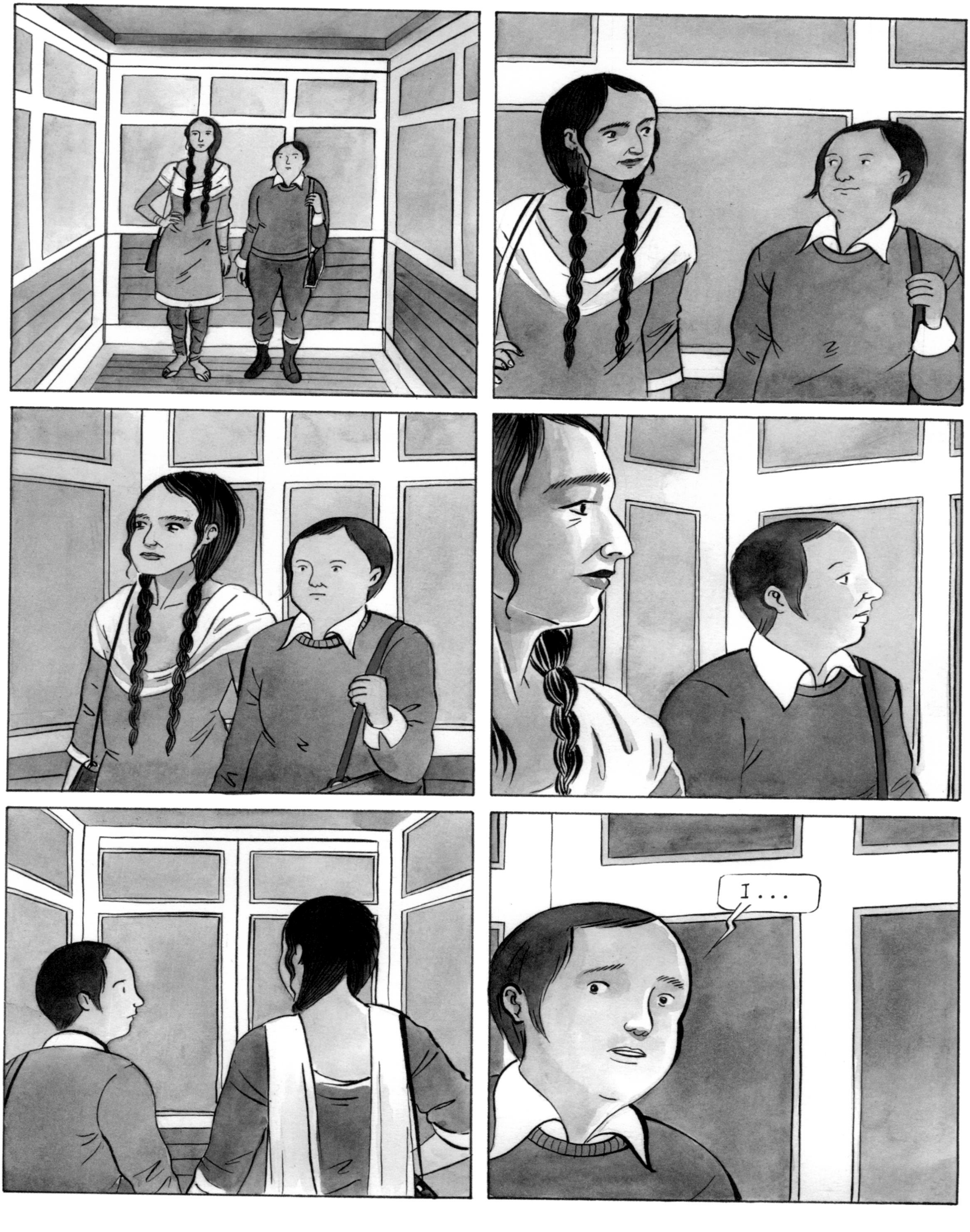
I...

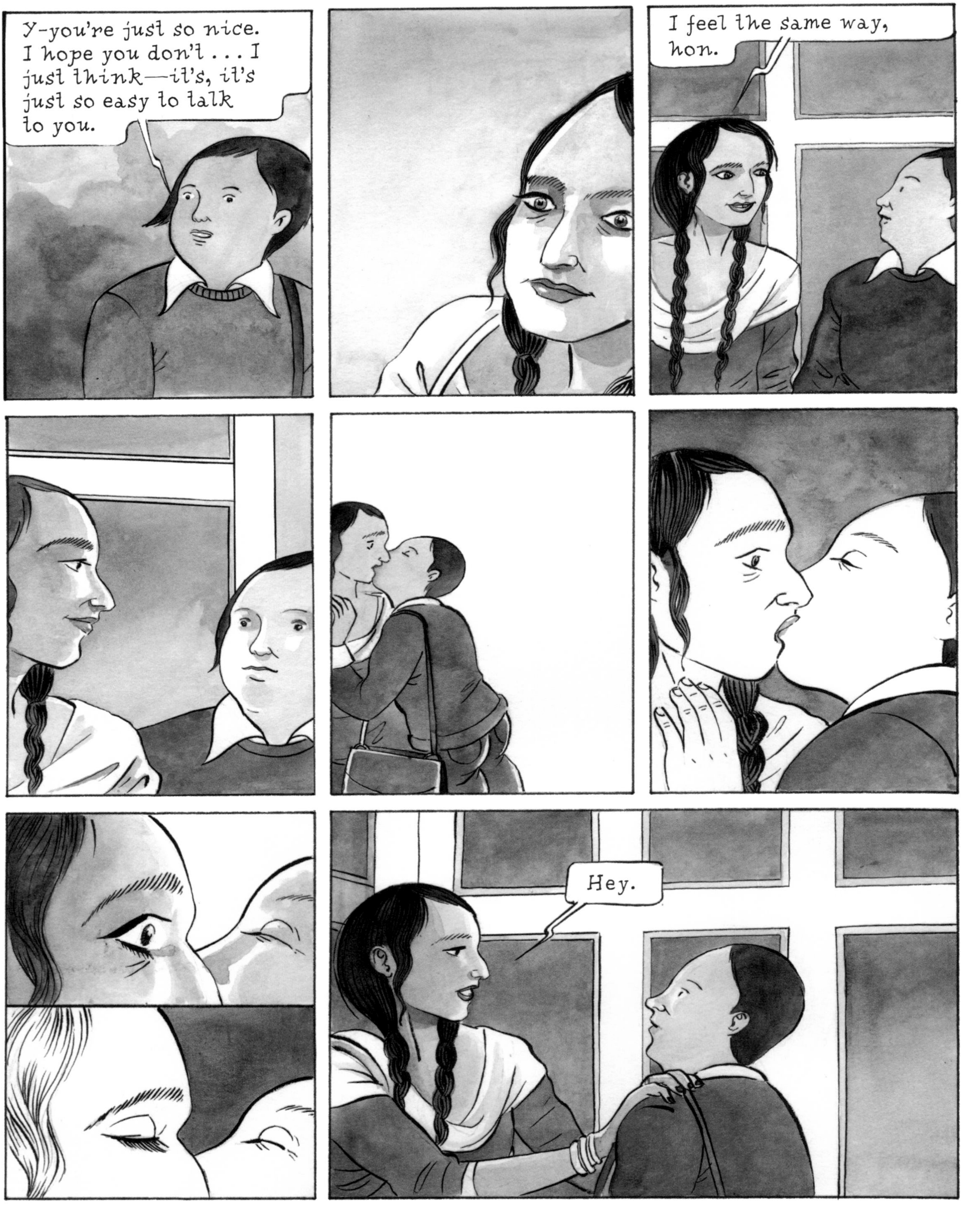
Y-you're just so nice. I hope you don't . . . I just think—it's, it's just so easy to talk to you.
I feel the same way, hon.
Hey.

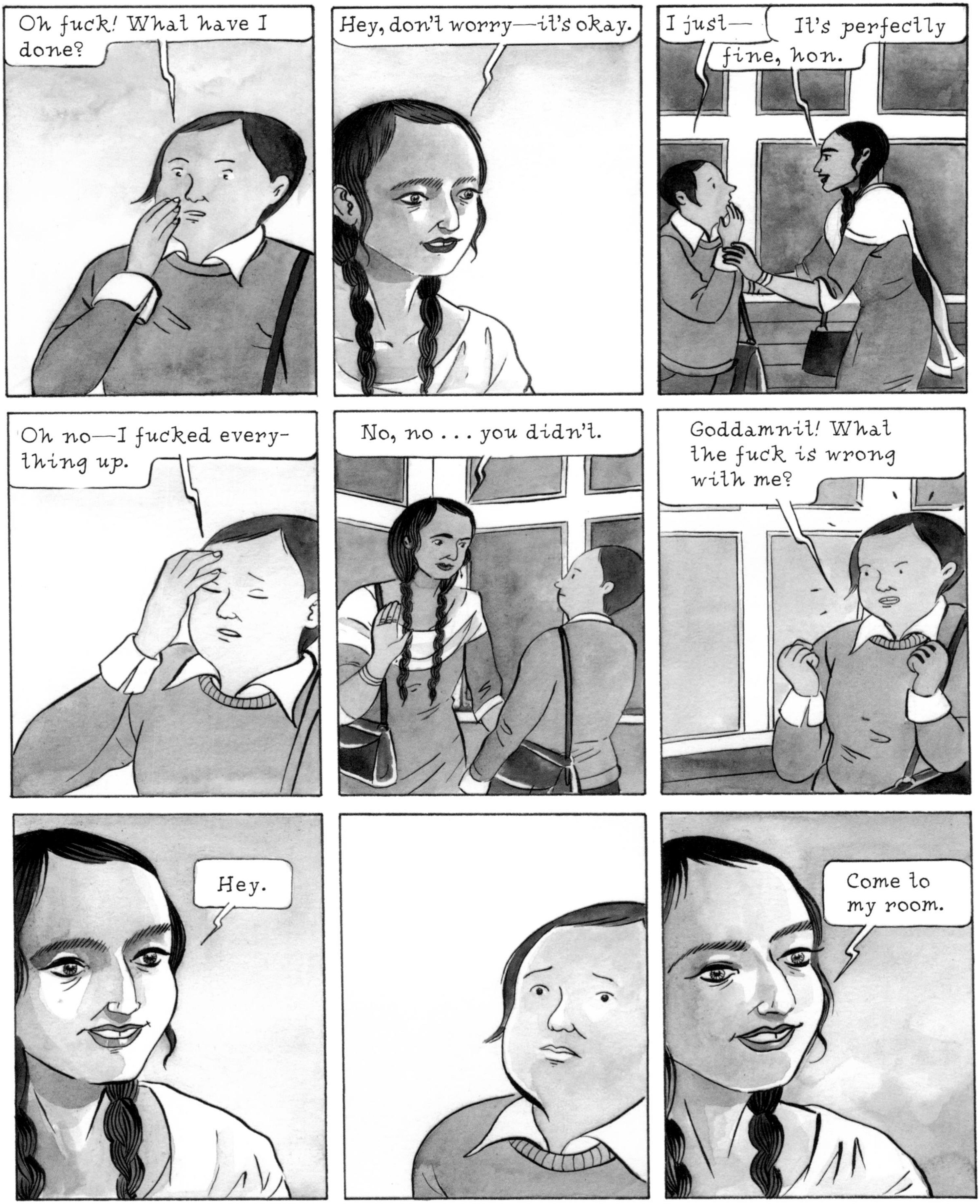
Oh fuck! What have I done?
Hey, don't worry—it's okay.
I just—
It's perfectly fine, hon.
Oh no—I fucked every-thing up.
No, no . . . you didn't.
Goddamnit! What the fuck is wrong with me?
Hey.
Come to my room.

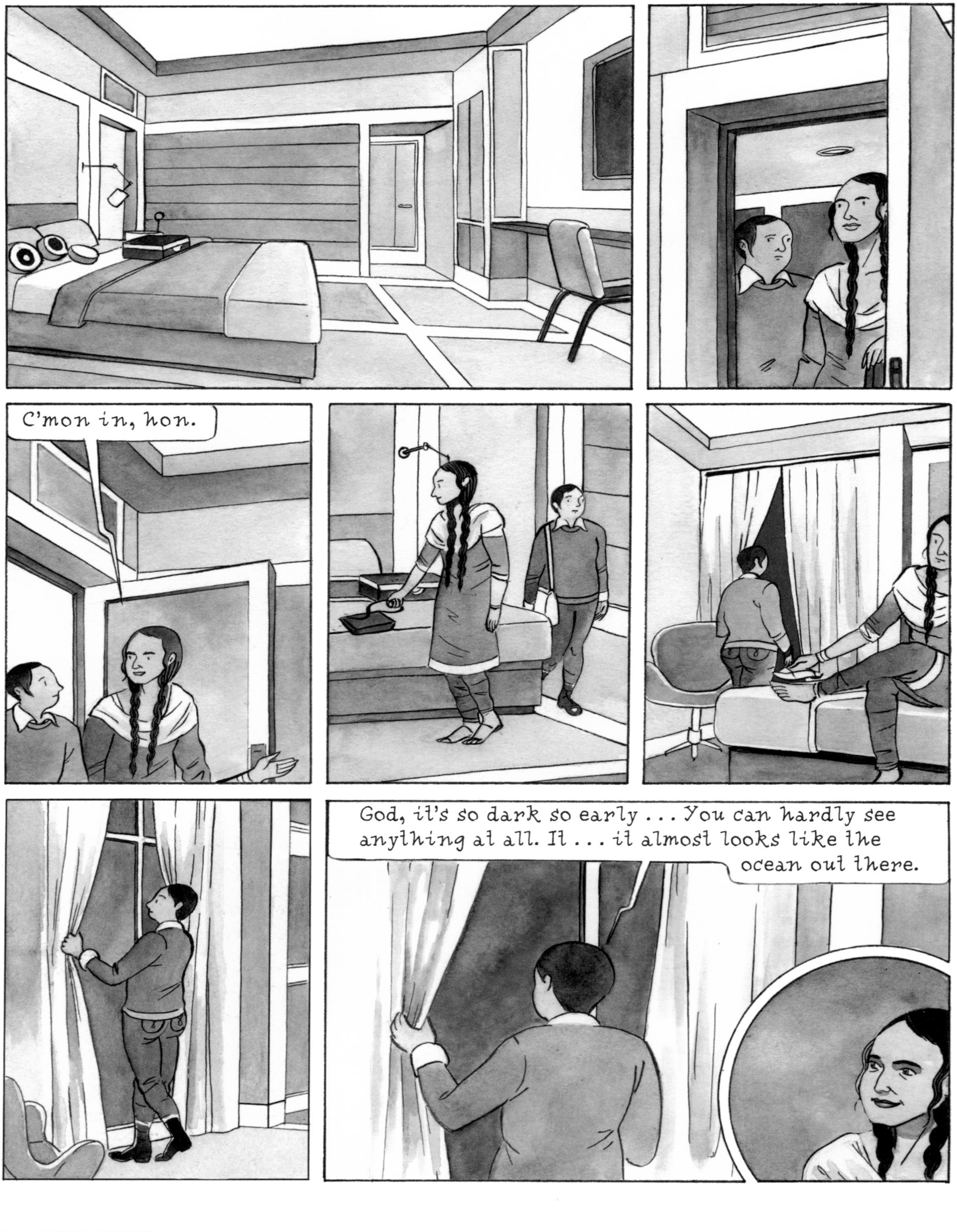
C'mon in, hon.
God, it's so dark so early . . . You can hardly see anything at all. It . . . it almost looks like the ocean out there.

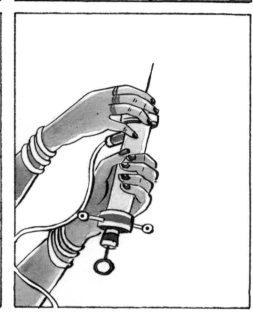

It's so strange ... you can't even see the city lights.

Hey, I want to show you something.

Holy shit! What the hell are you doing?

Wh—what—what's going on?

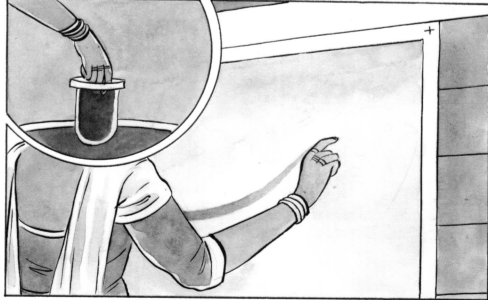

It's fine, hon—don't worry.

But how . . . ?

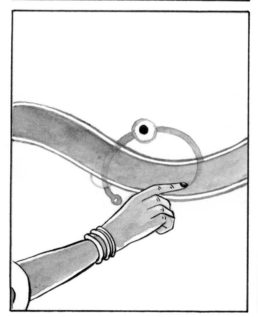

Maybe . . . this is the hub of the river, which runs east-west? There are coots and swans basking and sunning themselves.

Students, nomads, grannies having lunch on its banks. What do you think we should call it?

What? What are you doing —?

What's the name of the river?

What do you mean?

I mean, let's call it something.

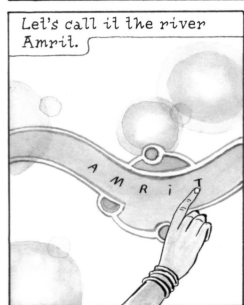

Oh my god—I don't understand what you're doing . . .

Let's call it the river Amrit.

And here, accessed by a narrow pedestrian bridge, is an island with record stores and a penny arcade, where they sell the best ice cream.

The bridge on the north bank leads to a round-about, surrounding a small park. Maybe there's a gang of trans girls who play soccer there on Sunday afternoons.

y—your arm...?

This avenue leads to a piazza—there's an alleé of bodhi trees, patches of neem, tulsi, rajani-gandha. Five streets that lead to different quadrants of the city.

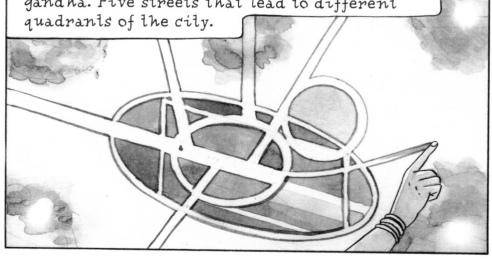

Ah—are you okay?

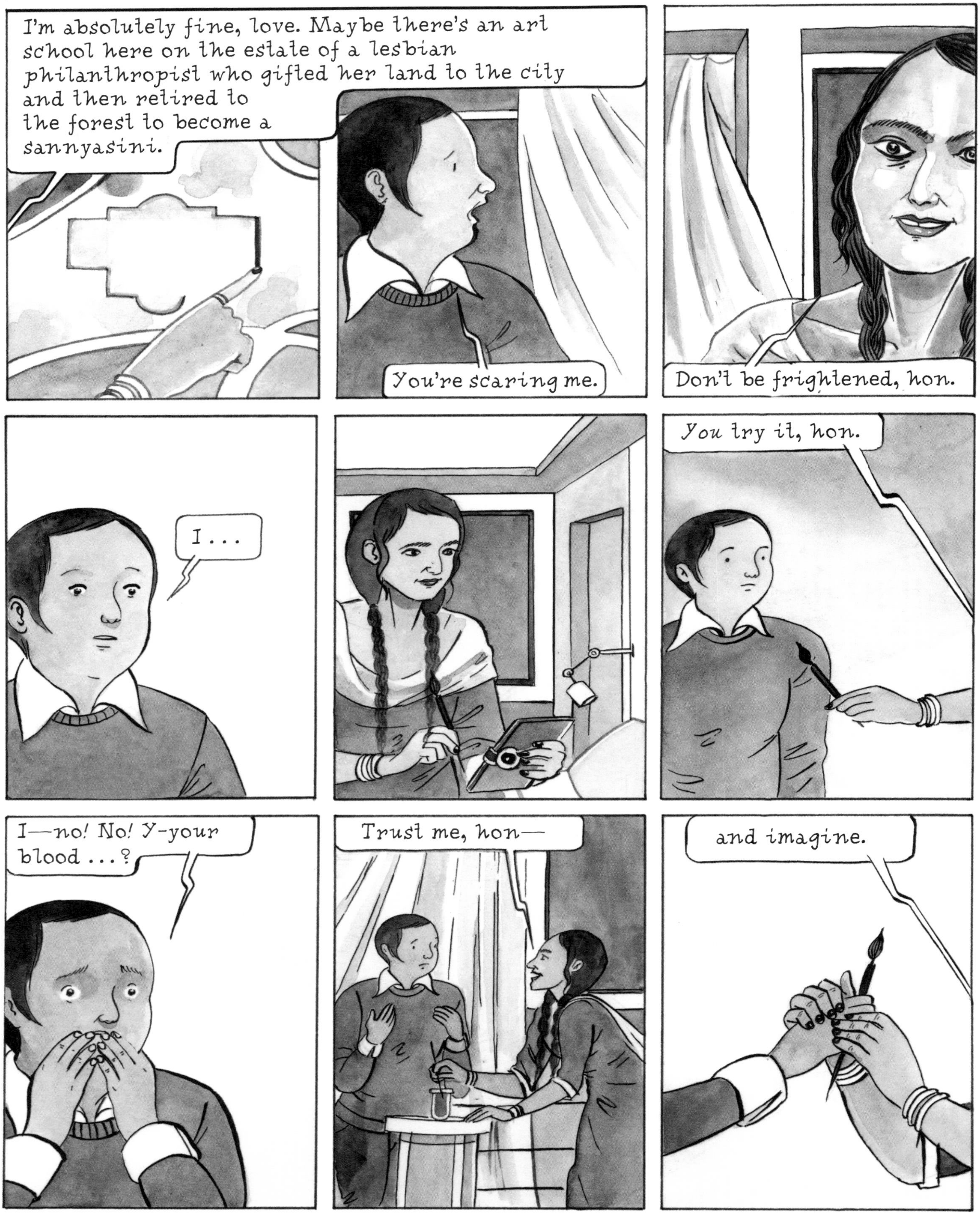
I'm absolutely fine, love. Maybe there's an art school here on the estate of a lesbian philanthropist who gifted her land to the city and then retired to the forest to become a sannyasini.
You're scaring me.
Don't be frightened, hon.
I . . .
You try it, hon.
I—*no!* No! Y-your blood . . . ?
Trust me, hon—
and imagine.

Um, okay ... here—here's a public garden where any-one can grow their own vegetables and stuff, and um ... anyone who needs food can have it. And there's a compound which has, um, free housing for trans and gender-nonconforming kids, and they have their own health clinic, a recording studio, and um, a bowling alley?

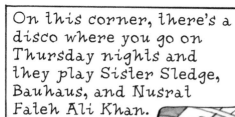

Mmm ...

On this corner, there's a disco where you go on Thursday nights and they play Sister Sledge, Bauhaus, and Nusrat Fateh Ali Khan.

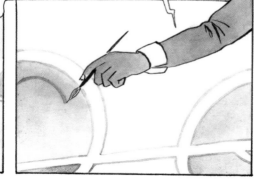

Here's a bohemian neighborhood that's bounded by the river on one side and this boulevard on another. There's a small hotel, a library, a museum of weather. Here's an old abandoned steel factory that's been taken over by a clowder of feral cats.

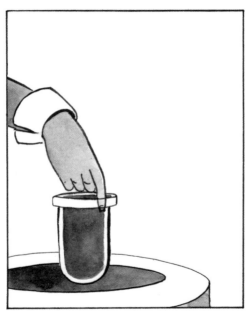

Umm . . . this is where my aunt—maybe her name is Bhabani—lives, across from this park—um, Madhubala Park, in her grand old family home. Sunday afternoons we go over there for tea and sit in a circle and sing ghazals.

Mmm . . . here's an urban beach where you can buy pani puri and stroll in the evenings under fairy lights with your friend Madhuri, who draws comics and smells like motor oil and sandalwood.

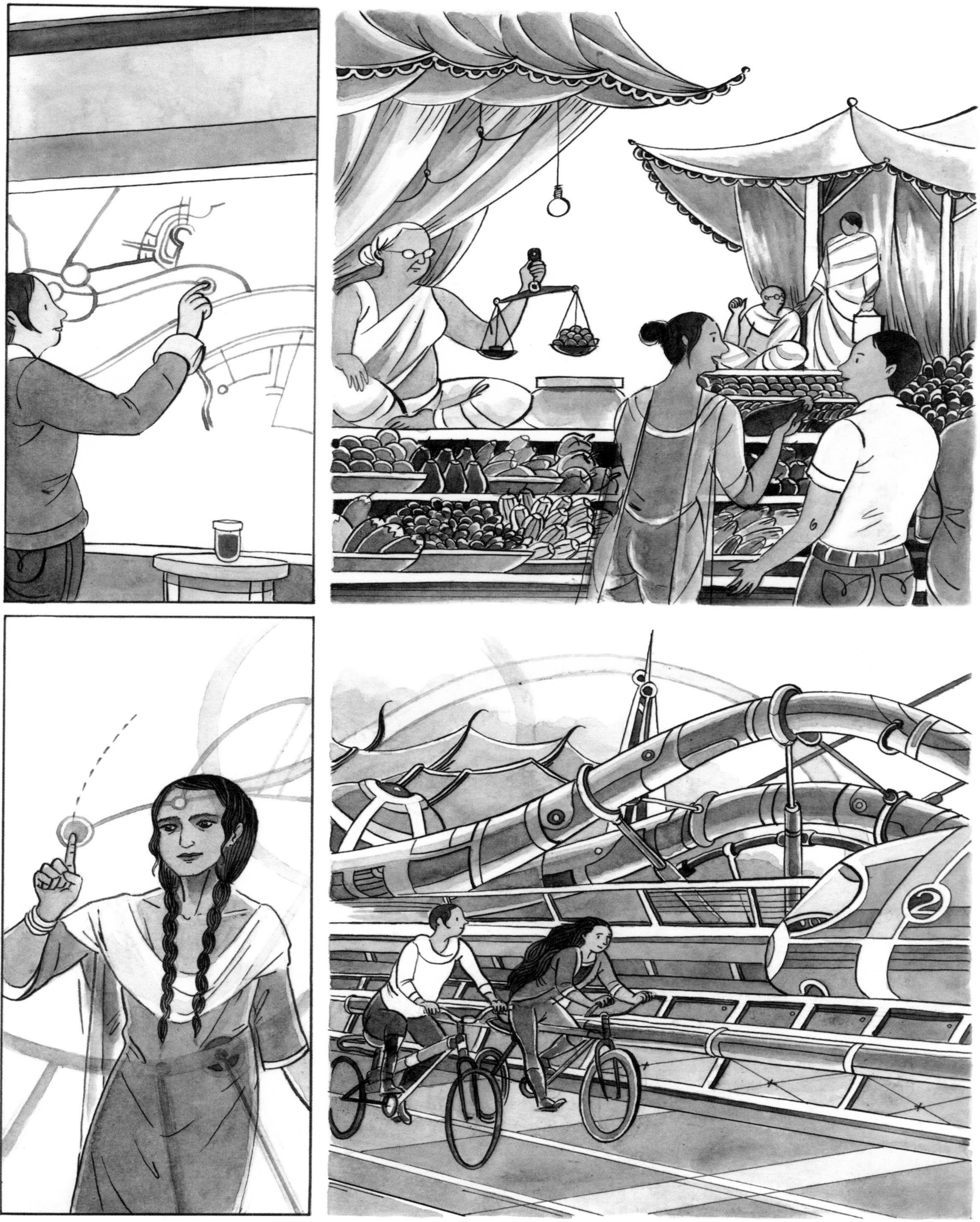

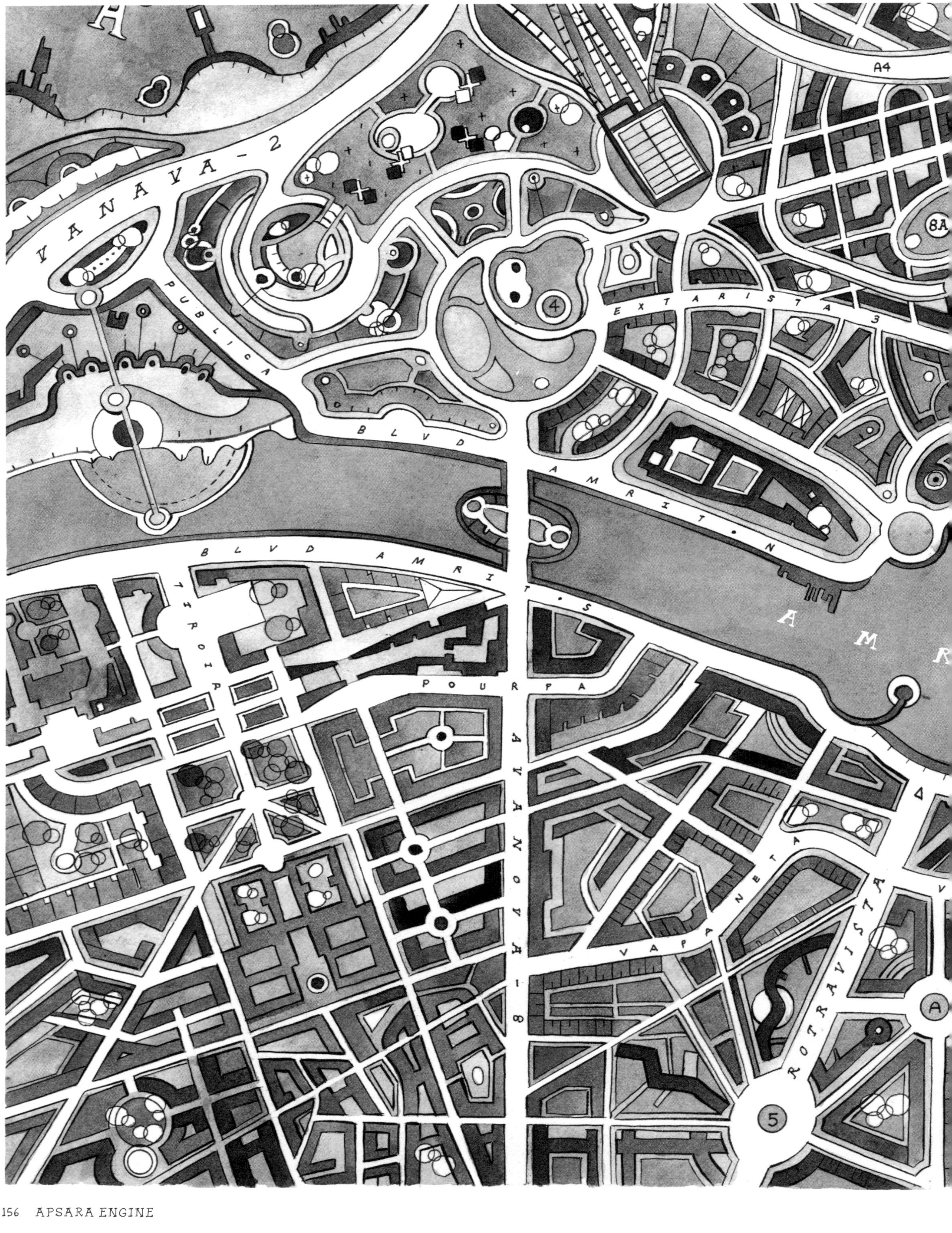
A4
8A
VANAVA-2
PUBLICA
EXTARISTA 3
4
BLVD
AMRIT.N
BLVD AMRIT.S
POURPA
AYANOVA-8
VAPPANETA
ROTRAVISTA
5
A

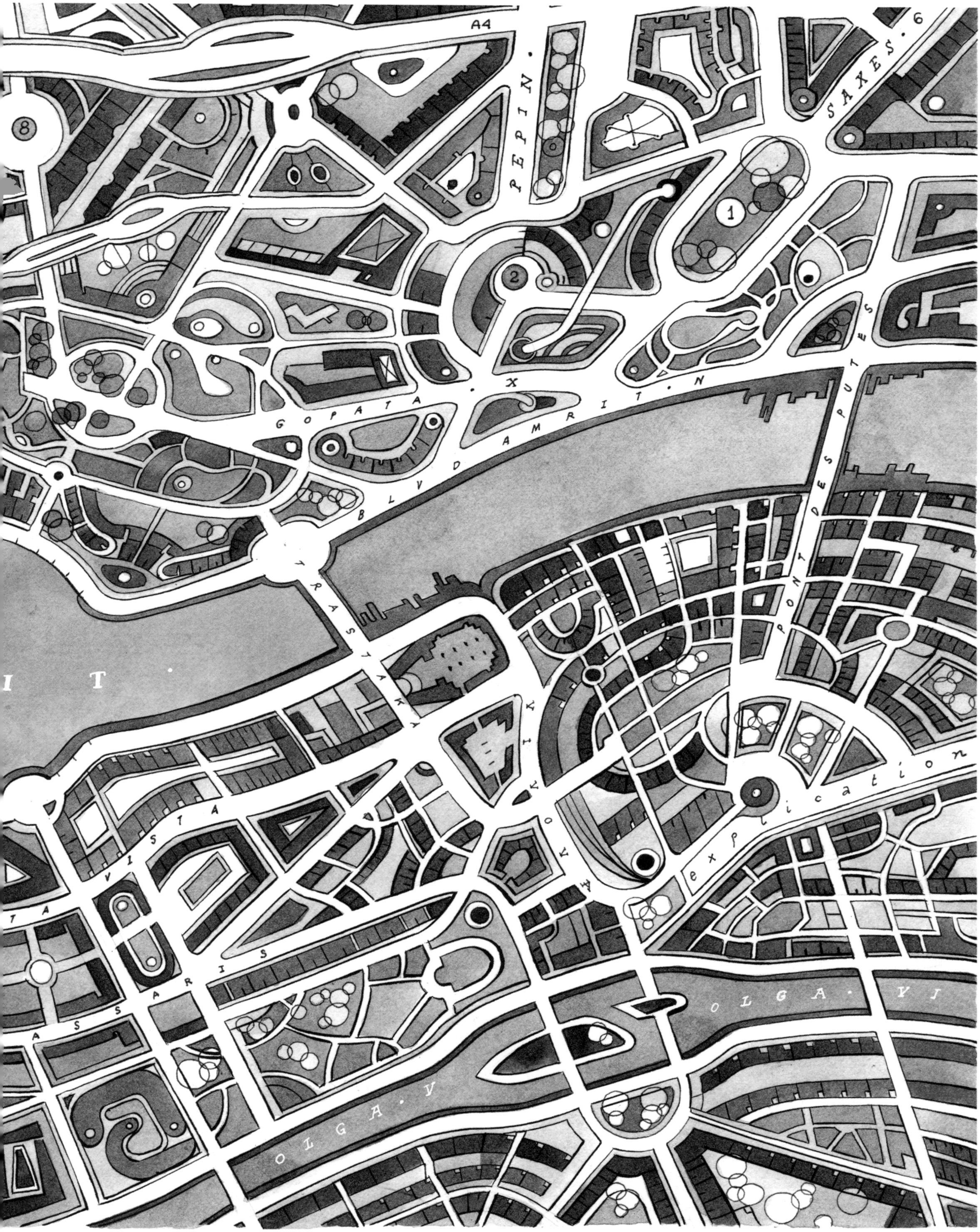
A4
PEPIN
SAXES.6
8
1
2
GOPATA.X
BLVD AMRIT.N
PONT DES PUTES
TRASTAKA
I T
VISTA
TA
ASSARIS
explication
OLGA.VI
OLGA.V

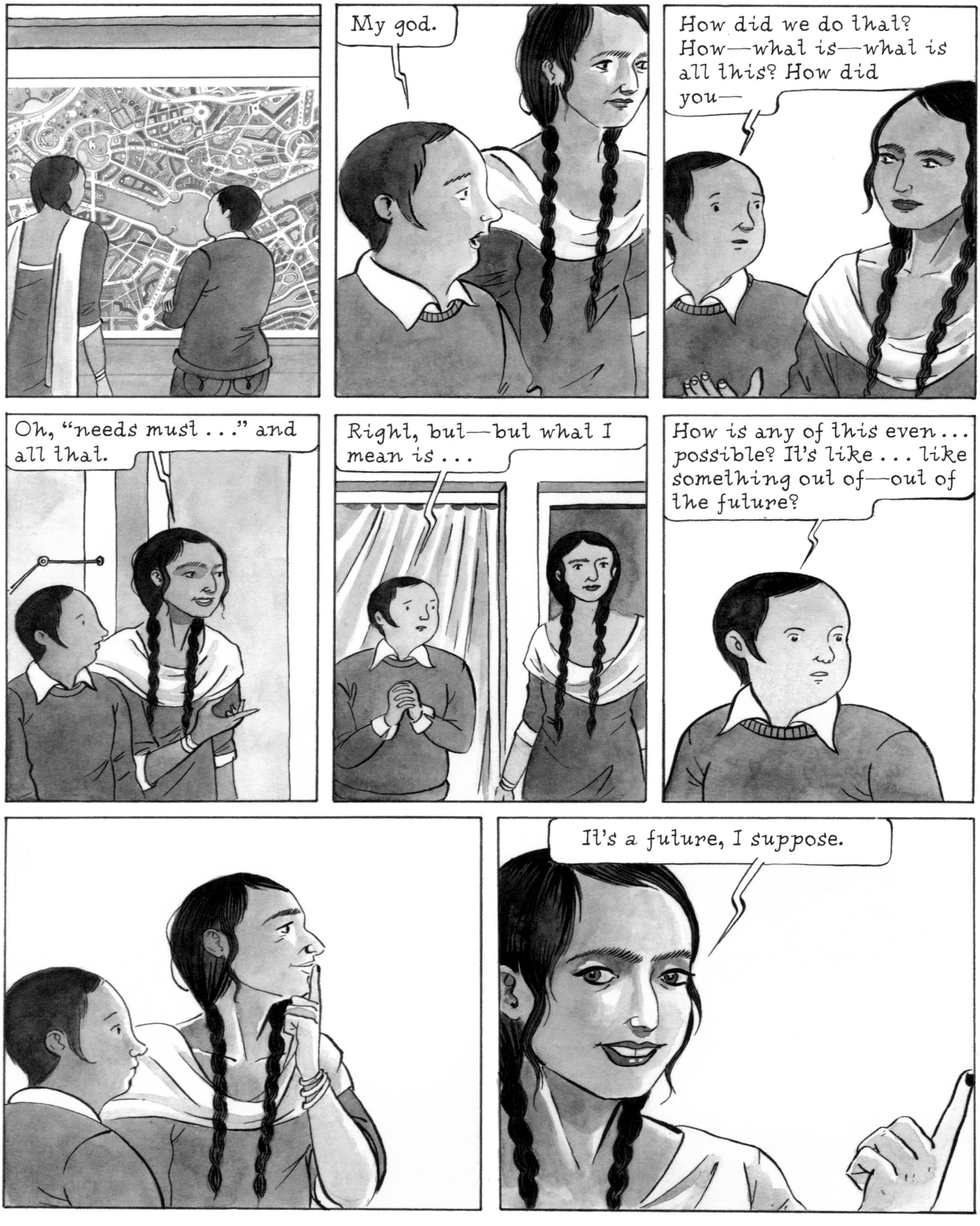
My god.
How did we do that? How—what is—what is all this? How did you—
Oh, "needs must . . ." and all that.
Right, but—but what I mean is . . .
How is any of this even . . . possible? It's like . . . like something out of—out of the future?
It's a future, I suppose.

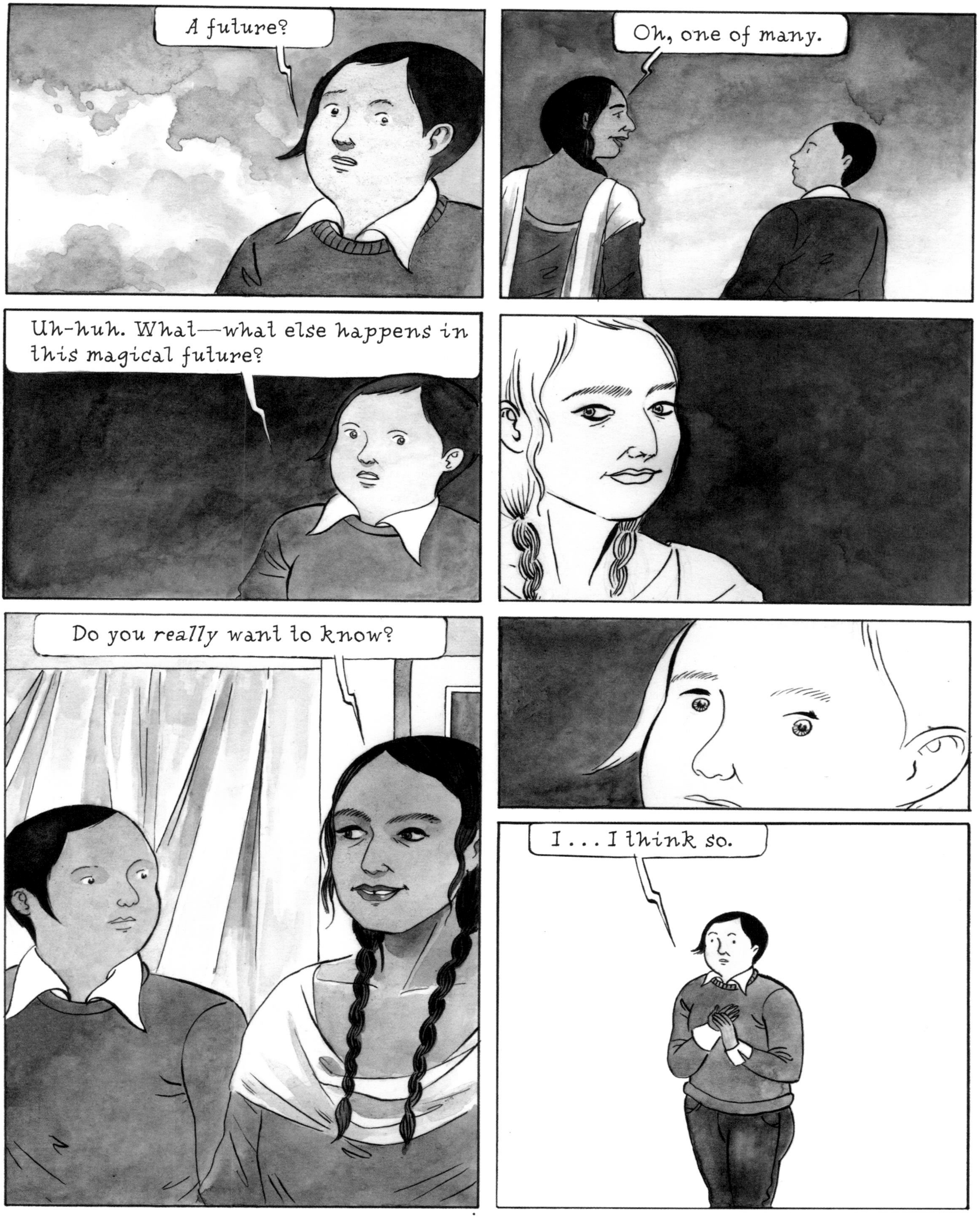
A future?
Oh, one of many.
Uh-huh. What—what else happens in this magical future?
Do you *really* want to know?
I . . . I think so.

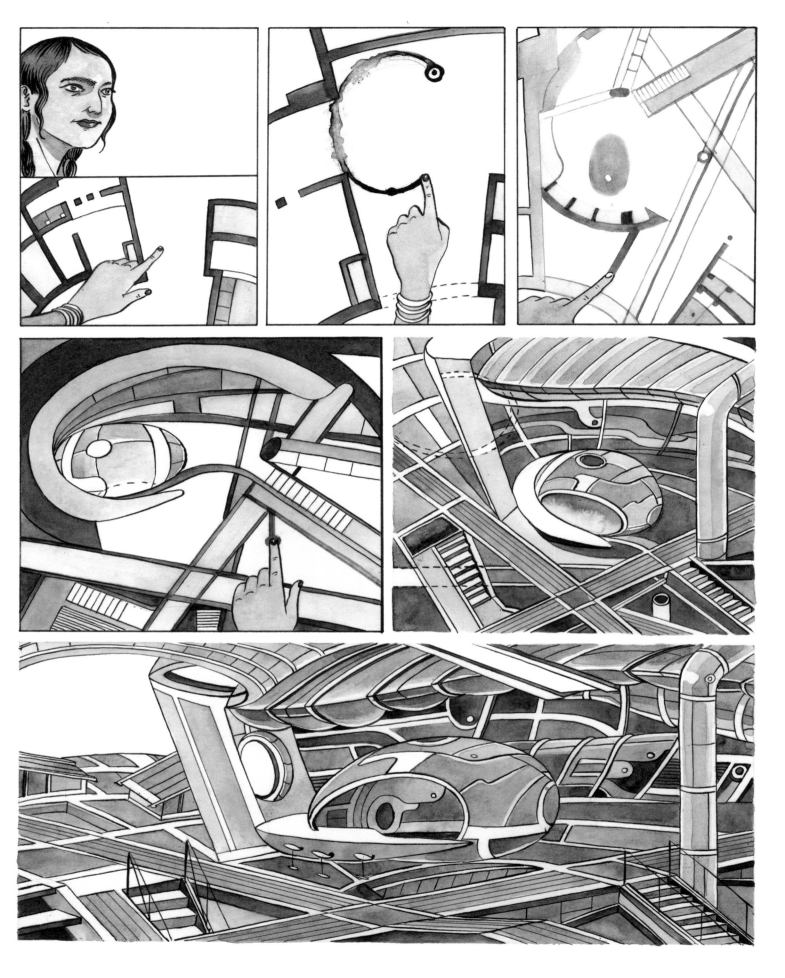

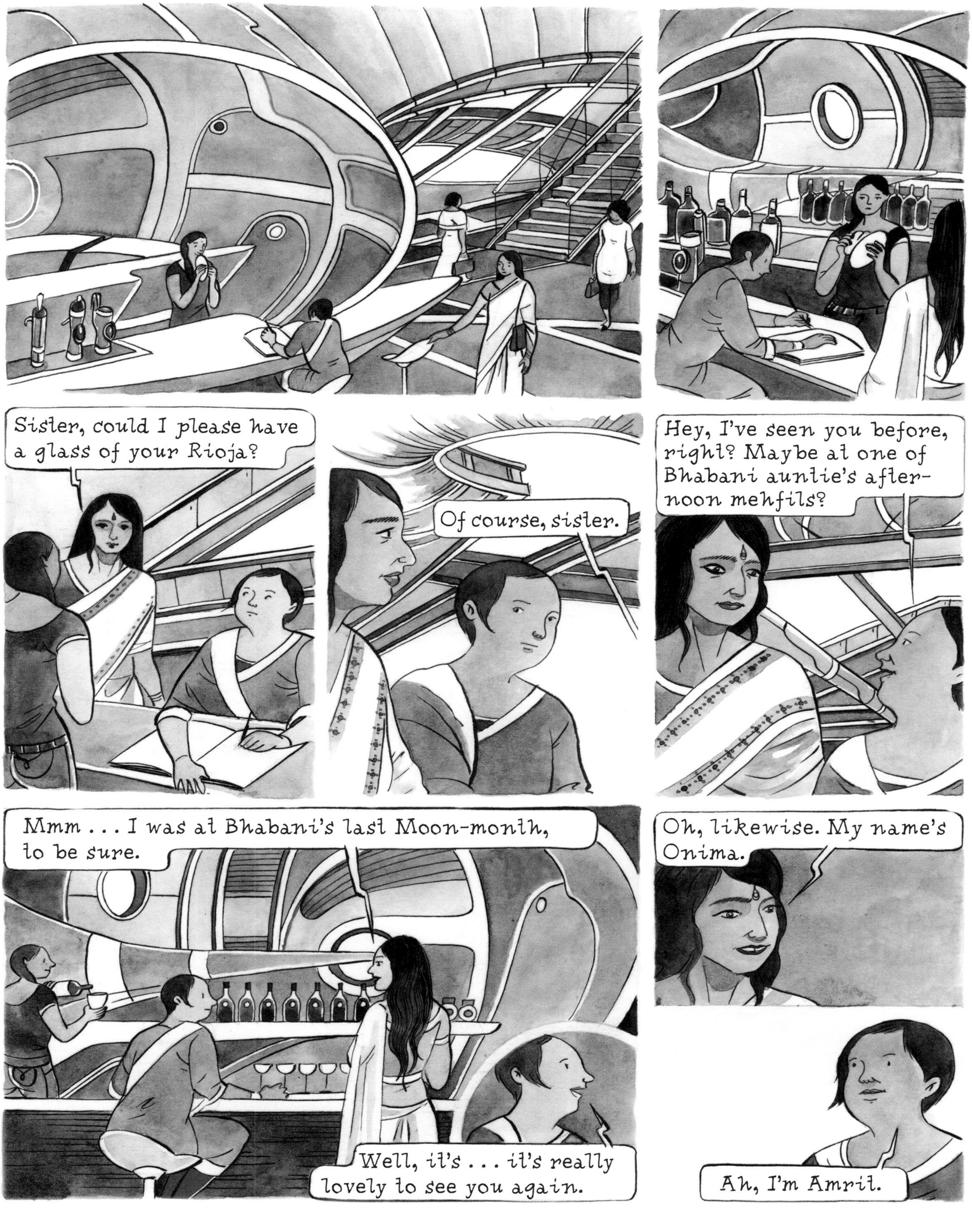
Sister, could I please have a glass of your Rioja?
Of course, sister.
Hey, I've seen you before, right? Maybe at one of Bhabani auntie's after-noon mehfils?
Mmm . . . I was at Bhabani's last Moon-month, to be sure.
Well, it's . . . it's really lovely to see you again.
Oh, likewise. My name's Onima.
Ah, I'm Amrit.

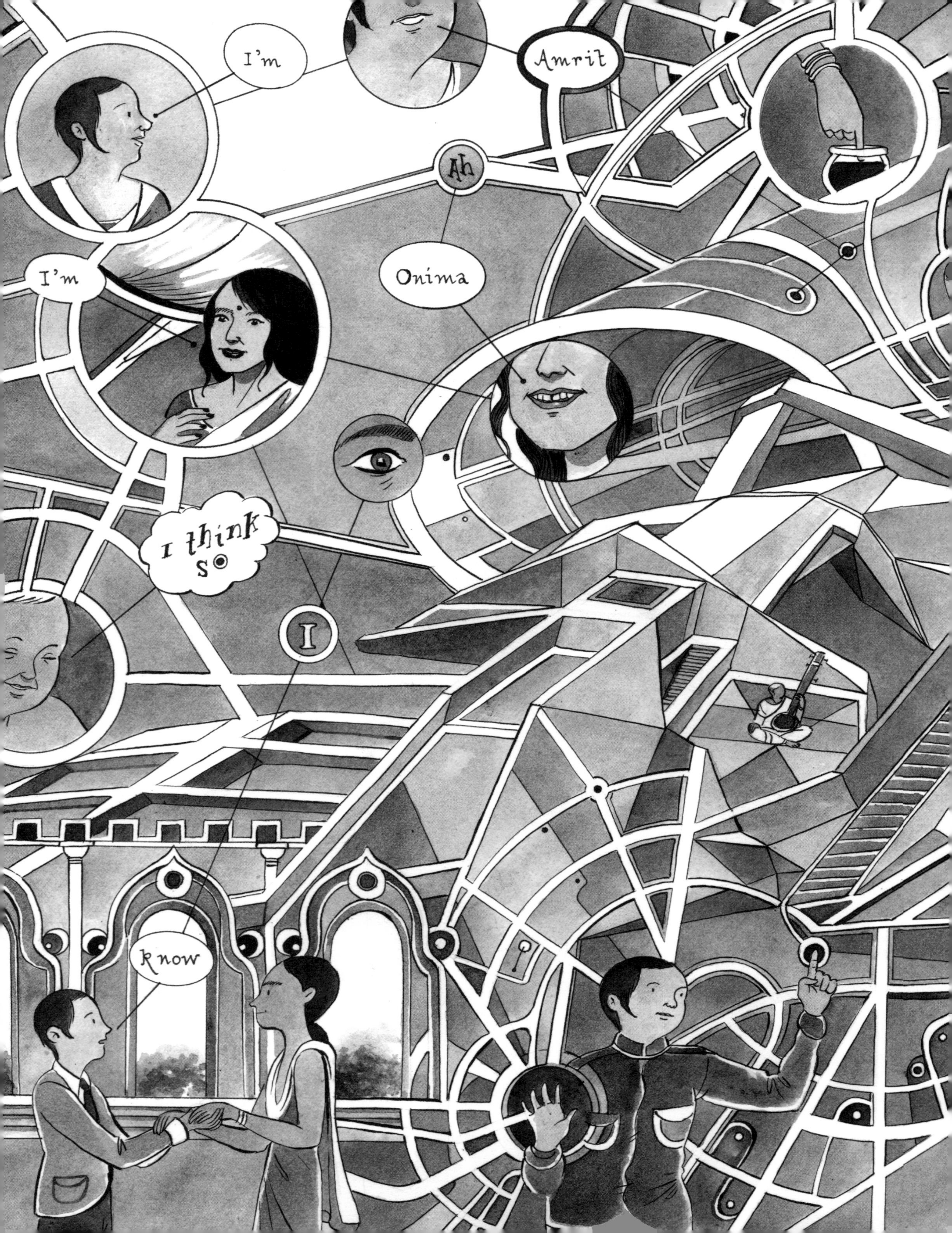
I'm
Amrit
Ah
I'm
Onima
I think so
I
know

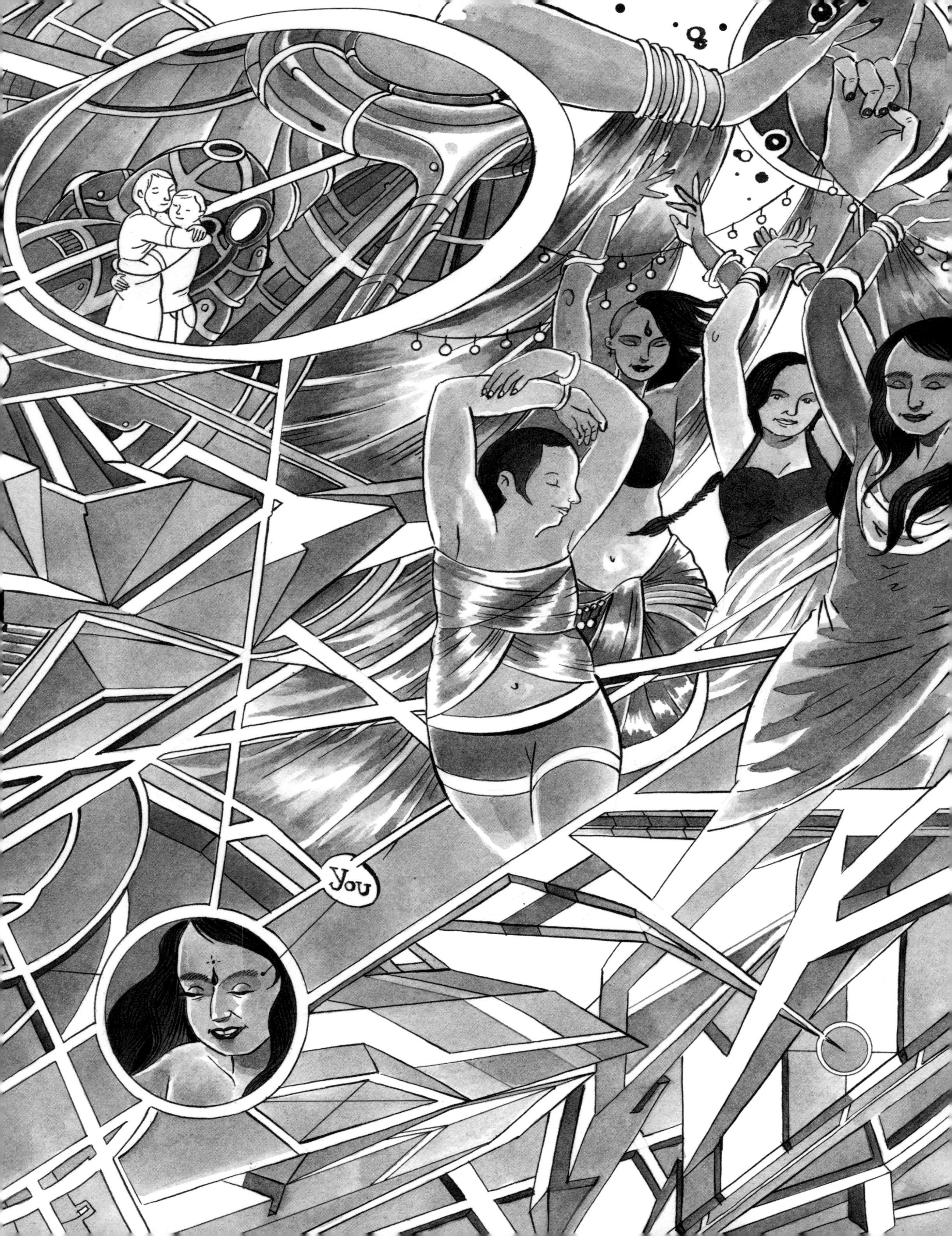
You

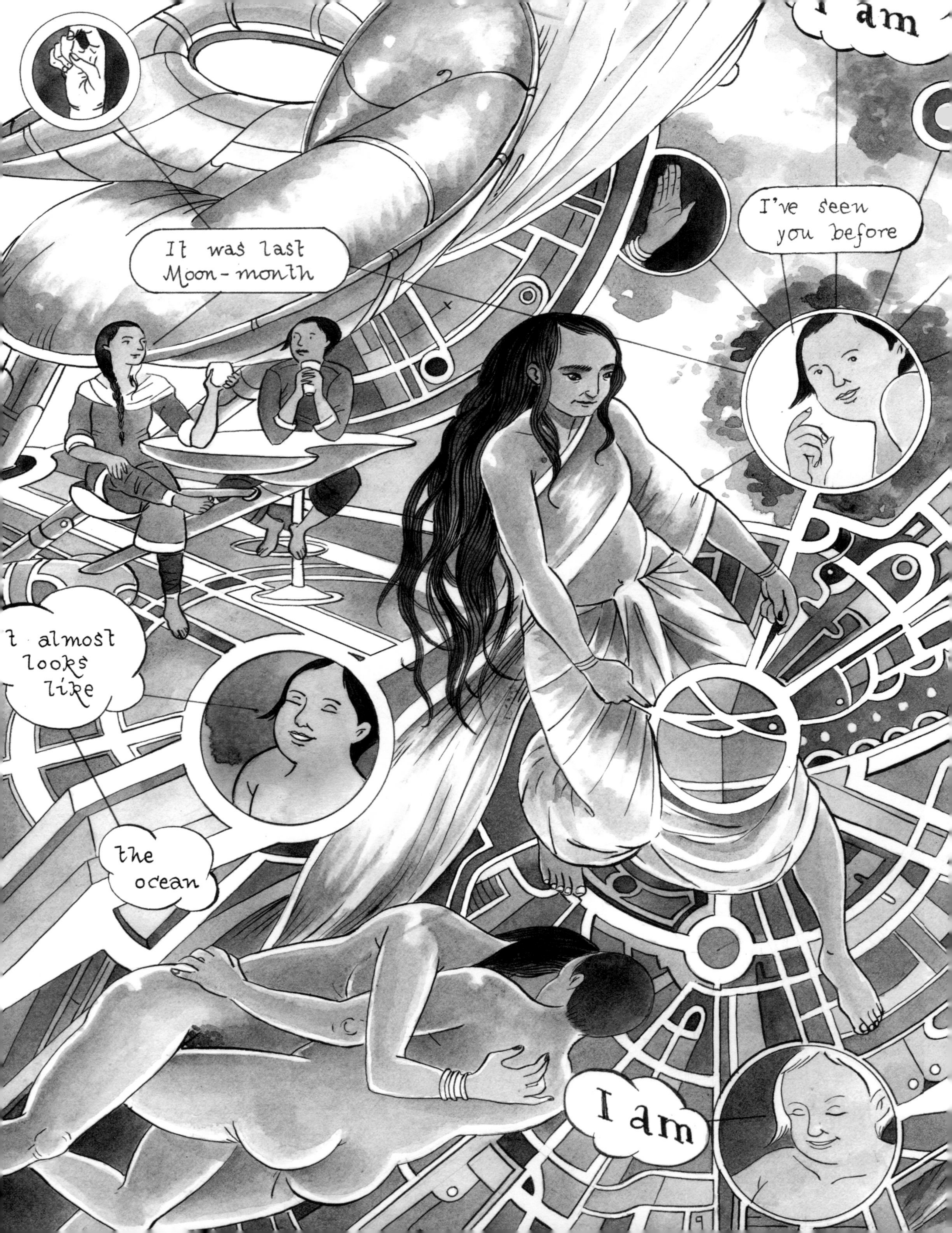
I am
It was last Moon-month
I've seen you before
t almost looks like
the ocean
I am

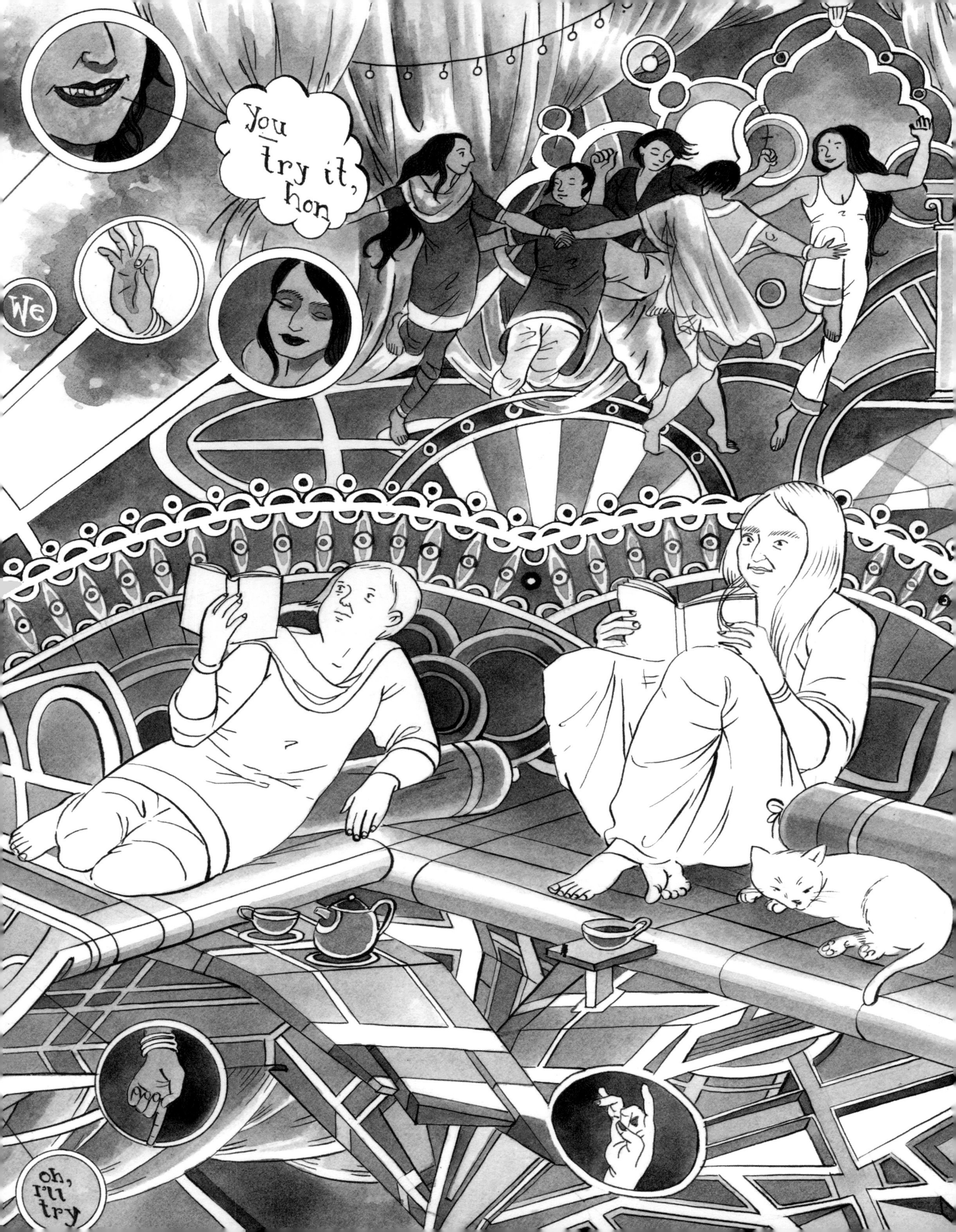
You try it, hon
We
oh, I'll try

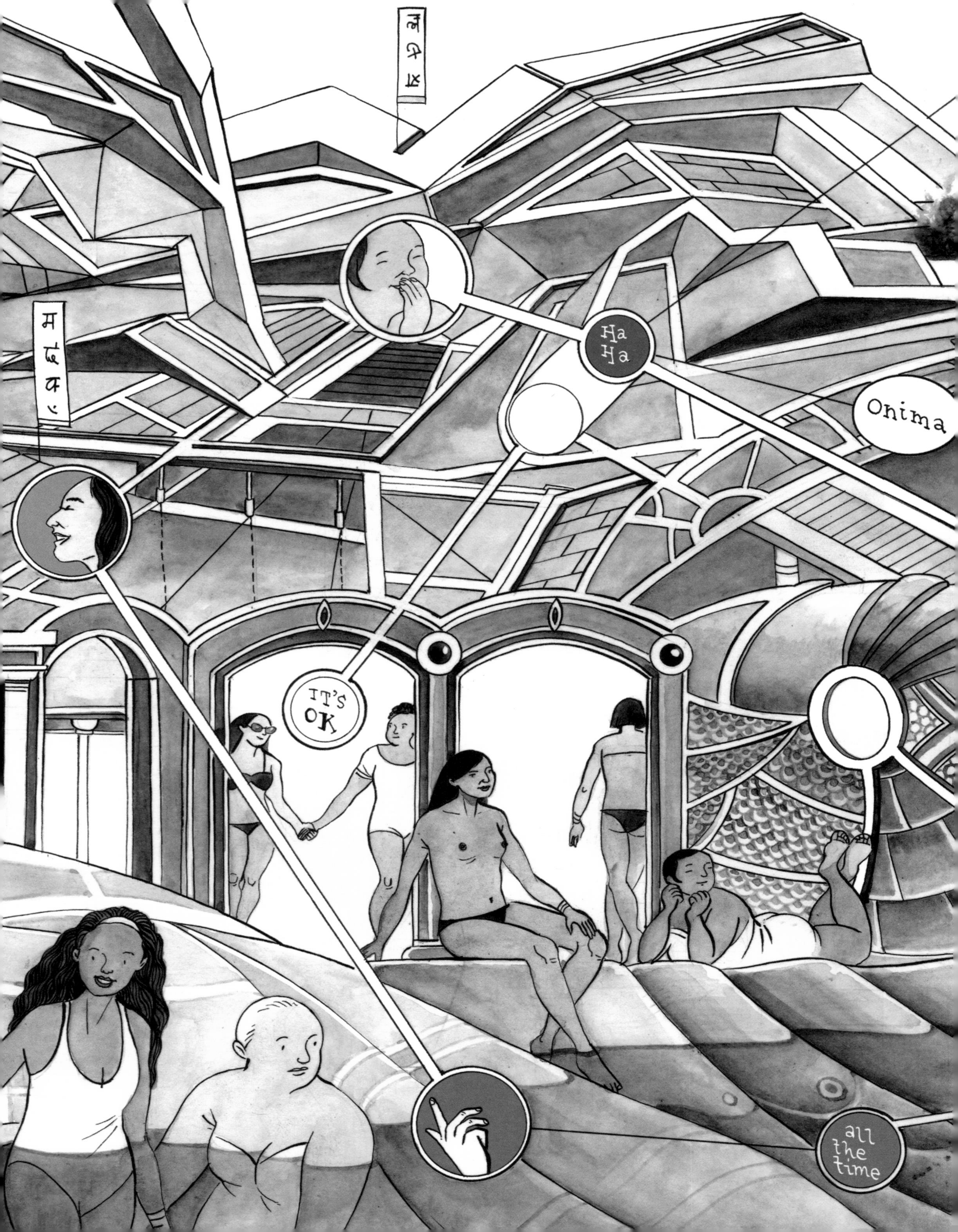
Ha Ha
Onima
IT'S OK
all the time

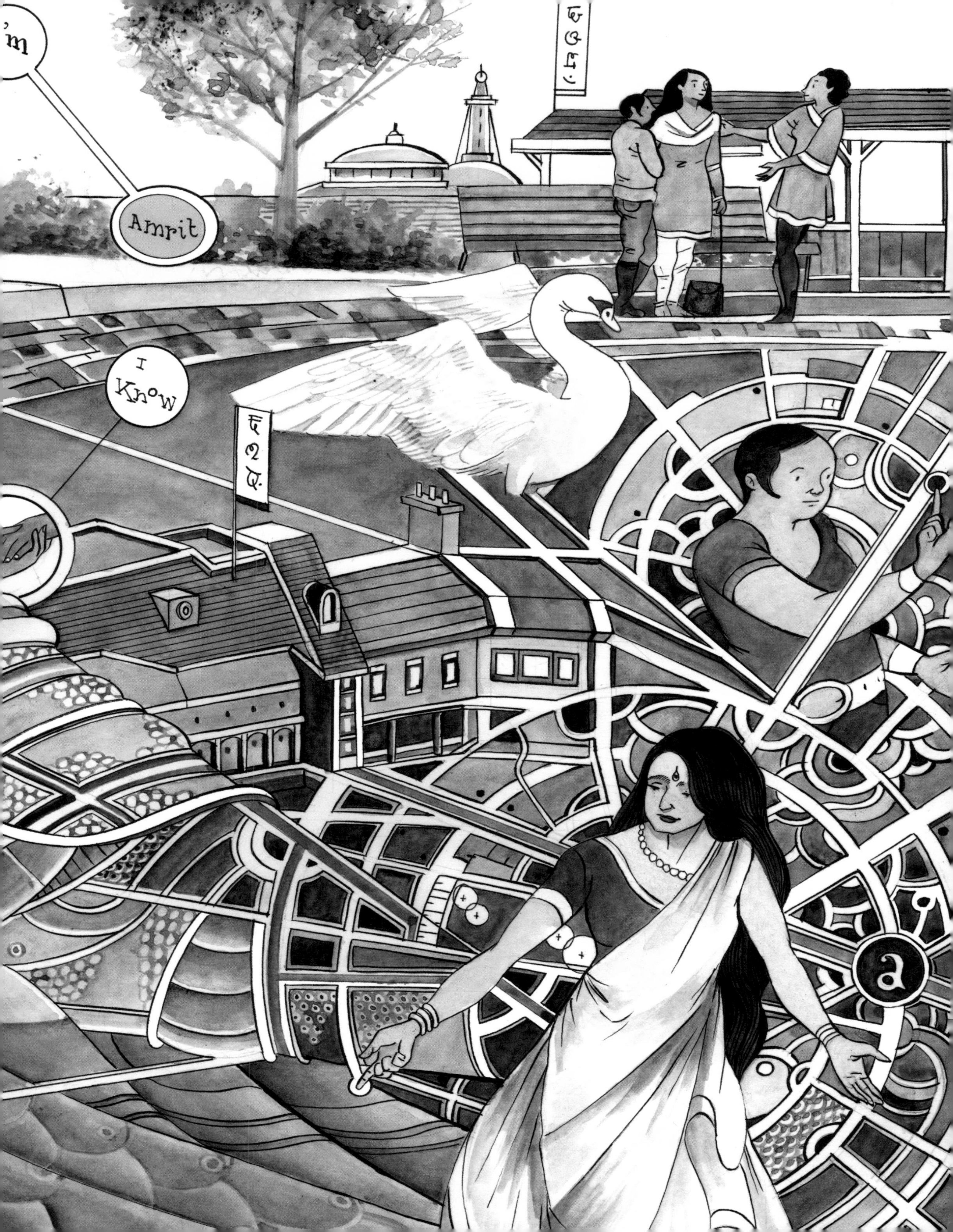
'm
Amrit
I Know
a

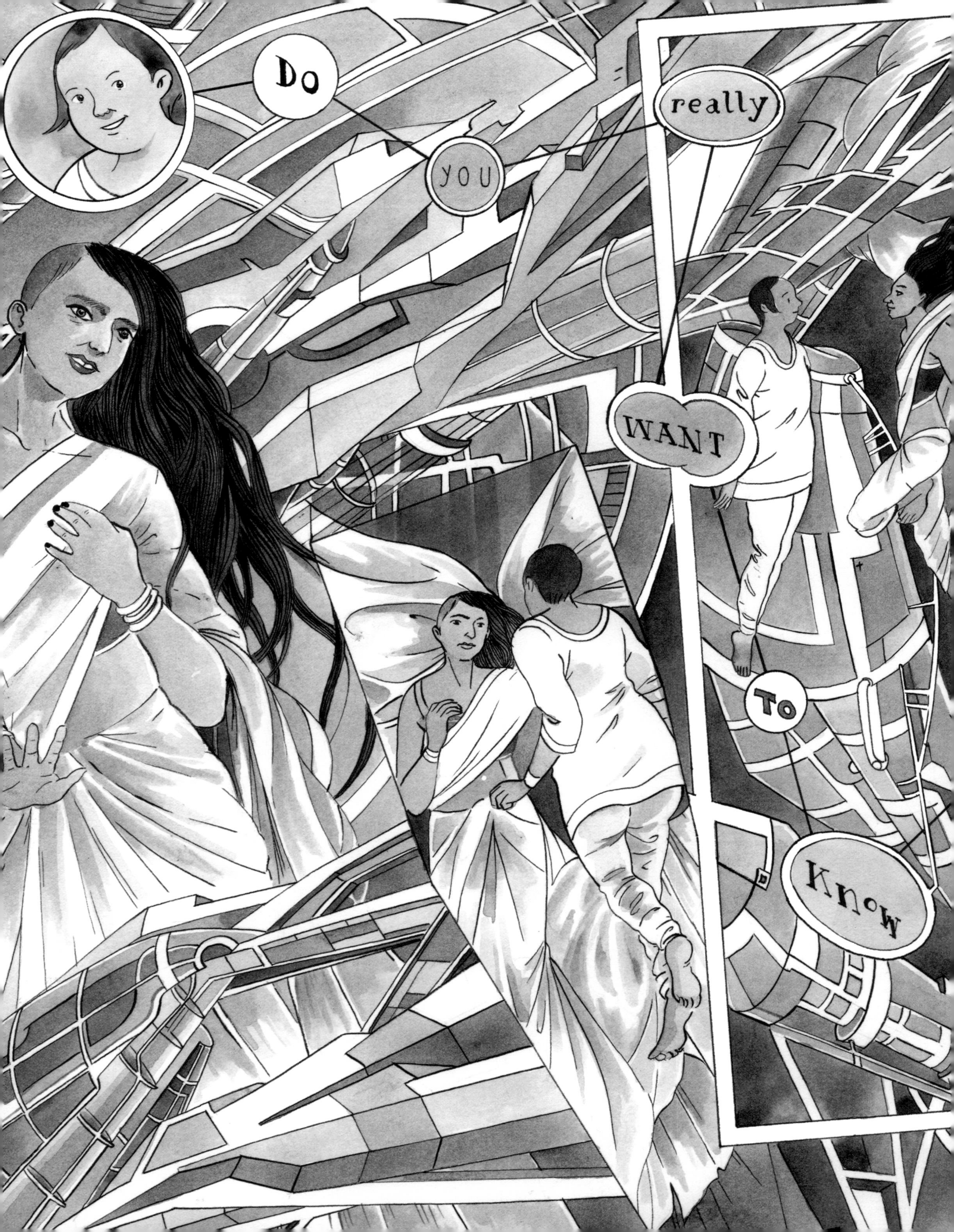
Do
you
really
WANT
TO
Know

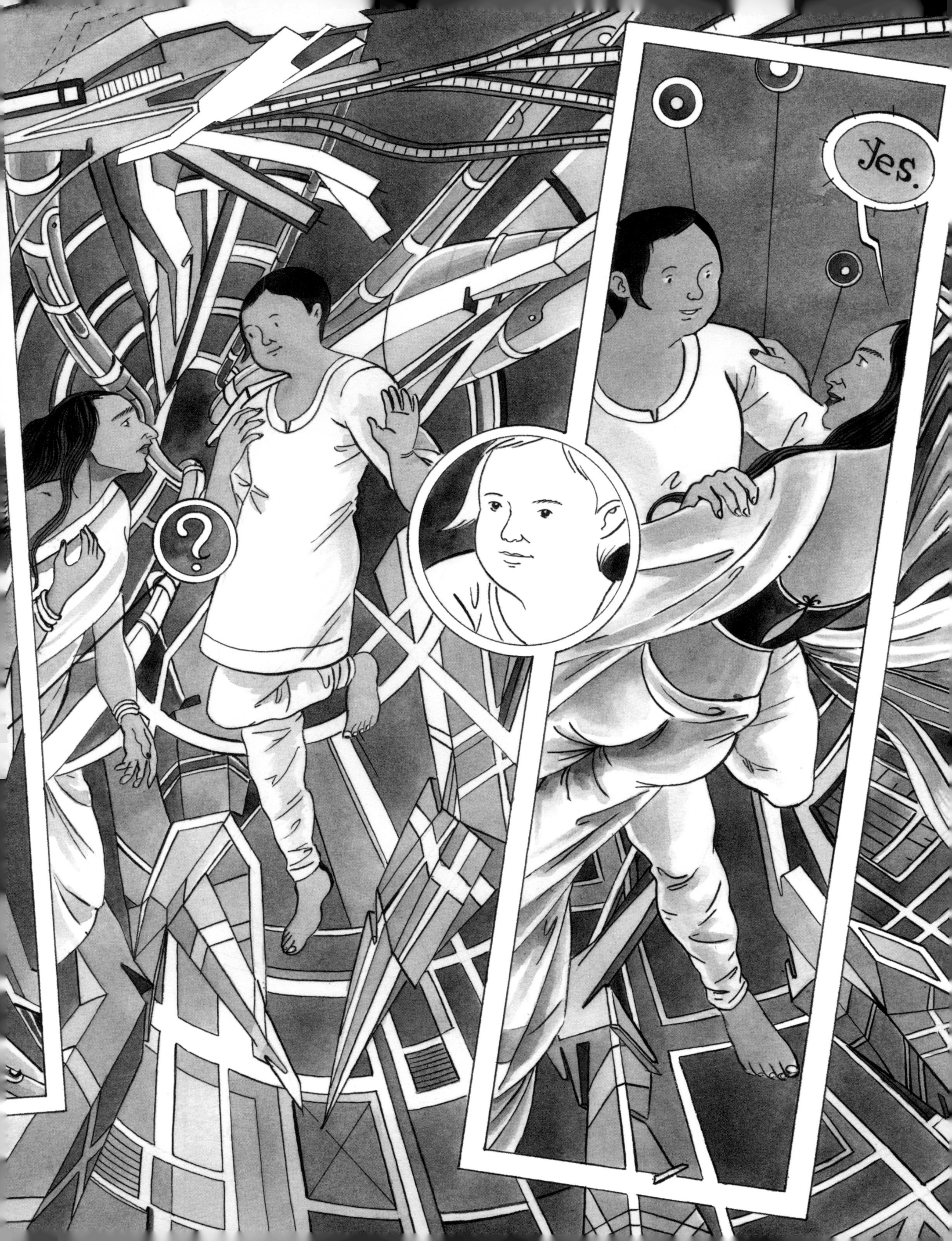
?
Yes.

Love Song

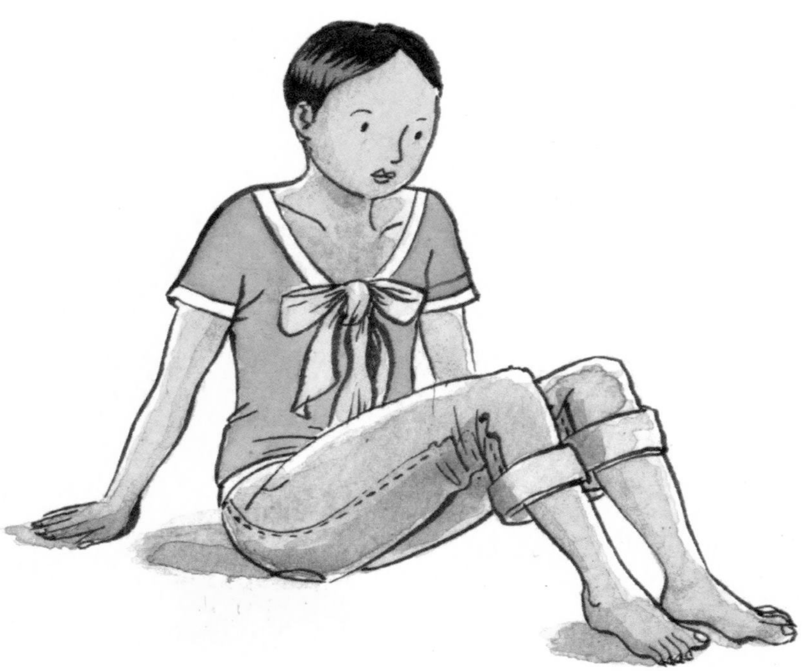

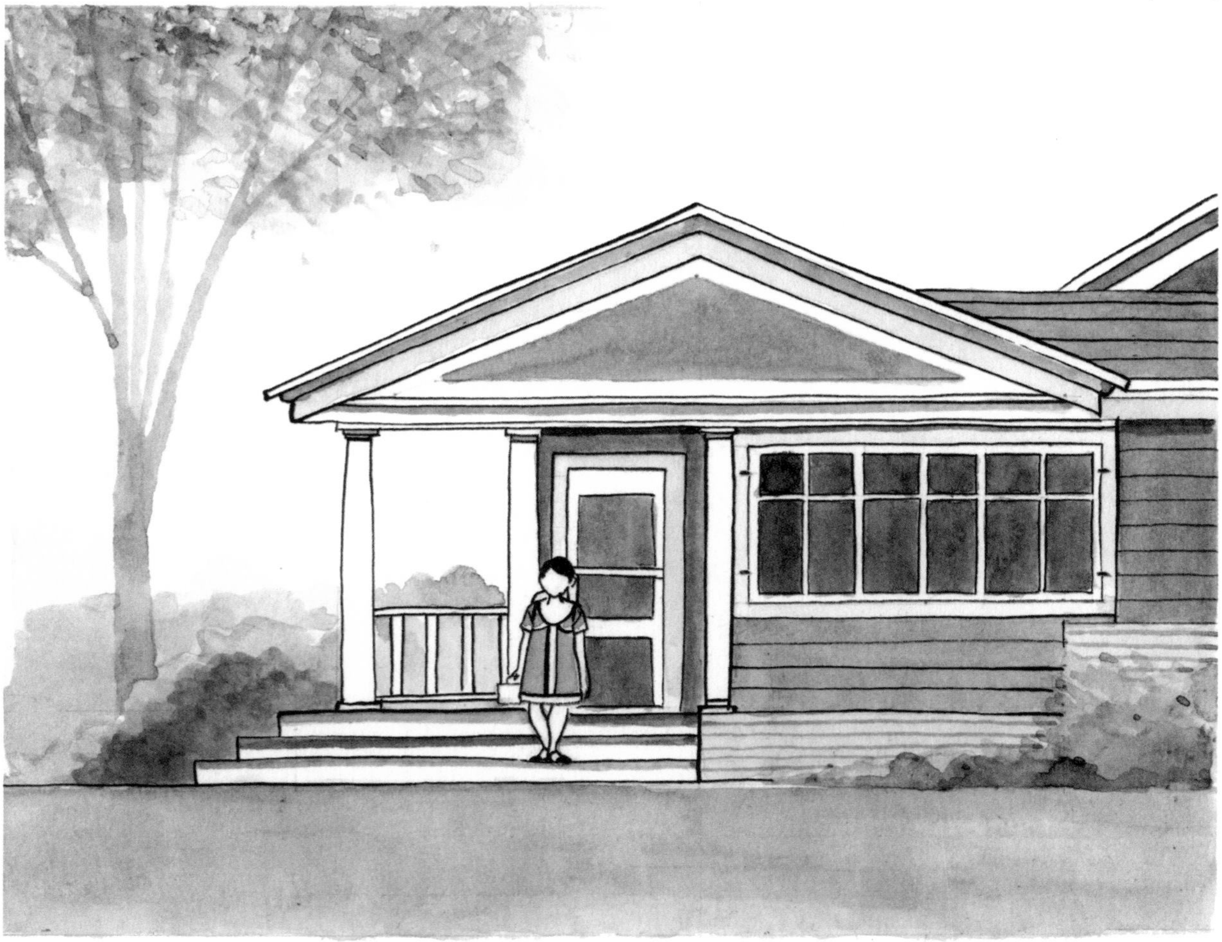

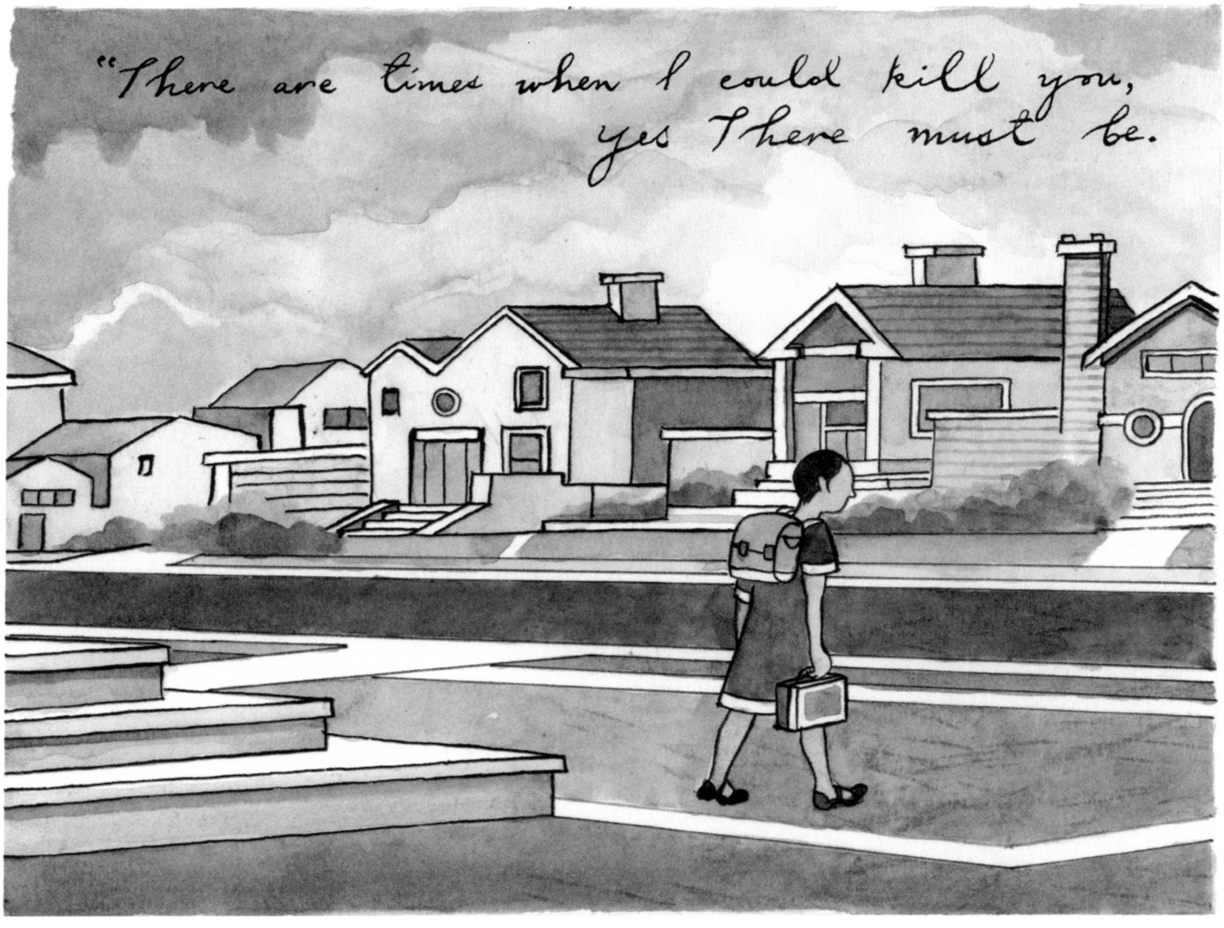
"There are times when I could kill you,
yes There must be.

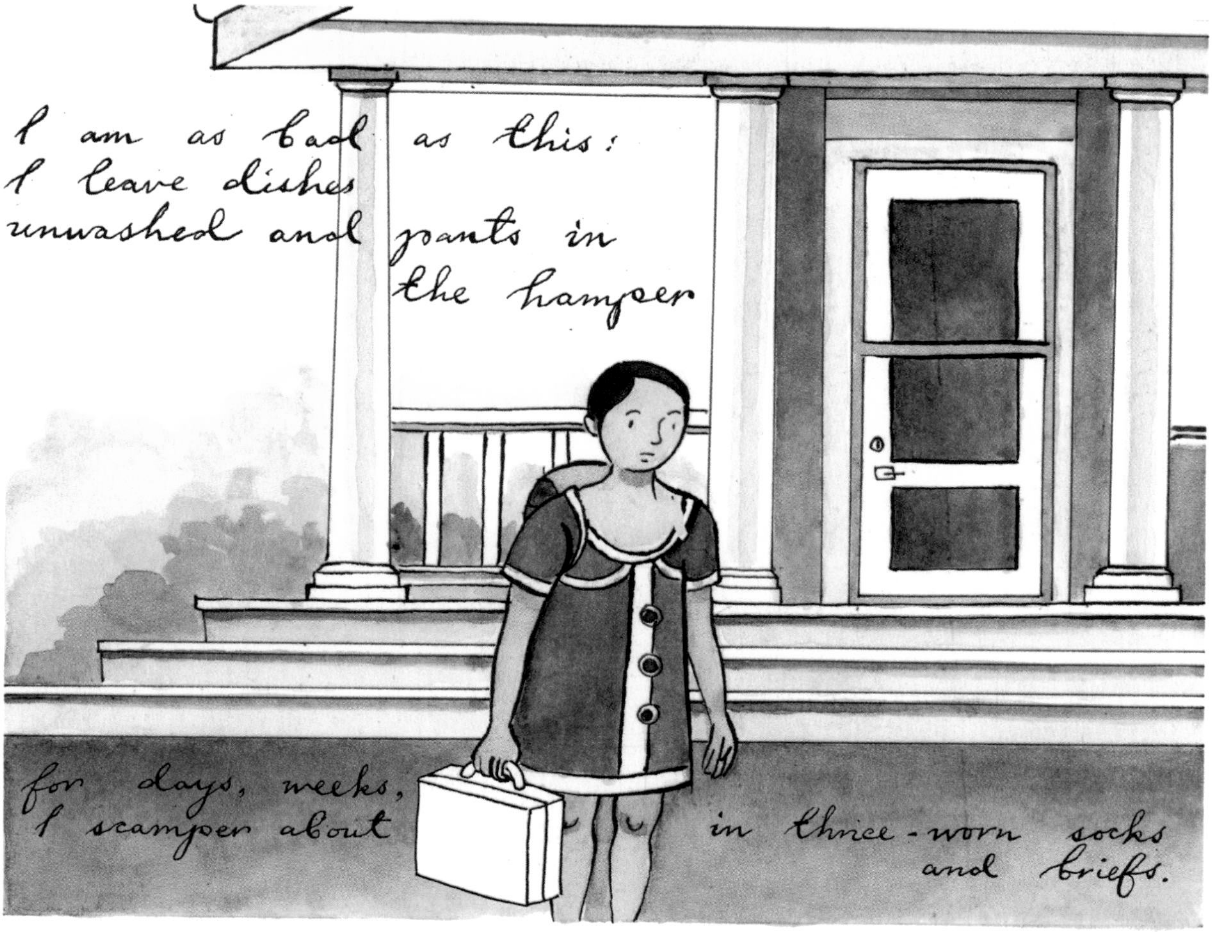
I am as bad as this:
I leave dishes
unwashed and pants in
the hamper
for days, weeks,
I scamper about
in three-worn socks
and briefs.

The listing clothes rack is about to give way —
bottles and cans, newspapers, food scraps.

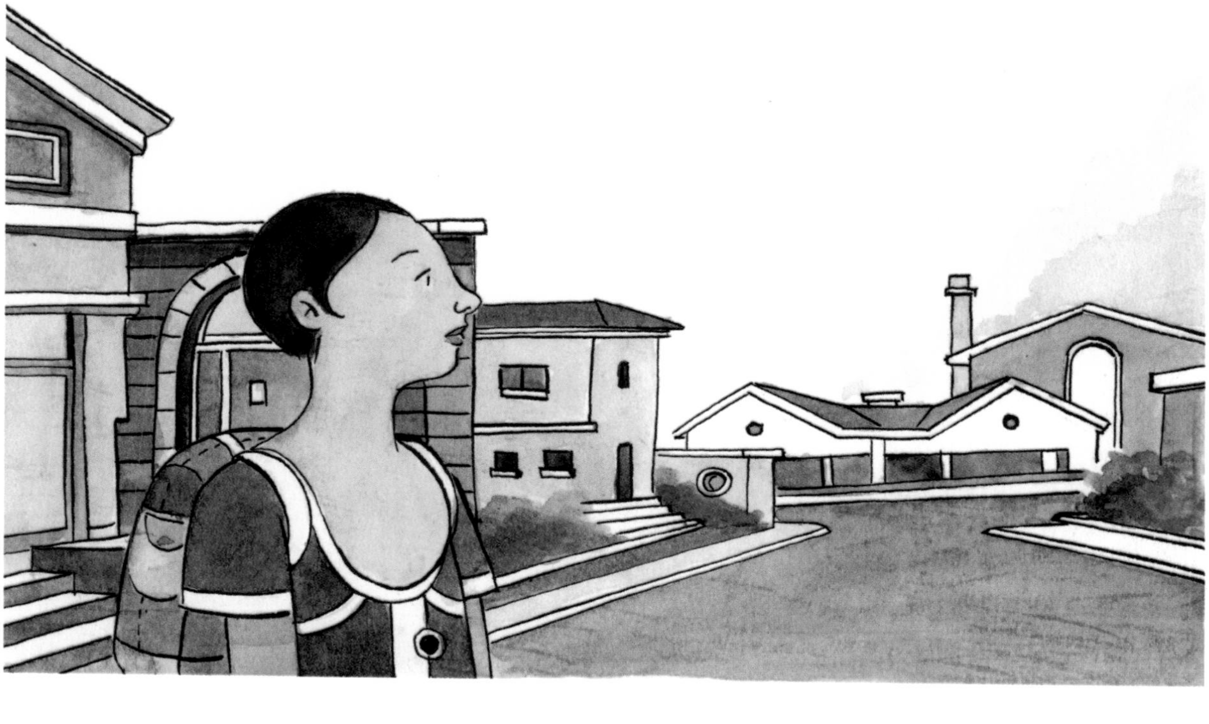

I am a great sluggard lying prone on the sofa.
My only excuse is that the Spiro makes me so.

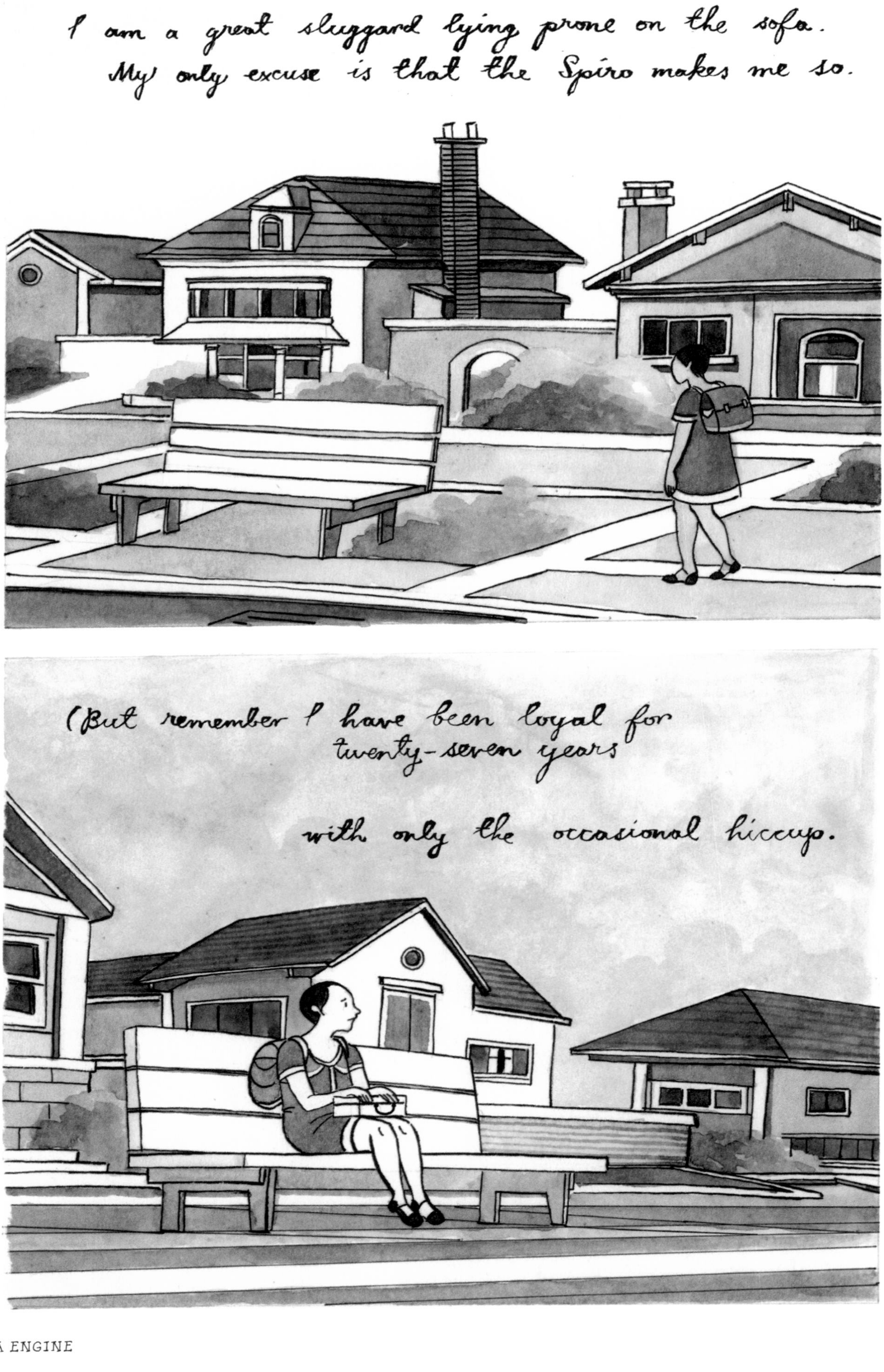
(But remember I have been loyal for
twenty-seven years
with only the occasional hiccups.

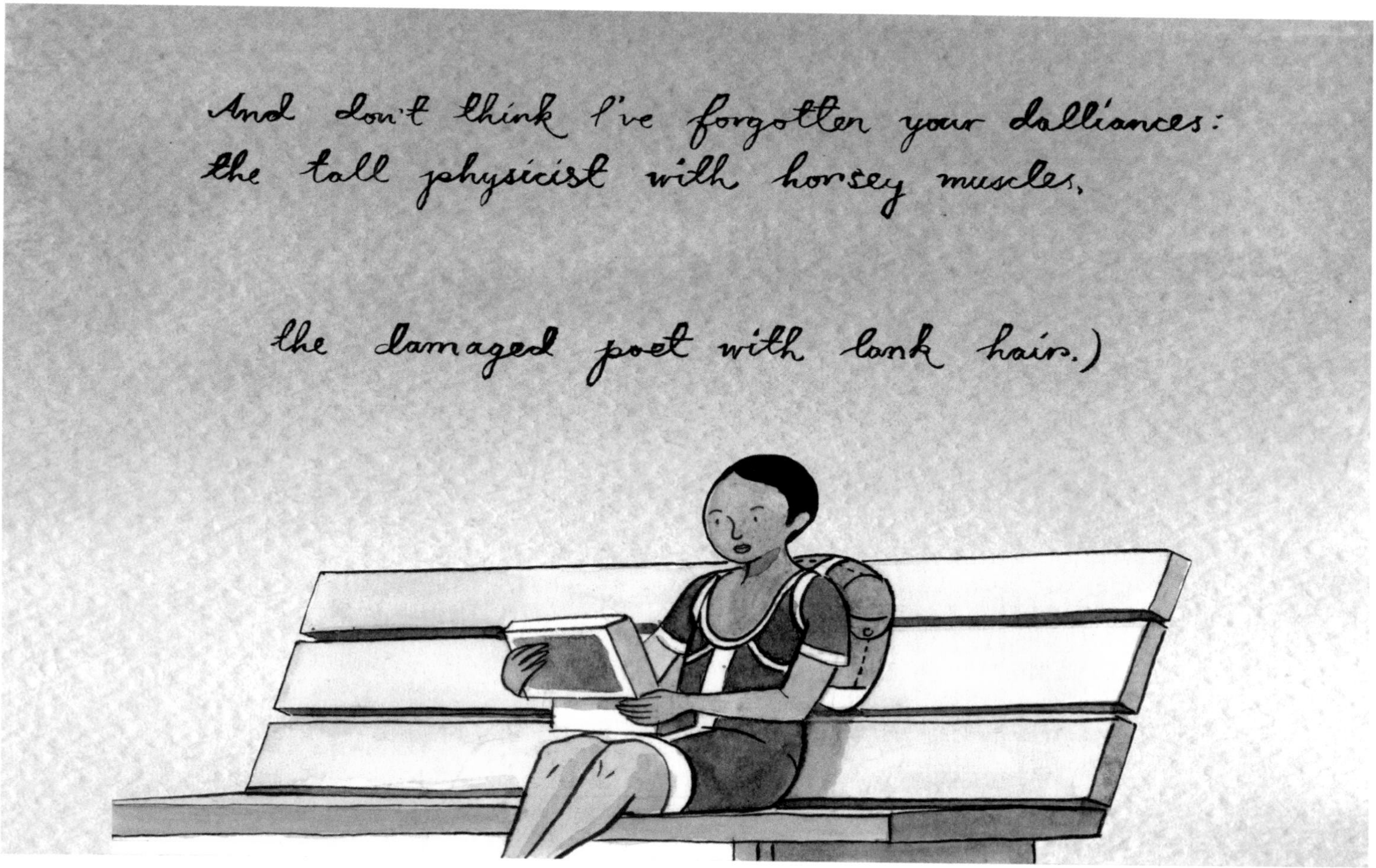
And don't think I've forgotten your dalliances:
the tall physicist with horsey muscles,
the damaged poet with lank hair.)

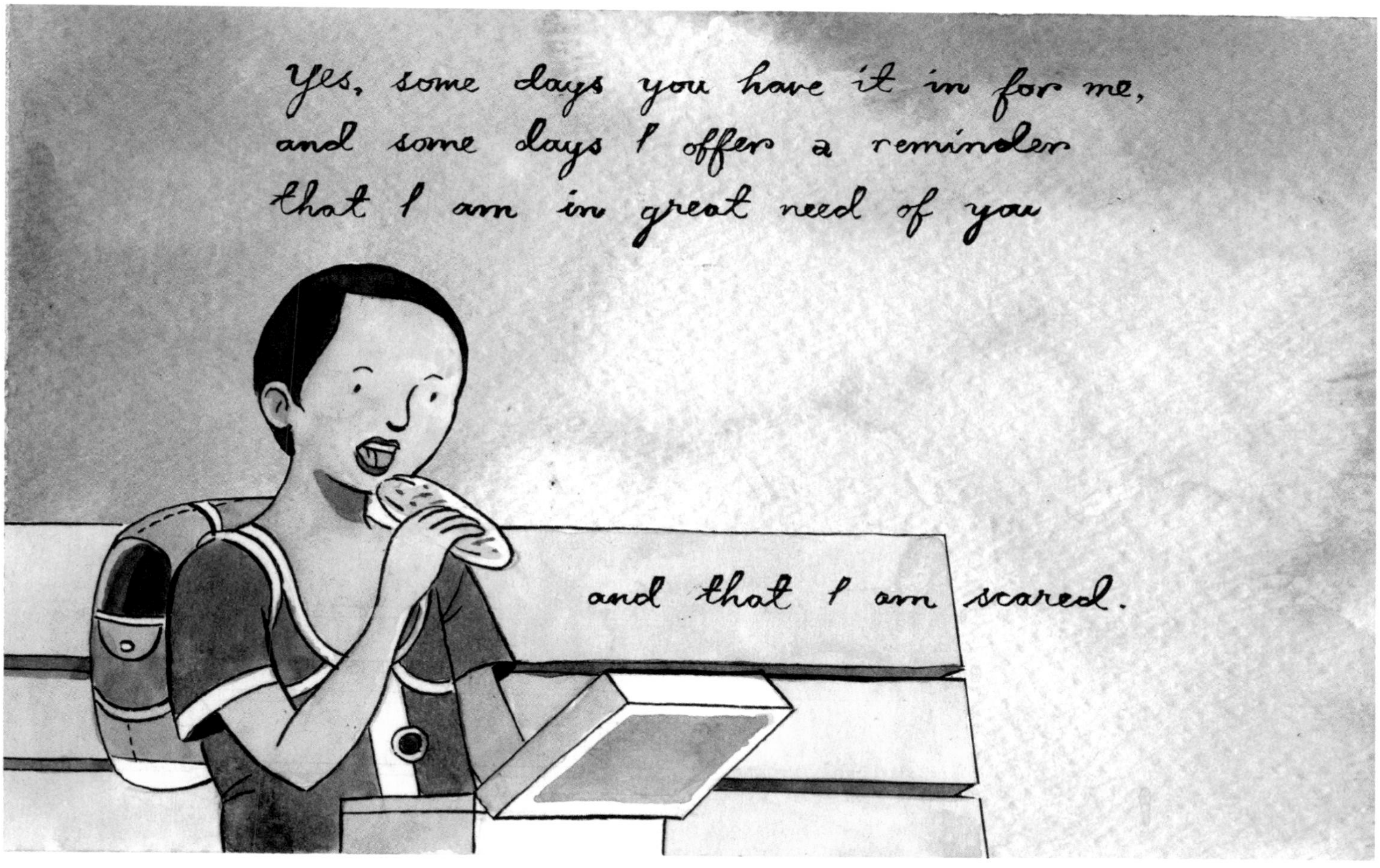
Yes, some days you have it in for me,
and some days I offer a reminder
that I am in great need of you
and that I am scared.

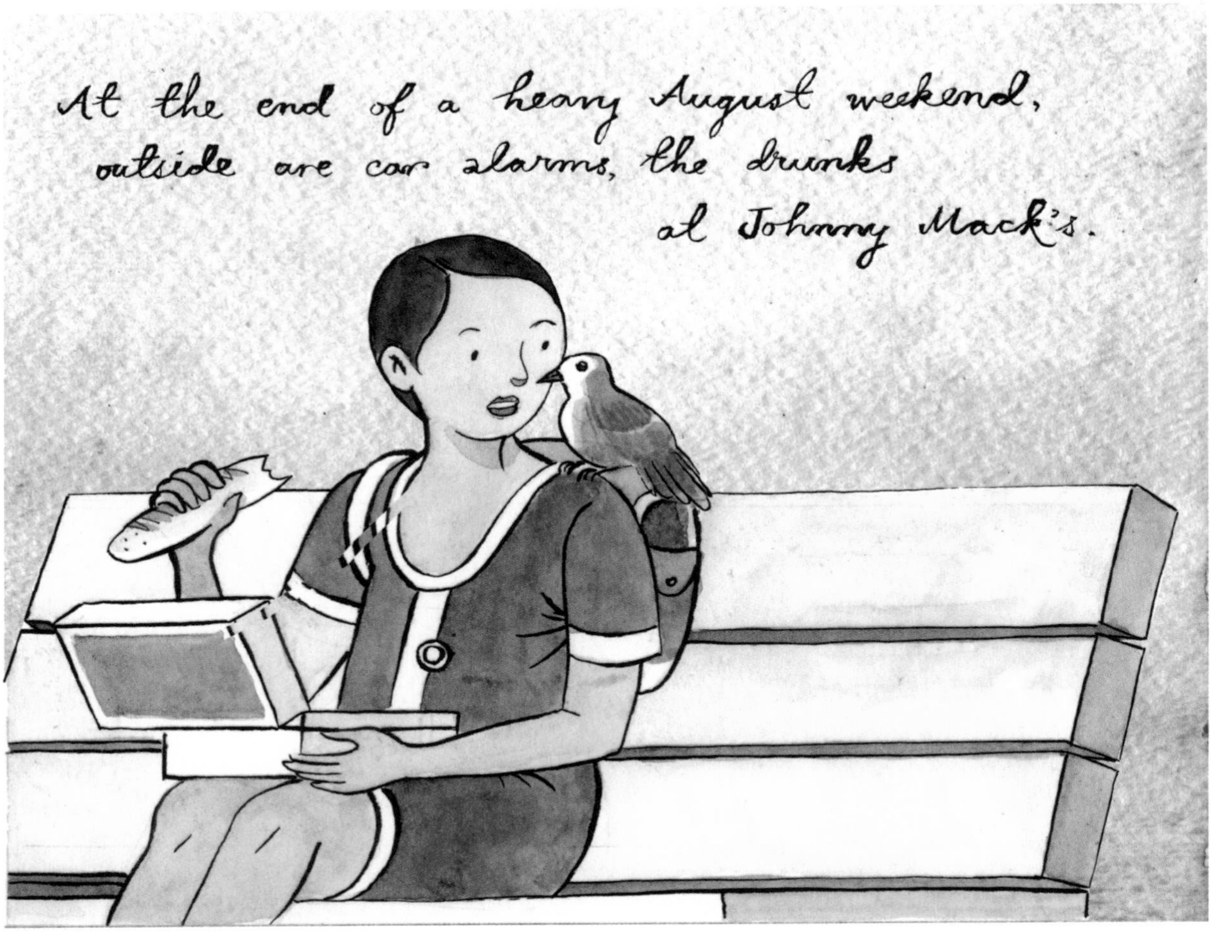
At the end of a heavy August weekend, outside are car alarms, the drunks at Johnny Mack's.

Inside, here you are, giving yourself a pedicure,

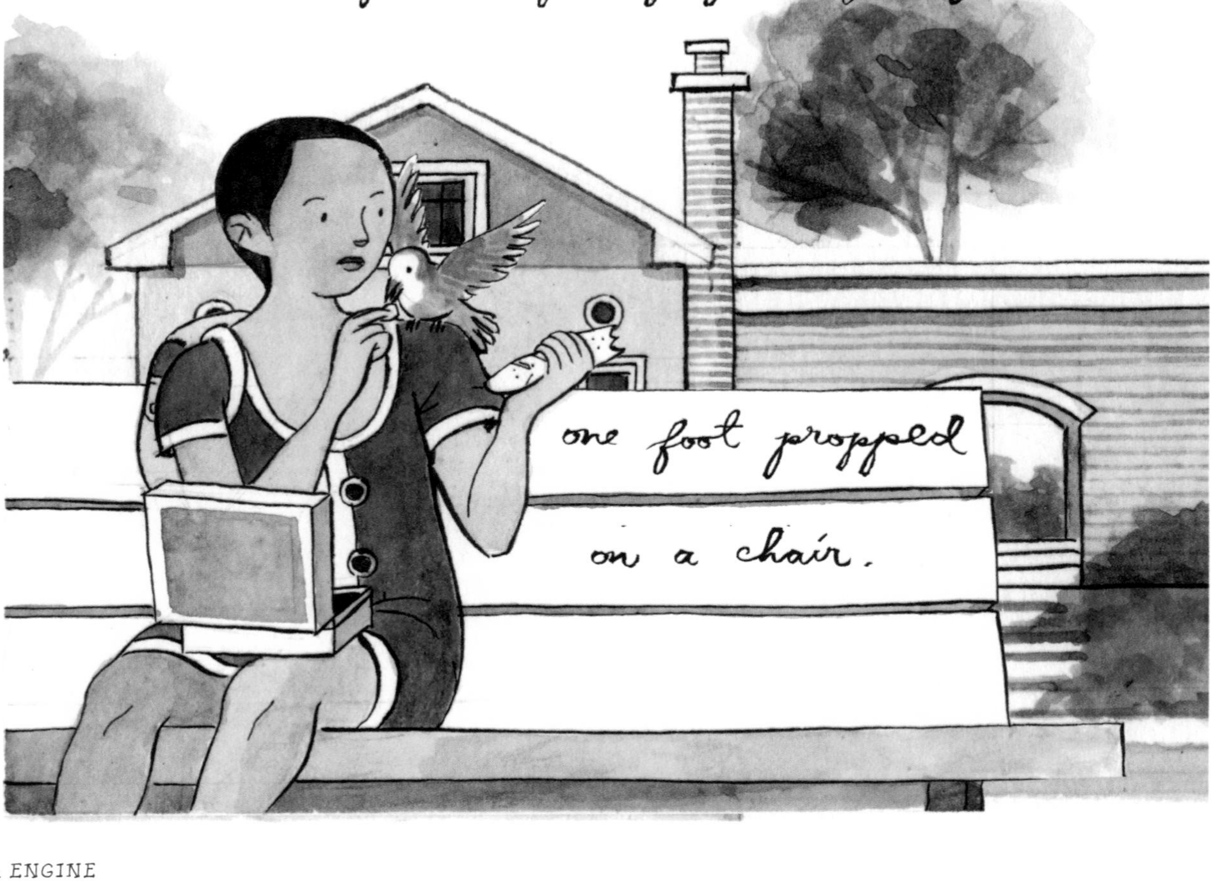
one foot propped on a chair.

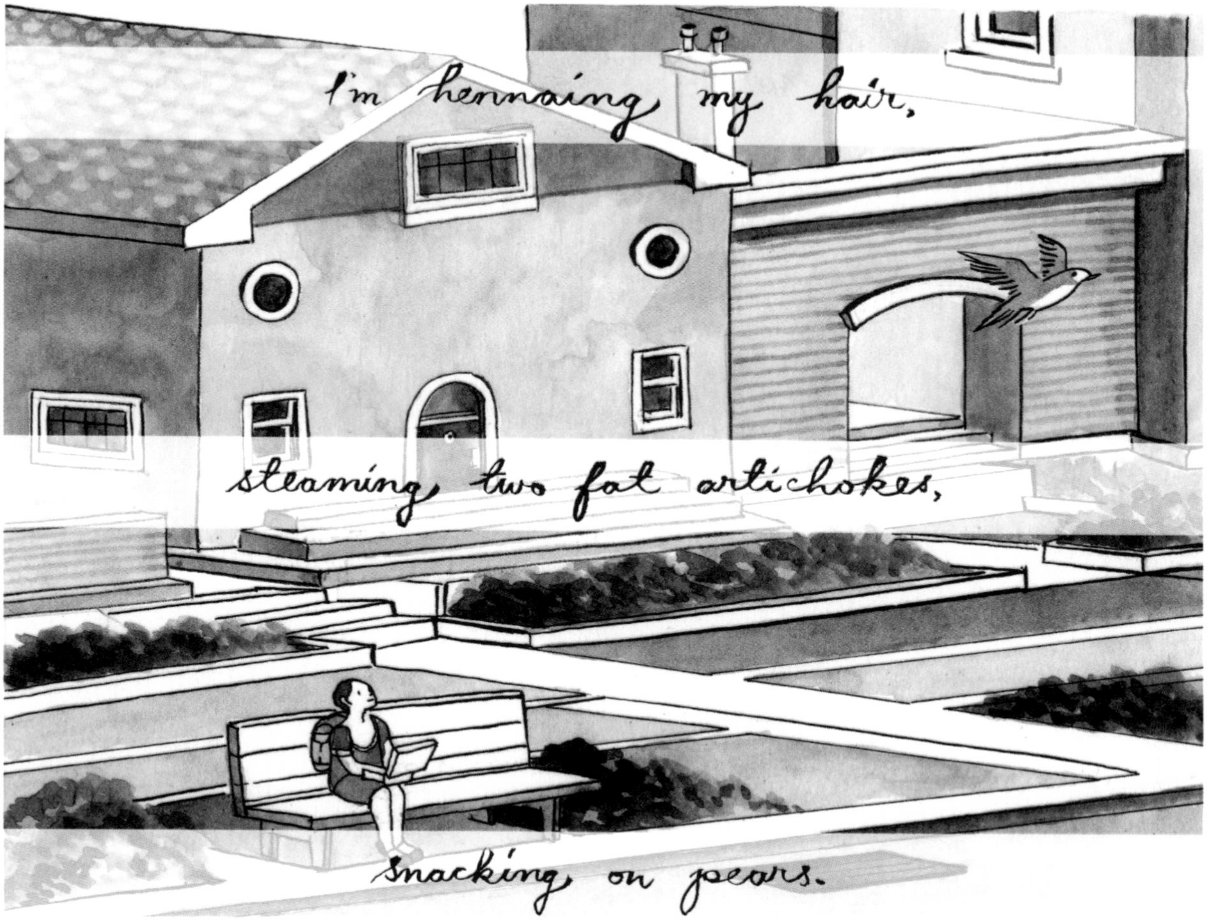
I'm hennaing my hair,
steaming two fat artichokes,
snacking on pears.

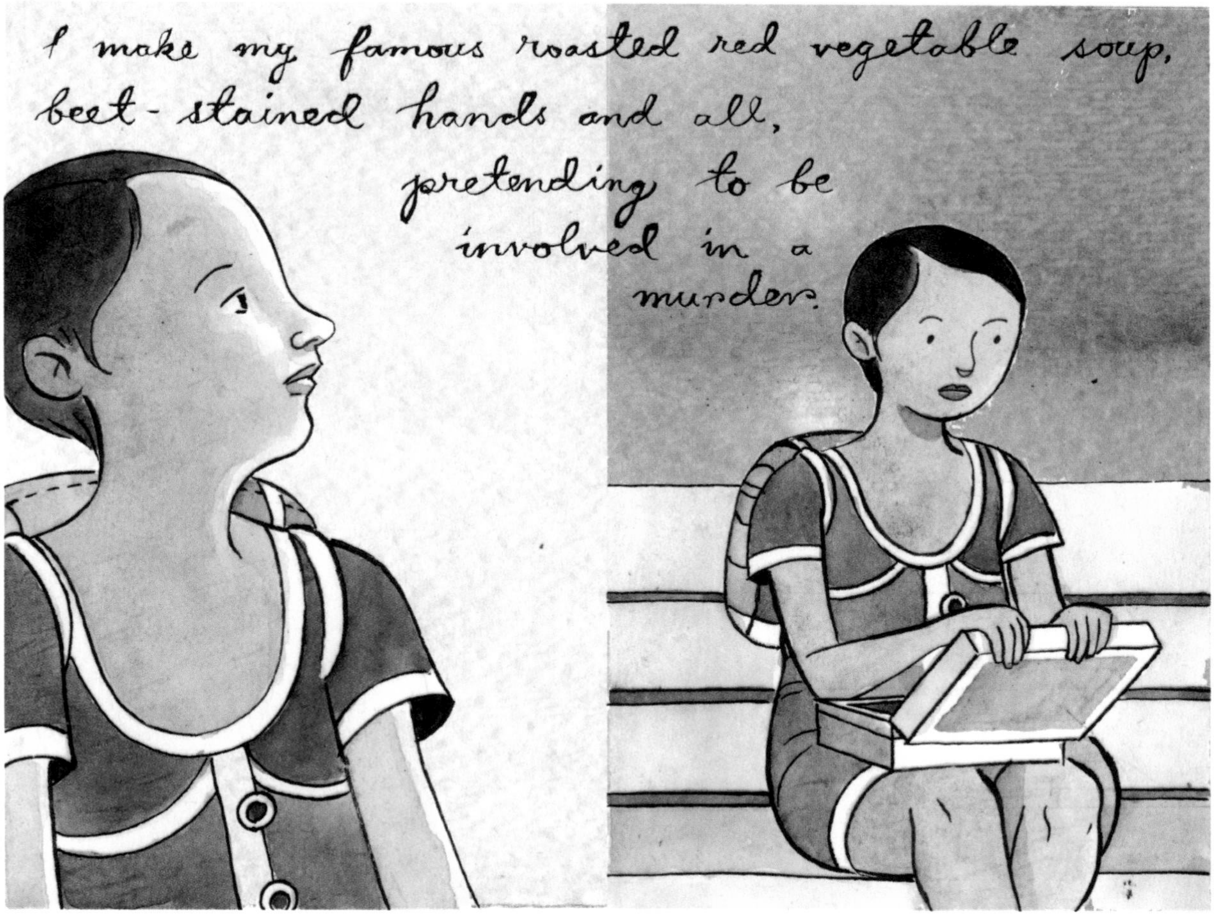
I make my famous roasted red vegetable soup,
beet-stained hands and all,
pretending to be
involved in a
murder.

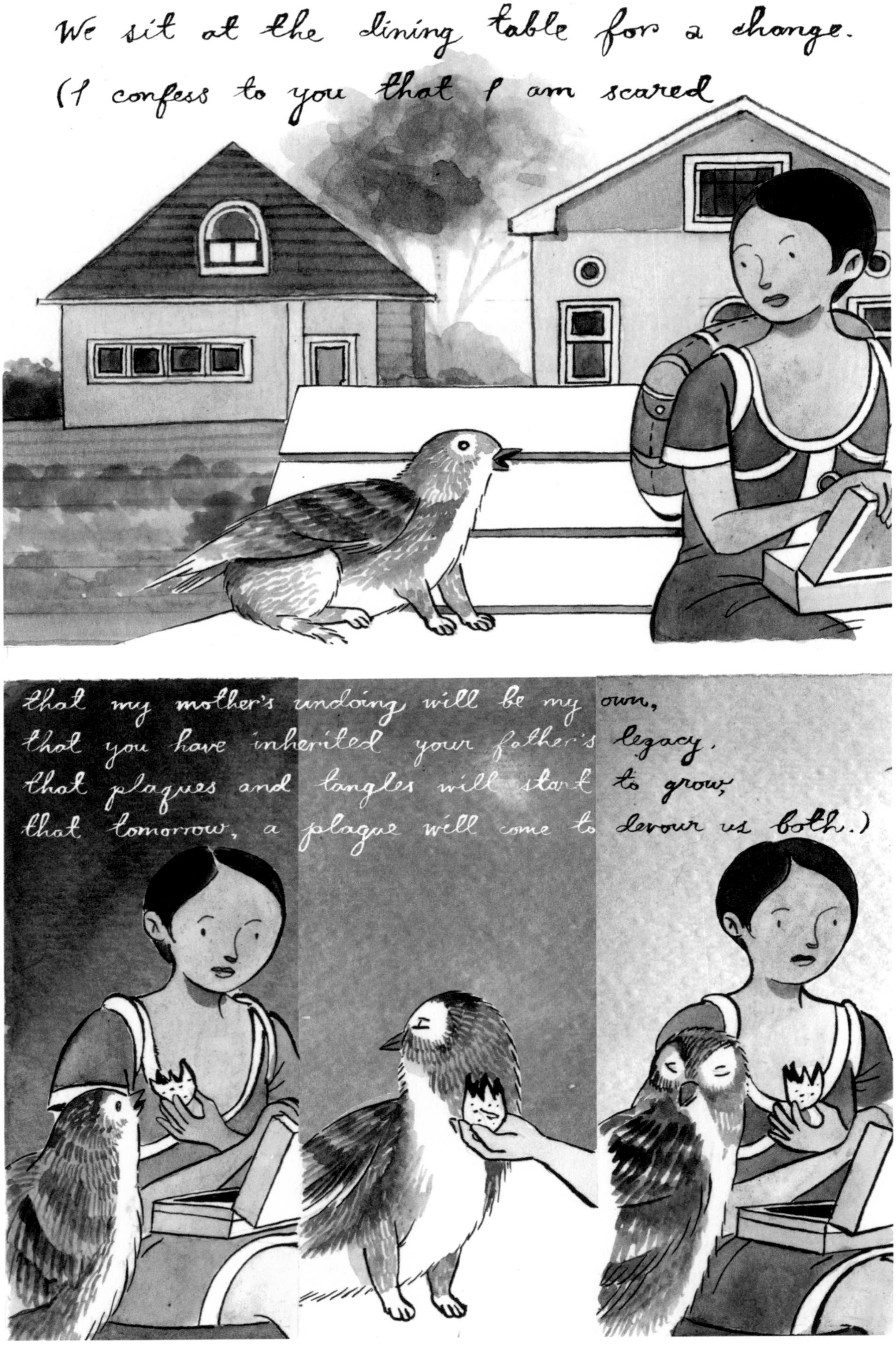
We sit at the dining table for a change.
(I confess to you that I am scared
that my mother's undoing will be my own,
that you have inherited your father's legacy,
that plaques and tangles will start to grow;
that tomorrow, a plague will come to devour us both.)

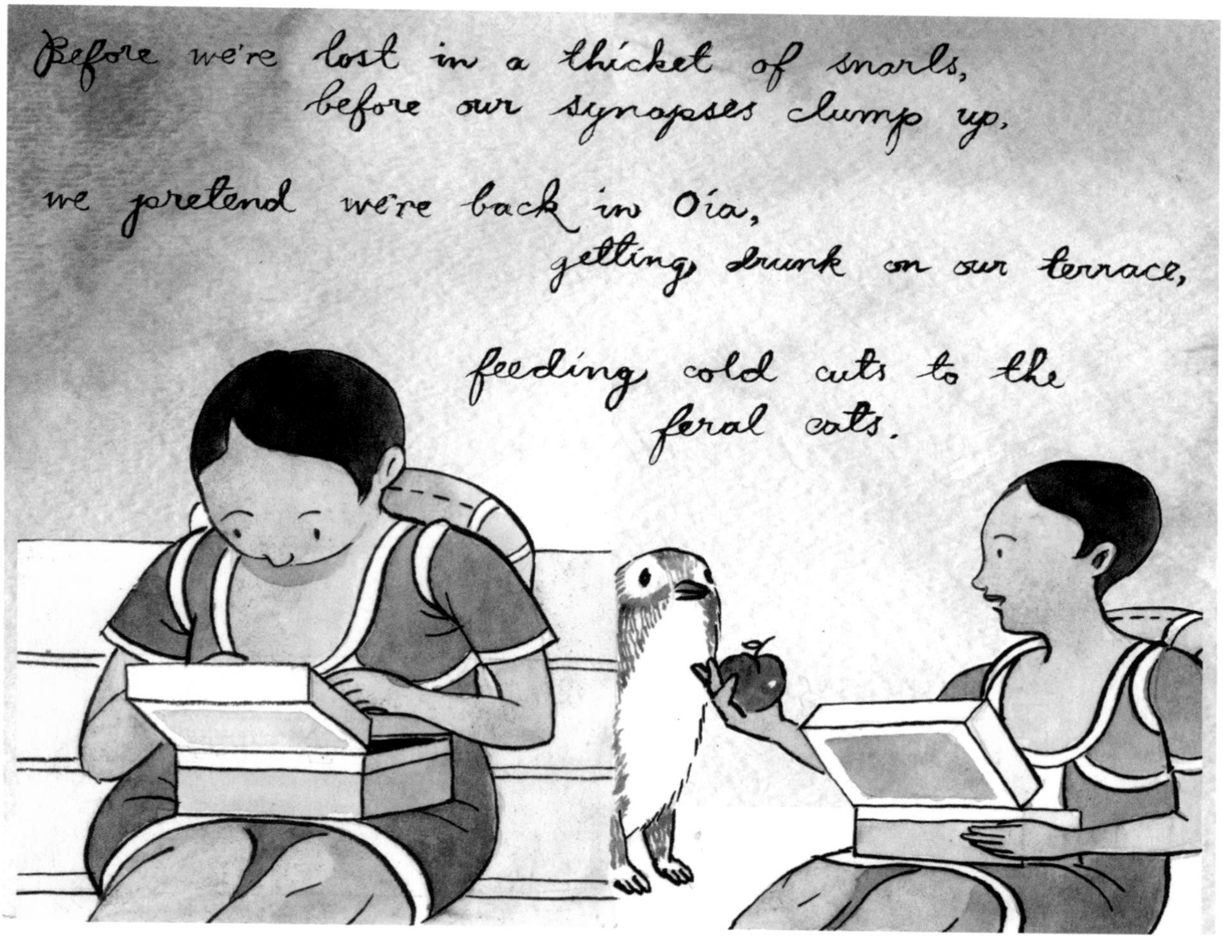
Before we're lost in a thicket of snarls,
before our synapses clump up,
we pretend we're back in Oia,
getting drunk on our terrace,
feeding cold cuts to the
feral cats.

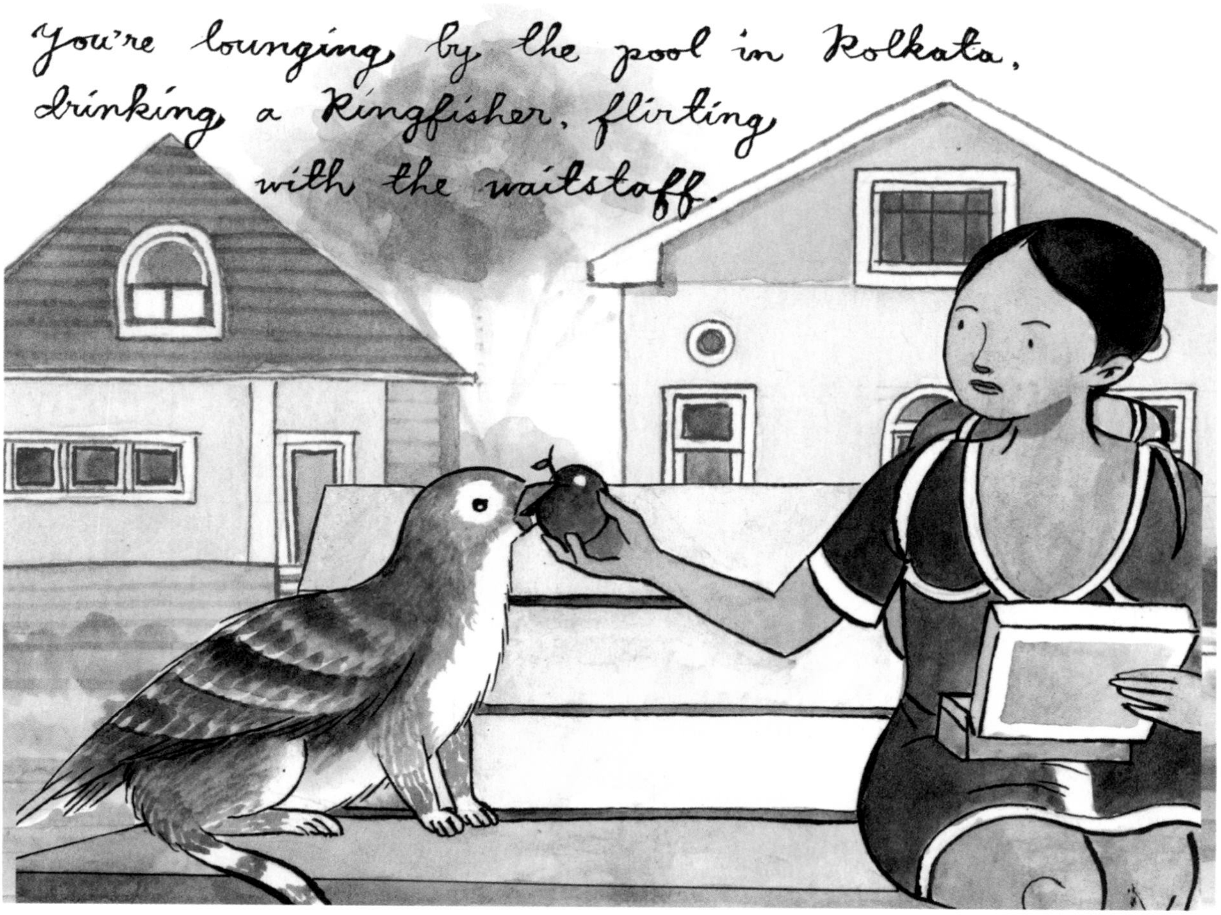
You're lounging by the pool in Kolkata,
drinking a Kingfisher, flirting
with the waitstaff.

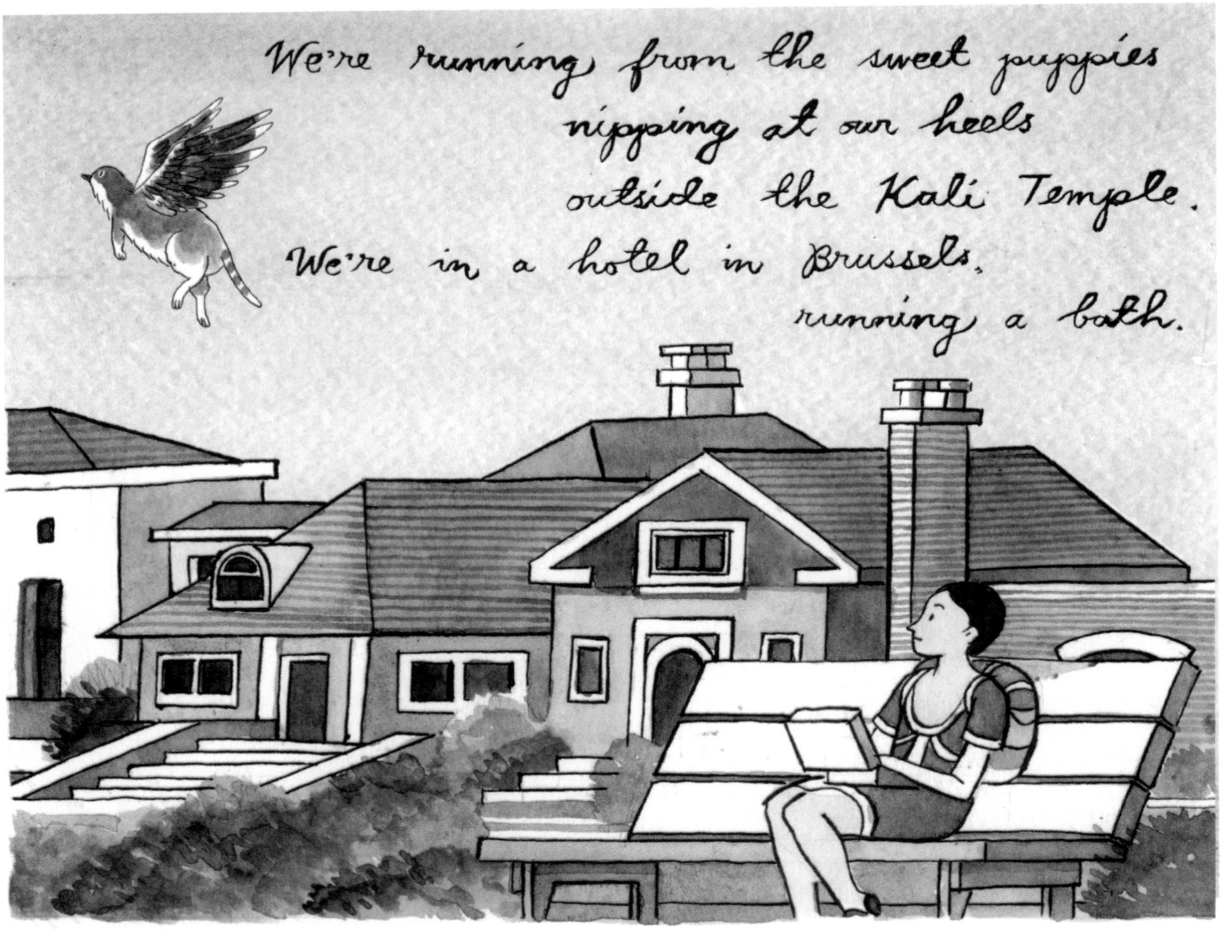
We're running from the sweet puppies
nipping at our heels
outside the Kali Temple.
We're in a hotel in Brussels,
running a bath.

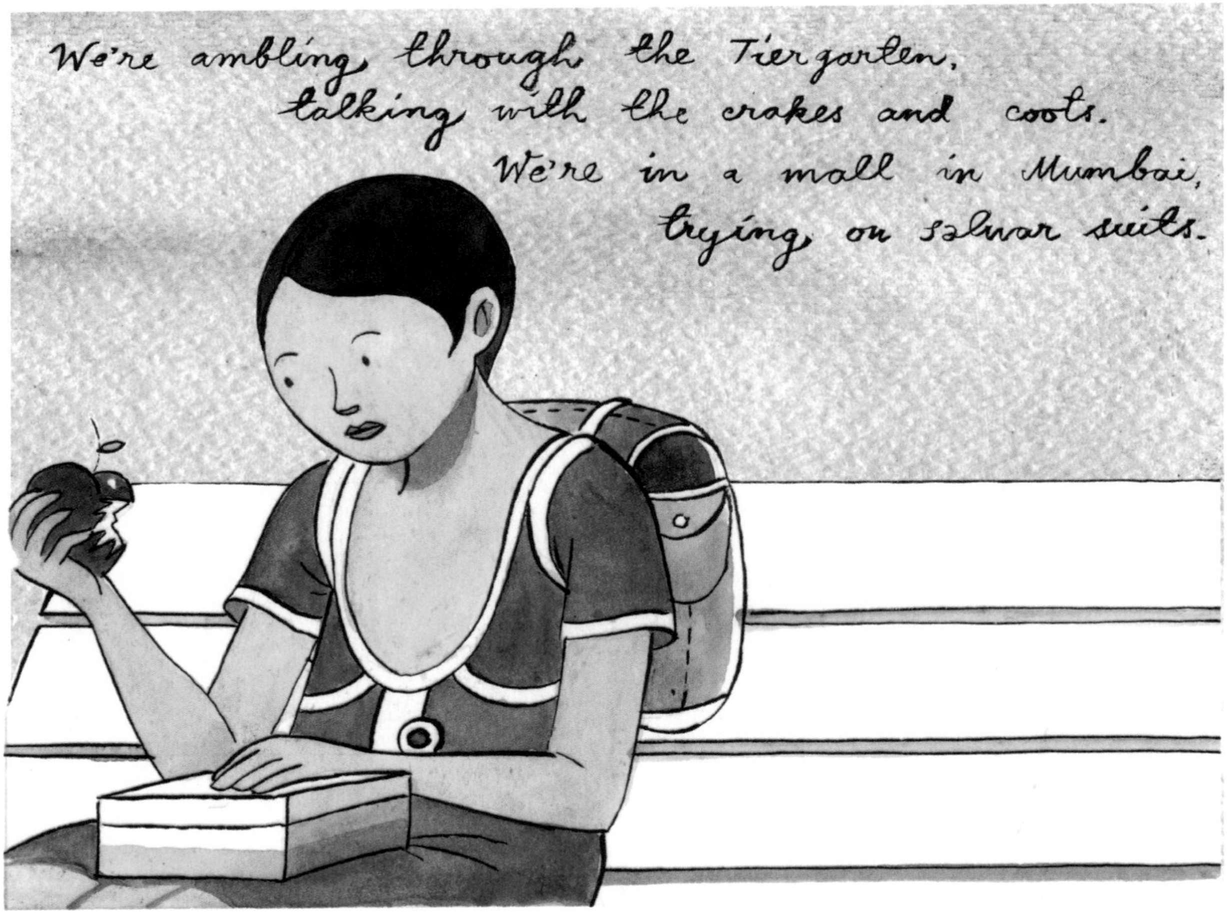
We're ambling through the Tiergarten,
talking with the crakes and coots.
We're in a mall in Mumbai,
trying on salwar suits.

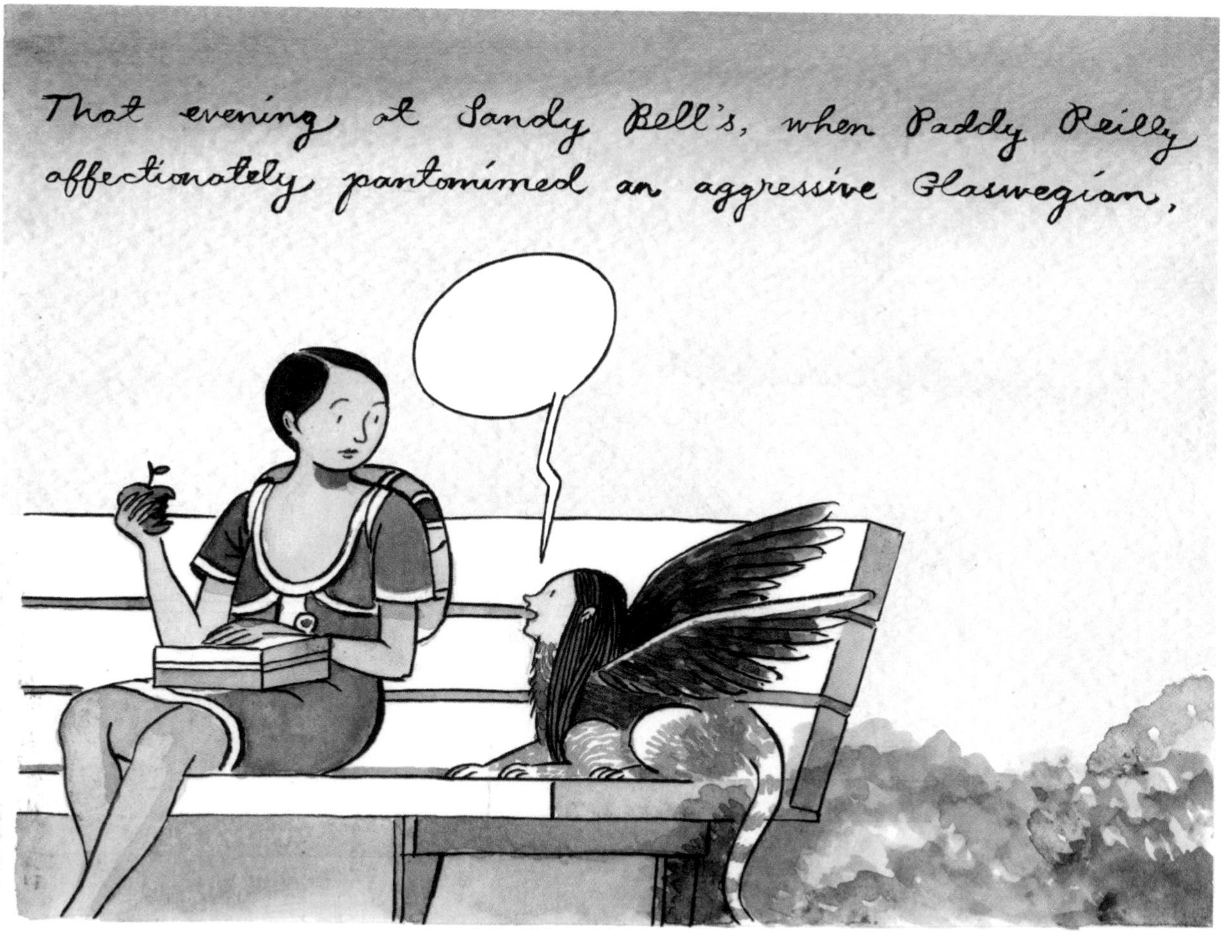
That evening, at Sandy Bell's, when Paddy Reilly affectionately pantomimed an aggressive Glaswegian,

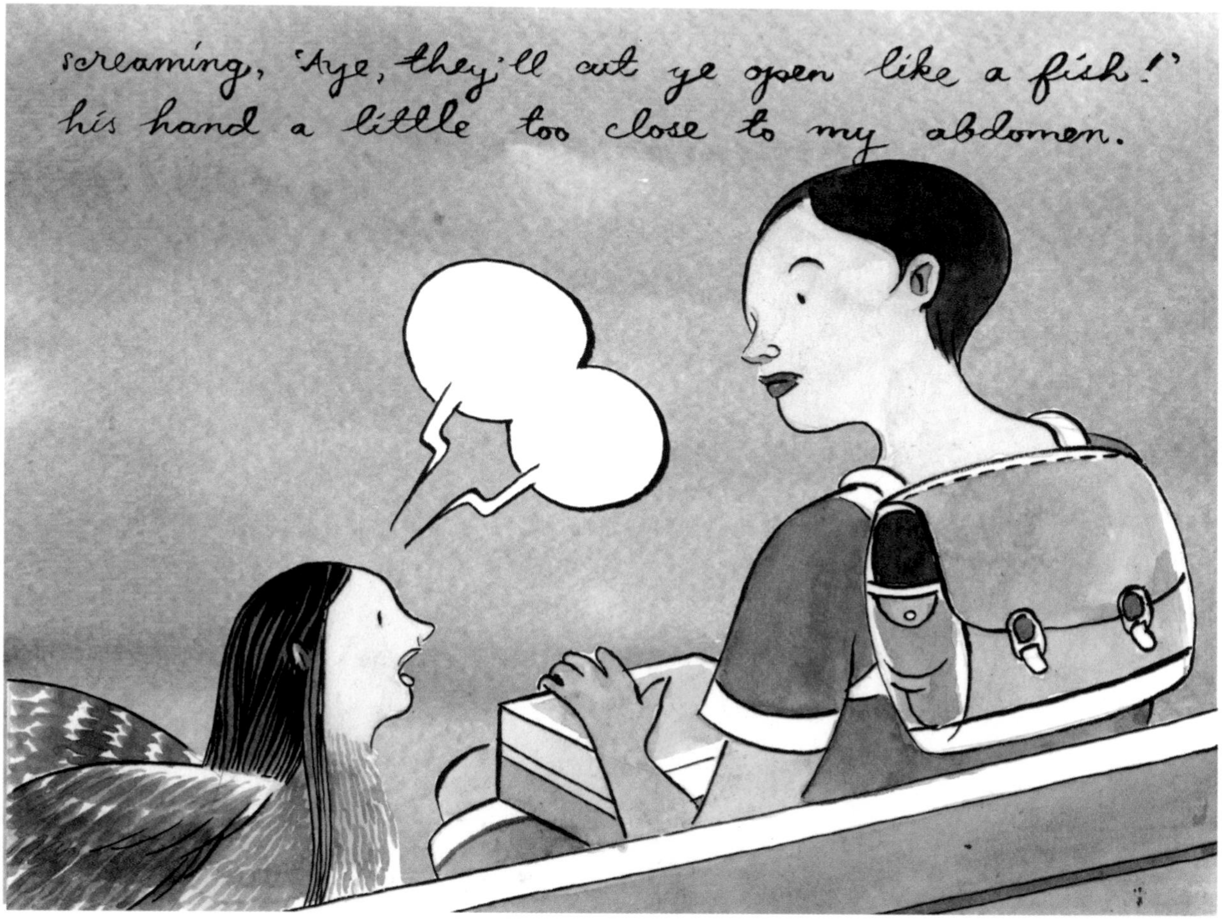
screaming, "Aye, they'll cut ye open like a fish!" his hand a little too close to my abdomen.

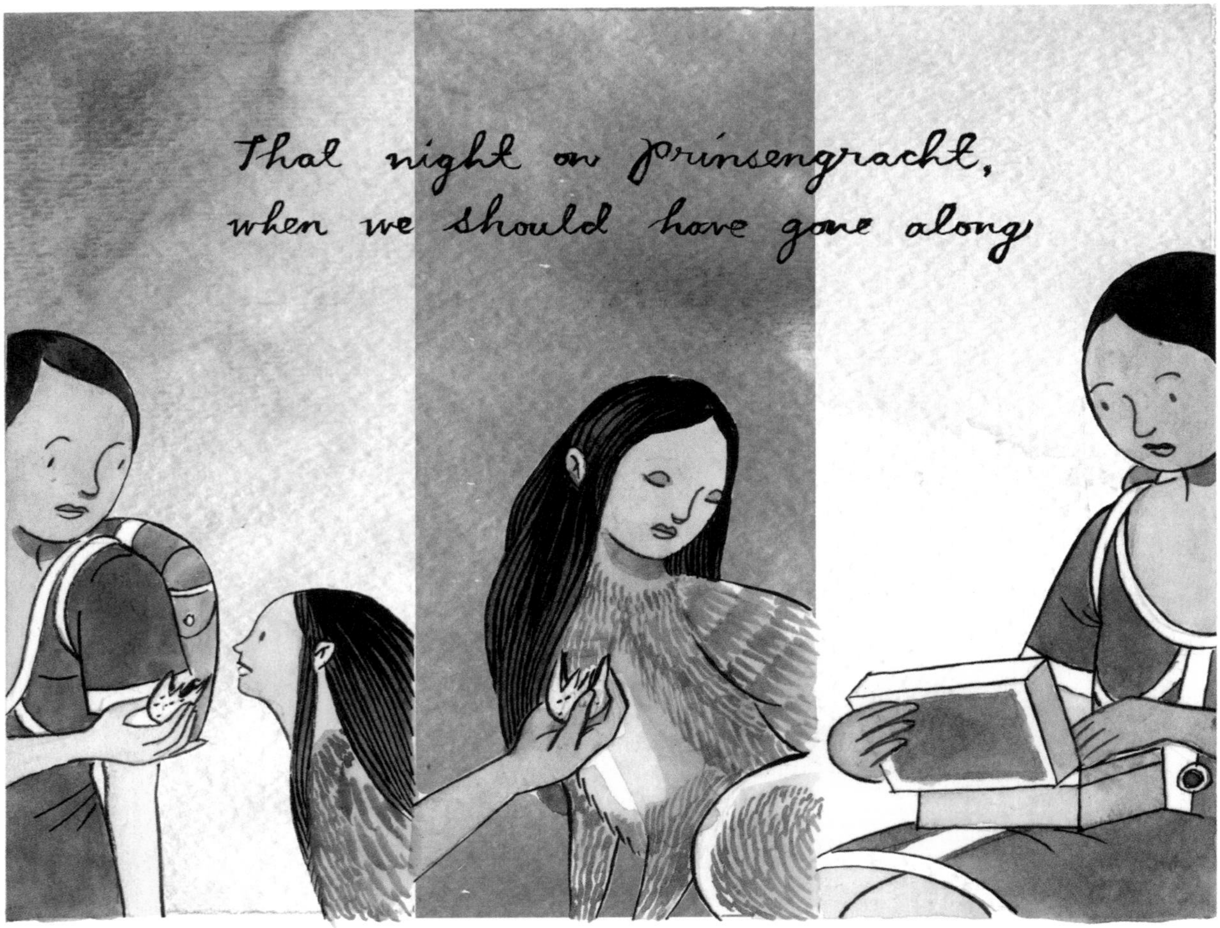
That night on Prinsengracht,
when we should have gone along

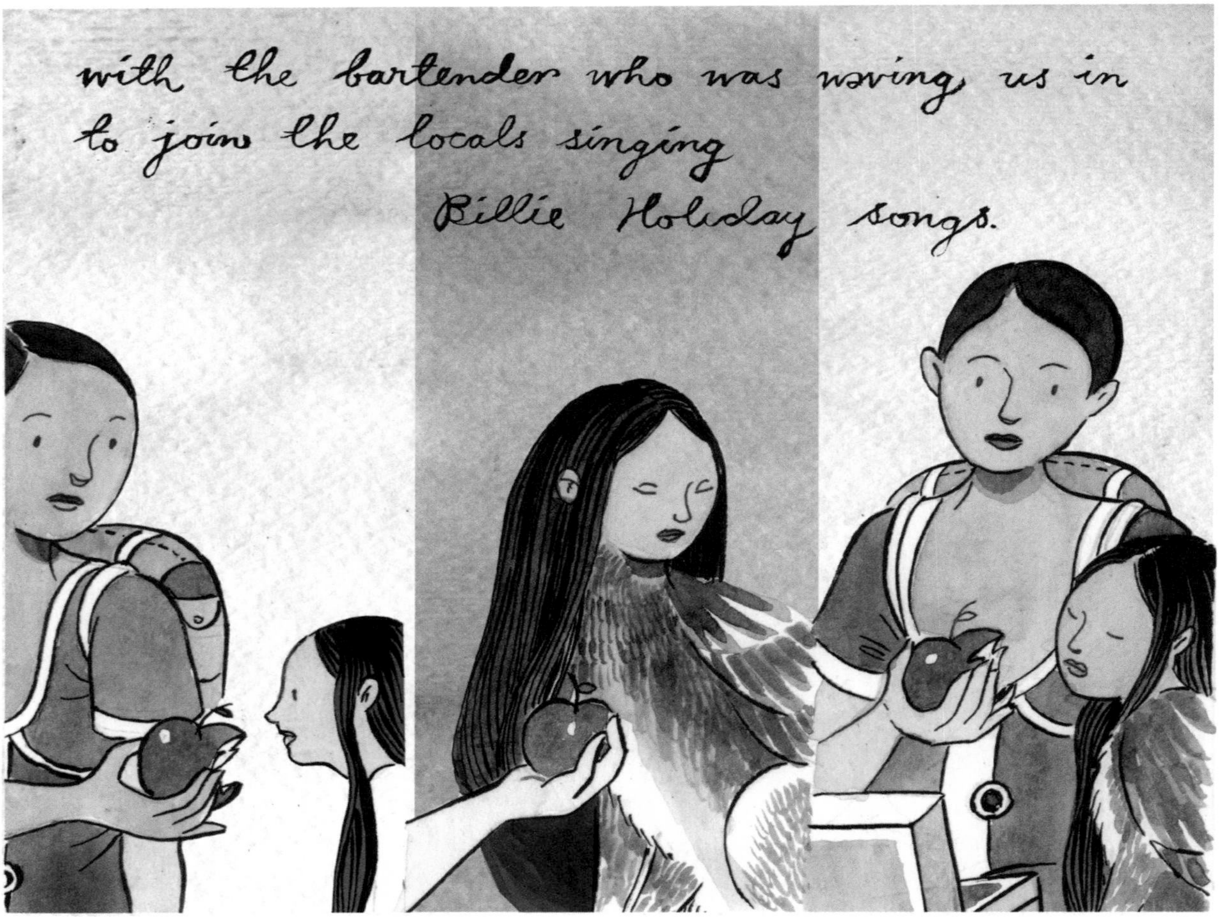
with the bartender who was waving us in
to join the locals singing
Billie Holiday songs.

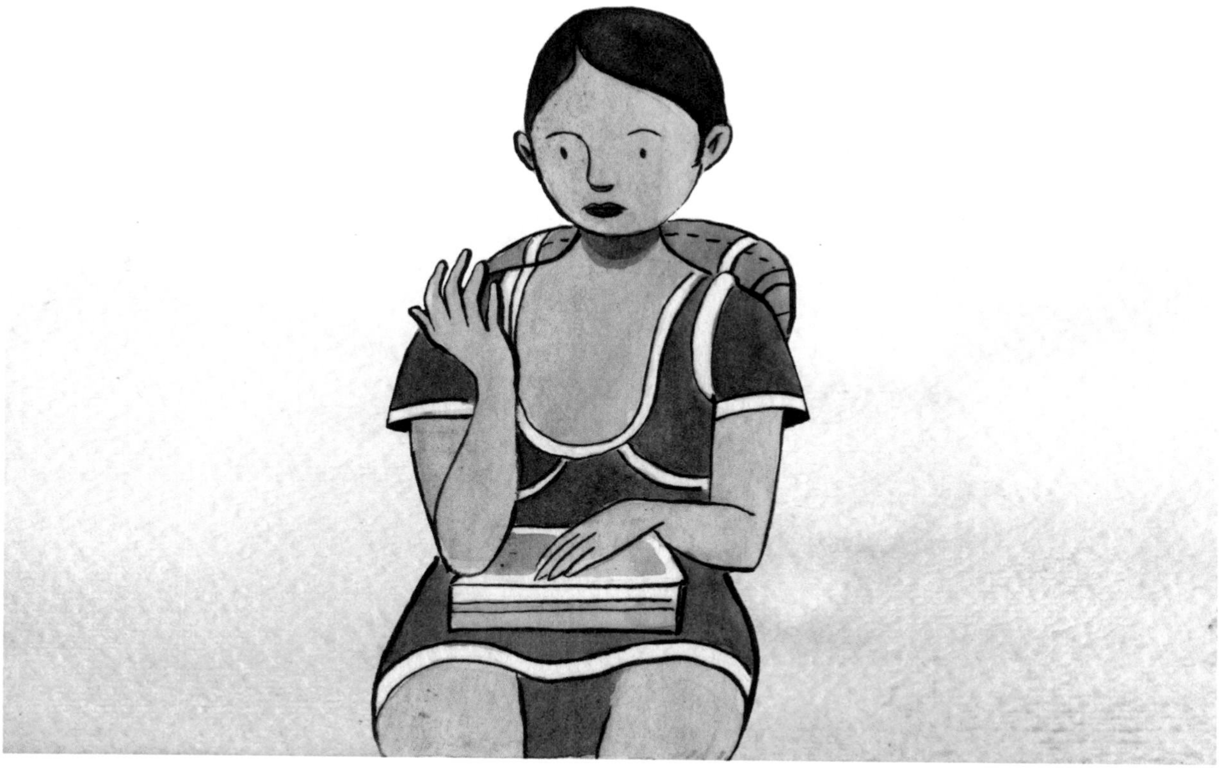

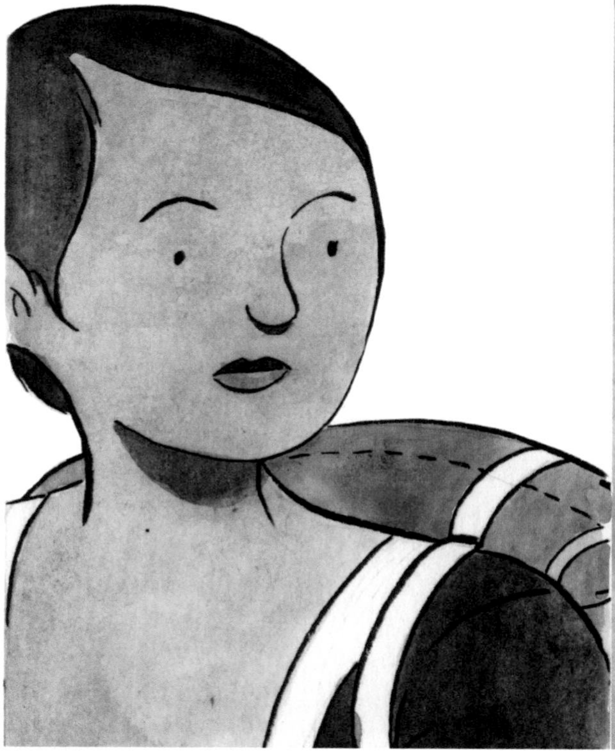

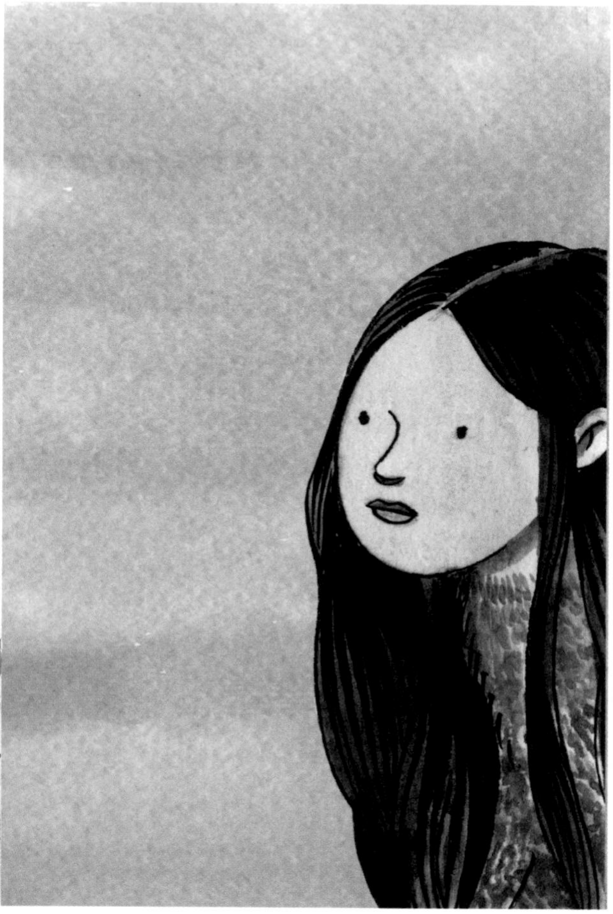

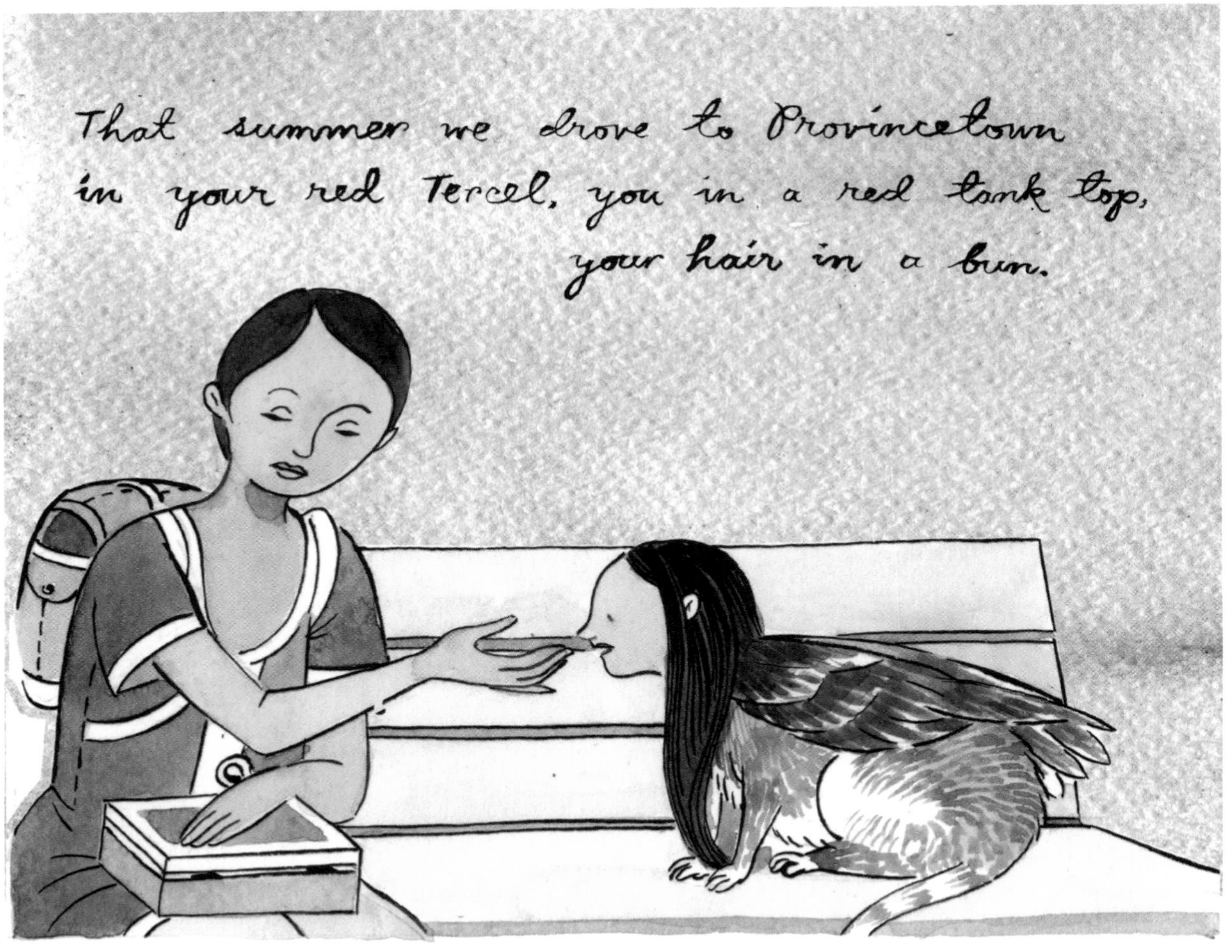
That summer we drove to Provincetown
in your red Tercel, you in a red tank top,
your hair in a bun.

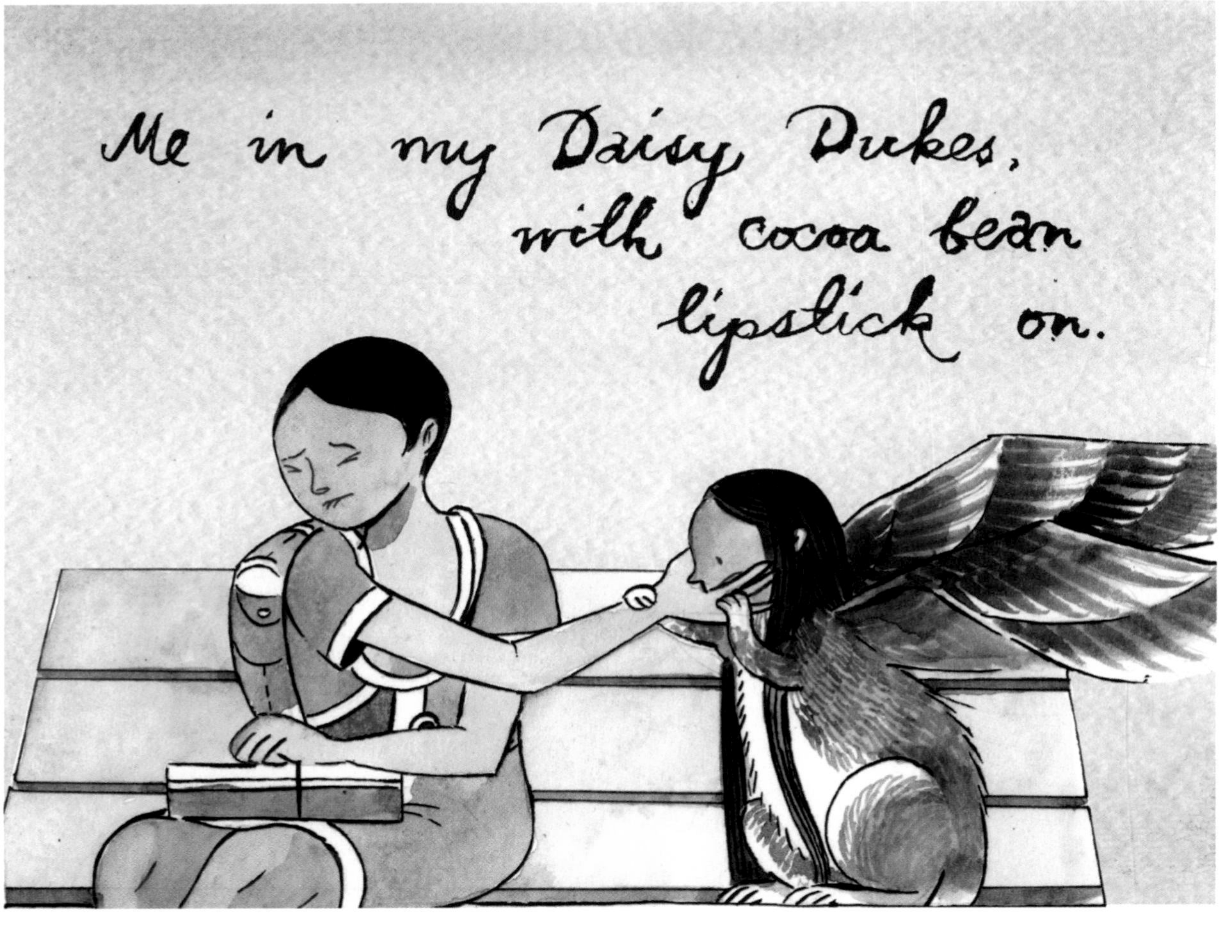
Me in my Daisy Dukes,
with cocoa bean
lipstick on.

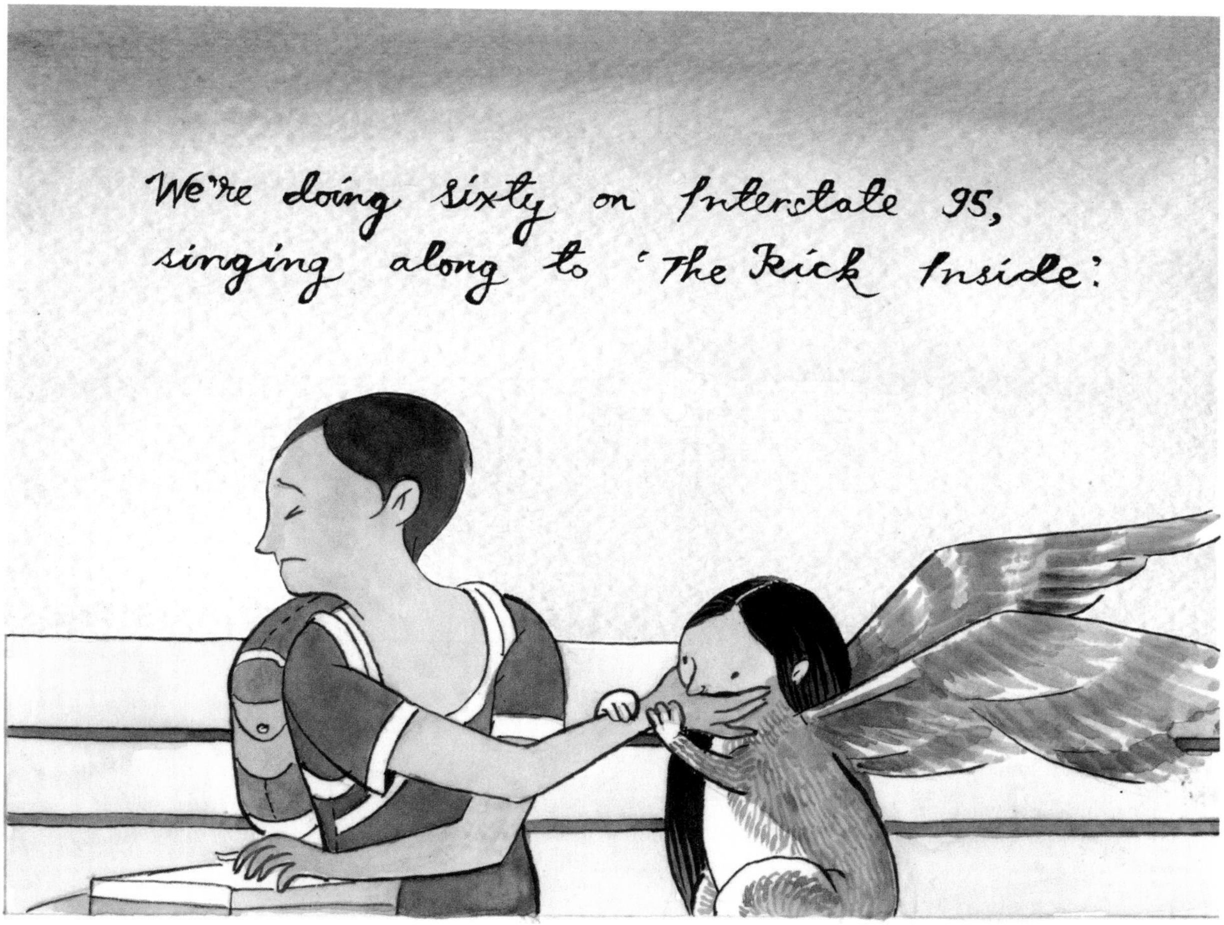
We're doing sixty on Interstate 95,
singing along to 'The Kick Inside.'

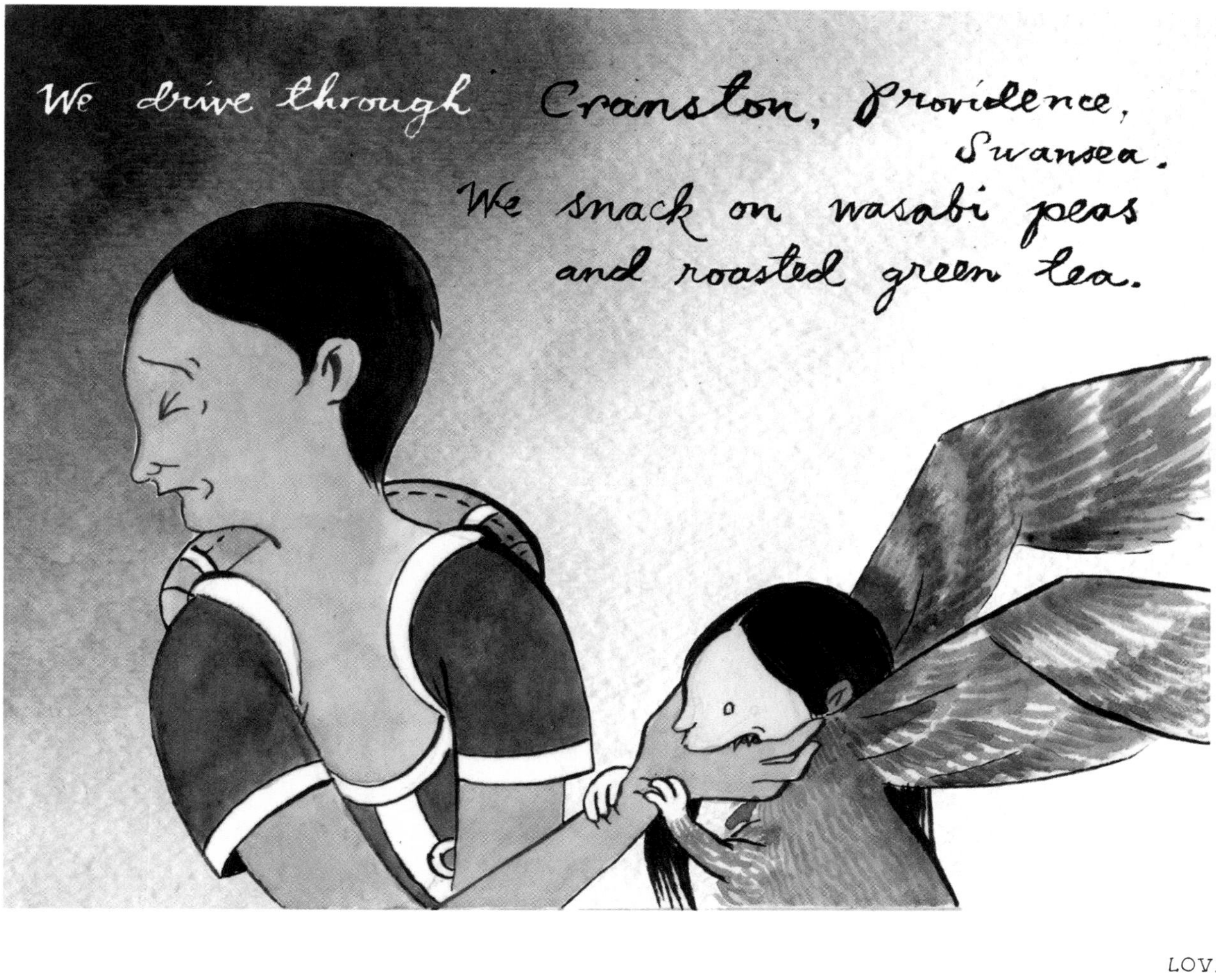
We drive through Cranston, Providence,
Swansea.
We snack on wasabi peas
and roasted green tea.

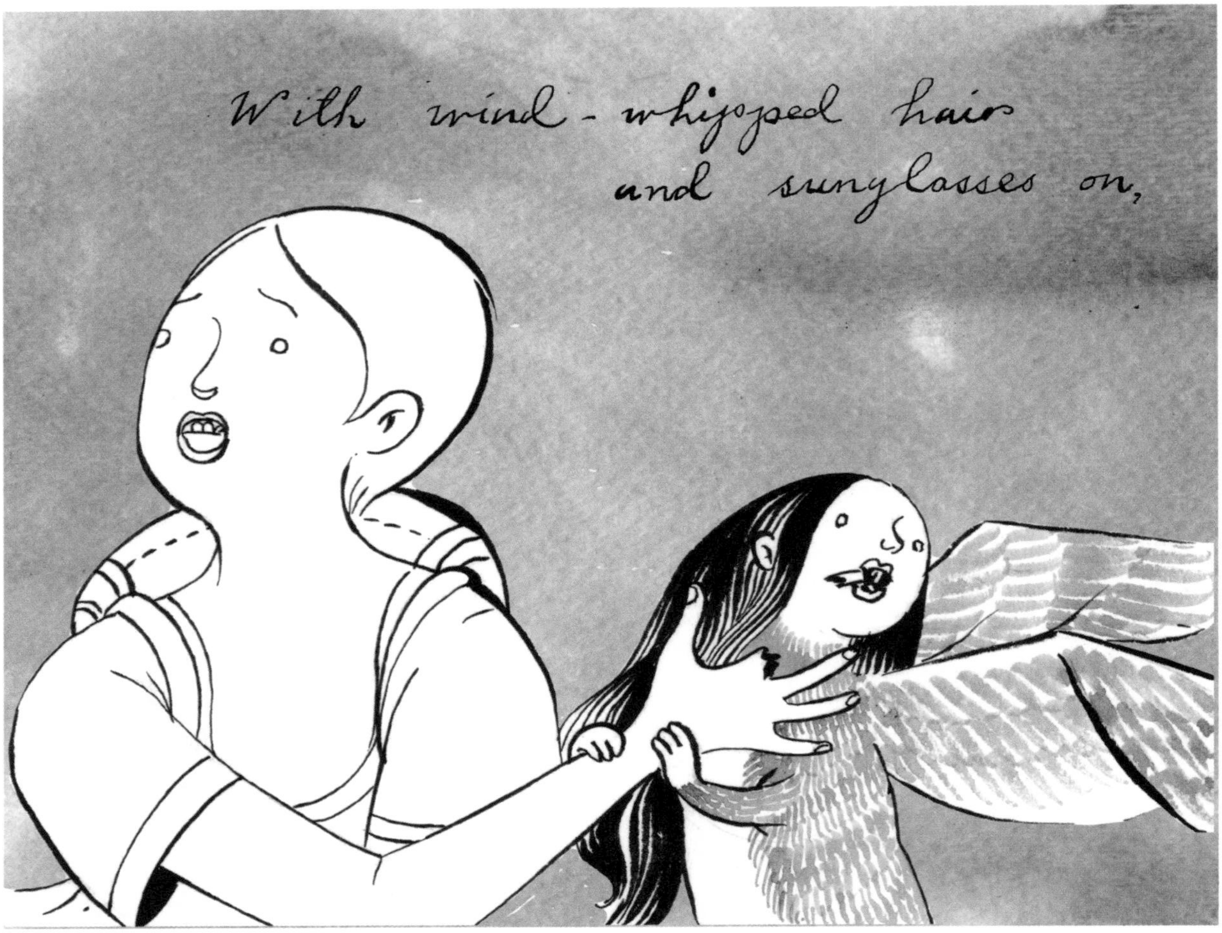
With wind-whipped hair
and sunglasses on,

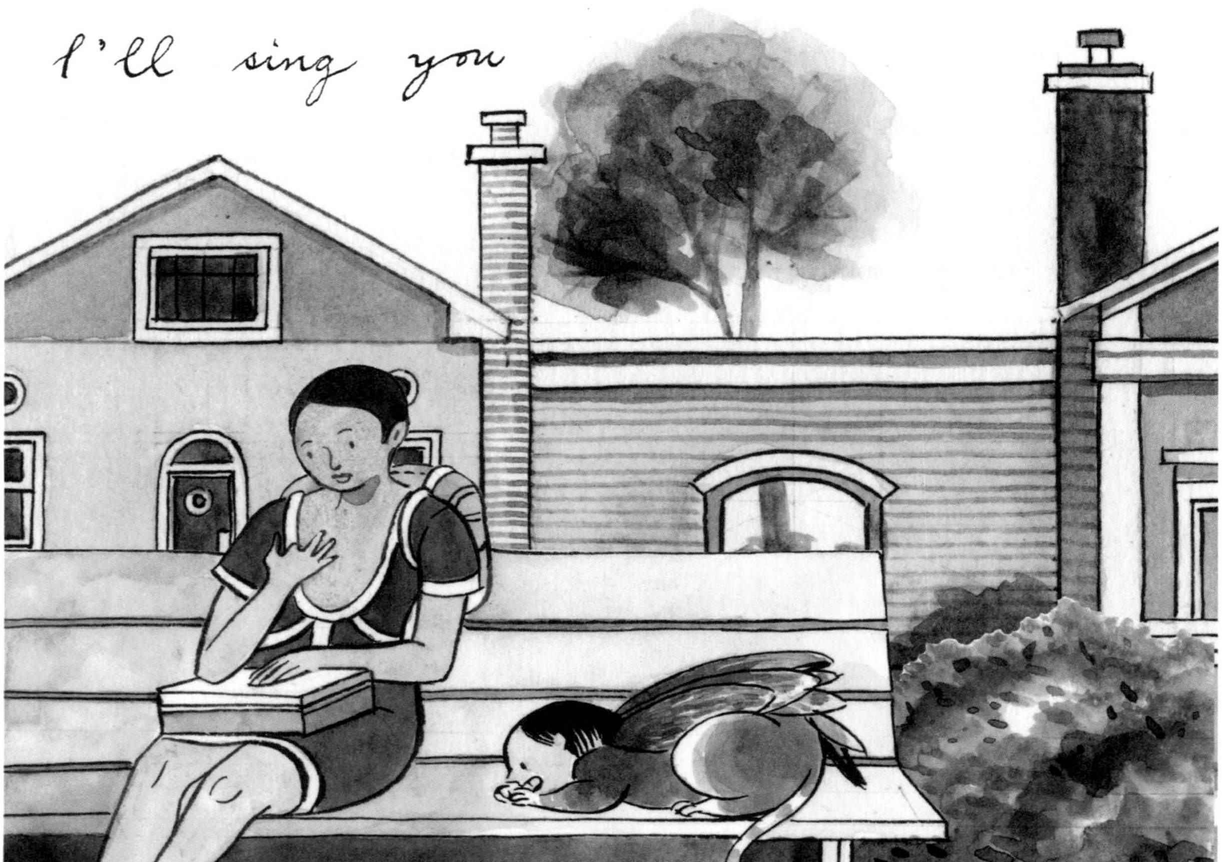
I'll sing you

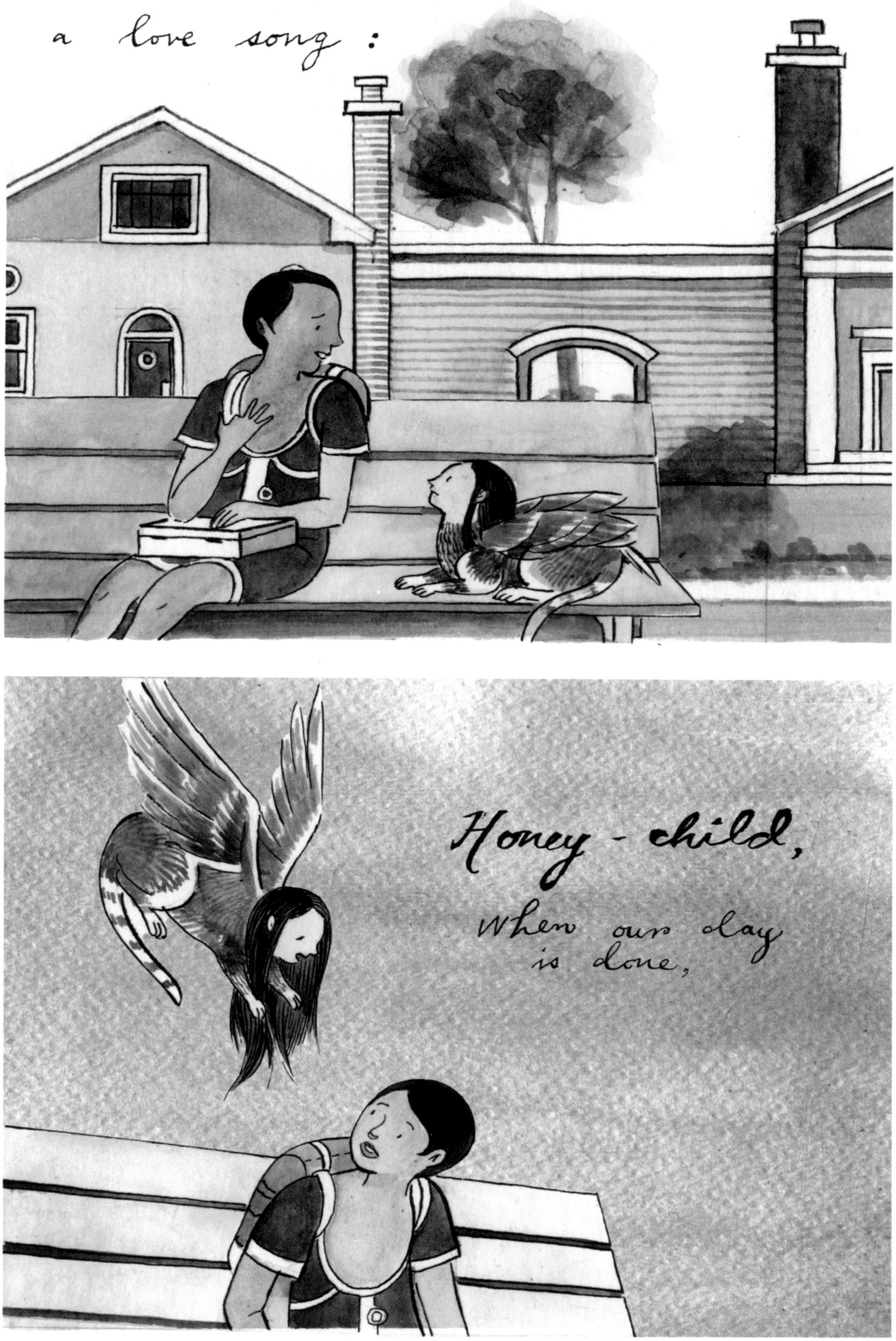
a love song:
Honey-child,
when our day is done,

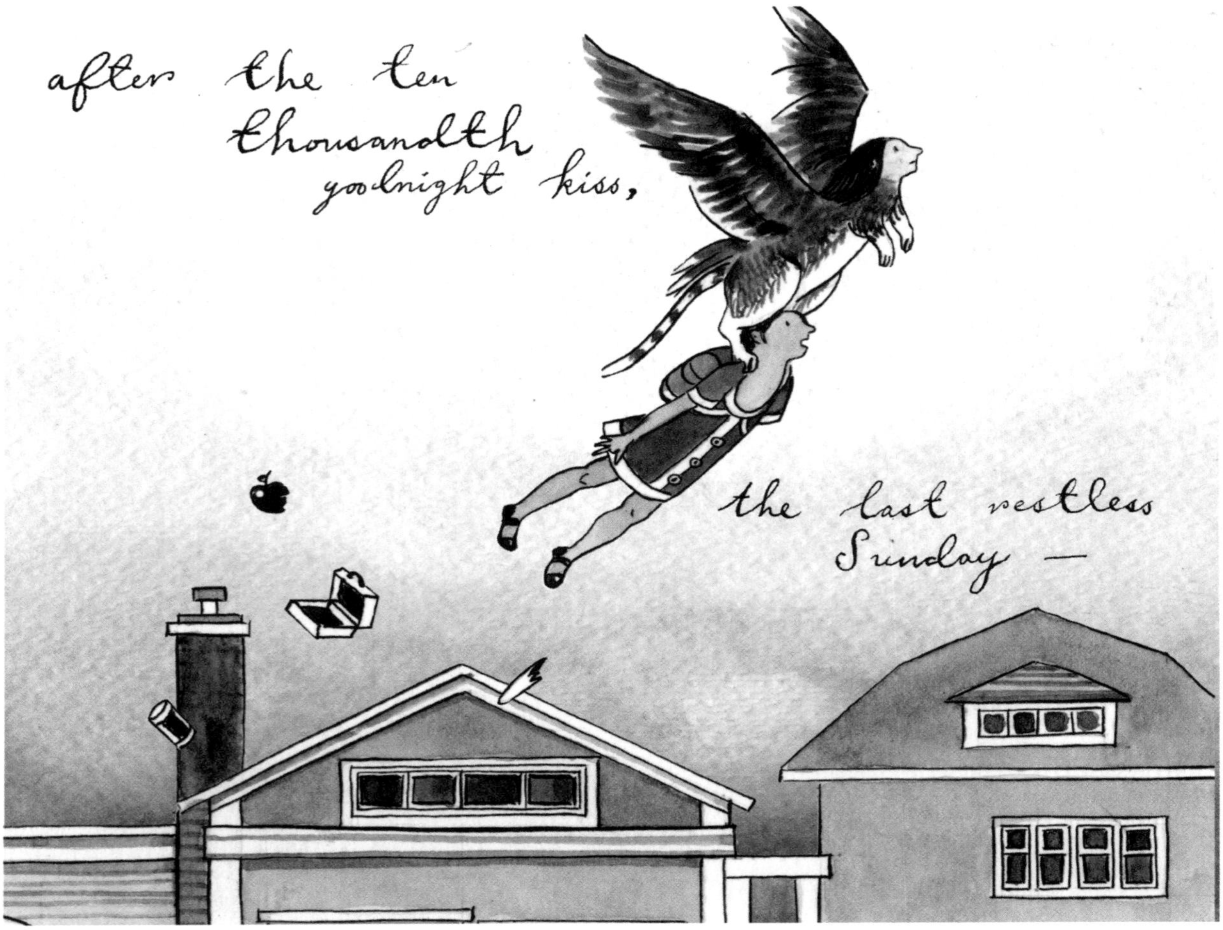
after the ten thousandth goodnight kiss,
the last restless Sunday —

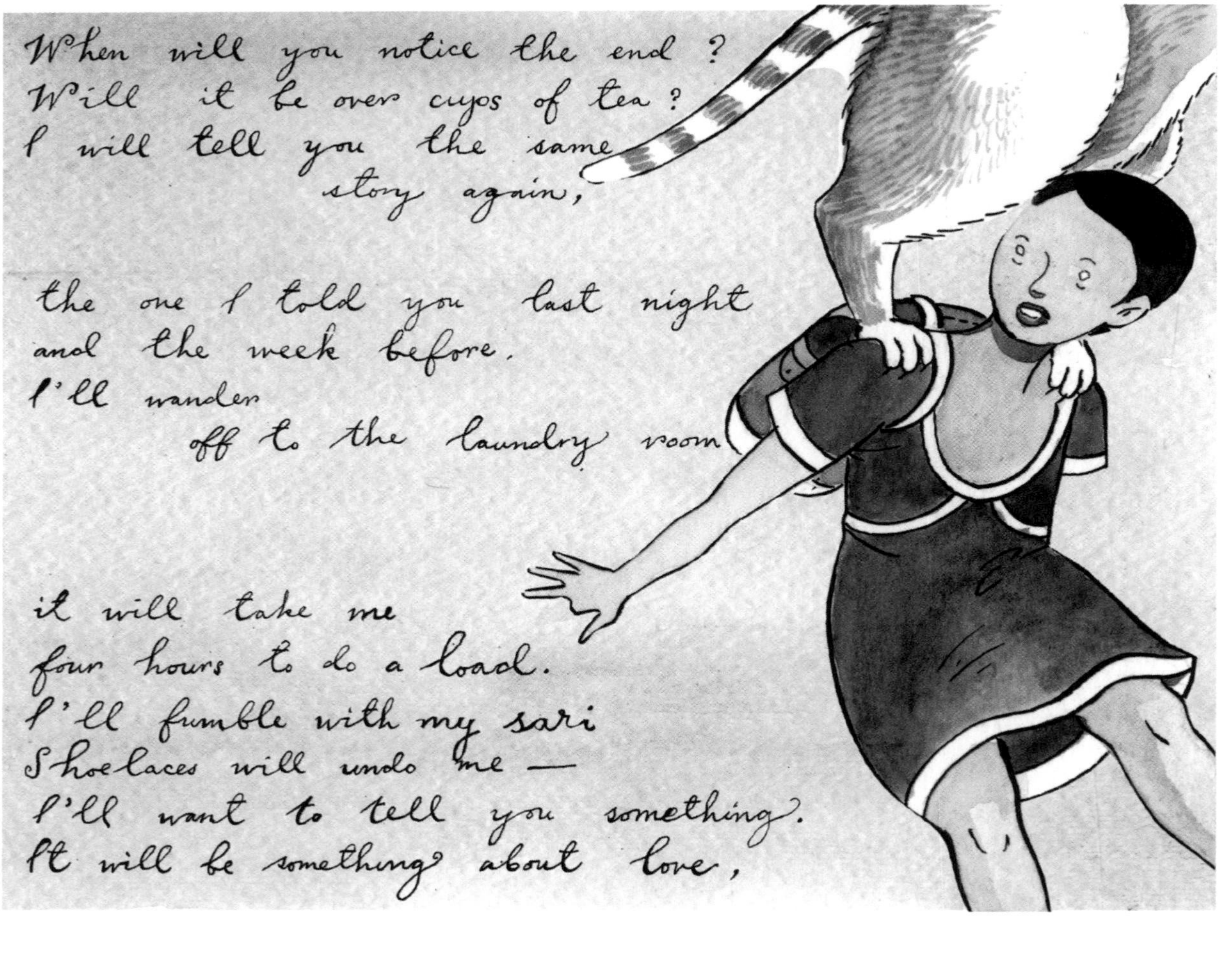
When will you notice the end?
Will it be over cups of tea?
I will tell you the same story again,
the one I told you last night and the week before.
I'll wander off to the laundry room
it will take me four hours to do a load.
I'll fumble with my sari
Shoelaces will undo me —
I'll want to tell you something.
It will be something about love,

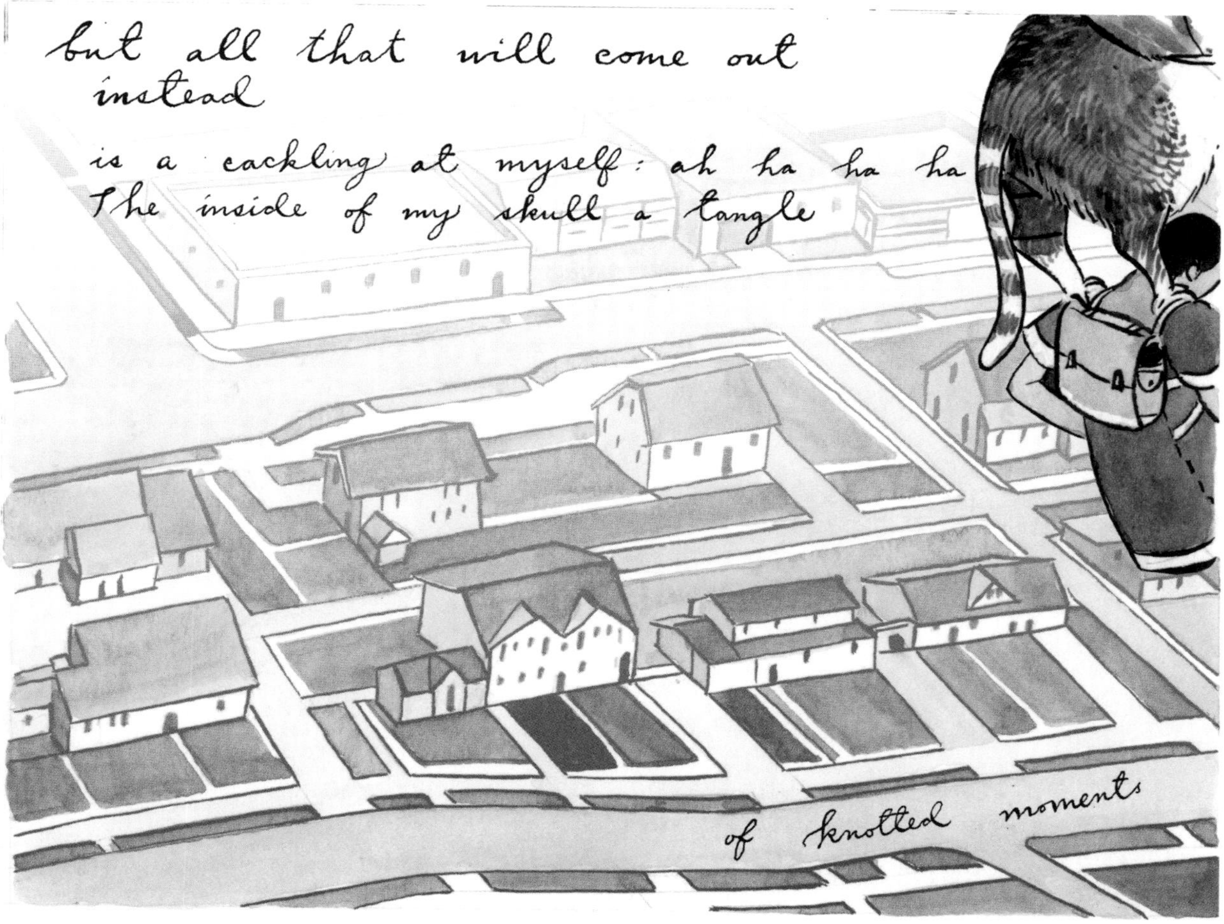
but all that will come out
instead
is a cackling at myself: ah ha ha ha
The inside of my skull a tangle
of knotted moments

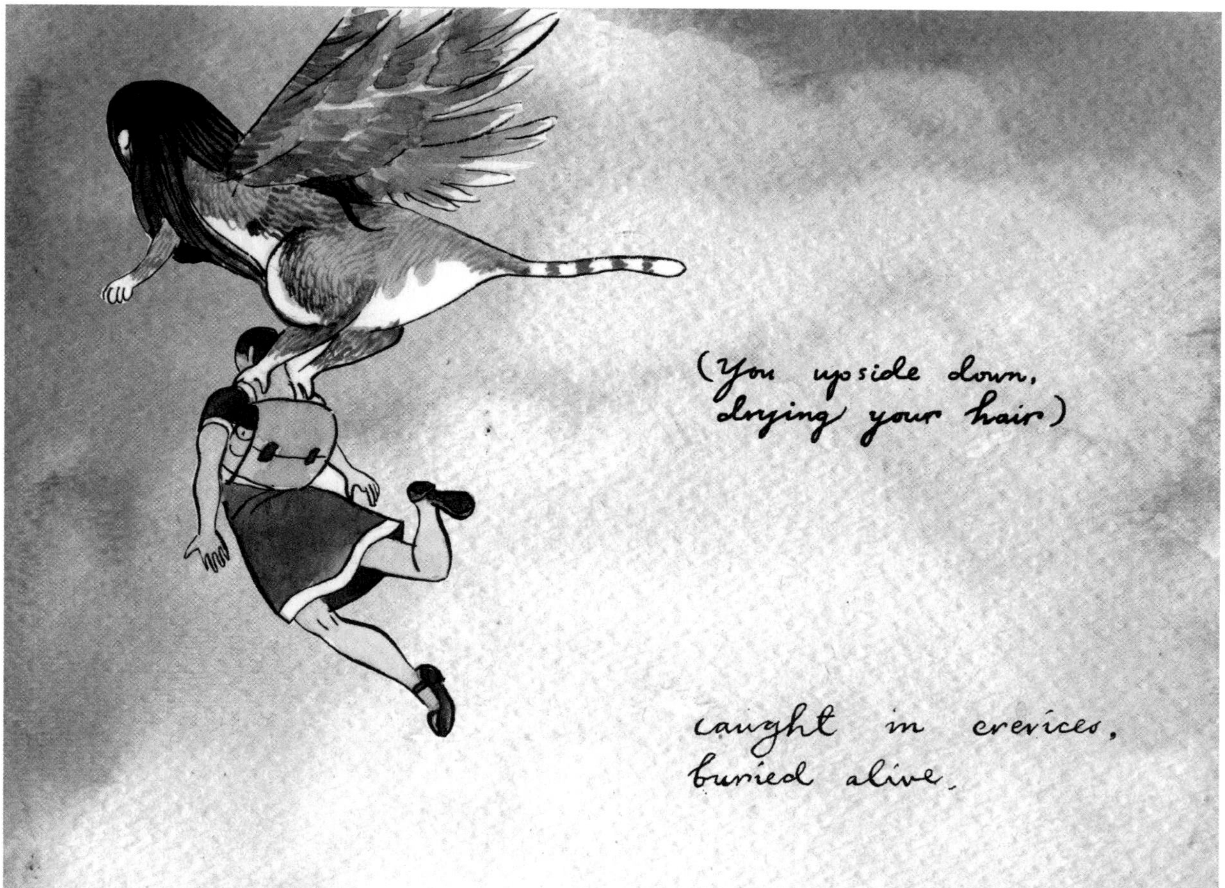
(You upside down,
drying your hair)
caught in crevices,
buried alive.

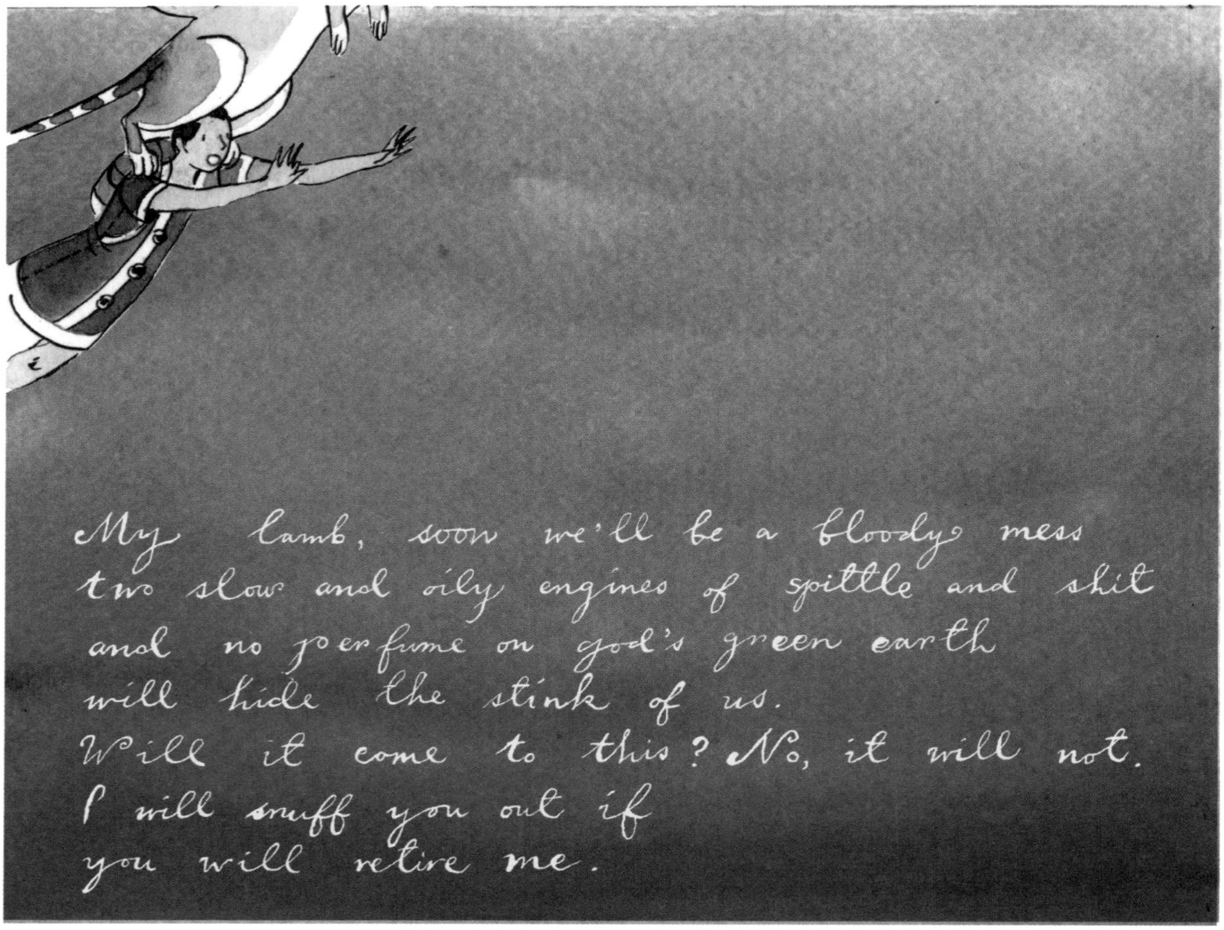
My lamb, soon we'll be a bloody mess
two slow and oily engines of spittle and shit
and no perfume on god's green earth
will hide the stink of us.
Will it come to this? No, it will not.
I will snuff you out if
you will retire me.

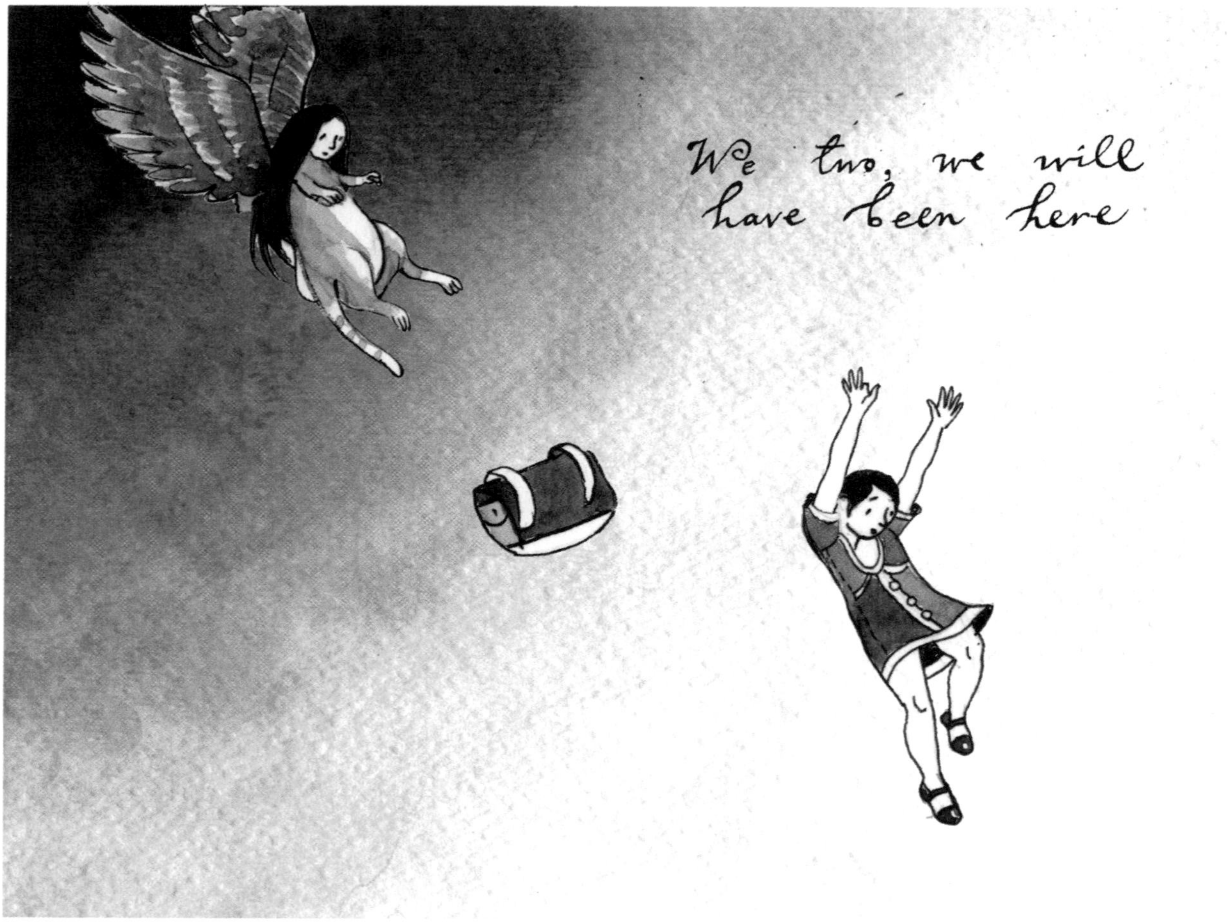
We two, we will
have been here

Long enough."

Look, here are cousins from car crashes.

Here are childhoods

that were cut in half.

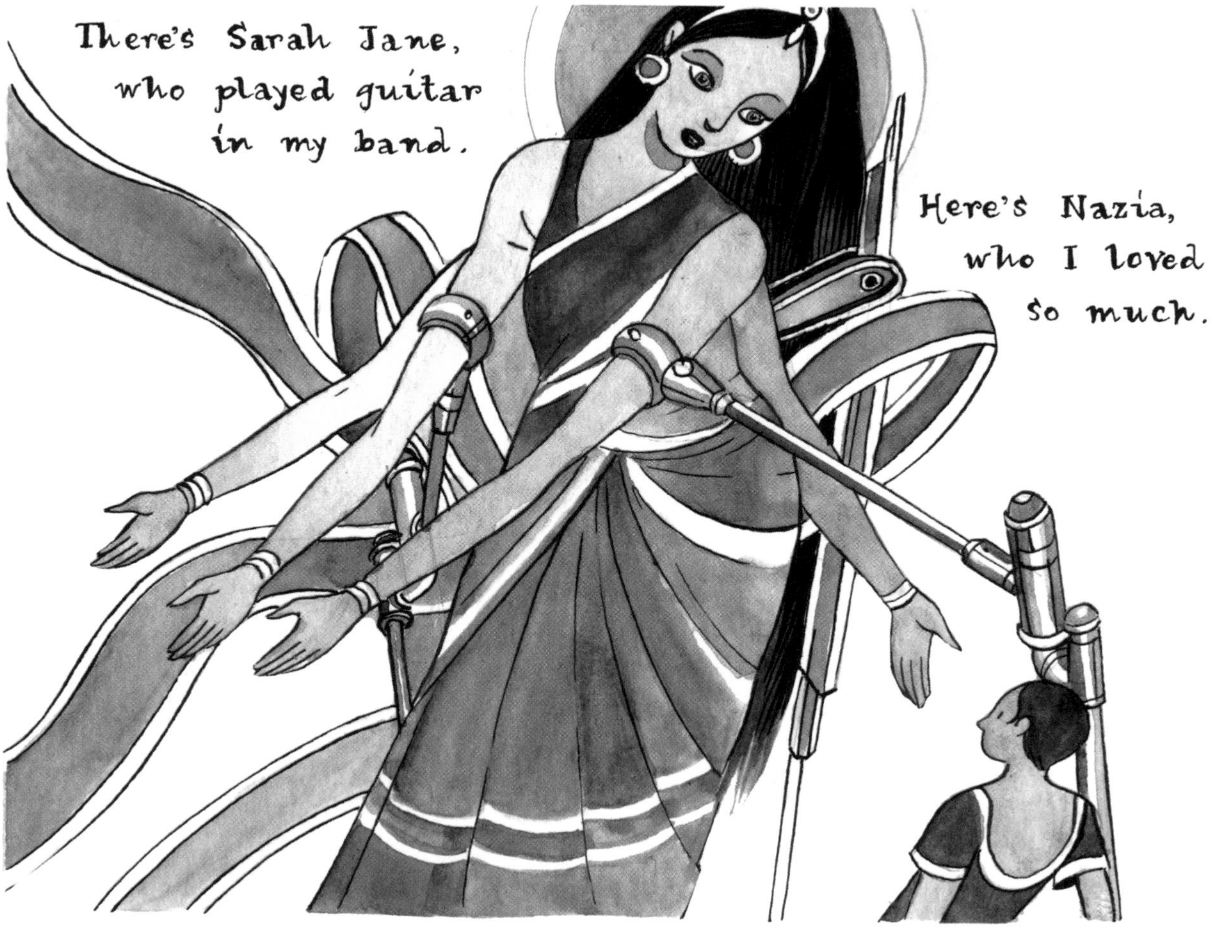
There's Sarah Jane, who played guitar in my band.
Here's Nazia, who I loved so much.

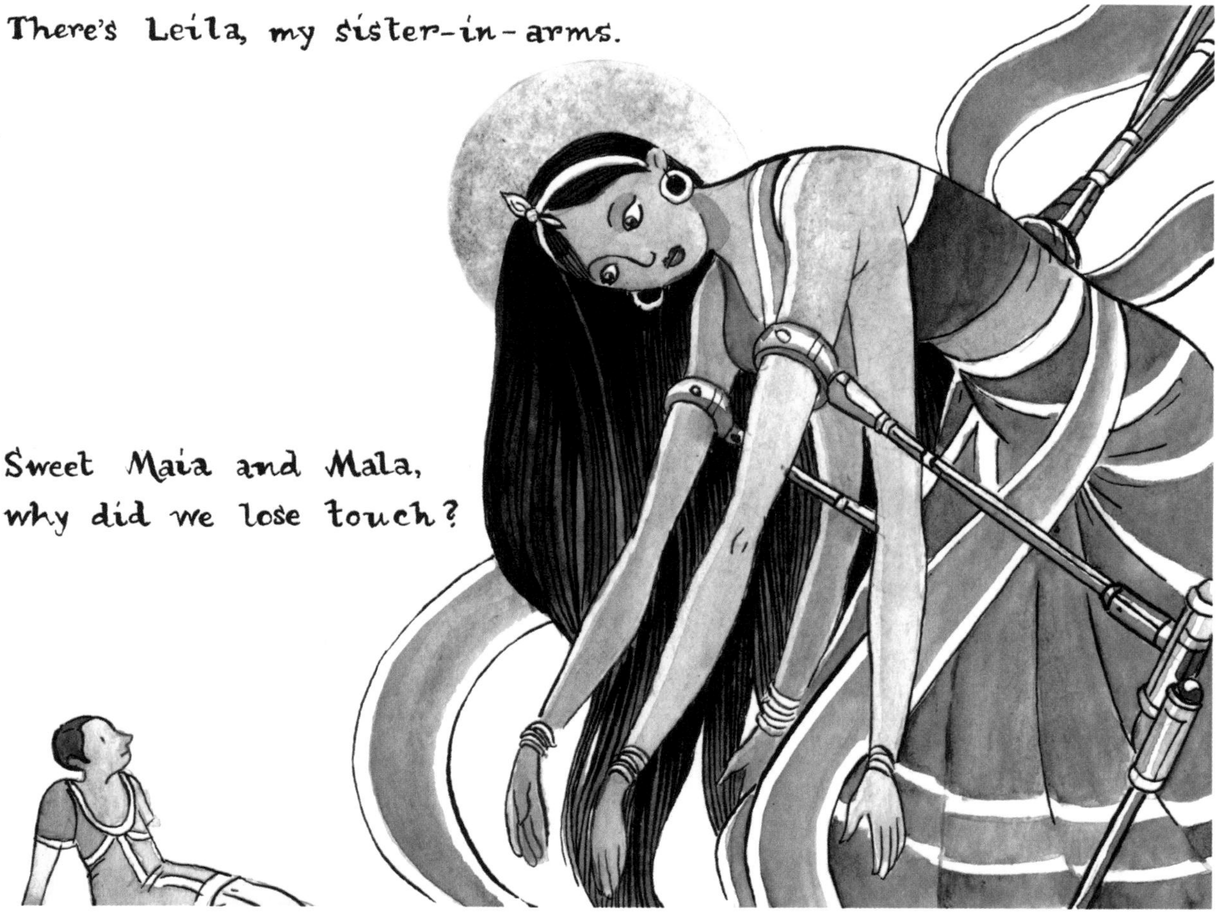
There's Leila, my sister-in-arms.
Sweet Maia and Mala, why did we lose touch?

There's Auntie Sarita in a shimmering kurta.

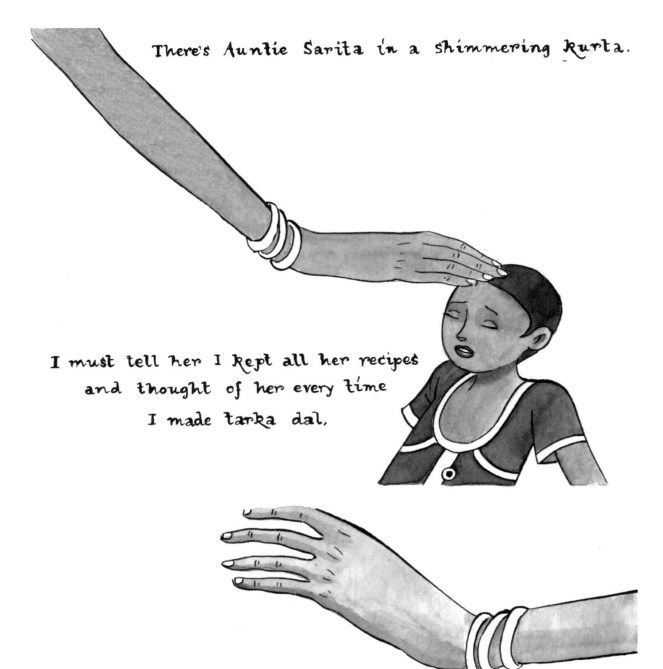

I must tell her I kept all her recipes
and thought of her every time
I made tarka dal.

Oh dear Lavinia,

you impetuous pup,

Where did you run off to
that hot August morning?

We scoured all of Scotia,
but there was no trace at all.

I never had a chance to take you
swimming in the falls.

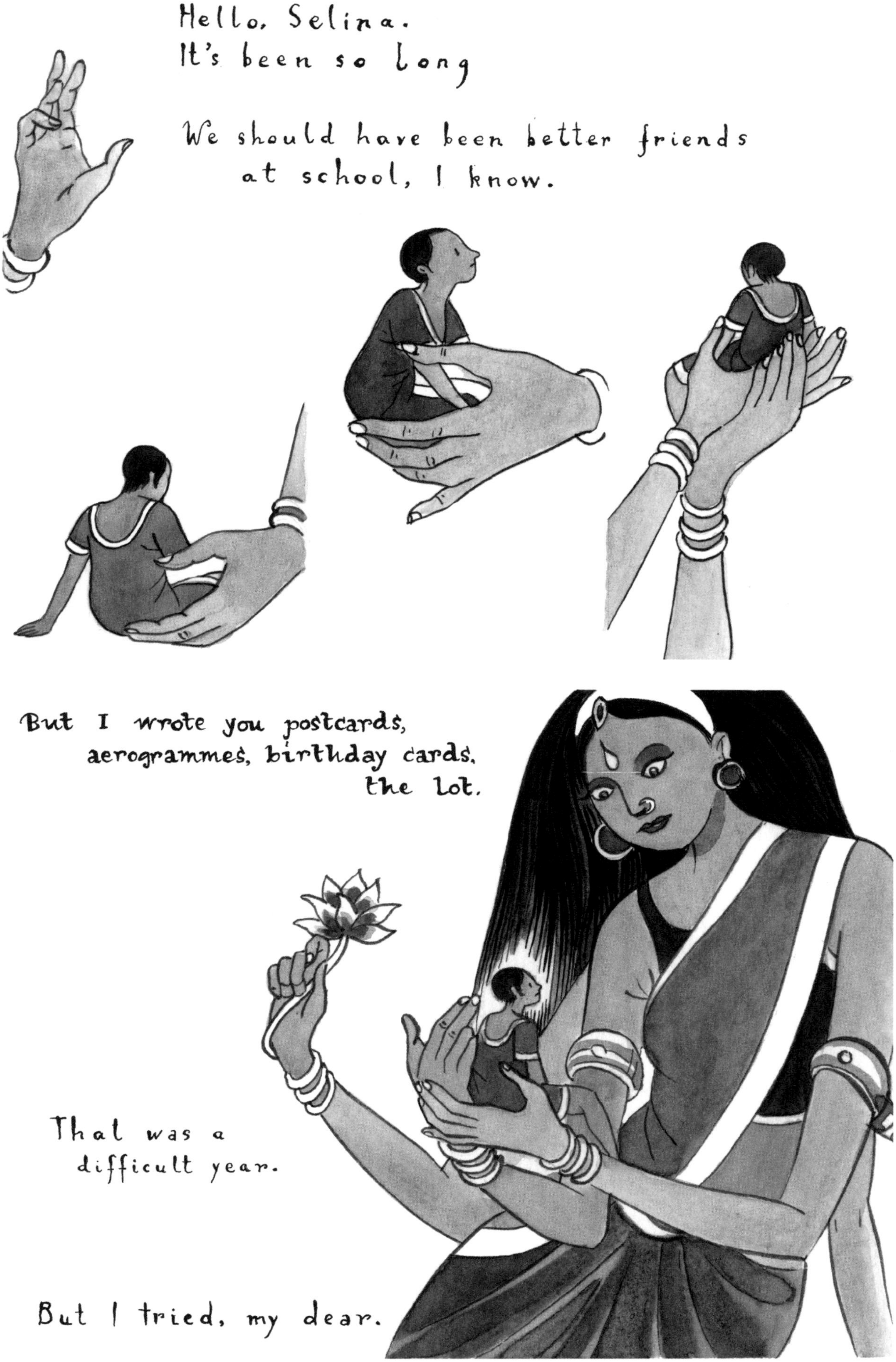
Hello, Selina.
It's been so long
We should have been better friends at school, I know.
But I wrote you postcards, aerogrammes, birthday cards, the lot.
That was a difficult year.
But I tried, my dear.

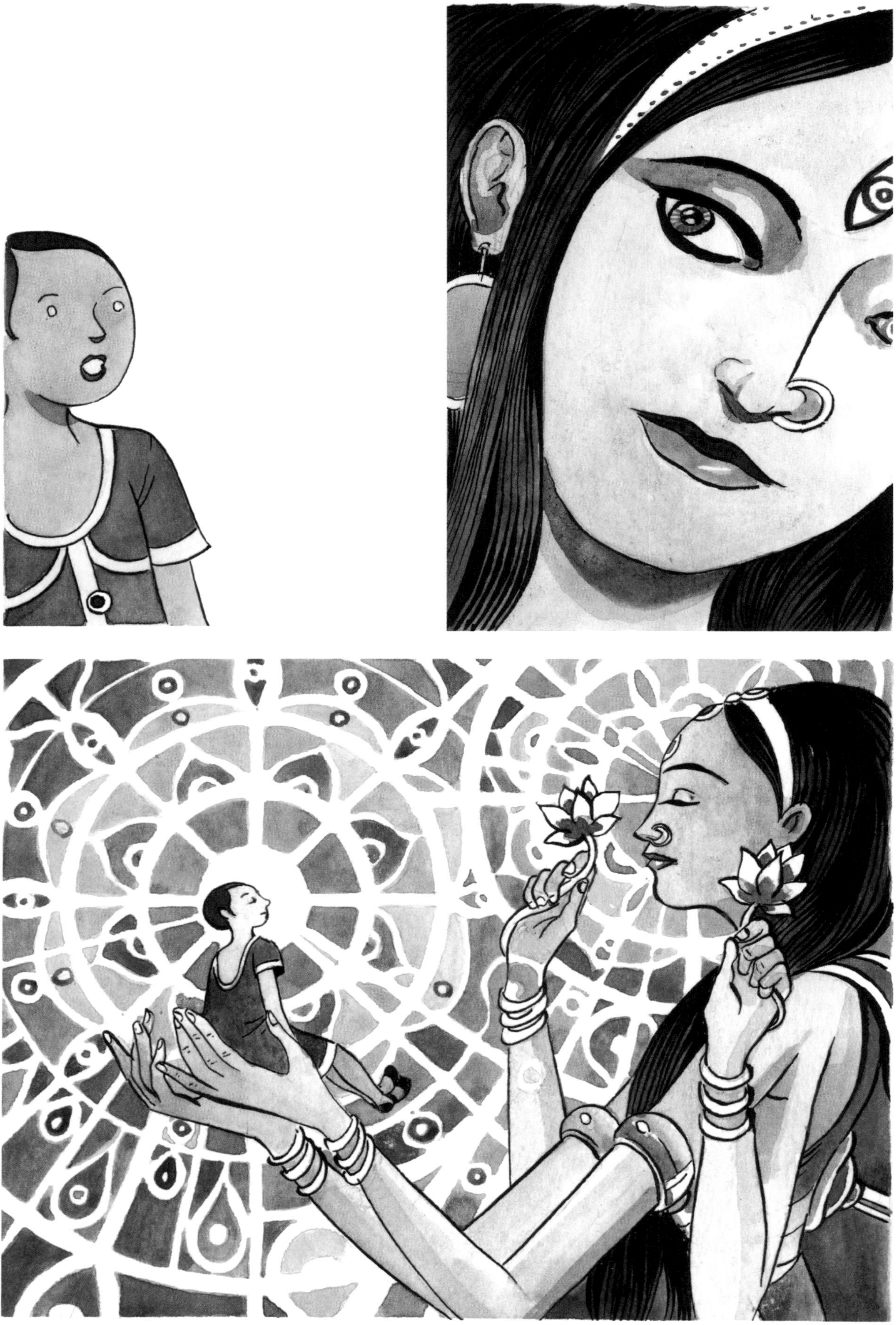

I tried.

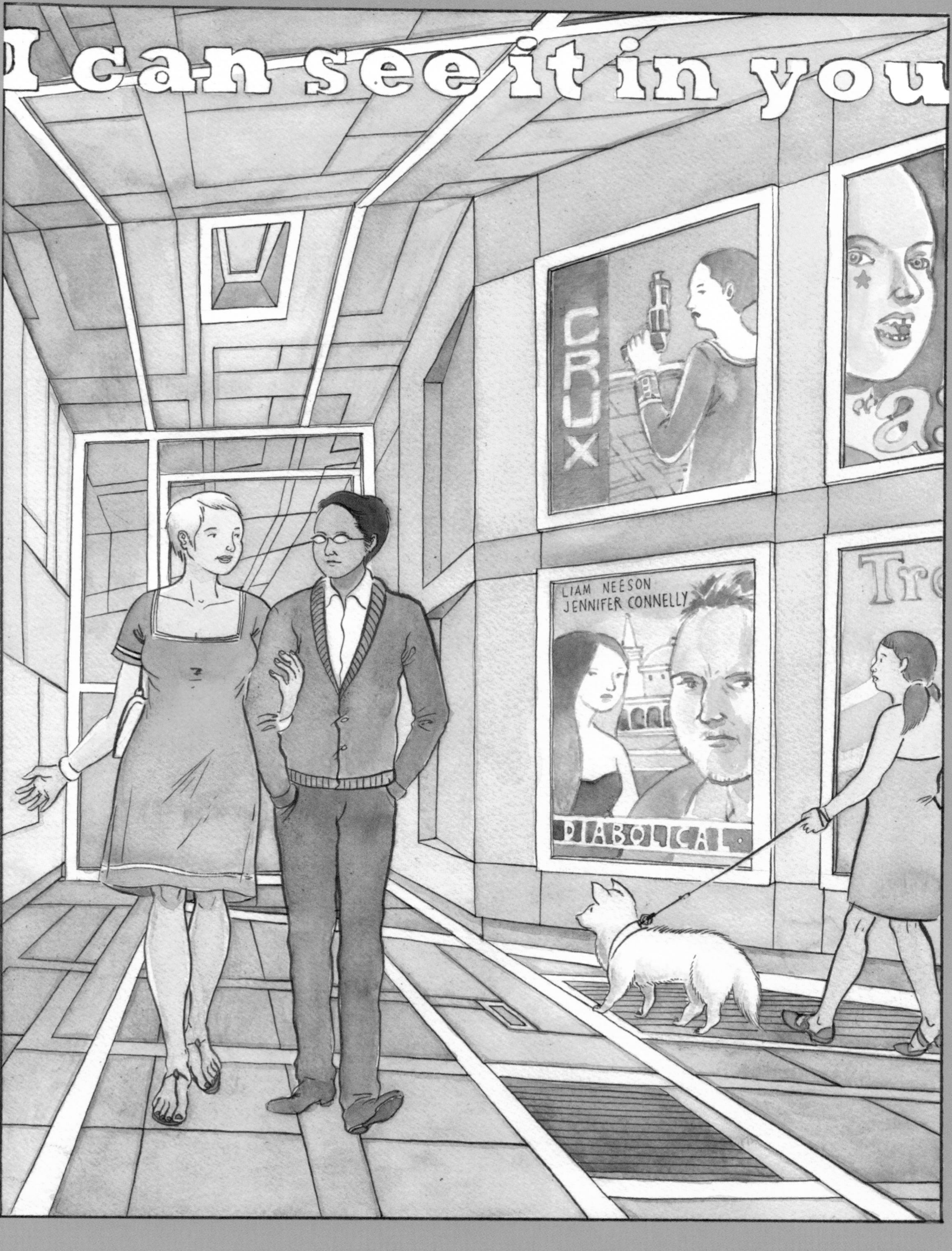
I can see it in you
CRUX
LIAM NEESON
JENNIFER CONNELLY
DIABOLICAL

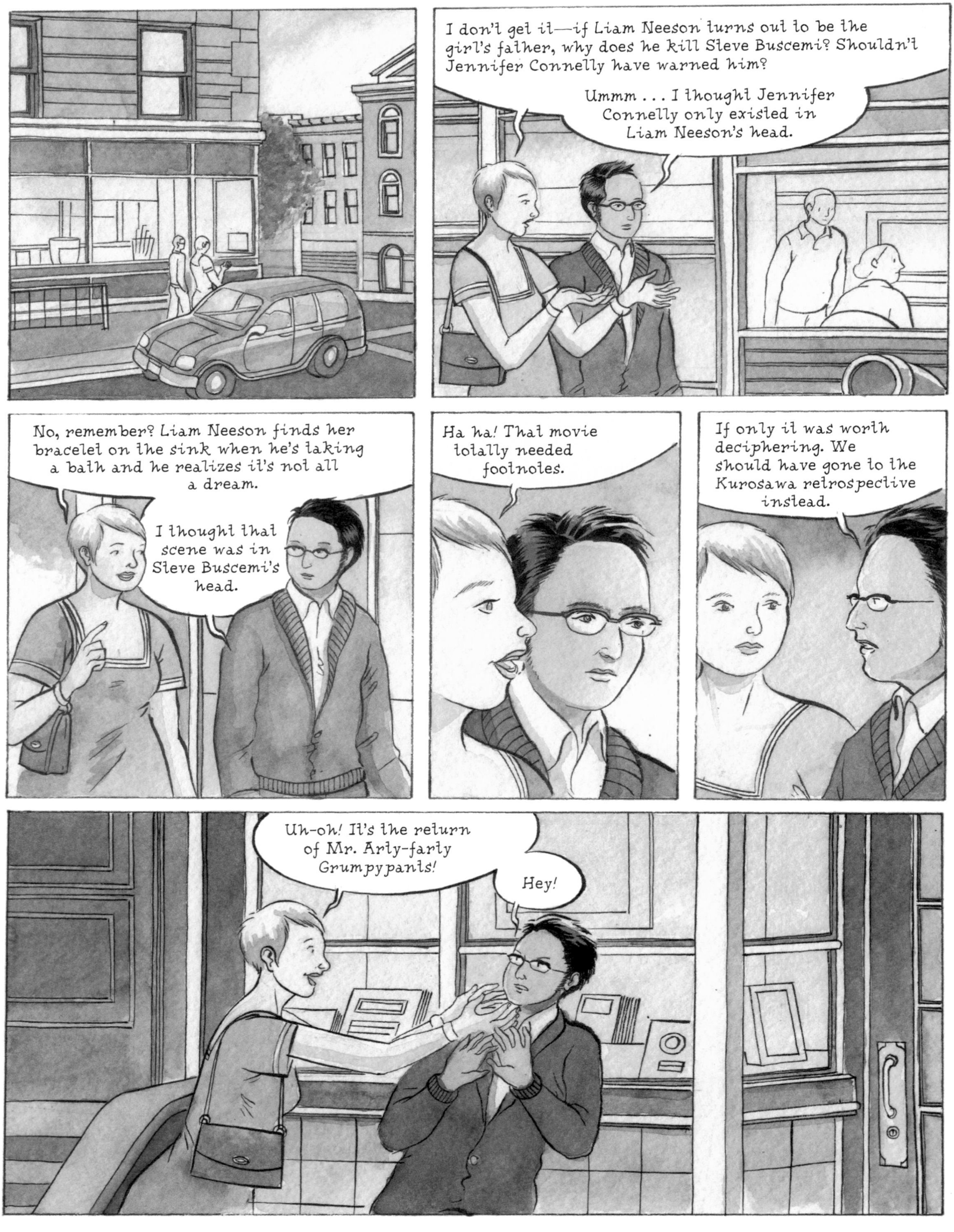
I don't get it—if Liam Neeson turns out to be the girl's father, why does he kill Steve Buscemi? Shouldn't Jennifer Connelly have warned him?
Ummm . . . I thought Jennifer Connelly only existed in Liam Neeson's head.
No, remember? Liam Neeson finds her bracelet on the sink when he's taking a bath and he realizes it's not all a dream.
I thought that scene was in Steve Buscemi's head.
Ha ha! That movie totally needed footnotes.
If only it was worth deciphering. We should have gone to the Kurosawa retrospective instead.
Uh-oh! It's the return of Mr. Arty-farty Grumpypants!
Hey!

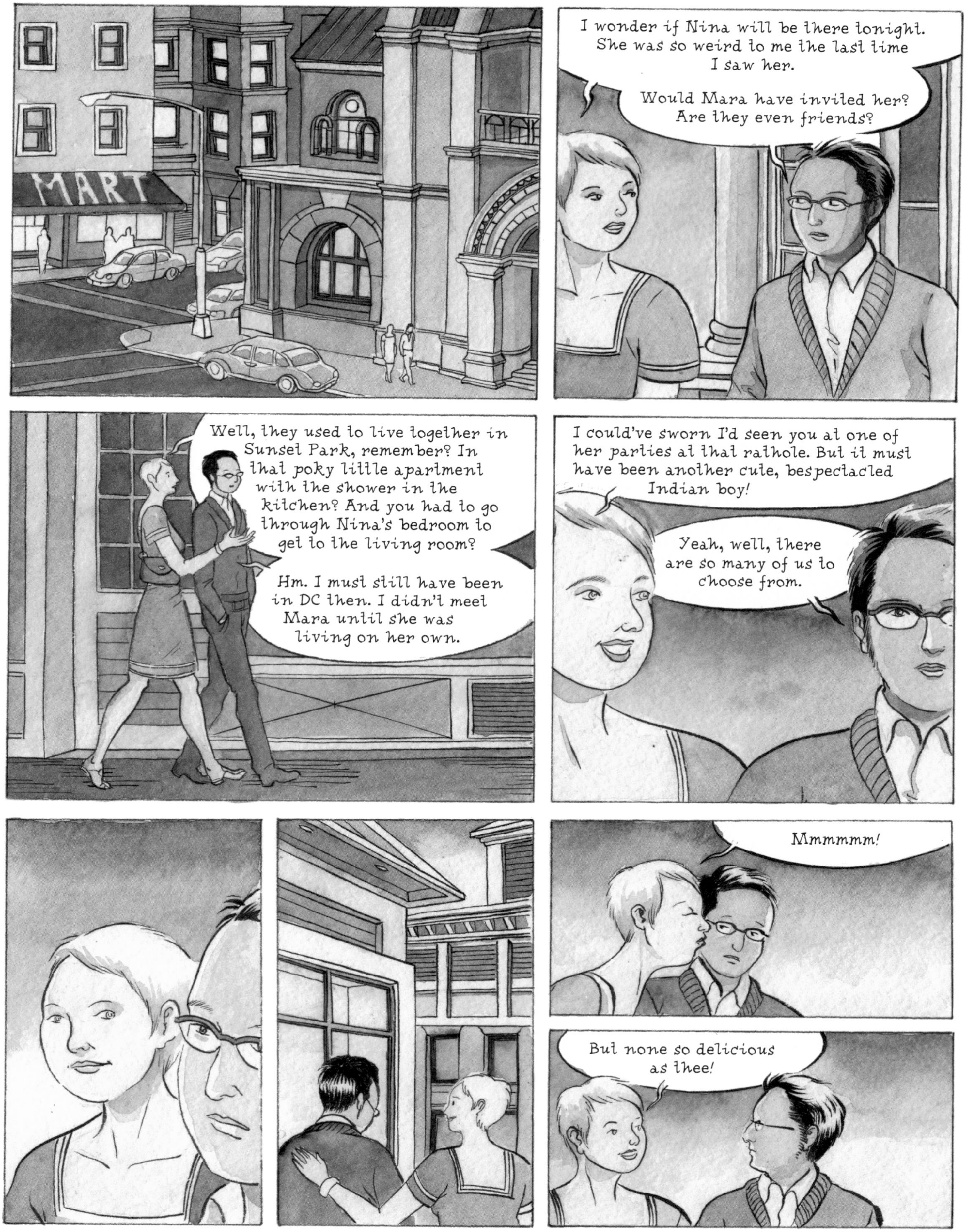
MART
I wonder if Nina will be there tonight. She was so weird to me the last time I saw her.
Would Mara have invited her? Are they even friends?
Well, they used to live together in Sunset Park, remember? In that poky little apartment with the shower in the kitchen? And you had to go through Nina's bedroom to get to the living room?
Hm. I must still have been in DC then. I didn't meet Mara until she was living on her own.
I could've sworn I'd seen you at one of her parties at that rathole. But it must have been another cute, bespectacled Indian boy!
Yeah, well, there are so many of us to choose from.
Mmmmmm!
But none so delicious as thee!

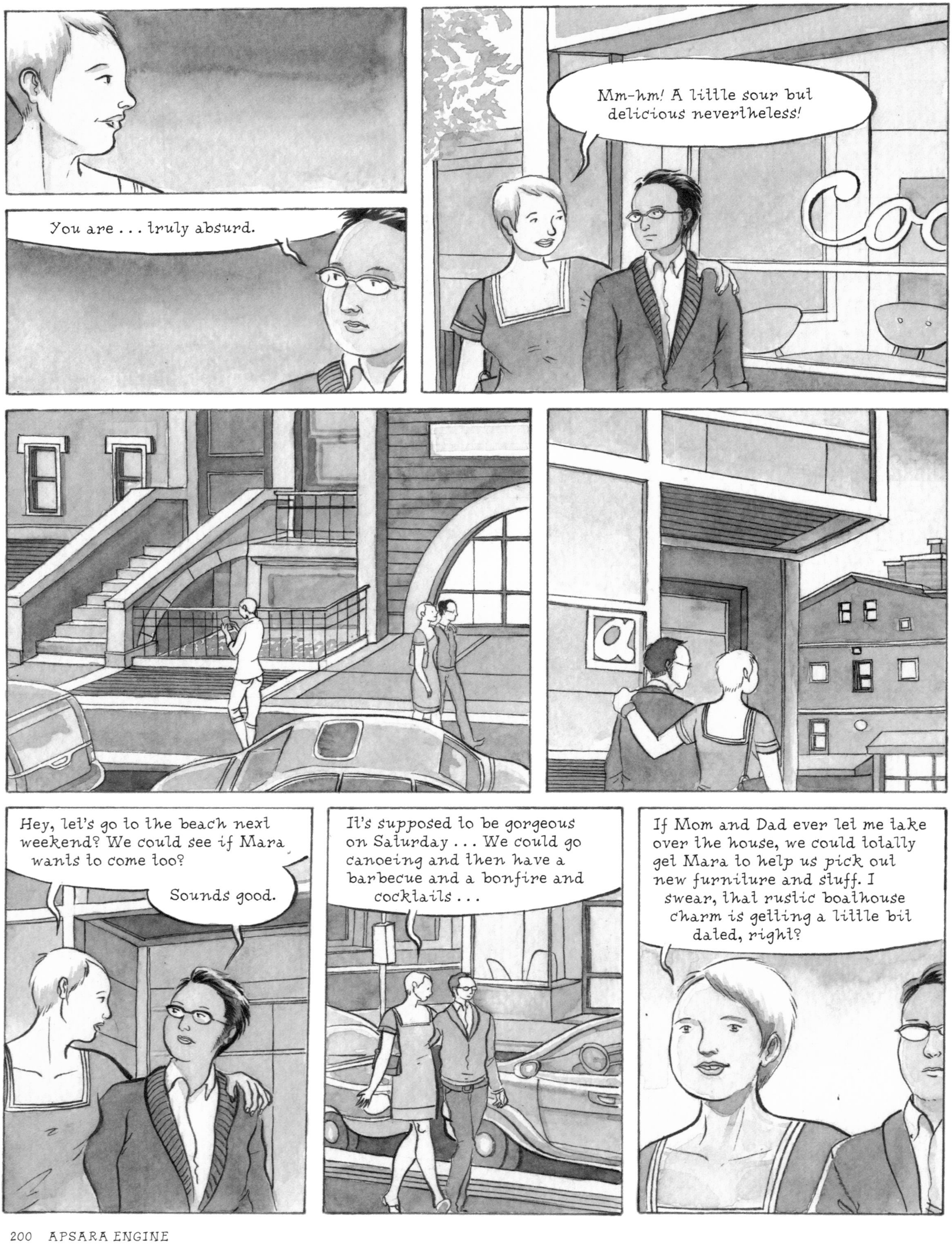
Mm-hm! A little sour but delicious nevertheless!
You are . . . truly absurd.
Hey, let's go to the beach next weekend? We could see if Mara wants to come too?
Sounds good.
It's supposed to be gorgeous on Saturday . . . We could go canoeing and then have a barbecue and a bonfire and cocktails . . .
If Mom and Dad ever let me take over the house, we could totally get Mara to help us pick out new furniture and stuff. I swear, that rustic boathouse charm is getting a little bit dated, right?

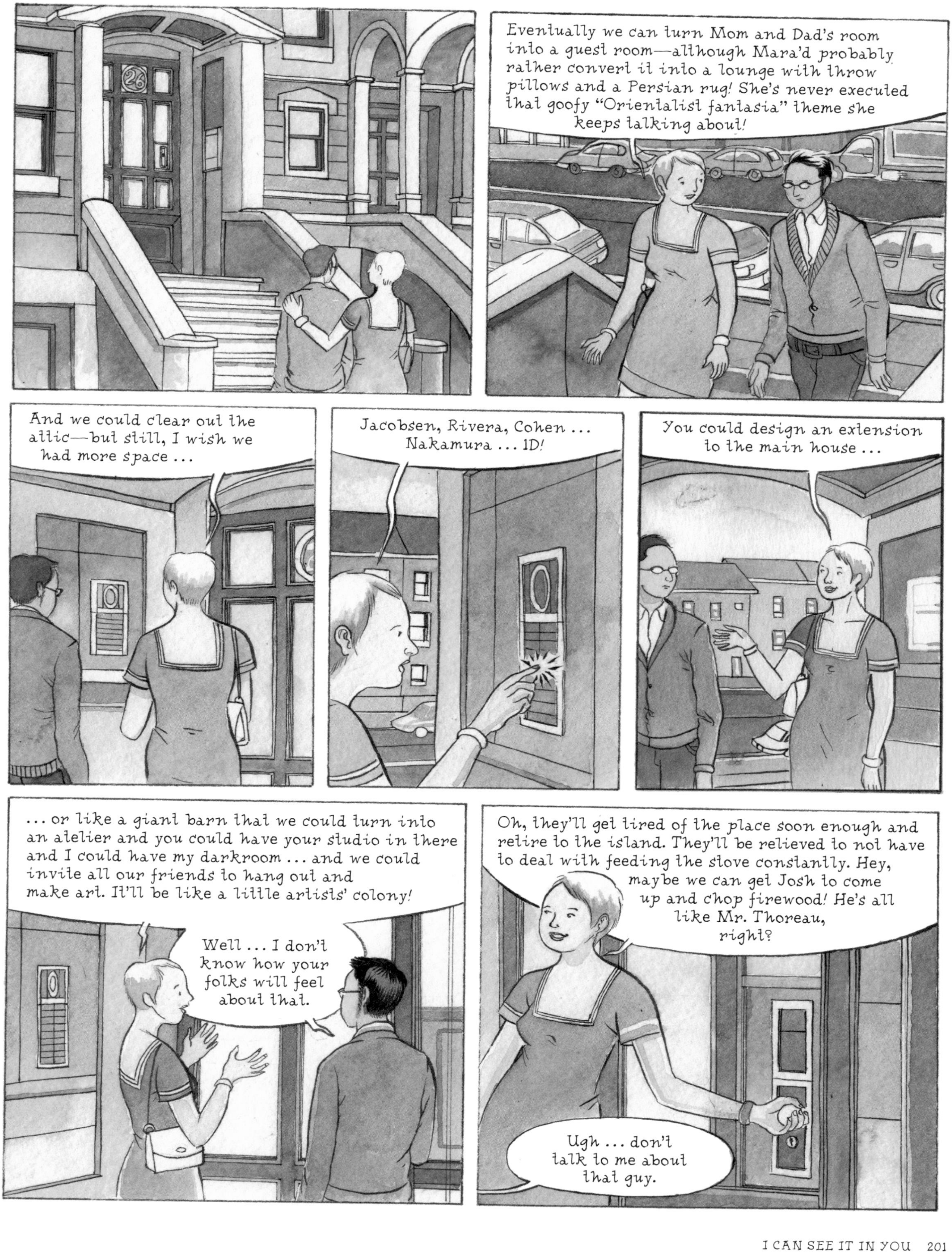
Eventually we can turn Mom and Dad's room into a guest room—although Mara'd probably rather convert it into a lounge with throw pillows and a Persian rug! She's never executed that goofy "Orientalist fantasia" theme she keeps talking about!
And we could clear out the attic—but still, I wish we had more space ...
Jacobsen, Rivera, Cohen ... Nakamura ... 1D!
You could design an extension to the main house ...
... or like a giant barn that we could turn into an atelier and you could have your studio in there and I could have my darkroom ... and we could invite all our friends to hang out and make art. It'll be like a little artists' colony!
Well ... I don't know how your folks will feel about that.
Oh, they'll get tired of the place soon enough and retire to the island. They'll be relieved to not have to deal with feeding the stove constantly. Hey, maybe we can get Josh to come up and chop firewood! He's all like Mr. Thoreau, right?
Ugh ... don't talk to me about that guy.

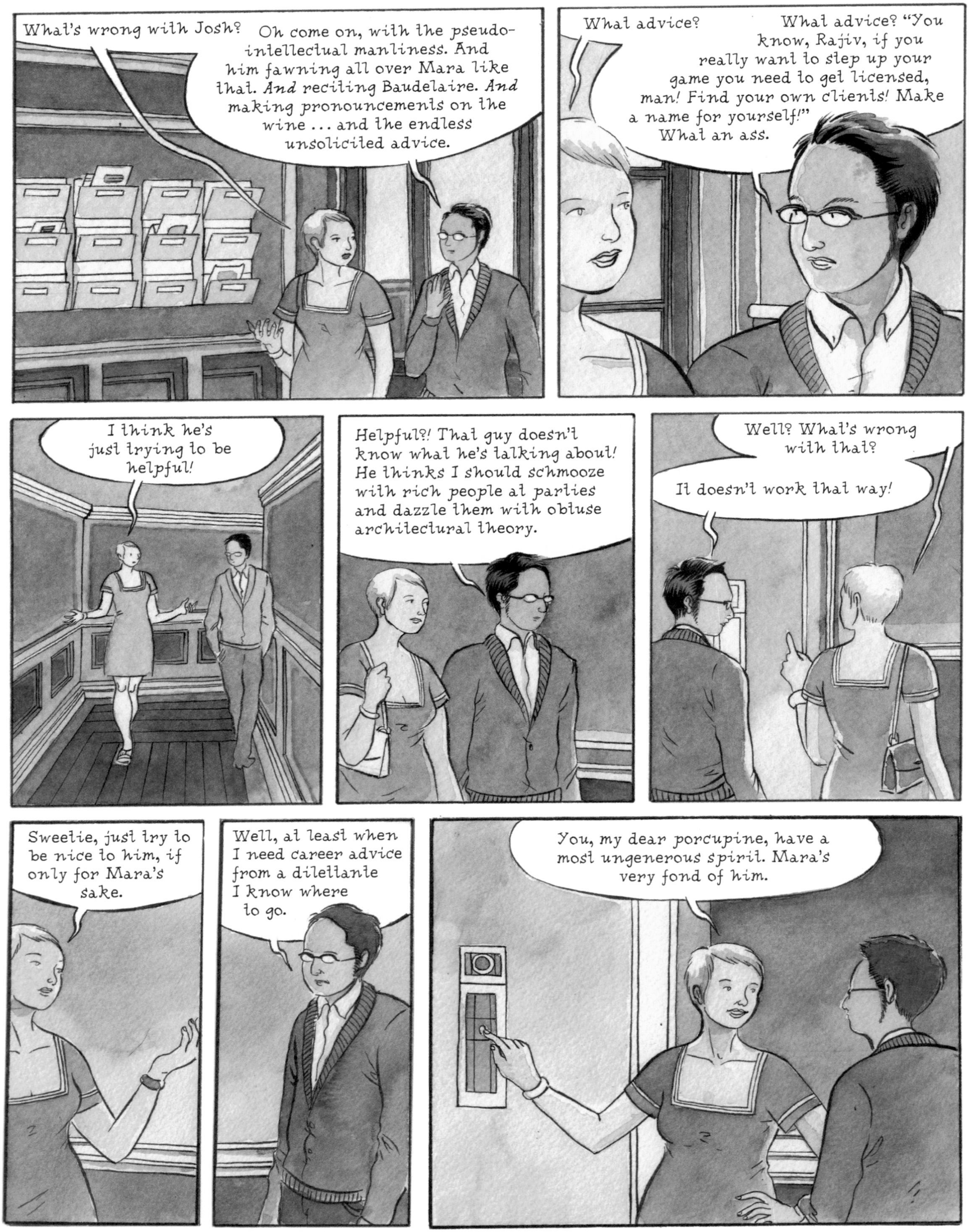
What's wrong with Josh?
Oh come on, with the pseudo-intellectual manliness. And him fawning all over Mara like that. And reciting Baudelaire. And making pronouncements on the wine ... and the endless unsolicited advice.
What advice?
What advice? "You know, Rajiv, if you really want to step up your game you need to get licensed, man! Find your own clients! Make a name for yourself!" What an ass.
I think he's just trying to be helpful!
Helpful?! That guy doesn't know what he's talking about! He thinks I should schmooze with rich people at parties and dazzle them with obtuse architectural theory.
Well? What's wrong with that?
It doesn't work that way!
Sweetie, just try to be nice to him, if only for Mara's sake.
Well, at least when I need career advice from a dilettante I know where to go.
You, my dear porcupine, have a most ungenerous spirit. Mara's very fond of him.

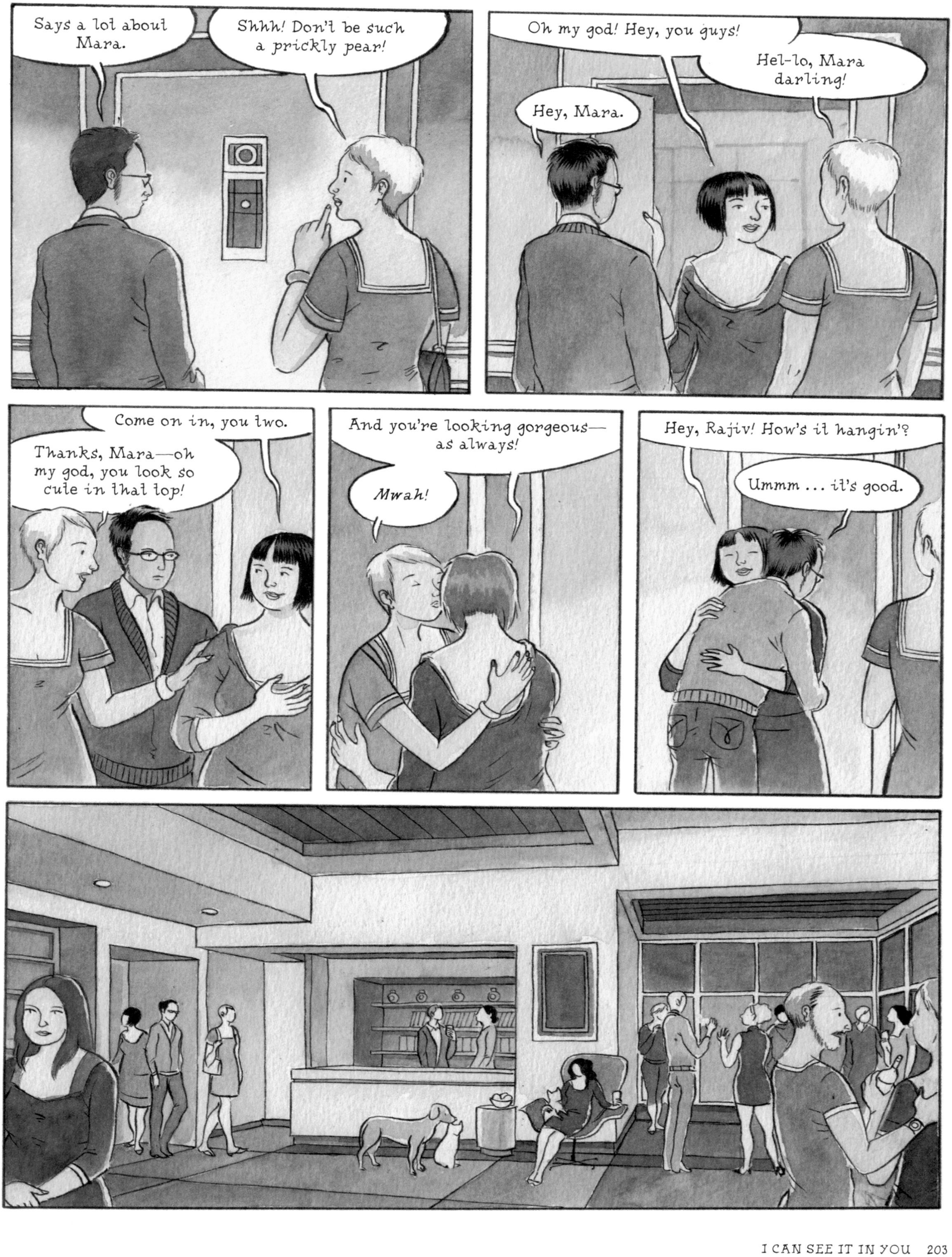
Says a lot about Mara.
Shhh! Don't be such a *prickly pear!*
Oh my god! Hey, you guys!
Hey, Mara.
Hel-lo, Mara darling!
Come on *in,* you two.
Thanks, Mara—oh my god, you look so cute in that top!
And you're looking gorgeous— as always!
Mwah!
Hey, Rajiv! How's it hangin'?
Ummm ... it's good.

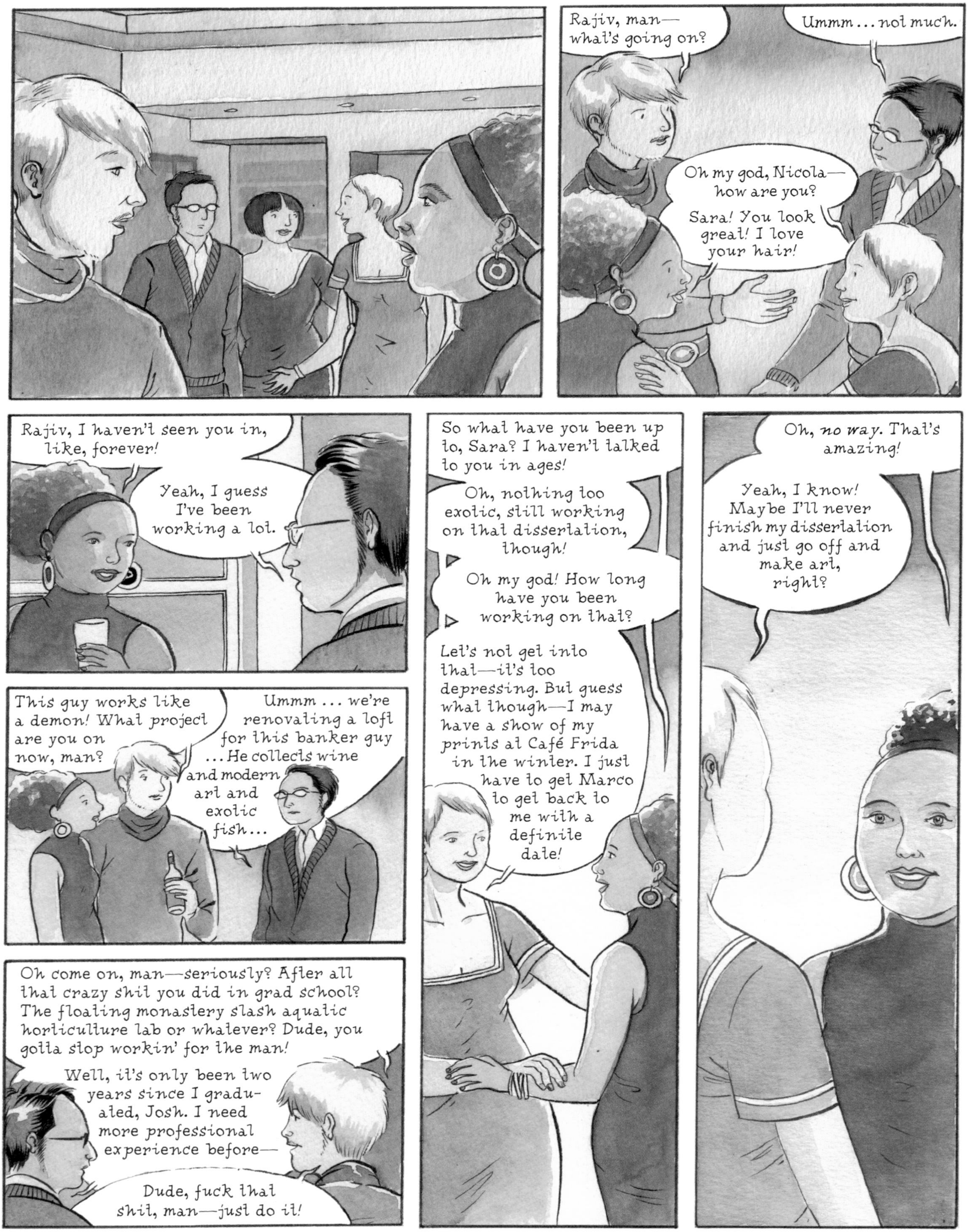
Rajiv, man—what's going on?
Ummm... not much.
Oh my god, Nicola—how are you?
Sara! You look great! I love your hair!
Rajiv, I haven't seen you in, like, forever!
Yeah, I guess I've been working a lot.
This guy works like a demon! What project are you on now, man?
Ummm ... we're renovating a loft for this banker guy ... He collects wine and modern art and exotic fish...
Oh come on, man—seriously? After all that crazy shit you did in grad school? The floating monastery slash aquatic horticulture lab or whatever? Dude, you gotta stop workin' for the man!
Well, it's only been two years since I graduated, Josh. I need more professional experience before—
Dude, fuck that shit, man—just do it!
So what have you been up to, Sara? I haven't talked to you in ages!
Oh, nothing too exotic, still working on that dissertation, though!
Oh my god! How long have you been working on that?
Let's not get into that—it's too depressing. But guess what though—I may have a show of my prints at Café Frida in the winter. I just have to get Marco to get back to me with a definite date!
Oh, *no way*. That's amazing!
Yeah, I know! Maybe I'll never finish my dissertation and just go off and make art, right?

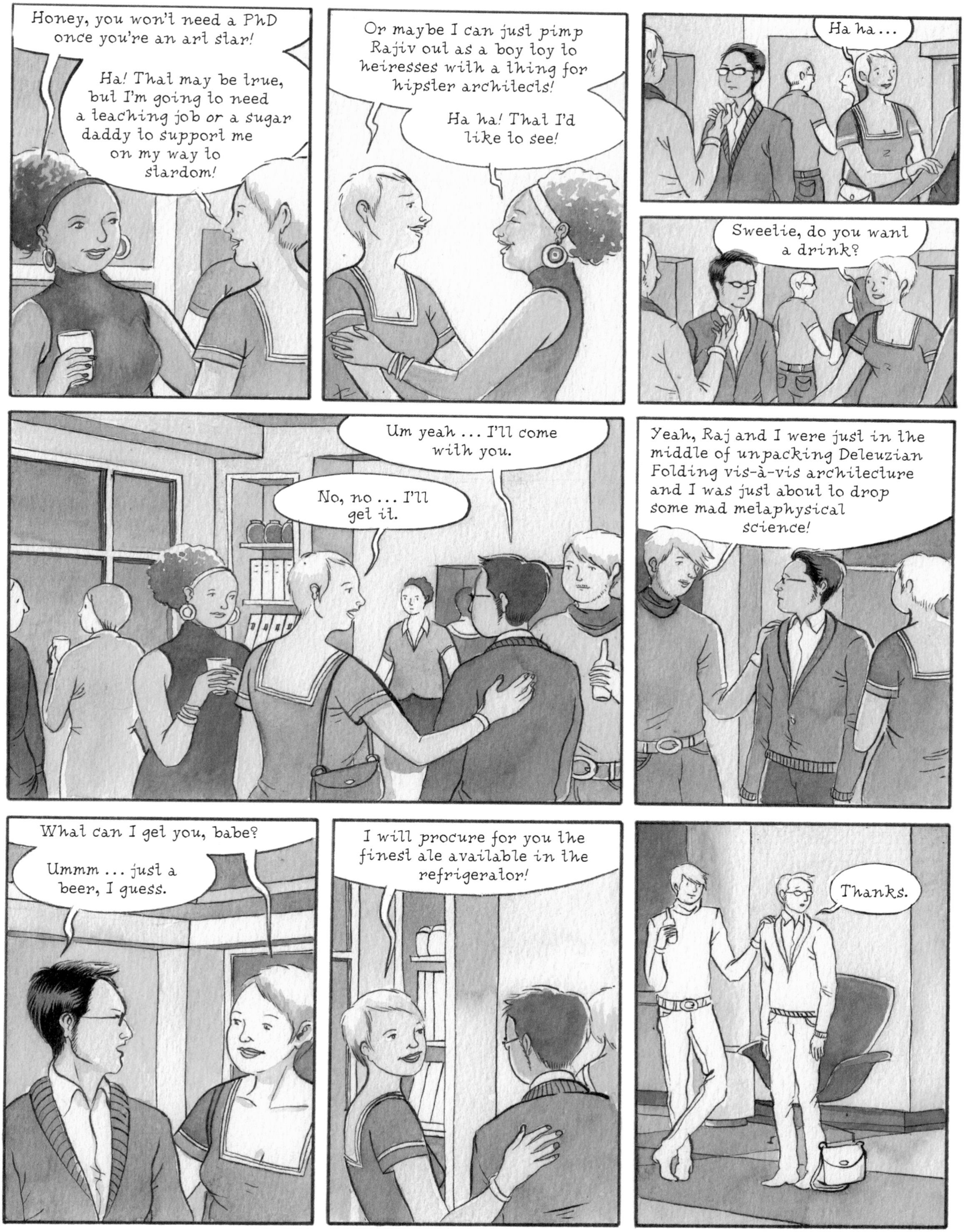
Honey, you won't need a PhD once you're an art star!
Ha! That may be true, but I'm going to need a teaching job or a sugar daddy to support me on my way to stardom!
Or maybe I can just *pimp* Rajiv out as a boy toy to heiresses with a thing for hipster architects!
Ha ha! That I'd like to see!
Ha ha ...
Sweetie, do you want a drink?
Um yeah ... I'll come with you.
No, no ... I'll get it.
Yeah, Raj and I were just in the middle of unpacking Deleuzian Folding vis-à-vis architecture and I was just about to drop some mad metaphysical science!
What can I get you, babe?
Ummm ... just a beer, I guess.
I will procure for you the finest ale available in the refrigerator!
Thanks.

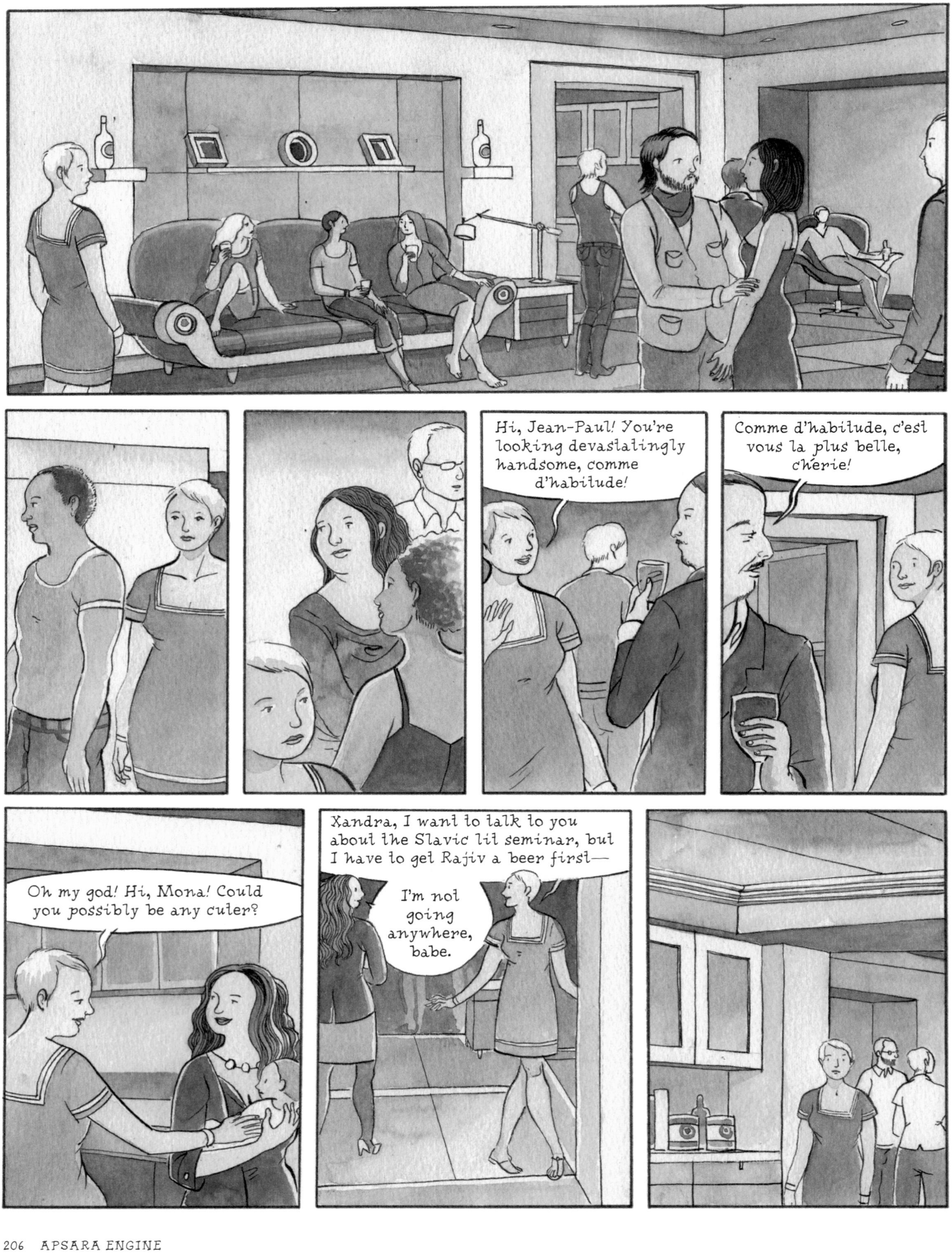
Hi, Jean-Paul! You're looking devastatingly handsome, comme d'habitude!
Comme d'habitude, c'est vous la plus belle, chérie!
Oh my god! Hi, Mona! Could you possibly be any cuter?
Xandra, I want to talk to you about the Slavic lit seminar, but I have to get Rajiv a beer first—
I'm not going anywhere, babe.

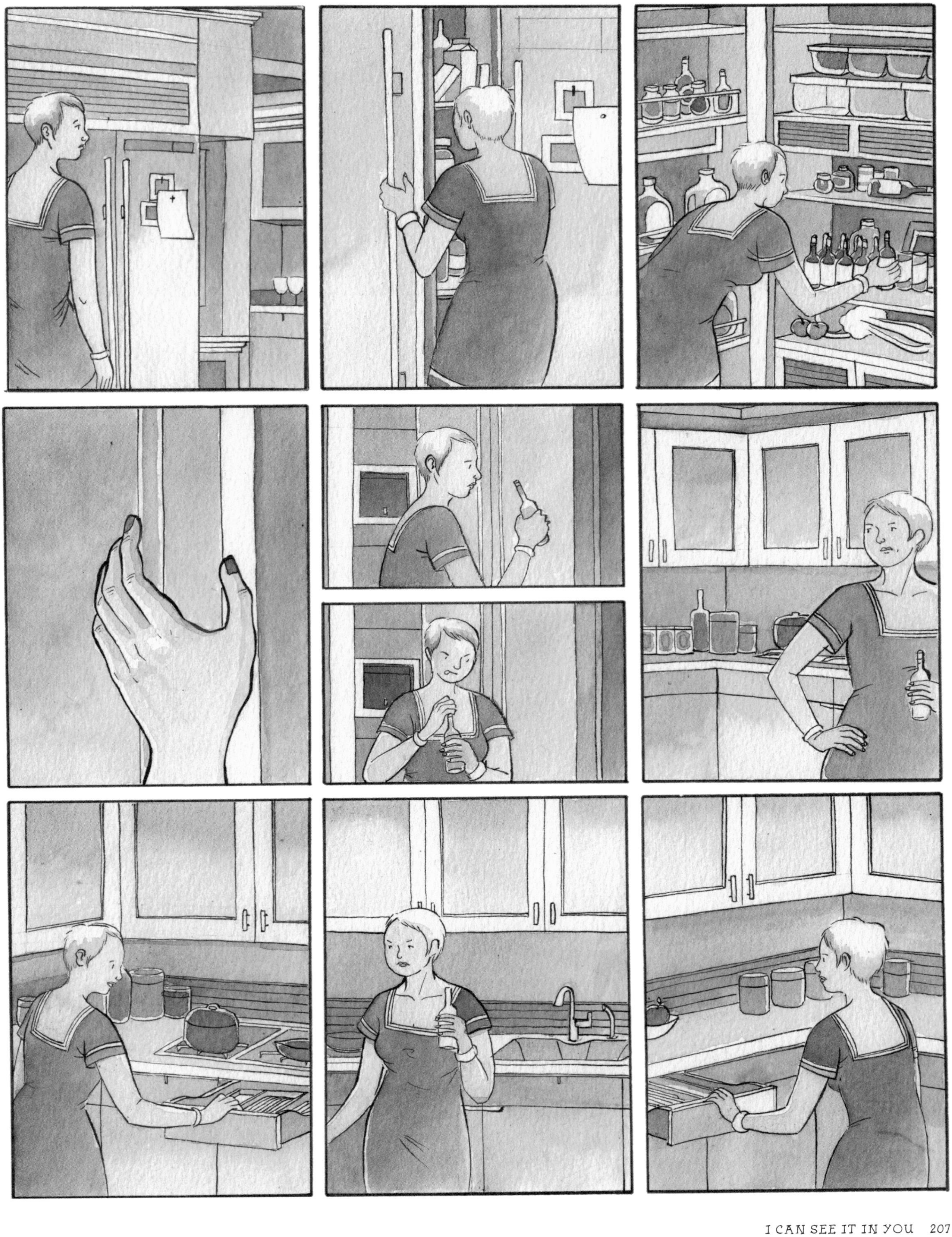

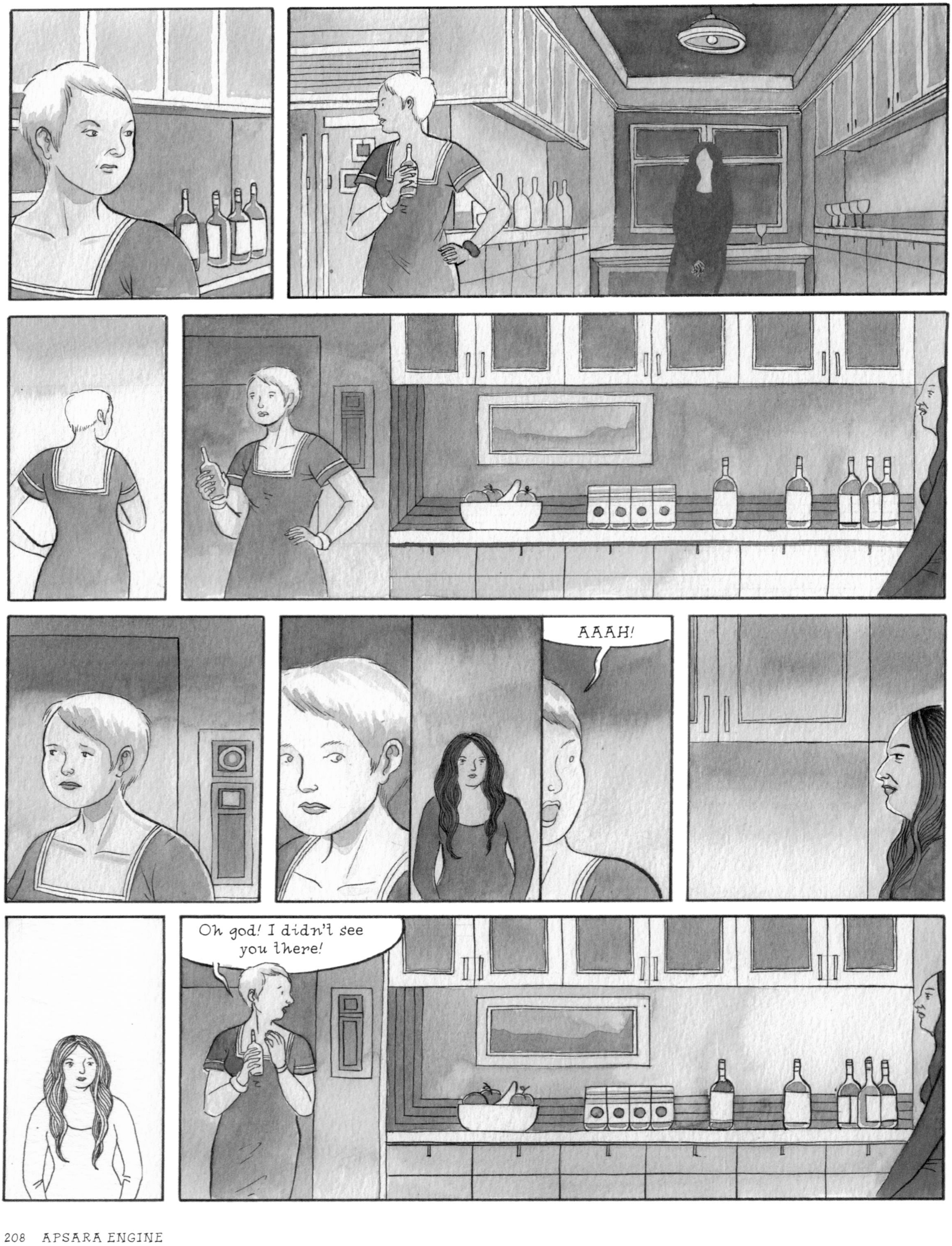
AAAH!
Oh god! I didn't see you there!

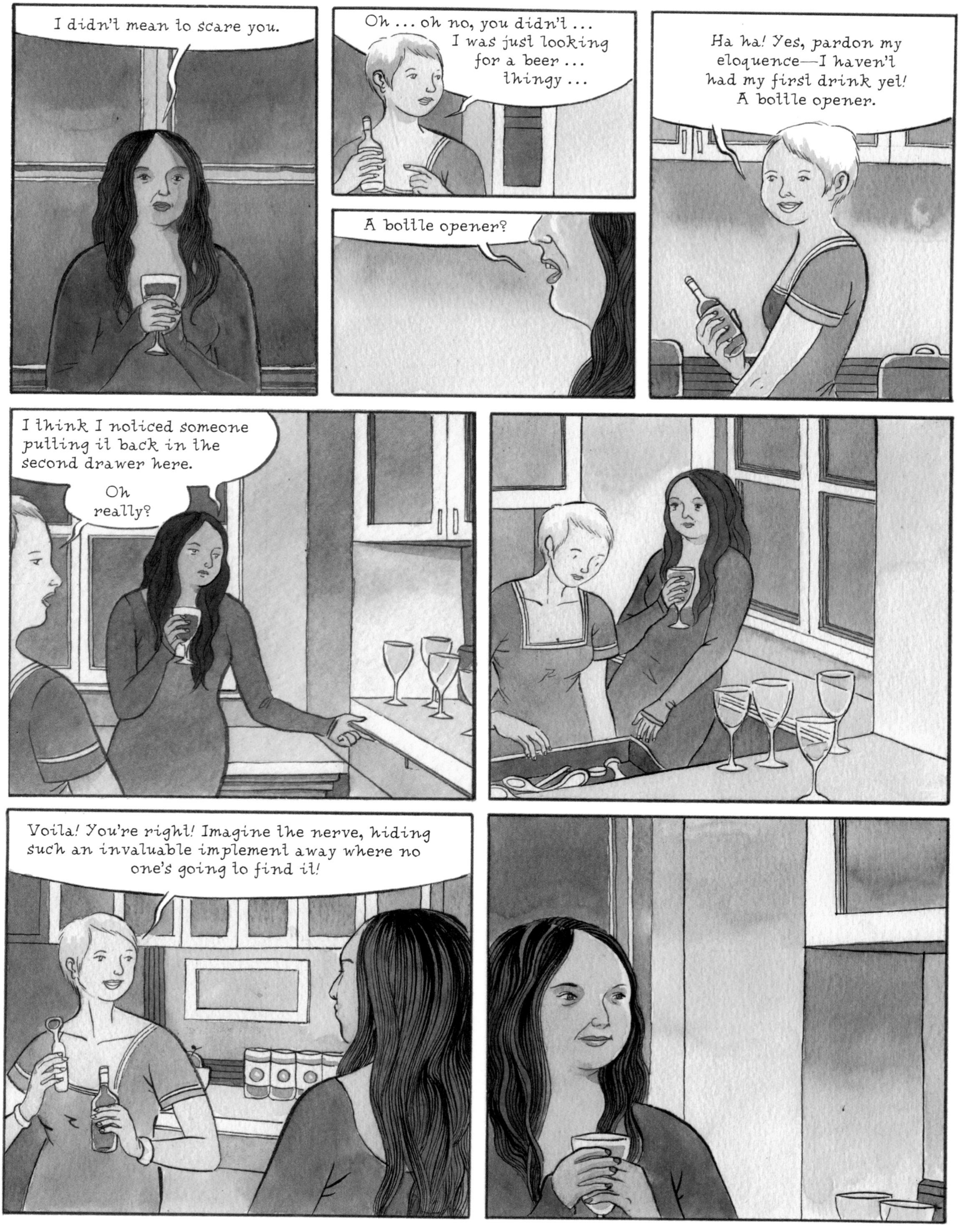
I didn't mean to scare you.
Oh ... oh no, you didn't ... I was just looking for a beer ... thingy ...
A bottle opener?
Ha ha! Yes, pardon my eloquence—I haven't had my first drink yet! A bottle opener.
I think I noticed someone putting it back in the second drawer here.
Oh really?
Voila! You're right! Imagine the nerve, hiding such an invaluable implement away where no one's going to find it!

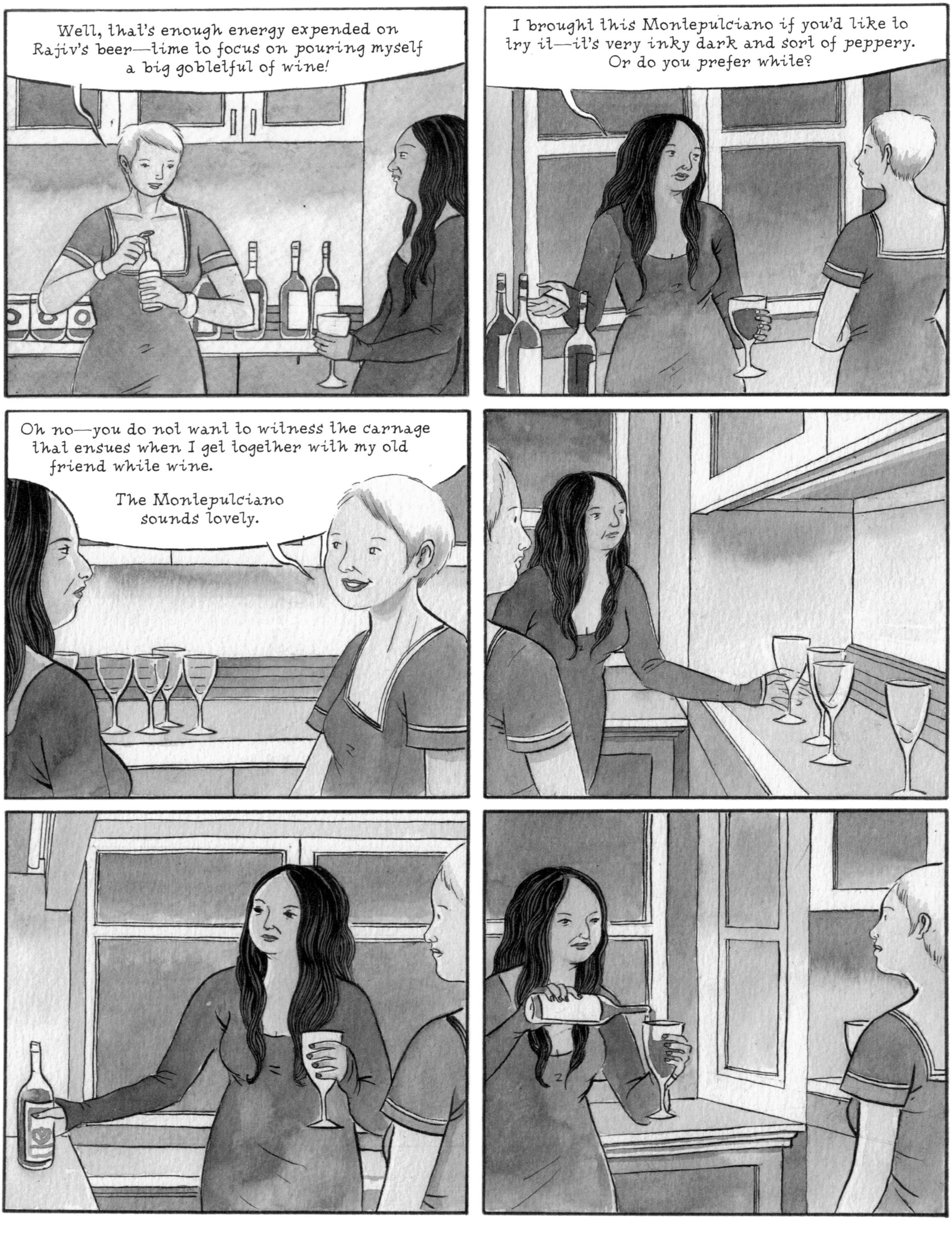
Well, that's enough energy expended on Rajiv's beer—time to focus on pouring myself a big gobletful of wine!
I brought this Montepulciano if you'd like to try it—it's very inky dark and sort of peppery. Or do you prefer white?
Oh no—you do not want to witness the carnage that ensues when I get together with my old friend white wine.
The Montepulciano sounds lovely.

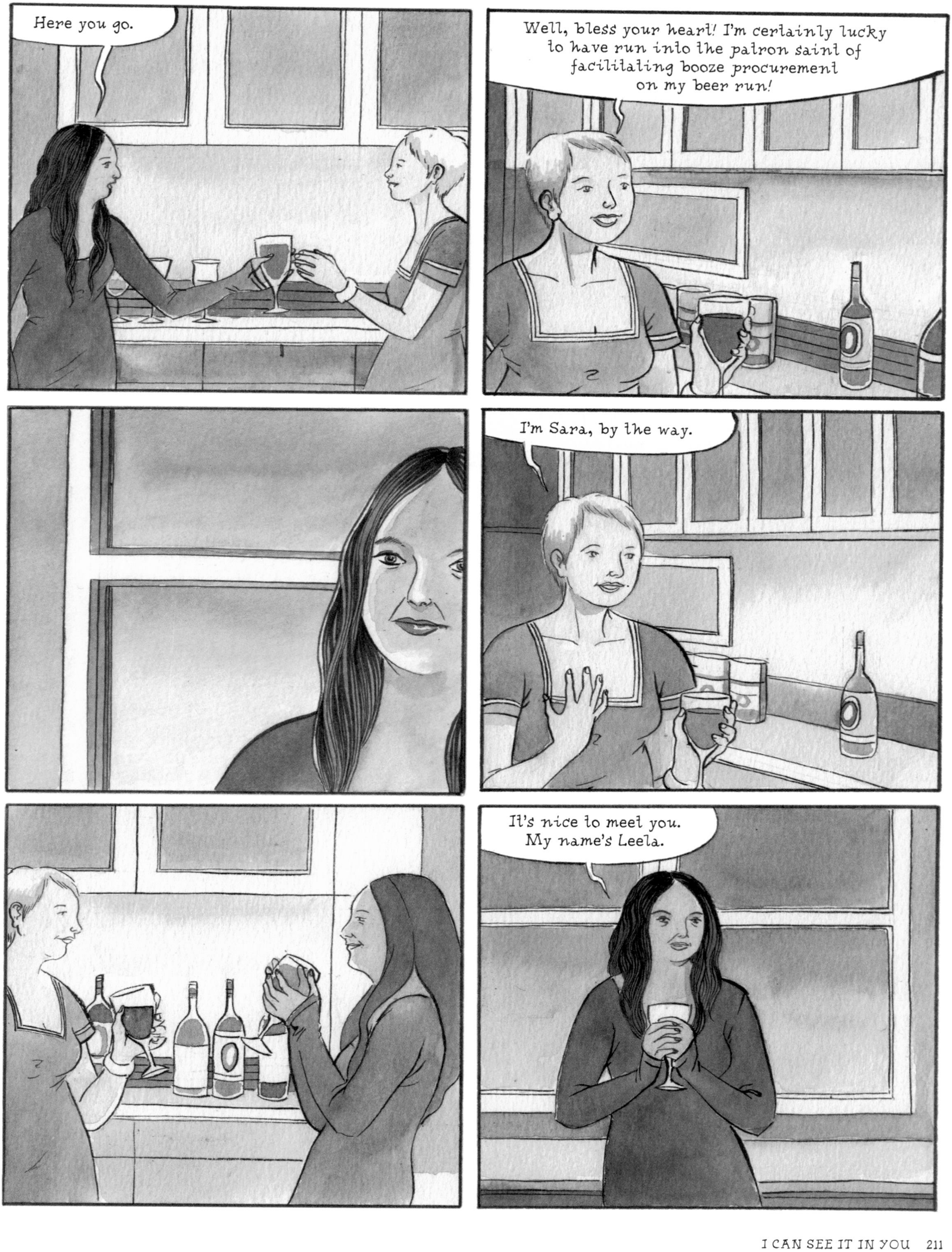
Here you go.
Well, bless your heart! I'm certainly lucky to have run into the patron saint of facilitating booze procurement on my beer run!
I'm Sara, by the way.
It's nice to meet you. My name's Leela.

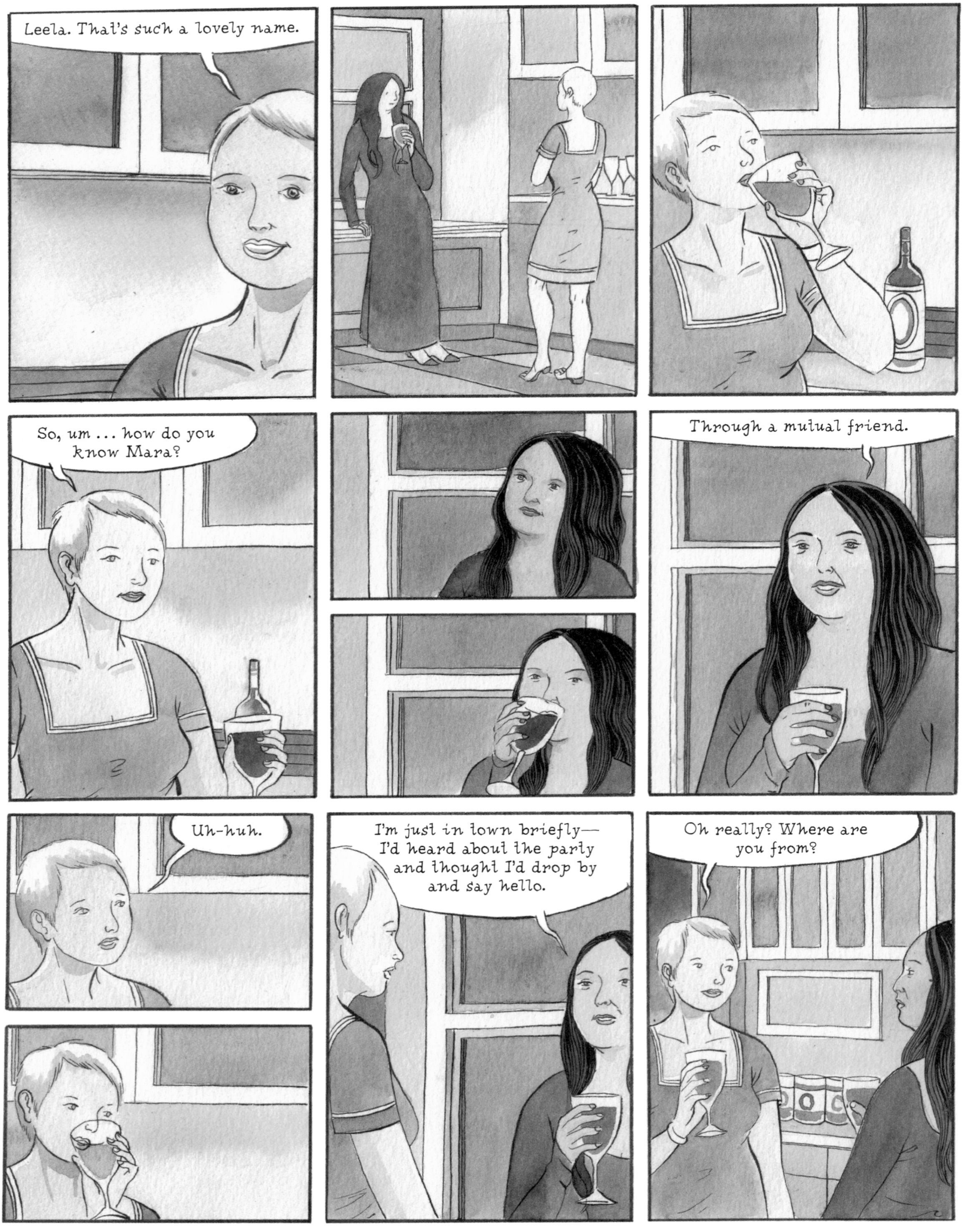
Leela. That's such a lovely name.
So, um ... how do you know Mara?
Through a mutual friend.
Uh-huh.
I'm just in town briefly—I'd heard about the party and thought I'd drop by and say hello.
Oh really? Where are you from?

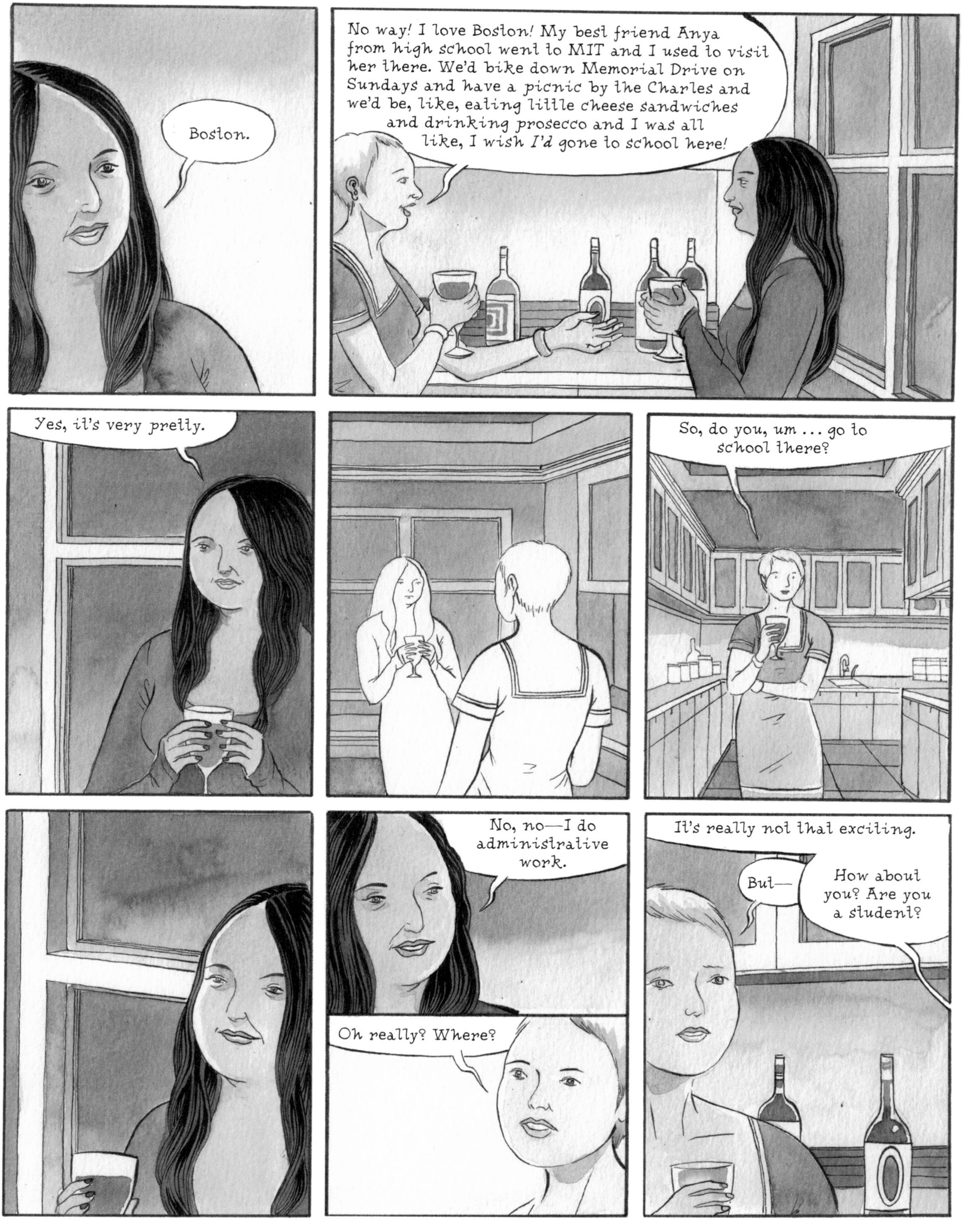
Boston.
No way! I love Boston! My best friend Anya from high school went to MIT and I used to visit her there. We'd bike down Memorial Drive on Sundays and have a *picnic* by the Charles and we'd be, like, eating little cheese sandwiches and drinking *prosecco* and I was all like, I wish *I'd* gone to school here!
Yes, it's very pretty.
So, do you, um ... go to *school* there?
No, no—I do administrative work.
Oh really? Where?
It's really not that exciting.
But—
How about you? Are you a student?

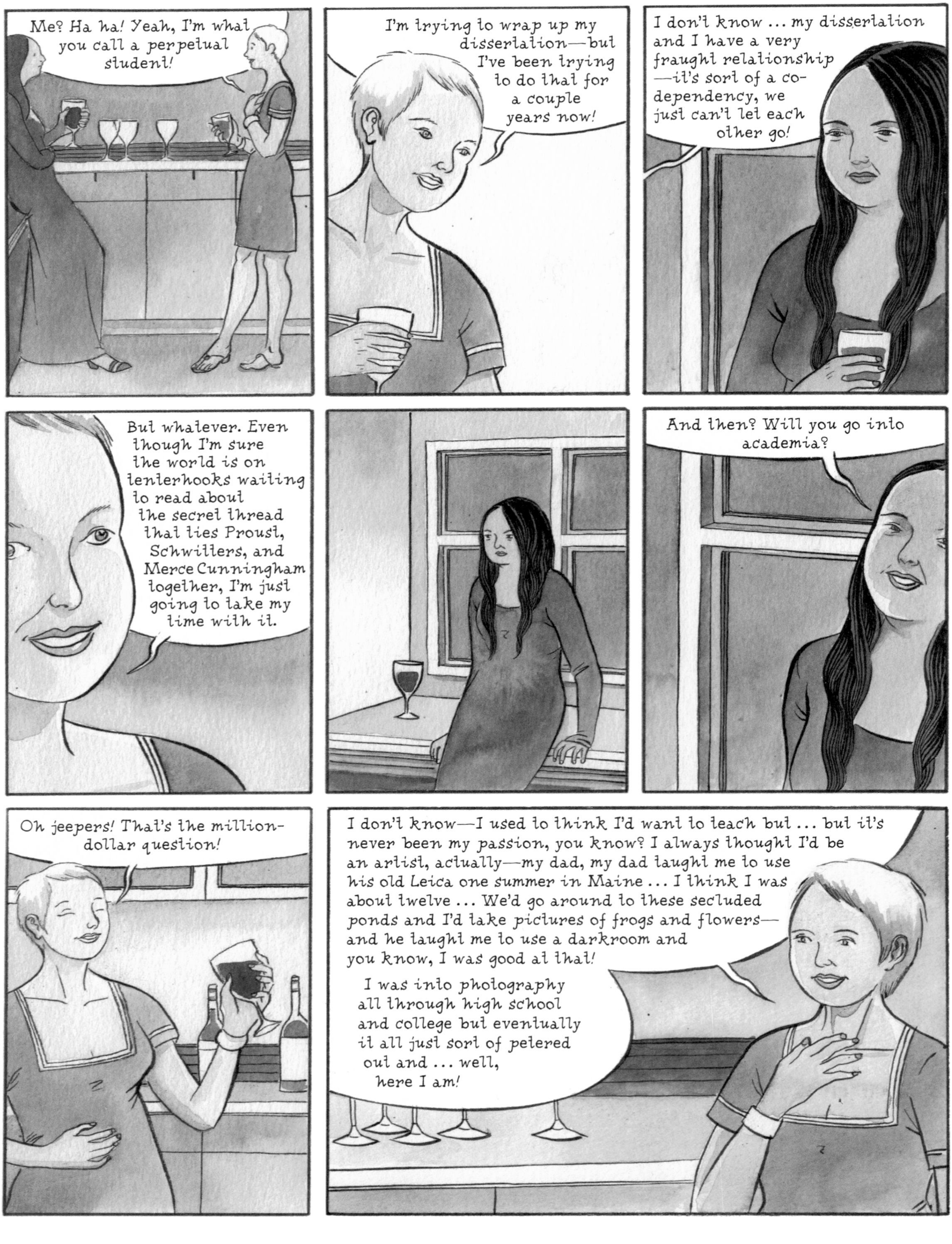
Me? Ha ha! Yeah, I'm what you call a perpetual student!
I'm trying to wrap up my dissertation—but I've been trying to do that for a couple years now!
I don't know ... my dissertation and I have a very fraught relationship —it's sort of a co-dependency, we just can't let each other go!
But whatever. Even though I'm sure the world is on tenterhooks waiting to read about the secret thread that ties Proust, Schwitters, and Merce Cunningham together, I'm just going to take my time with it.
And then? Will you go into academia?
Oh jeepers! That's the million-dollar question!
I don't know—I used to think I'd want to teach but ... but it's never been my passion, you know? I always thought I'd be an artist, actually—my dad, my dad taught me to use his old Leica one summer in Maine ... I think I was about twelve ... We'd go around to these secluded ponds and I'd take pictures of frogs and flowers—and he taught me to use a darkroom and you know, I was good at that!
I was into photography all through high school and college but eventually it all just sort of petered out and ... well, here I am!

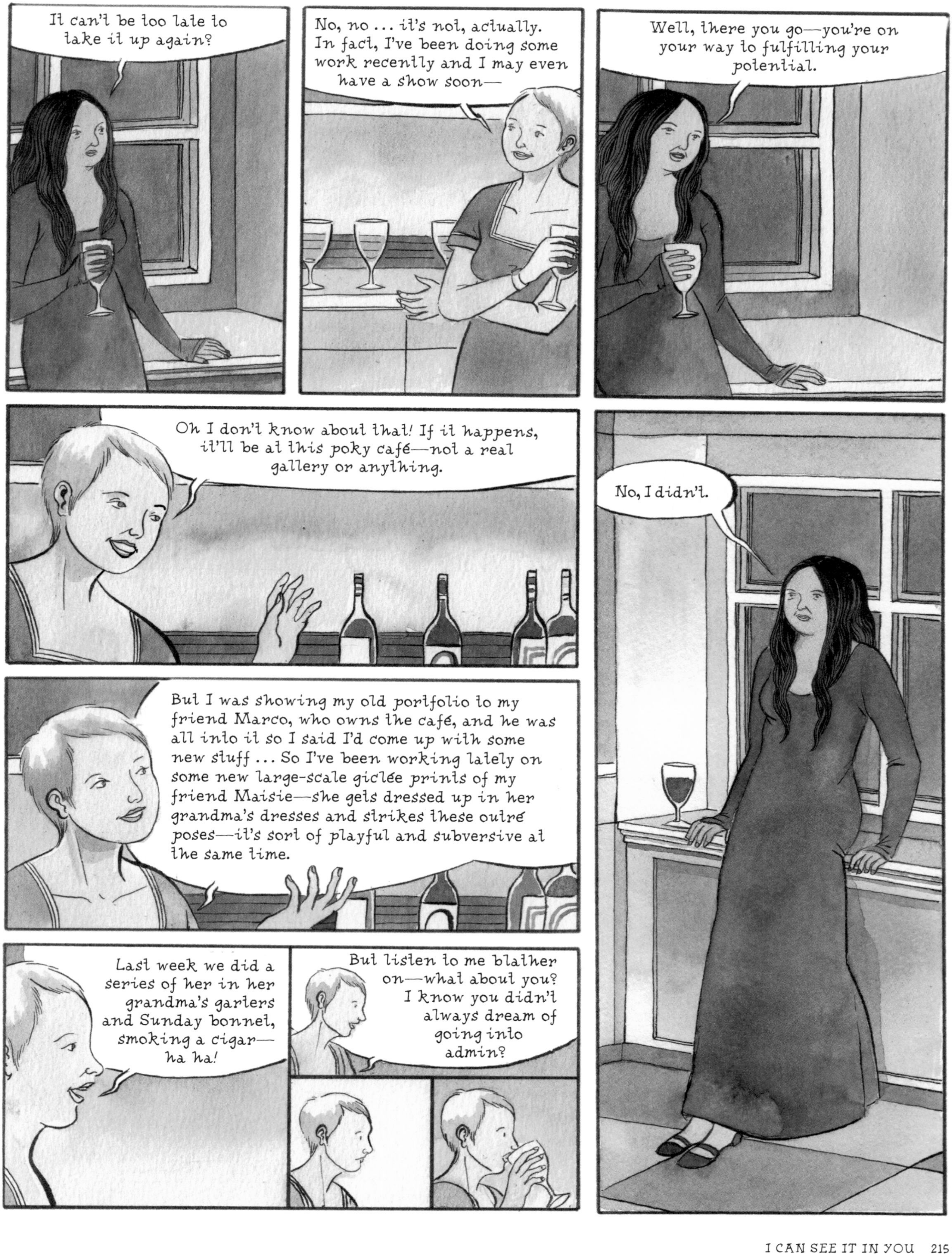
It can't be too late to take it up again?
No, no ... it's not, actually. In fact, I've been doing some work recently and I may even have a show soon—
Well, there you go—you're on your way to fulfilling your potential.
Oh I don't know about that! If it happens, it'll be at this poky café—not a real gallery or anything.
But I was showing my old portfolio to my friend Marco, who owns the café, and he was all into it so I said I'd come up with some new stuff ... So I've been working lately on some new large-scale giclée prints of my friend Maisie—she gets dressed up in her grandma's dresses and strikes these outré poses—it's sort of playful and subversive at the same time.
Last week we did a series of her in her grandma's garters and Sunday bonnet, smoking a cigar—ha ha!
But listen to me blather on—what about you? I know you didn't always dream of going into admin?
No, I didn't.

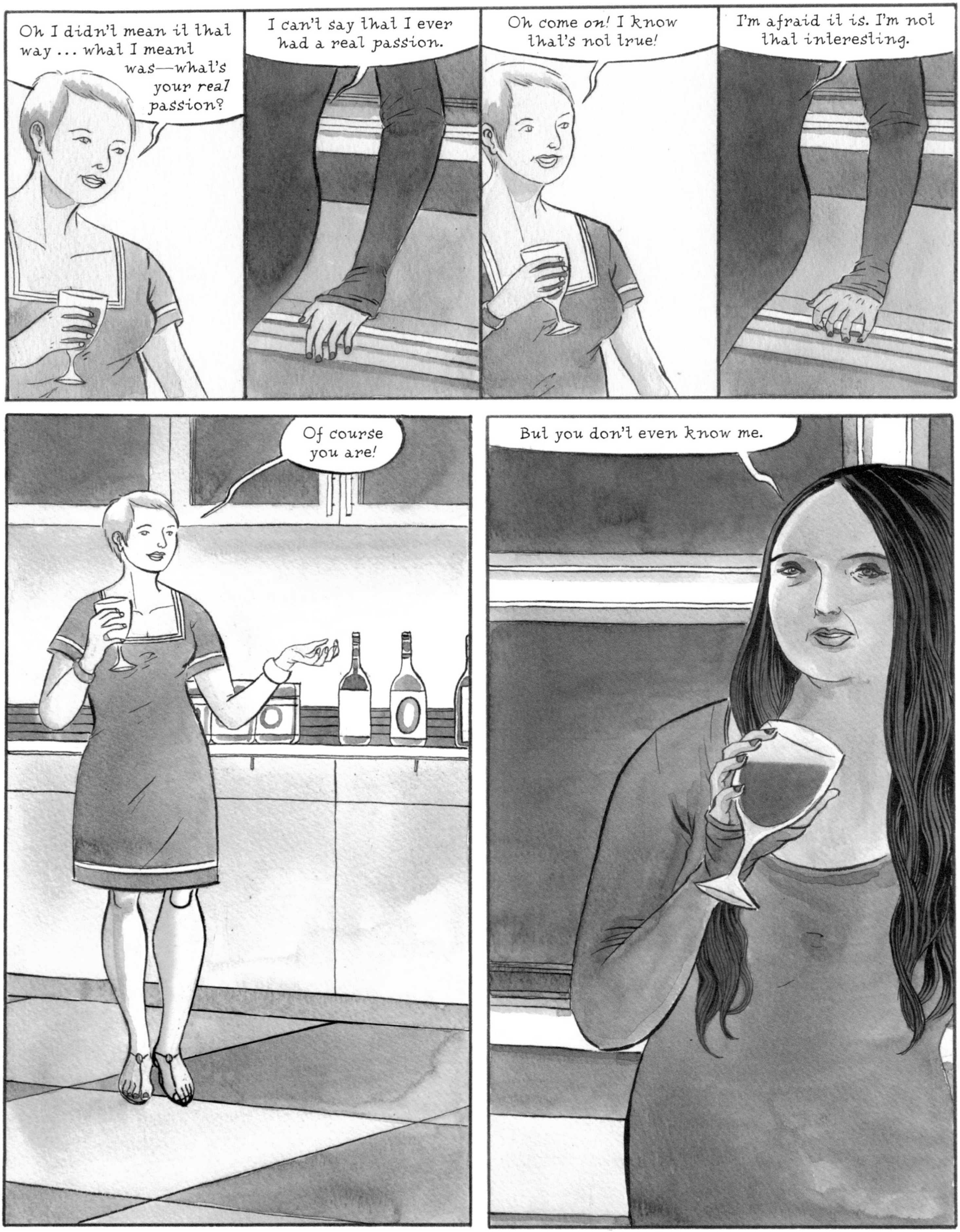
Oh I didn't mean it that way ... what I meant was—what's your *real* passion?
I can't say that I ever had a real passion.
Oh come *on!* I know that's not true!
I'm afraid it is. I'm not that interesting.
Of course you are!
But you don't even know me.

I can see it in you.

I look at you and I know—inside you there's a ... writer waiting to come out! Or a chef! Or a bassist! Or a painter! Or ... a dancer!

Right?

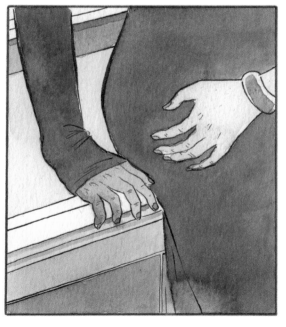

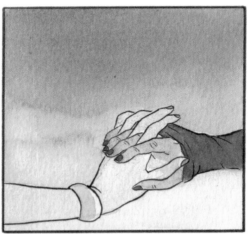
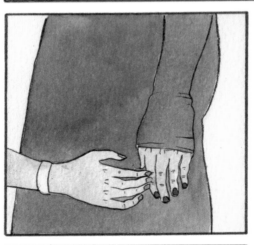
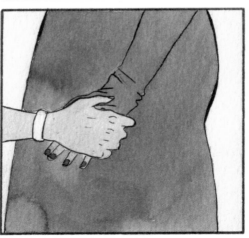

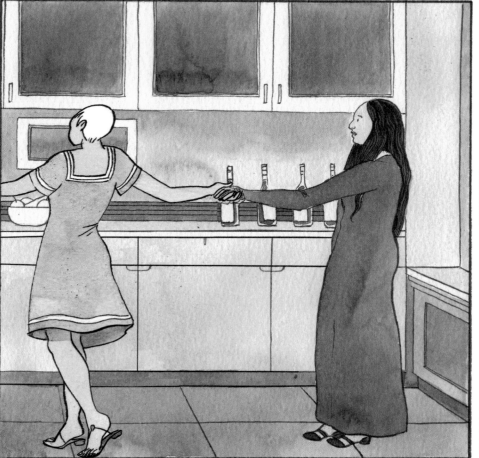

Cha-cha-cha!

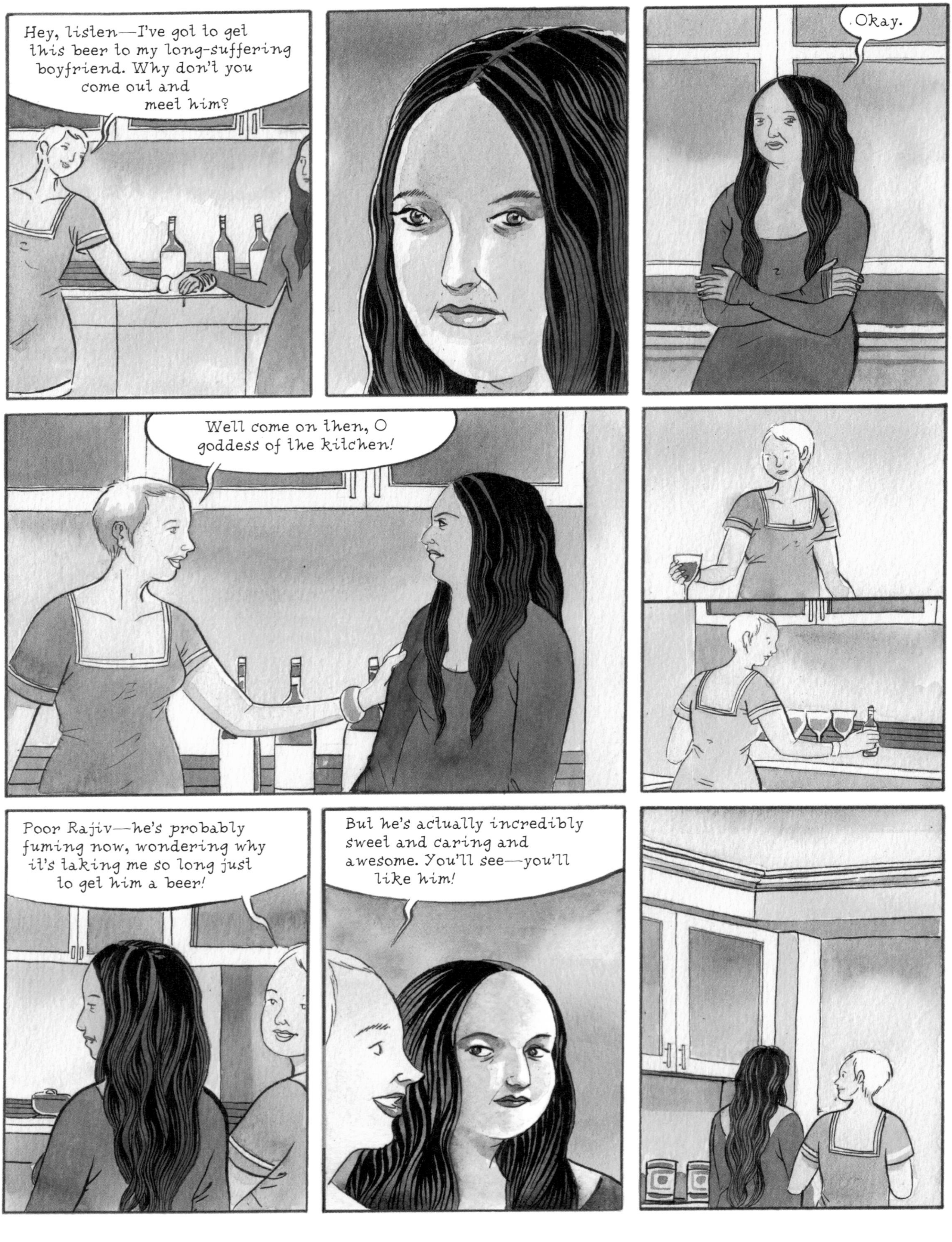
Hey, listen—I've got to get this beer to my long-suffering boyfriend. Why don't you come out and meet him?
Okay.
Well come on then, O goddess of the kitchen!
Poor Rajiv—he's probably fuming now, wondering why it's taking me so long just to get him a beer!
But he's actually incredibly sweet and caring and awesome. You'll see—you'll like him!

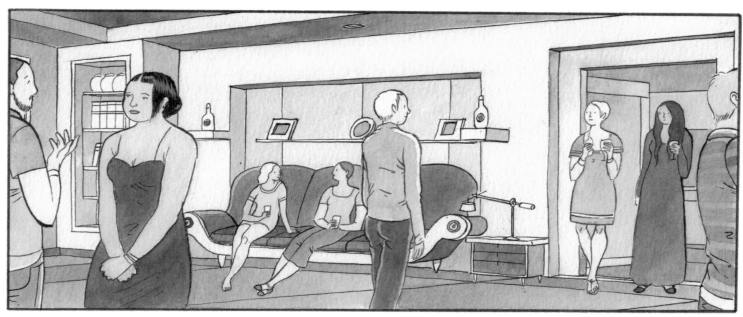

Oh my god—that guy over there totally had a creepy affair with my thesis advisor! So gross. He'd be all like, "I just had *office hours* with Tania!"

Hey, Bernard! How's tricks?

I have no tricks, Sara. What you see is what you get.

Ha ha!

Oh my god— so cheesy!

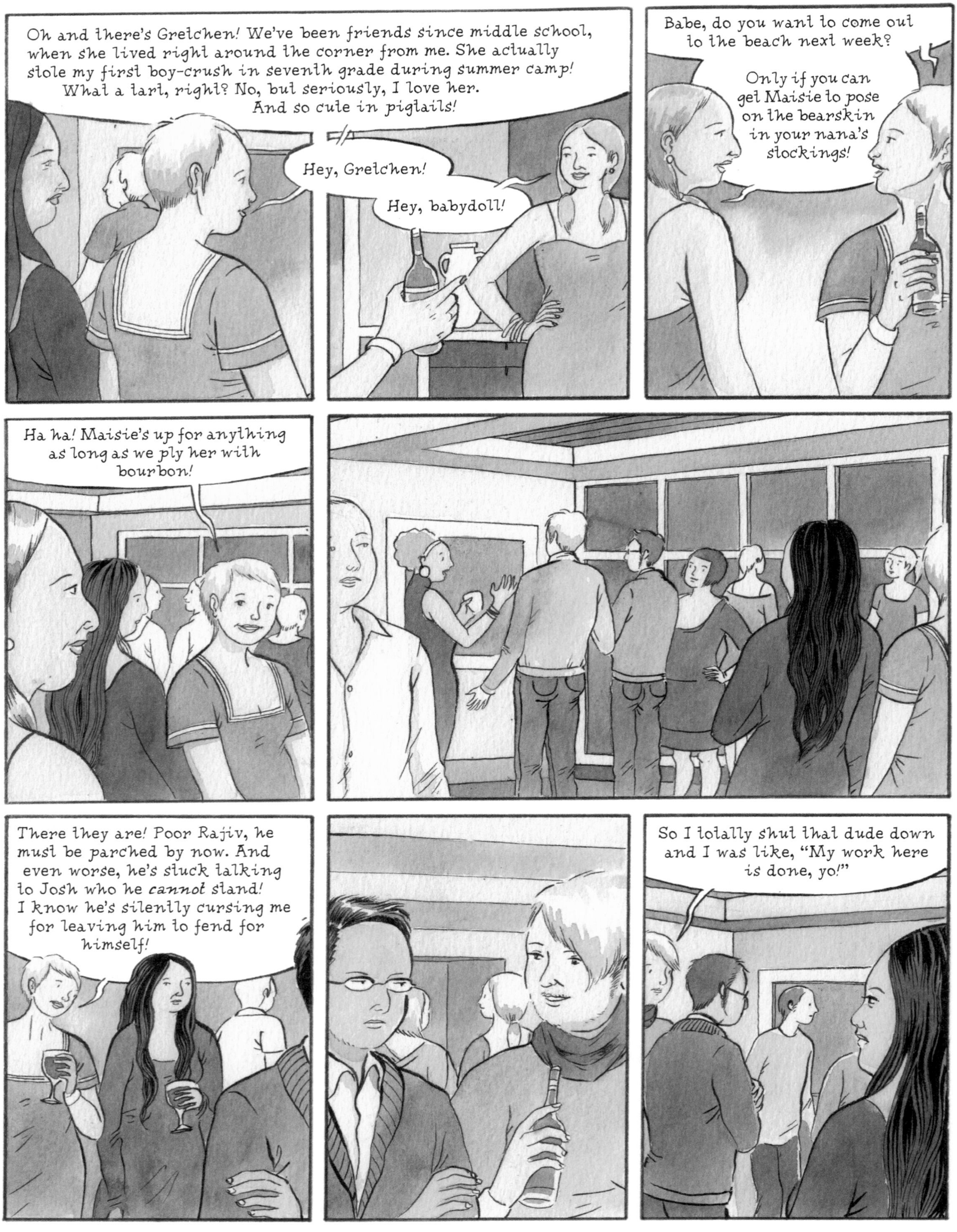
Oh and there's Gretchen! We've been friends since middle school, when she lived right around the corner from me. She actually stole my first boy-crush in seventh grade during summer camp! What a tart, right? No, but seriously, I love her. And so cute in pigtails!
Hey, Gretchen!
Hey, babydoll!
Babe, do you want to come out to the beach next week?
Only if you can get Maisie to pose on the bearskin in your nana's stockings!
Ha ha! Maisie's up for anything as long as we ply her with bourbon!
There they are! Poor Rajiv, he must be parched by now. And even worse, he's stuck talking to Josh who he *cannot* stand! I know he's silently cursing me for leaving him to fend for himself!
So I totally shut that dude down and I was like, "My work here is done, yo!"

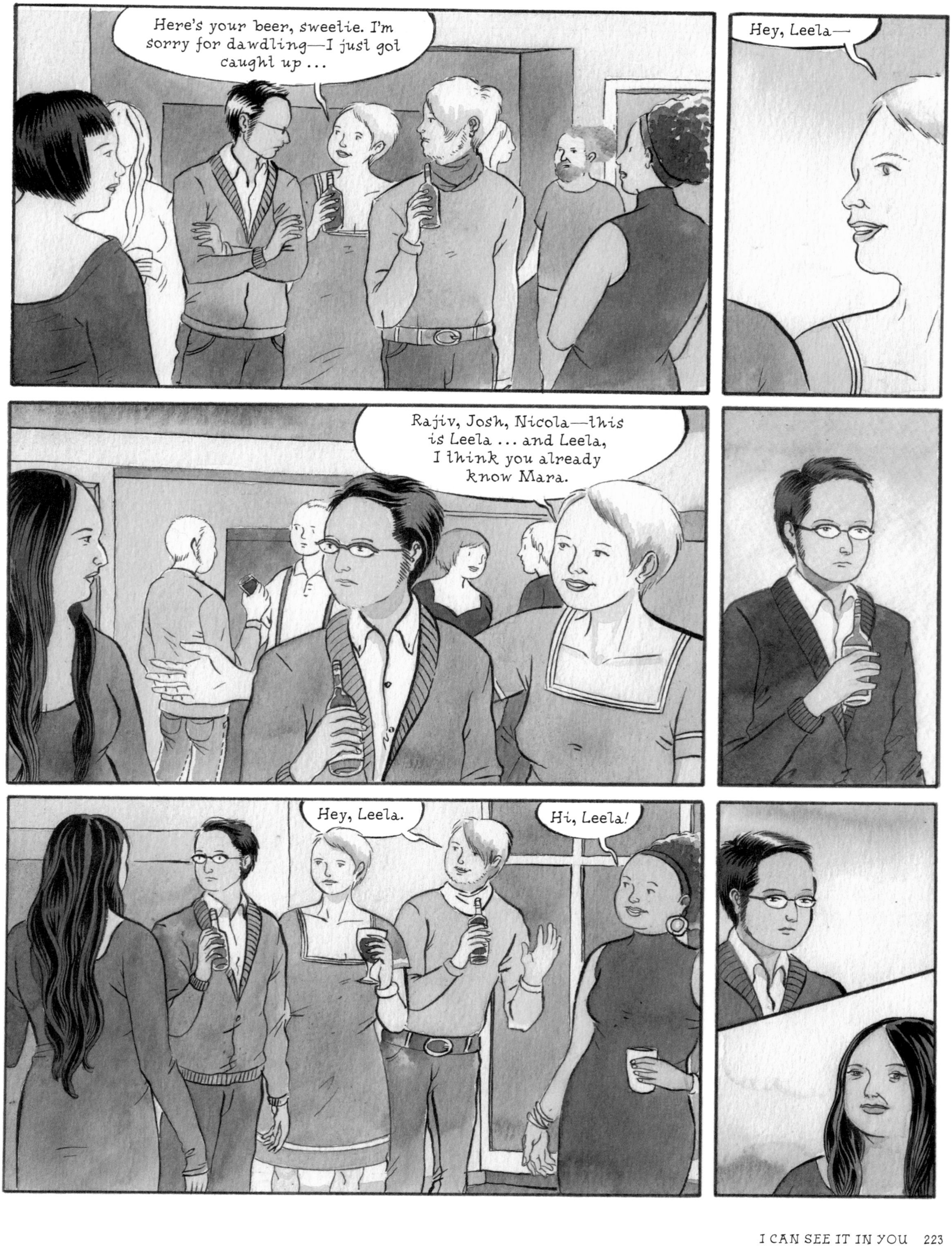
Here's your beer, sweetie. I'm sorry for dawdling—I just got caught up . . .
Hey, Leela—
Rajiv, Josh, Nicola—this is Leela . . . and Leela, I think you already know Mara.
Hey, Leela.
Hi, Leela!

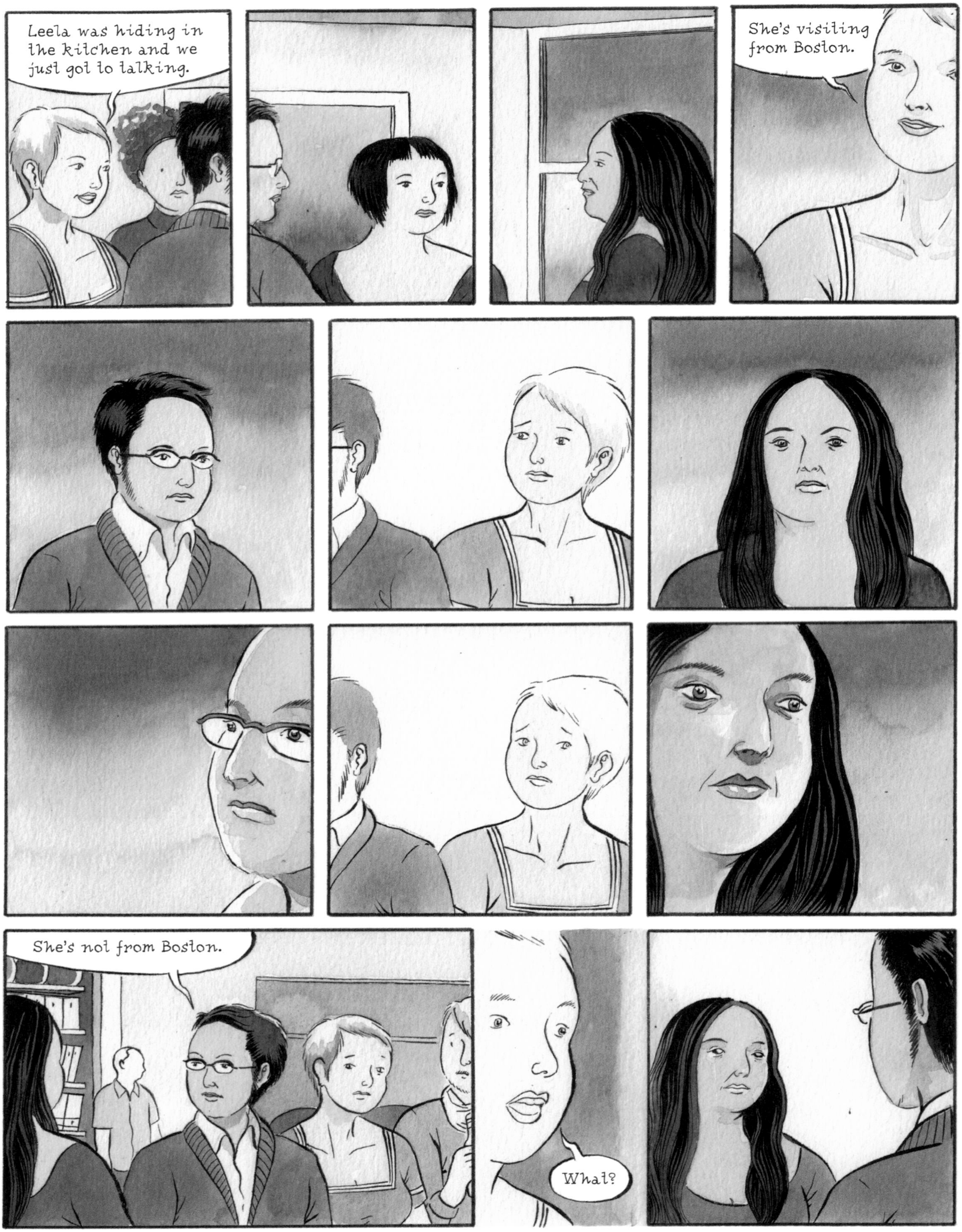
Leela was hiding in the kitchen and we just got to talking.
She's visiting from Boston.
She's not from Boston.
What?

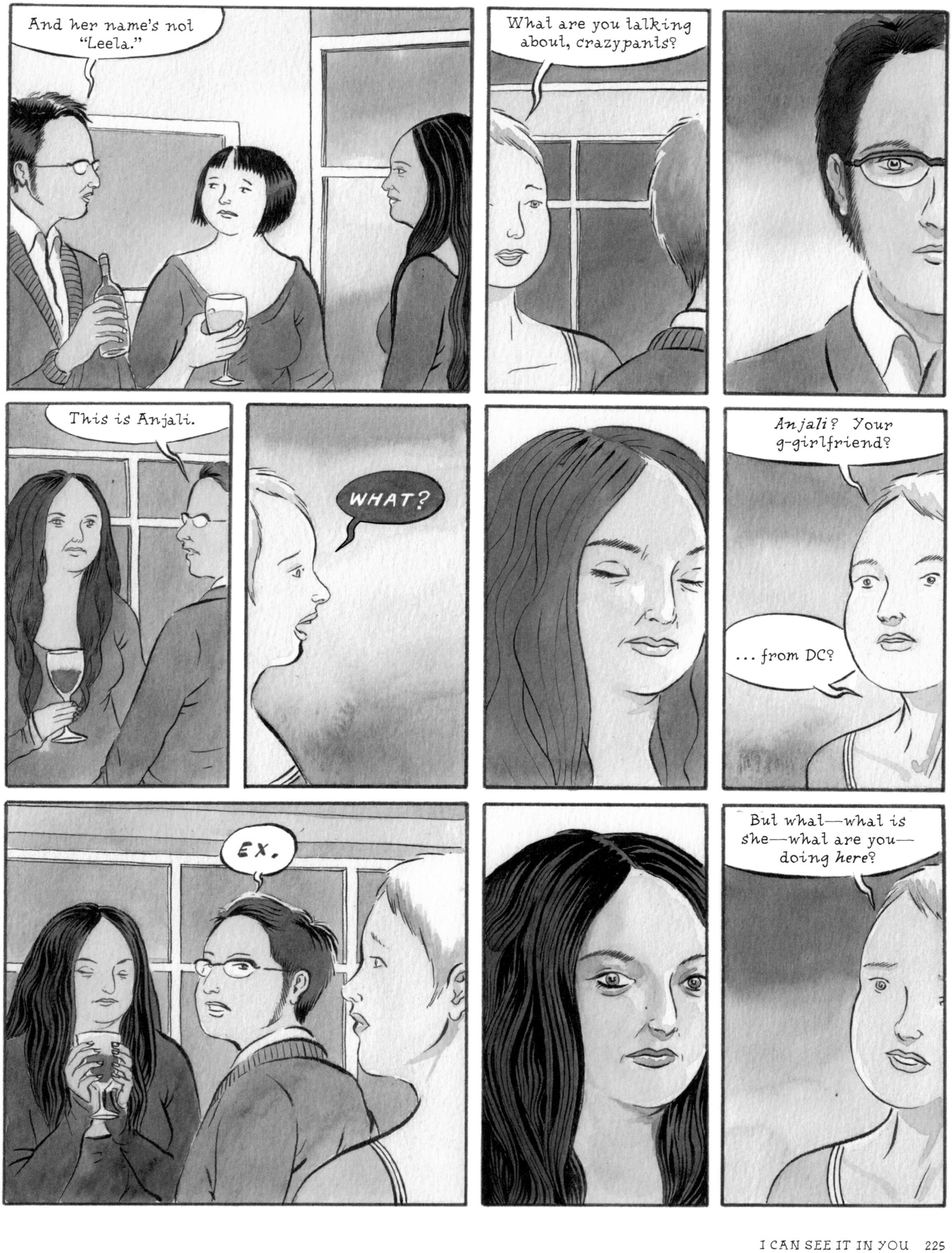
And her name's not "Leela."
What are you talking about, crazypants?
This is Anjali.
WHAT?
Anjali? Your g-girlfriend?
... from DC?
EX.
But what—what is she—what are you—doing here?

 I don'l undersland.

 I'm sorry, Sara.

 Can I lalk lo you *outside*, please?

 Yes.

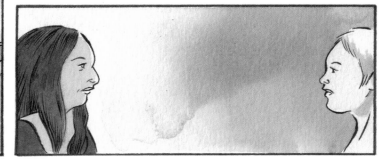

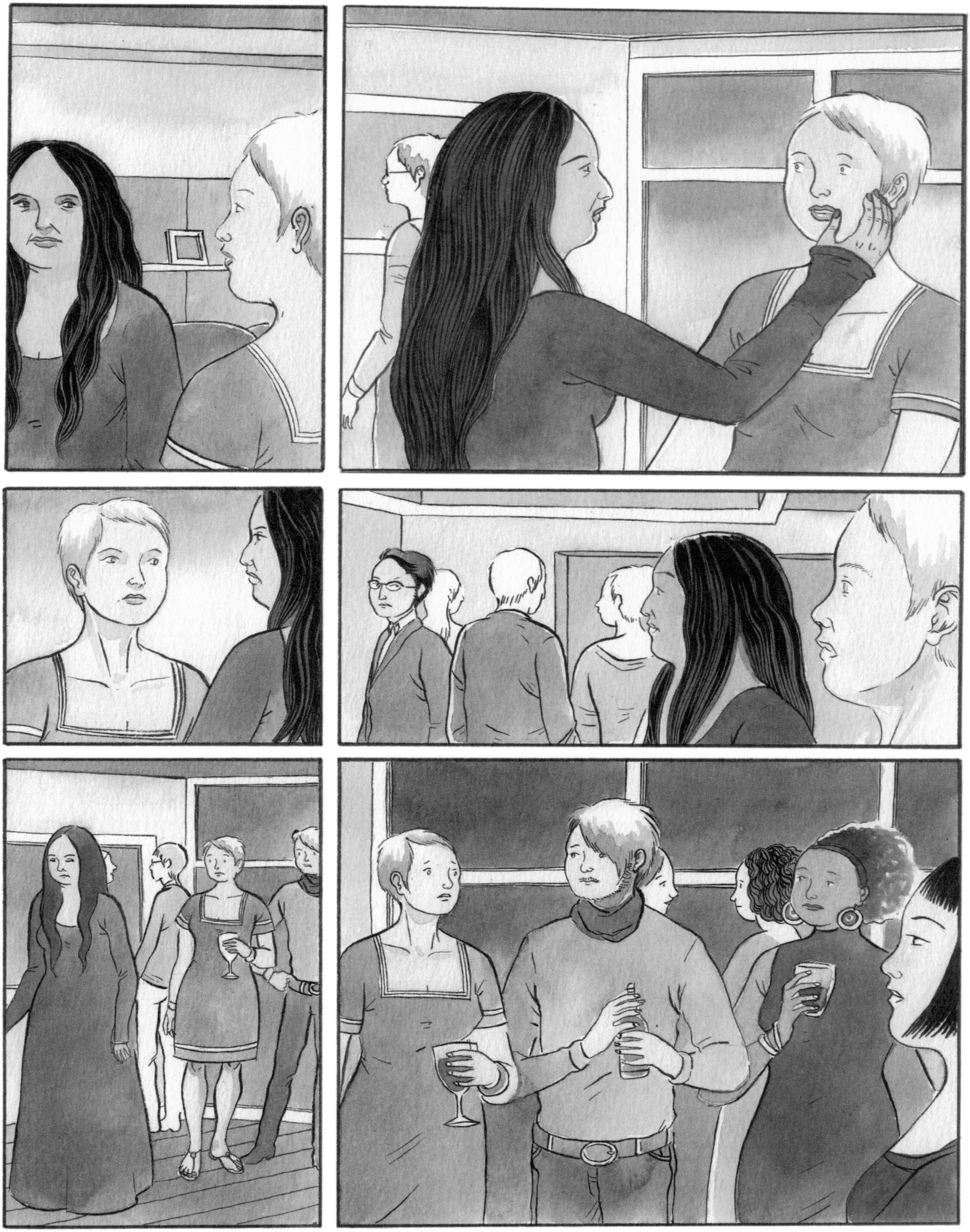

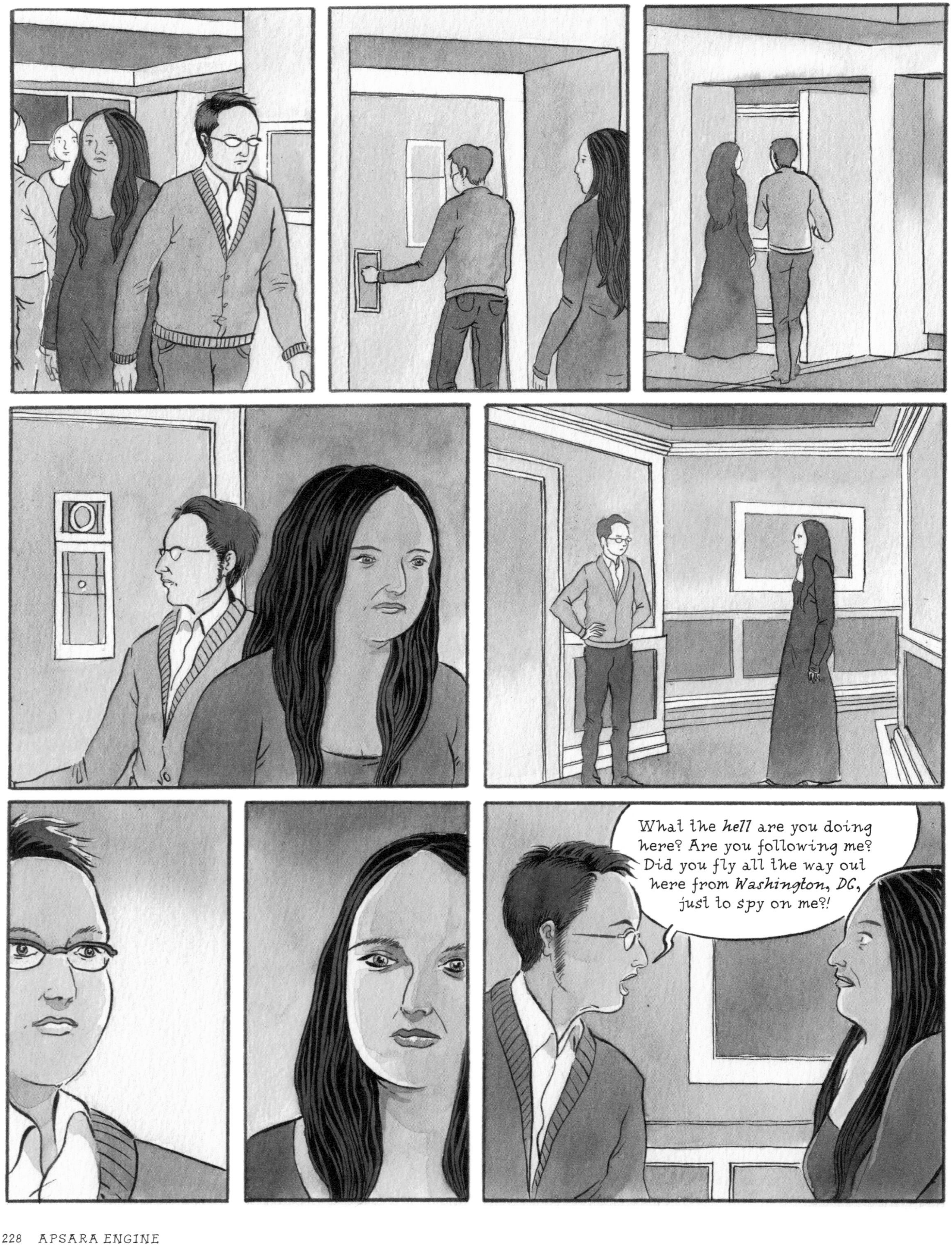
What the *hell* are you doing here? Are you following me? Did you fly all the way out here from *Washington, DC,* just to spy on me?!

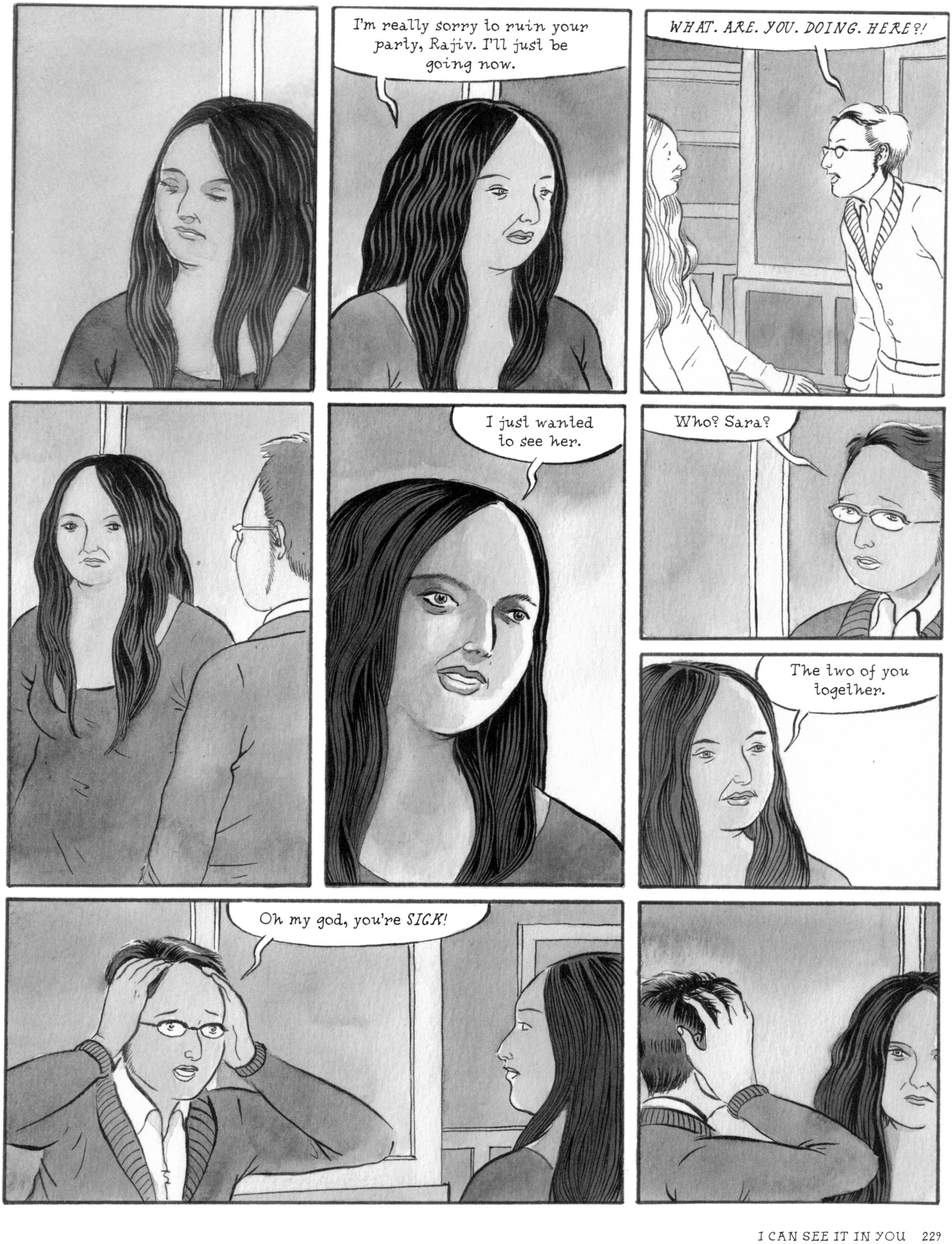
I'm really sorry to ruin your party, Rajiv. I'll just be going now.
WHAT. ARE. YOU. DOING. HERE?!
I just wanted to see her.
Who? Sara?
The two of you together.
Oh my god, you're SICK!

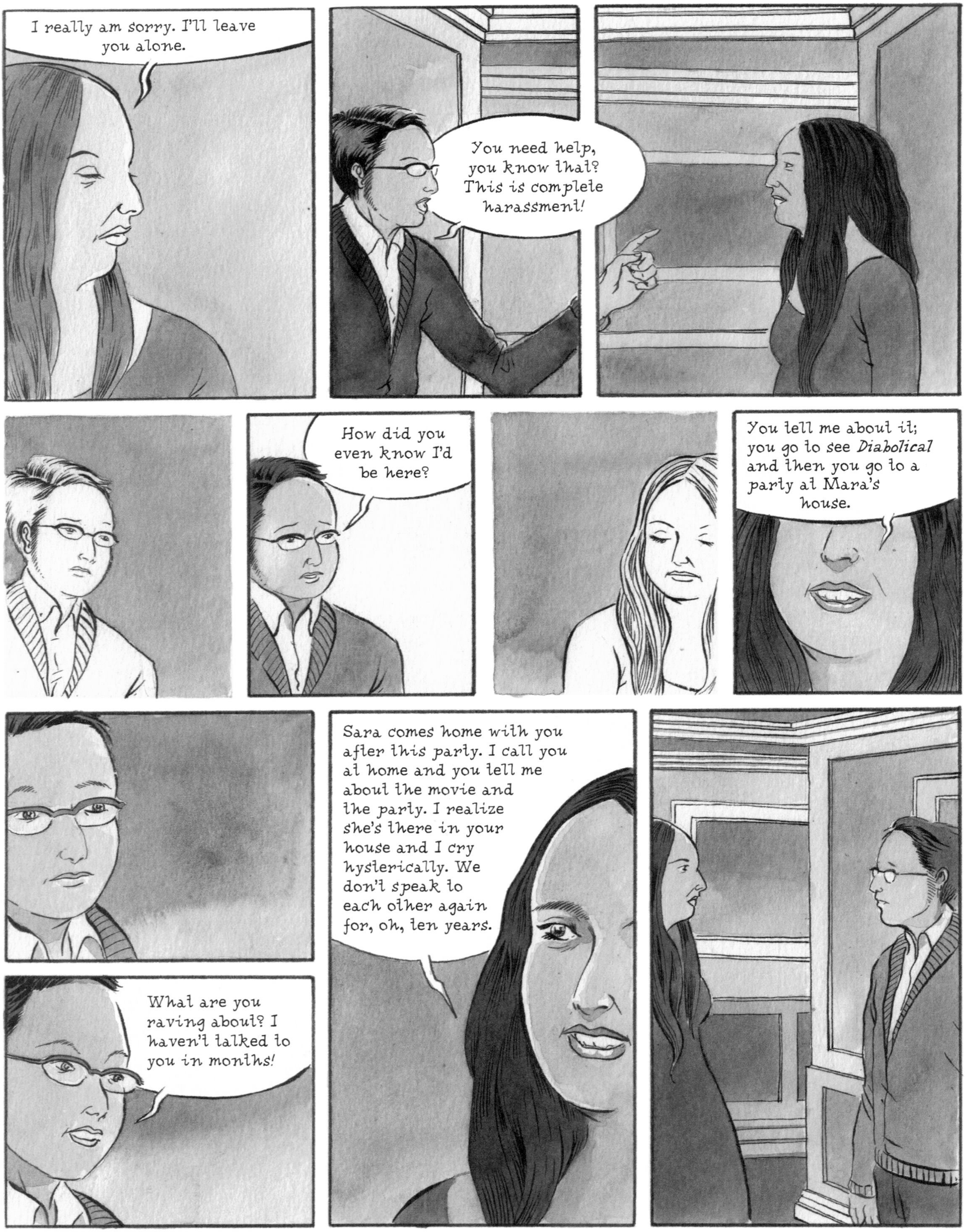
I really am sorry. I'll leave you alone.
You need help, you know that? This is complete harassment!
How did you even know I'd be here?
You tell me about it; you go to see *Diabolical* and then you go to a party at Mara's house.
Sara comes home with you after this party. I call you at home and you tell me about the movie and the party. I realize she's there in your house and I cry hysterically. We don't speak to each other again for, oh, ten years.
What are you raving about? I haven't talked to you in months!

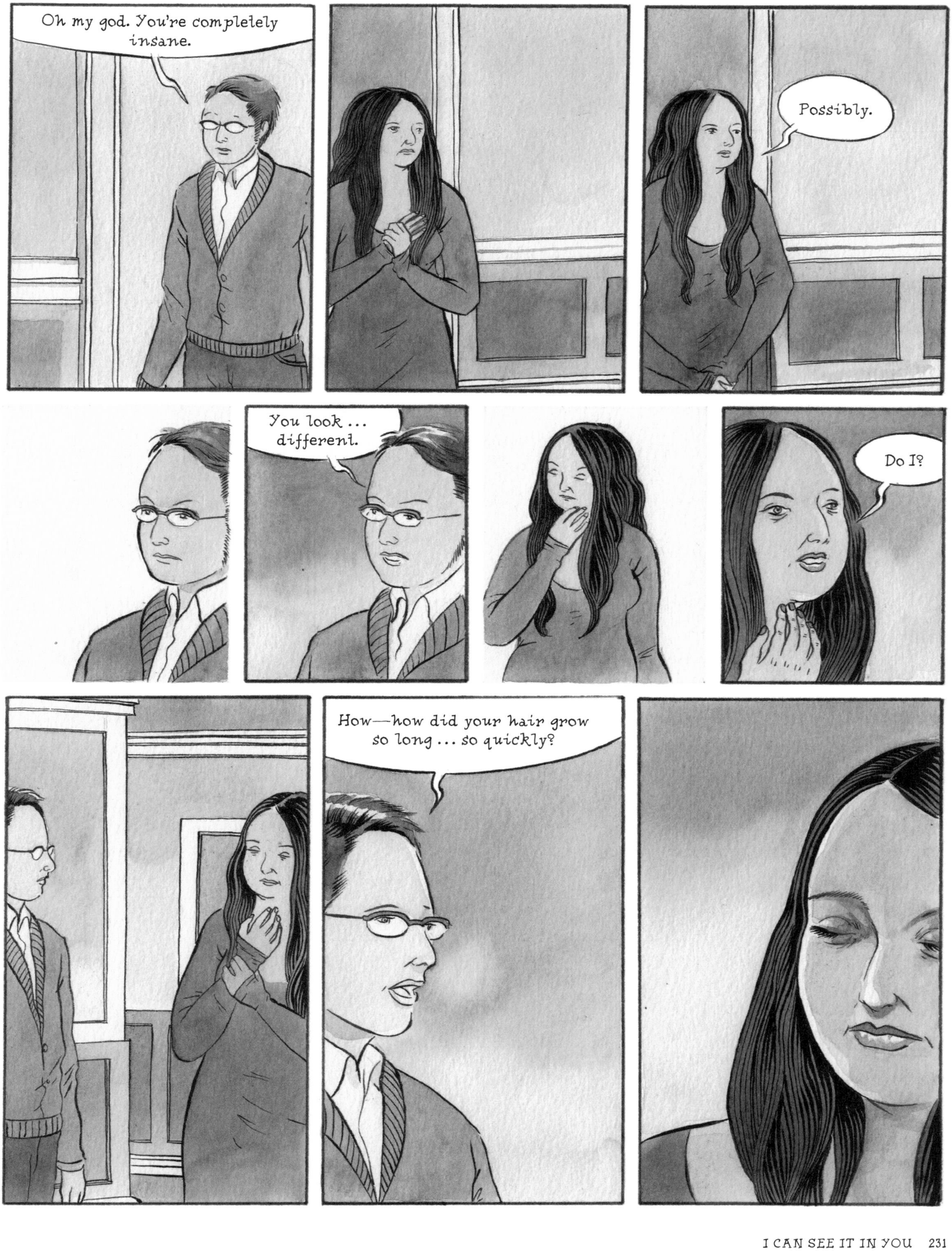
Oh my god. You're completely insane.
Possibly.
You look ... different.
Do I?
How—how did your hair grow so long ... so quickly?

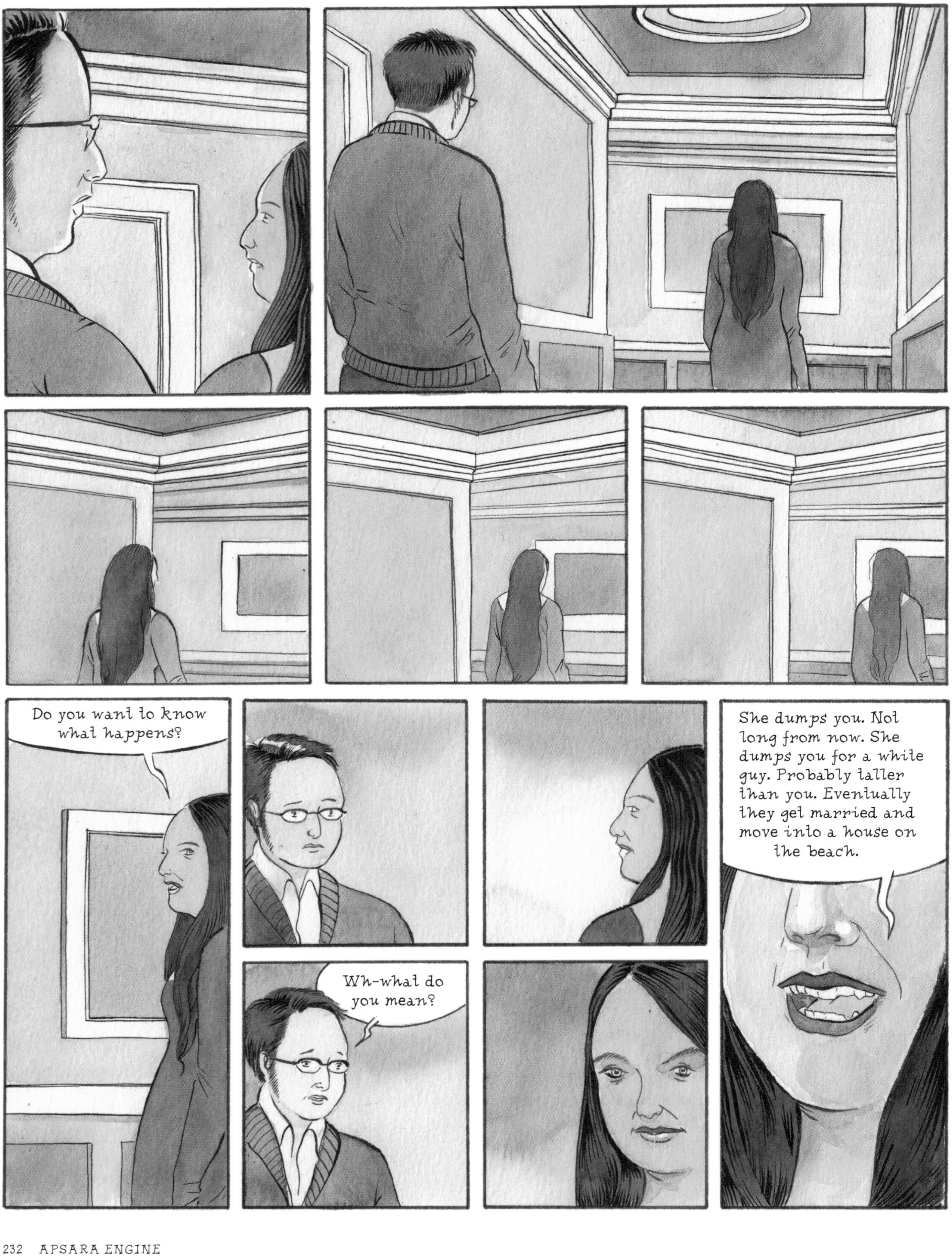
Do you want to know what happens?
Wh-what do you mean?
She dumps you. Not long from now. She dumps you for a white guy. Probably taller than you. Eventually they get married and move into a house on the beach.

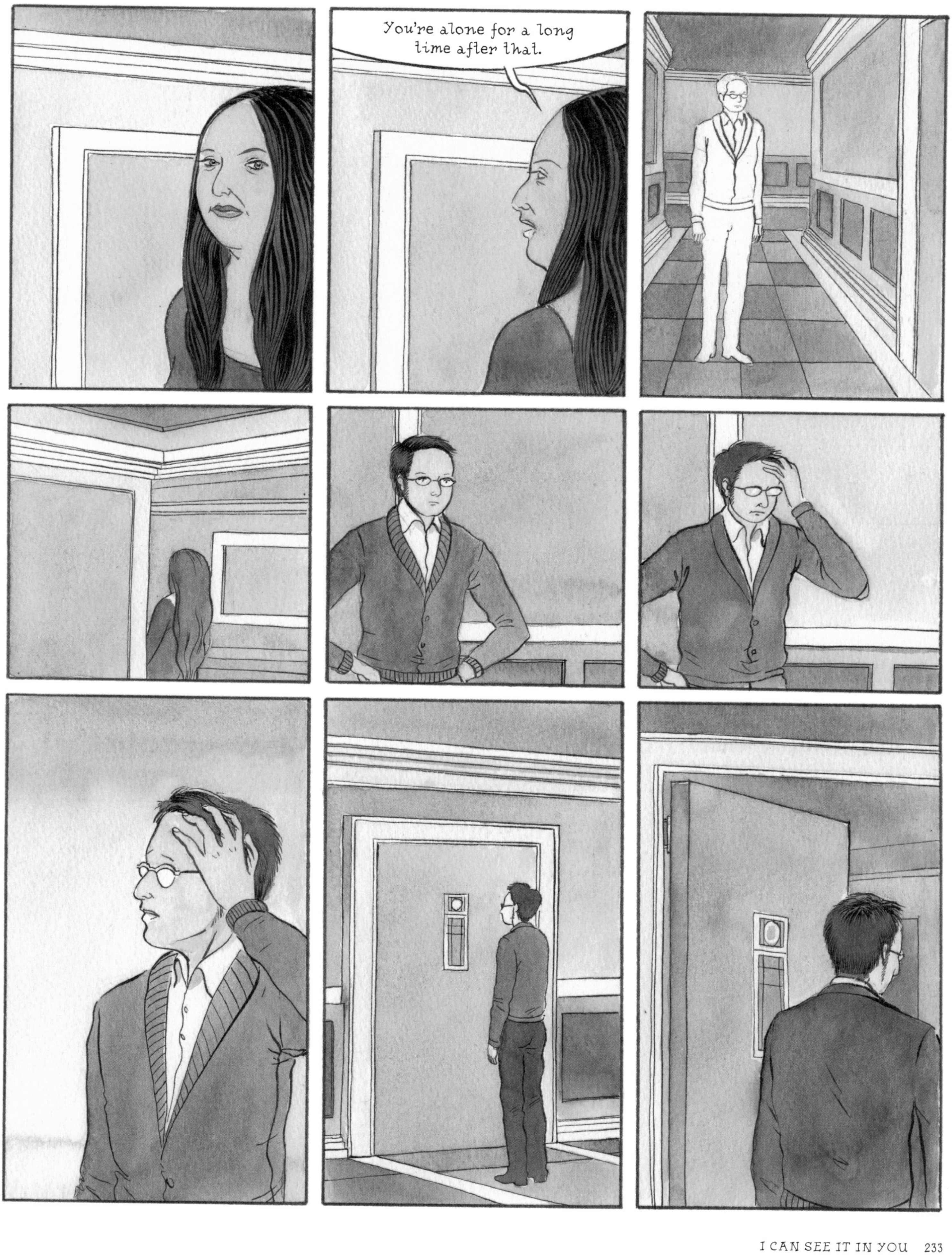
You're alone for a long time after that.

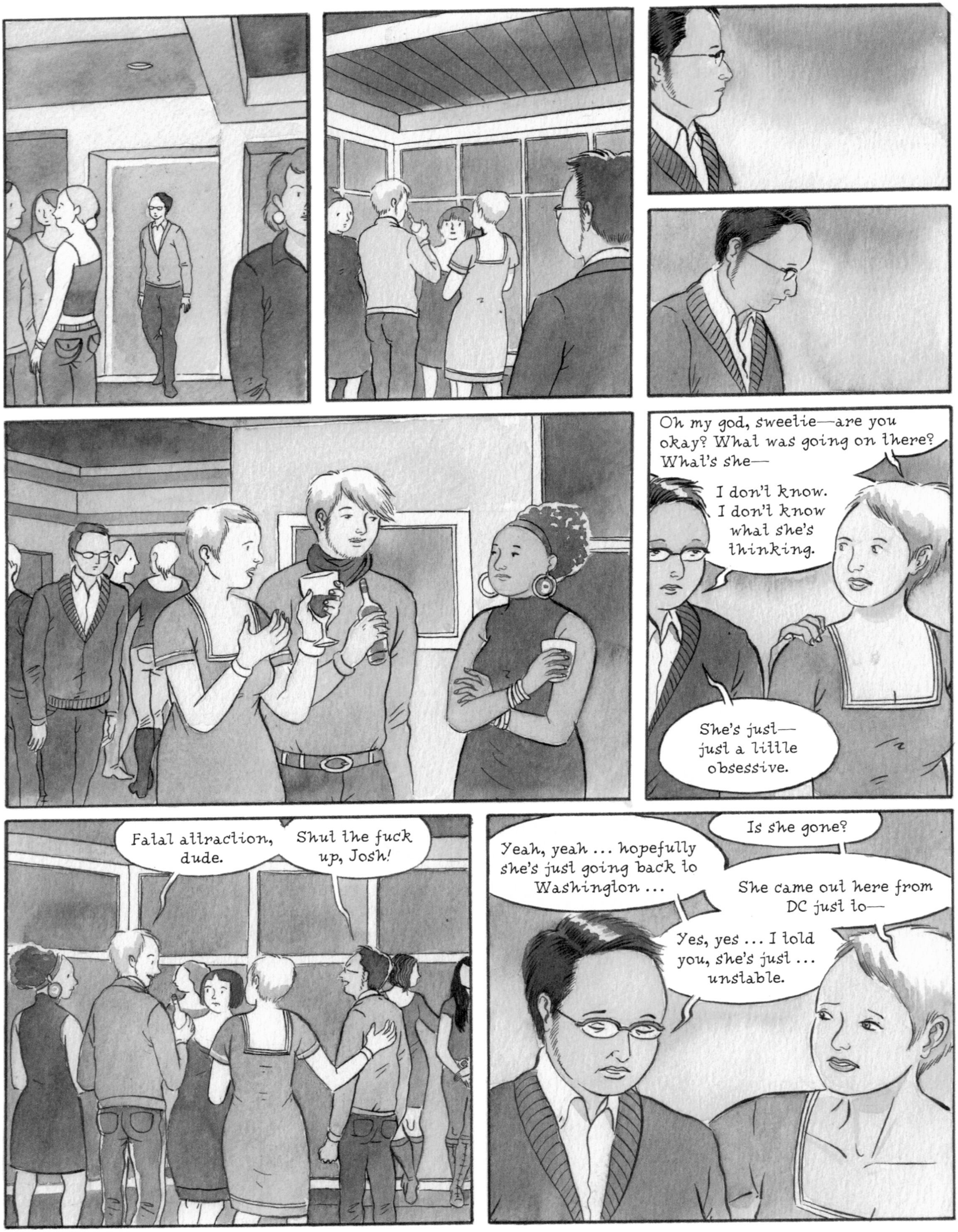
Oh my god, sweetie—are you okay? What was going on there? What's she—
I don't know. I don't know what she's thinking.
She's just— just a little obsessive.
Fatal attraction, dude.
Shut the fuck up, Josh!
Is she gone?
Yeah, yeah ... hopefully she's just going back to Washington ...
She came out here from DC just to—
Yes, yes ... I told you, she's just ... unstable.

Did you tell her we'd be here?

God, no ... why would I do that?

Then how did she—

I don't know!

She told me you'd invited her, Rajiv!

We haven't spoken to each other in ages!

I'm going to go home—I'm ... I'm not really up for a party now.

I'll come with you.

No, please ... you stay and have fun. I ... I just need to chill out for a while.

Don't be stubborn! I'll make us some caipirinhas.

I'd really rather be alone.

I'll just talk to you tomorrow, okay?

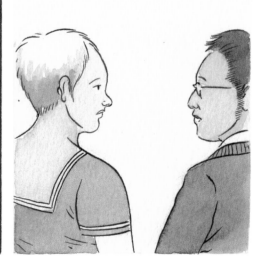

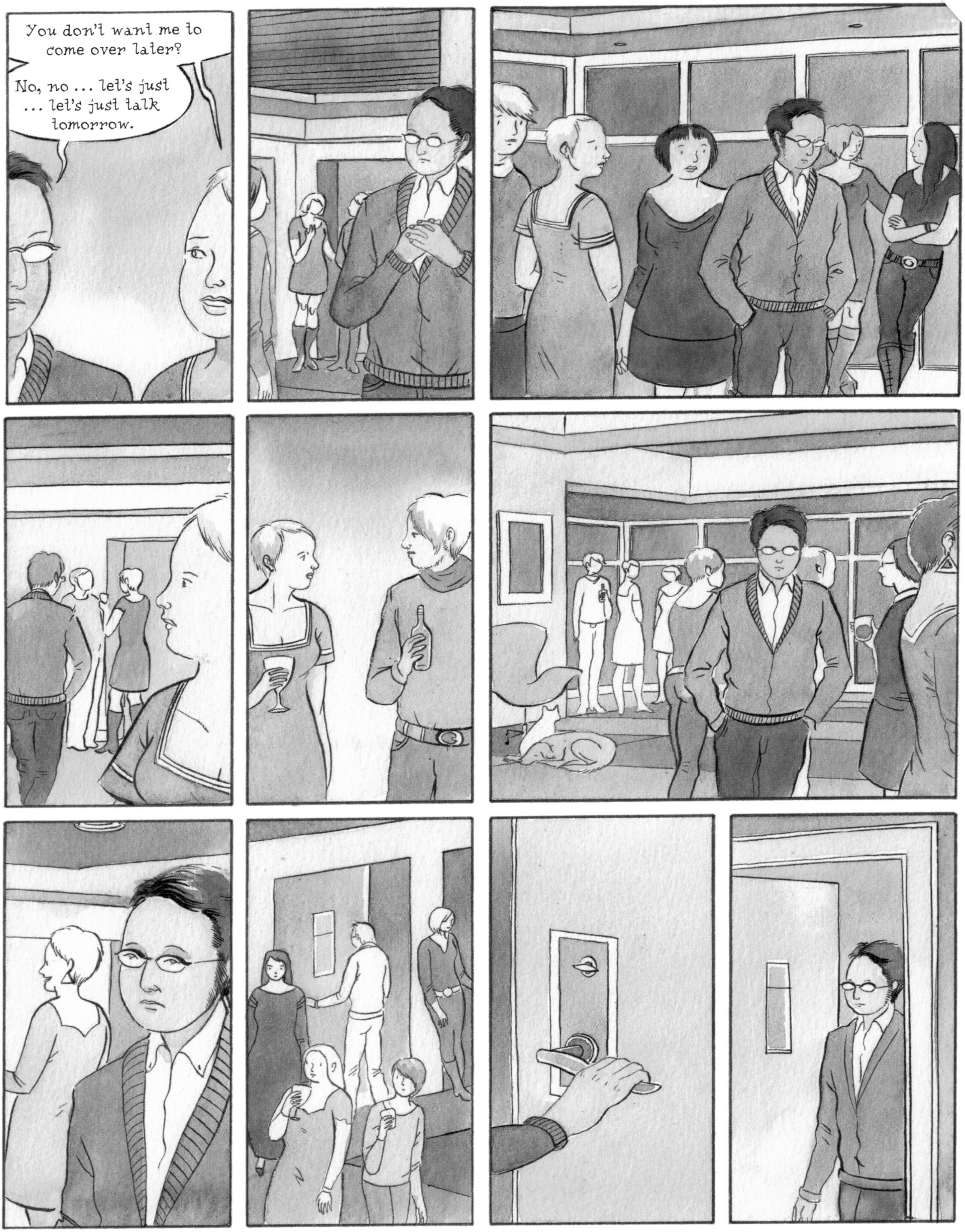
You don't want me to come over later?
No, no ... let's just ... let's just talk tomorrow.

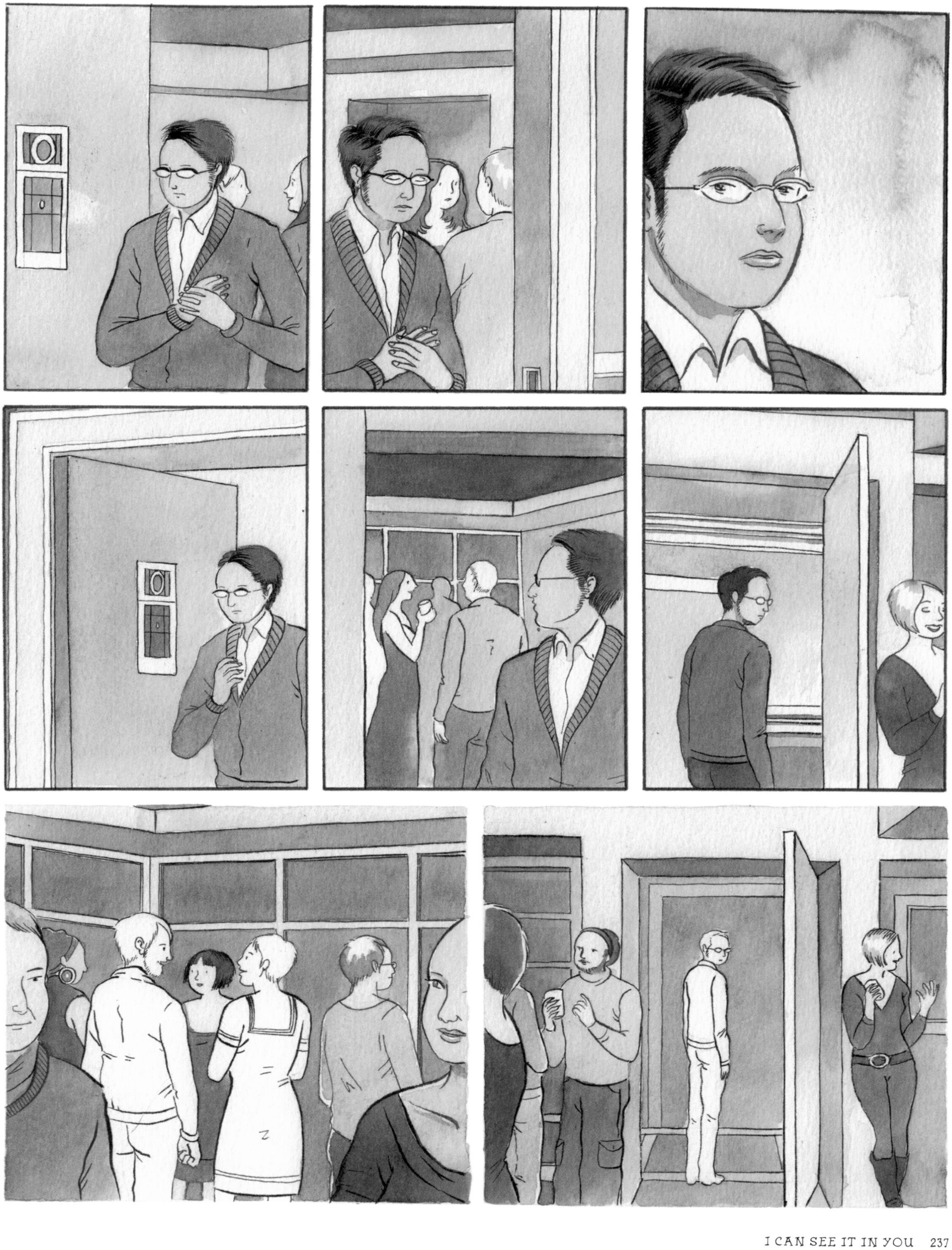

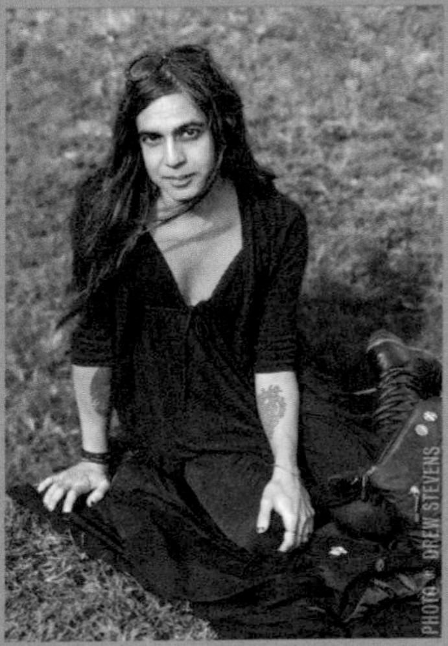
PHOTO © DREW STEVENS

BISHAKH SOM is an artist, illustrator, and writer whose work has appeared in the *New Yorker*, the *Boston Review*, and the *Brooklyn Rail*, among others. Her books include *Spellbound: A Graphic Memoir* and *The Prefab Bathroom: An Architectural History*, and she was also a contributor to *We're Still Here: An All-Trans Comics Anthology*. Som is currently based in Brooklyn, NY.

The Feminist Press publishes books that ignite movements and social transformation. Celebrating our legacy, we lift up insurgent and marginalized voices from around the world to build a more just future.

See our complete list of books at
feministpress.org

THE FEMINIST PRESS
AT THE CITY UNIVERSITY OF NEW YORK
FEMINISTPRESS.ORG

Published in 2020 by the Feminist Press
at the City University of New York
The Graduate Center
365 Fifth Avenue, Suite 5406
New York, NY 10016

feministpress.org

First Feminist Press edition 2020

 This book is supported in part by an award from the
ART WORKS. National Endowment for the Arts.

 Council on This book was made possible thanks to a grant from New York State Council on the Arts
the Arts with the support of Governor Andrew M. Cuomo and the New York State Legislature.

First printing April 2020

Cover art by Bishakh Som
Design and production by Drew Stevens

Library of Congress Cataloging-in-Publication Data
Names: Som, Bishakh, 1968- author, artist.
Title: Apsara engine / Bishakh Som.
Description: First Feminist Press edition. | New York, NY : The Feminist
   Press, 2020.
Identifiers: LCCN 2019035431 | ISBN 9781936932818 (paperback)
Subjects: LCSH: Comic books, strips, etc.
Classification: LCC PN6727.S566 A85 2020 | DDC 741.5/973--dc23
LC record available at https://lccn.loc.gov/2019035431

PRINTED IN THE UNITED STATES OF AMERICA